KYOTO CSEAS SERIES ON ASIAN STUDIES 3
Center for Southeast Asian Studies, Kyoto University

TRAVELING NATION-MAKERS

Transnational Flows and Movements in the Making of Modern Southeast Asia

KYOTO CSEAS SERIES ON ASIAN STUDIES 3
Center for Southeast Asian Studies, Kyoto University

TRAVELING NATION-MAKERS

Transnational Flows and Movements in the Making of Modern Southeast Asia

Edited by
Caroline S. Hau and Kasian Tejapira

NUS PRESS
Singapore
in association with
KYOTO UNIVERSITY PRESS
Japan

NUS Press
National University of Singapore
AS3-01-02, 3 Arts Link
Singapore 117569
www.nus.edu.sg/nuspress

ISBN 978-9971-69-547-7 (Paper)

Kyoto University Press
Kyodai-Kaikan (Kyoto University Hall)
15-9 Yoshida-Kawaramachi, Sakyo-ku
Kyoto-city 606-8305
Japan
www.kyoto-up.or.jp

ISBN 978-4-87698-352-0

National Library Board Singapore Cataloguing in Publication Data

Traveling nation-makers: transnational flows and movements in the making of modern Southeast Asia / edited by Caroline S. Hau and Kasian Tejapira. – Singapore: NUS Press in association with Kyoto University Press, c2011.
p. cm. – (Kyoto CSEAS series on Asian studies; 3)
Includes index.
ISBN: 978-9971-69-547-7 (pbk.)

1. Southeast Asians – Biography. 2. Southeast Asians – Foreign countries – Biography. 3. Southeast Asians – Travel. 4. Southeast Asia – Civilization – 21st century. I. Hau, Caroline S. II. Kasian Techaphira. III. Series: Kyoto CSEAS series on Asian studies; 3.

DS524.2
920.059 — dc22 OCN698434678

The front cover is taken from a children's book series on heroes in Vietnamese history. It depicts the young Vietnamese revolutionary Phạm Hồng Thái fleeing from the Hotel Victoria in the British concession of Guangzhou after a failed attempt to assassinate the Governor-General of Indochina in June 1924 (Hà Nội: Nhà Xuất Bản Trẻ [Hanoi: Youth Publishing House], 2004).

Typeset by: Scientifik Graphics
Printed by : Mainland Press Pte Ltd

CONTENTS

ACKNOWLEDGMENTS

This book originated in a panel at the March 2004 Center for Southeast Asian Studies, Kyoto University Core University Program workshop on "Flows and Movements in East Asia," sponsored by the Japan Society for the Promotion of Science and the National Research Council of Thailand, where the chapters by Caroline Hau, Kasian Tejapira, Khoo Boo Teik, and Onimaru Takeshi were presented. We thank Ishikawa Noboru for co-organizing the "Flows and Movements" project, and the staff and students of Kyoto University for their contribution to the success of the workshop. We also thank Yoshikawa Asuna and Jafar Suryomenggolo for their great help in the preparation of the manuscript.

The publication of this volume was made possible by a "Grant-in-Aid for Publication of Scientific Research Results" by the Japan Society for the Promotion of Science, whose support we gratefully acknowledge. We thank the anonymous readers for their constructive comments and suggestions, as well as Hayami Yoko, Mario Lopez, Paul Kratoska, Sunandini Arora Lal, Lena Qua, the staff of Kyoto University Press, and Trans Pacific Press for their editorial support.

Introduction

Caroline S. Hau and Kasian Tejapira

Cross-border circulations of people and ideas have been the object of increasing scholarly attention and debate in recent decades as discourses and practices of globalization have made substantial inroads in the academic and popular imagination. To some extent, this interest in transnational mobility is a logical outcome of a world of "flows," a world "fundamentally characterized by objects in motion,"[1] propelled by advances in transportation and communication; diffusion of technology and ideologies; large-scale movements of capital, labor, tourists, commodities, and cultural artifacts; expansion of mass education; creation of transnational public spheres and institutions; and relocation of production facilities "abroad."

Far from being merely a description of current empirical realities, this scholarly focus also has a normative import in its critique of the limitations of the nation-state as a collective agent; as a geopolitical, economic, and cultural system; and as a unit of study and analysis. The sheer volume and speed of flows, it is said, have eroded the sovereignty and capabilities of the nation-state, rendering its borders far more permeable than is popularly assumed and opening it to the world far beyond the reaches and control of the territorially rooted state.[2] As an intellectual framework, the nation-state has been criticized for promoting an intellectual parochialism that downplays or ignores the long history and ever-growing breadth of interactions among societies within and beyond its borders.[3] Nation-states have also been criticized for imposing repressive, territorialized, and homogenized identities on the fluid, polyglot condition of existence of much of the world before, and since, the advent of the inter-state system.[4]

Not surprisingly, terms such as "cosmopolitanism," "deterritorialization," and "postnationalism" have gained purchase by offering themselves as theoretical alternatives to the constraining fixities and rigidities of nation-centred categories, perspectives, and policies. Almost all of these terms rely in part on the idea of travel, not only as a metaphor but as a literal means of realization: for example, some definitions of cosmopolitanism presuppose movement across space as the pre-eminent form of encounter and exchange with different peoples and cultures,[5] while Gilles Deleuze and Felix Guattari's concept of deterritorialization[6] has been used in discussions of cultural dislocation, as ties between culture and place are weakened by globalization.[7] The challenges of European integration — including the lowering of barriers in trade, the movement of workers and capital, and the partial surrender of national sovereignty in the name of legal harmonization (in conformity with the *acquis communautaire*, or body of European Union laws) — are the central concern of Habermas' essays on the "post-national constellation."[8] Migrants and diasporic communities have received special attention as exemplary articulations of the "transnational moment."[9] In the wake of the events of 11 September 2001, profiling of Muslim radical activists has routinely highlighted their "de-territorialized" backgrounds: "they may be born in a country, then educated in another country, then go to fight in a third country and take refuge in a fourth country."[10]

In Southeast Asian studies, flows and movements have had a central place in the construction of the field as well as the characterization of the area. Elasticity has been a hallmark of the field, since "Southeast Asia" at different times encompassed different boundaries according to specific cartographic, scholarly, and geopolitical demands.[11] Its definition has been partly shaped by external actors and references. Western travelers and scholars understood it as the region lying between the better-known civilizations of India and China. The Chinese saw it as a site of trade, immigration, and activism. The Japanese considered it a resource-rich and geopolitically strategic part of its co-prosperity sphere. The British and their allies mapped it as a regional theater of the Pacific War. The Americans treated it as the southern bulwark of anti-Communist "Free Asia" and the third party in the post-war triangular trade system involving the United States and Japan. The neighboring dialogue partners (China, Japan, South Korea, India, Australia, and New Zealand) of the Association of Southeast Asian Nations view it as the hub of regional cooperation and region-making in the name of an "East Asia Community."

Moreover, scholars of Southeast Asia have long theorized the region, particularly its premodern and colonial histories, as a contact zone within a larger global context of economic, cultural, and intellectual flows and movements, with travels to, from, and through the region by traders, laborers, pilgrims, tourists, officials, scholars, activists, soldiers, and immigrants playing important roles in the history — and theorizing — of the area.[12] Concerns with excavating the "bedrock" of an "original" Southeast Asian cultural substratum beneath "foreign influences," with ideas of agency through "localization" and other concepts of selective and creative appropriation, and with the writing of "autonomous history" all reflect a critical awareness of the difficulty, if not impossibility, of studying Southeast Asia as a self-contained and self-enclosed unit.[13]

This leitmotif in Southeast Asian studies resonates with the paradigm shift in international scholarship that has sought to overcome the constraints posed by nation-centered studies by calling for transnational, comparative, and cross-cultural analyses, and for careful consideration of cross-border "networks and synchronisms" across space and time.[14] Shaped by the historical experience of decolonization and the strategic imperatives of the Cold War, nation-centered studies have tended to privilege national(ist) narratives to the exclusion of other theoretical alternatives, while area studies have sought to defend their institutional existence by upholding the feasibility of "Southeast Asia" as a unit of study and analysis through discussions of the regional distinctiveness of its processes of hybridization, localization, and translation of "foreign influences."[15] The call for a broader perspective is both the product of a post-Cold War epoch, with its new geopolitical, spatial, economic, social, and cultural arrangements that stress — and capitalize on — a broader geographic expanse of commonalities and differences among peoples across the world, and an attempt at clearing a critical space for thought and writing that would be "more self-generative and less over-determined by cold-war history."[16]

This call has been answered by nuanced research, particularly in the emergent field of world history and global history in which Southeast Asia is now nested as a sub-region. Inspired by Fernand Braudel and Immanuel Wallerstein,[17] scholars such as Kenneth Pomeranz, Andre Gunder Frank, and R. Bin Wong have criticized the Eurocentrism of social and political theories and employed "two-way" or reciprocal comparisons (between geographical units such as Europe and China, or their parts) to offer new insights and ask new questions about industrialization and other issues.[18] Attention has focused particularly on the sea lanes that enabled long-distance trade. K.N. Chaudhuri, Ashin Das Gupta, and Michael Pearson have drawn on archival research to theorize the "Indian Ocean" as an economic and cultural unit and explore the ways in which trade and other contacts linked peoples and knitted communities across broad expanses of sea and land that included Southeast Asia.[19] Where civilizational discourses have come into use, the emphasis has generally been on hybridity and pluralism, encounter and engagement,[20] rather than the polarizing "clash of civilizations"[21] thesis that gained currency following the events of

11 September 2001. Special attention has been accorded the traveler, who is often also merchant, migrant, missionary, student, or activist, as a key agent of economic, political, cultural, and intellectual flows and exchange.[22] World-regional approaches to economic history have highlighted the systemic nature, densities, and spatial reach and limits of interconnections and interactions among countries within a "region" and between the "region" and the world, effectively eroding country boundaries while heuristically positing "regions" as units of study, analysis, and collective action that mediate between the global and the local.[23] The salience of understanding a "world of regions"[24] resonates with the current trend toward regionalism (institution-building) and regionalization (economic integration) in Europe and, more recently, in East Asia, the formulation of which has come to encompass both Northeast and Southeast Asia, with the Association of Southeast Asian Nations playing the role of institutional hub for community-building in the name of "East Asia."[25]

The understandable frustration with the narrowness of national studies has, however, come at a price. Research inspired by cross-cultural and cross-border frameworks has tended to bracket off the nation-states and concentrate on early and colonial histories to produce "prehistories" of contemporary globalization, or on contemporary transnationalism and connections between migrant or diasporic communities and their real and imagined homelands. Relatively little sustained attention has been paid to the question of how nation-states themselves were constituted out of, and crisscrossed by, these multidirectional material, cultural, and intellectual flows, circulations, and interactions across space and time; how various nationalists and nation-making projects sought to tap into, appropriate, rechannel, or truncate these flows; how shared as well as differing visions of community may arise out of contacts among people from different "territories" within a given space; and what implications these questions have for rethinking commonsensical understandings of national identities, nation-states, and nationalism.[26] Leaving nation-formation and the nation form largely unexamined and unexplored has meant consigning nations and nationalism to the category of an ideological ruse, theorized solely in terms of their constraints on research, their parochialism and homogenizing impulses, and their ethico-political opposition to universal ideals of hybrid cosmopolitanism.

Critical interest in local, regional, and global flows can, in fact, complicate and revise nation-centered studies of political movements by showing how flows in, through, and across Southeast Asia enabled forms of identification and activism among different political actors in ways that promoted thinking, feeling, and making nation during much of the twentieth century.[27] The ten essays in this book seek to fill the gap in current scholarship by viewing the "national" politics of Southeast Asia in terms of the historical flows and movements of activists, ideas, and cultural artifacts. They are concerned with the political salience of "travel" in, from, to, and through Southeast Asia, and with the question of how biographical accounts of "travel" might contribute to a more nuanced understanding of the modern history and politics of nationness in Southeast Asia.

The central organizing concept of this book is "travel" (which need not be defined as physical movement of people, since the term encompasses circulations of ideas and discourses enabled by inflows of goods and commodities such as books, films, and other consumer items) within and beyond Southeast Asia,[28] and its transformative effect on individual lives and their intellectual, political, religious, and cultural projects, and on the trajectories of nationalist, Communist, Islamic, and other movements in the region.[29] The contributors grapple with the notion of "travel" beyond one that is paradigmatically defined as elite, European, male, bourgeois, scientific, heroic, or recreational movement across space.[30] We consider the salience not only of time (or, more specifically, historical timing), but of space (say, Shanghai, as discussed by Lorraine Paterson and Onimaru Takeshi in this book) as well, in structuring the experience of travel and the visions and projects that travel helps enable. We are interested in how auto/biographies of local, regional, and global flows might unsettle or re-invent long-standing or modern concepts not only of personhood and identity but of forms of belonging and community-making, and thereby complexify the use of the nation as a unit of analysis in Southeast Asian studies. We also hope to offer a number of perspectives — whether local, national, regional, or global — from which to understand the various political projects engendered by encounters and exchanges that bring people and ideas together in a given space and across boundaries.

Travel has been central to the theorizing of nationalism, Communism, and Islam, three of the most important political movements and ideologies in the region. In the case of nationalism, Benedict Anderson has argued in favor of the interpretive force of "journeys" and their ability to turn administrative units into meaningful "fatherlands." Drawing on the analogy of religious pilgrimages, in which devotees from different places of origin come together in the act of traversing and worshipping in sacred spaces, Anderson talks about Creole government officials whose travels, delimited within the territories of their colonies, brought them into contact with fellow Creoles. The connectedness generated by these journeys is determined not only by the particular routes traveled, but by the Creoles' consciousness of the "shared fatality of trans-Atlantic birth."[31] The spread of print capitalism provided the technological and linguistic cement to bind territory with homeland-as-nation, even as its serial logic endowed the nation form and nationalism with a modularity that enabled it to travel, and be adapted, around the world.

While travel within the administrative bounds of a territory helped define the scope and reach of the nationalist imagination, anti-colonial and nationalist movements themselves were not confined strictly within the boundaries of the colonial state. An important component of the theorizing and mobilizing of these movements took place, as in the case of the Philippines[32] and Vietnam (see the chapters by Paterson and Resil Mojares) and to some extent Indonesia, outside the colonies, usually but not necessarily among communities of exiles and emigrants, and beyond the purview of their colonial states. Activists also traveled to obtain international sympathy and aid for anti-colonial movements. In Asia, this international component of anti-colonialism took shape in the early years of the twentieth century around a pan-Asianist regional network (see the chapter by Mojares) linked by regional hubs such as Tokyo, Canton, Shanghai, Hong Kong, and Siam.[33] This network was active from the late nineteenth century until World War II and would, at various times, include Pak Yong-hyo and An Kyong-su of Korea, Inukai Tsuyoshi and Miyazaki Tōten of Japan, Sun Yat-sen of China, Phan Bội Châu of Vietnam, and Rash Behari Bose of India. Pan-Asianism capitalized on the sense of crisis created by Western encroachment in Asia and by the imperatives of cooperation and solidarity in bringing about social transformation across the region.

Internationalism is an essential component of the Communist movements in Asia. This global "socialist ecumene," as Susan Bayly has called it, is anchored in "shared practices of cultural circulation" and powered by the belief in, and claims to, a worldwide fraternal community based on revolutionary solidarities, long-distance exchange, and friendship.[34] Lenin's *Imperialism, the Highest Stage of Capitalism* (1916) was one of the earliest attempts to link the anti-imperialist liberation struggles in the "East" to proletarian world revolution.[35] The Third International, founded in 1919, sought to tap the political passions of anti-colonial nationalist movements to build a world party of Communists. Its Second Congress in 1920 explicitly addressed the colonial and national questions and encouraged collaboration with revolutionary nationalism.[36] In the 1920s and early 1930s, the Comintern, whose Far Eastern Bureau was headquartered in Shanghai, relied on traveling activists such as Hồ Chí Minh and Tan

Malaka to help midwife the birth of some of the radical movements in Asia during the interwar period (see the chapter by Onimaru).[37]

Christopher Goscha has shown how Vietnamese nationalist and Communist revolutionaries relied on pre-existing regional networks of Vietnamese migrants, traders, and activist-exiles centered in Thailand, but also extending to southern China and as far as Japan.[38] Nguyen Ai Quoc (Hồ Chí Minh), who along with Tan Malaka was a key "regional facilitator" (to use Onimaru's term) of the Comintern's Far Eastern Bureau, was instrumental in the creation of the Communist parties of Vietnam, Siam, and Laos. In the post-war period, Maoist movements in Thailand, Malaysia, Burma, Cambodia, Vietnam, and the Philippines drew on the support of the Chinese Communist Party in financial, military, and ideological terms (see the chapters by Caroline Hau and Kasian Tejapira)[39] to challenge, and attempt to capture, the state.

Travel also figures prominently in the religious doctrine and practices of Islam. Terms such as "Hajj" (pilgrimage), "hijra" (emigration), "rihla" (travel for learning and other purposes), and "ziyara" (visits to shrines) give us some idea of the complex and subtle ways in which travel, as a form of social and political action, entailed not simply physical, but simultaneously spiritual and temporal, movement. These travels brought pilgrims from different cultures and societies into contact with each other, simultaneously generating awareness of their membership in a universal community while also strengthening their sense of their differences from each other. Motives for travel were diverse but by no means mutually exclusive: the rihla, for example, was often undertaken in connection, or concurrently, with trade, as traders and intellectuals followed the trade routes that brought Islam to Southeast Asia, among other regions.

Travel also had political implications, as Muslim returnees brought back with them new ideas and practices or else sought and forged new conceptions of religious community "at home," some of which threatened to undermine the existing authority and prestige not only of the ruling elites but of local Islamic leaders and organizations.[40] New communication technologies, mass education, the translation and circulation of Islamic texts, and increased opportunities for travel have been instrumental in creating global activist networks while also enabling Muslim political participation in their "home" countries.[41] In the Philippines, for example, travel has shaped the character of the separatist movements that challenged the Philippine state. US colonial rule laid the foundations for the development of Muslim ethno-religious identity among Moro Filipinos through contacts established among Muslims of different ethnic groupings within the institutions of public and tertiary education, notably through contacts among Muslims in universities in Manila. This integration politics may account for why the separatism of the Moro National Liberation Front was not specifically Islamic, but was rather nationalist. Between 1955 and 1970, however, the Egyptian government provided some 200 scholarships for Muslim Filipinos to study abroad, and the Islamic resurgence of the 1970s — with the transnational Islamic political movement of the Society of Muslim Brothers (Jamaat al-Ikhwan al-Muslimun) gaining mainstream status in the Middle East in the 1980s[42] — would come to shape the politics of the splinter group Moro Islamic Liberation Front, which nevertheless had to contend with local resistance to its attempts to purify Islamic rituals.[43]

On the international front, a number of Organization of the Islamic Conference member-states have provided financial aid to promote Islamic activities and foster pan-Islamic awareness and solidarity, with official institutions as well as philanthropic associations in Saudi Arabia, Kuwait, and the United Arab Emirates serving as major sources of funding and organizational support.[44] Using routes created by trade, labor migration, and education, militant Islamic groups have made Afghanistan, Pakistan, Mindanao, and Malaysia their bases for military operations and training camps.[45] The revolution that established an Islamic republic in Iran and the Soviet occupation of Afghanistan in 1979 provided important crucibles for Islamist awakening and activism (see the chapter by Shiraishi Takashi). The Salafi movement, which began among students studying in Lebanon, Syria, and Egypt, challenged state interpretations of Islam; where jihadi thought had made inroads into the social movement, the movement has relied on informal social networks rather than formal organizations to pursue collective action.[46] Moreover, following September 11, the US-led global "war on terror" trained the spotlight on Islamist movements and their global, regional, national, and local networks, turning Islamism's cross-country, cross-cultural features into an international policy concern.[47]

Nationalist, Communist, and Islamic activisms are by no means exclusive categories. Characterized as much by intellectual and organizational cross-fertilization as by tensions and contestations, these intellectual and political struggles are themselves shaped by flows and movements of people and ideas, particularly in the region that we now call East Asia, which includes both Northeast and Southeast Asia and is linked to South Asia. The late nineteenth century was not only characterized by large-scale migration of Chinese and Indians to Southeast Asia (as discussed by Hau and Khoo Boo Teik in this book), but transcontinental and transoceanic contacts — not just between European metropole and colonial Asia but in particular among the colonies and countries within the region during the later nineteenth to early twentieth centuries — played a crucial role in the economic modernization of Japan, China, and Southeast Asia.[48] The salience of region as a unit of study and analysis that is larger than specific countries but smaller than the planet becomes clear when we consider that the patterns and density of flows and connections are unevenly spread out across space. The economic historian Kaoru Sugihara has cogently shown that between 1883 and 1913, intra-Asian trade grew at a rate that outstripped trade within Europe, Latin America, Africa, and other regions,[49] prefiguring economic integration in the post-Cold War era.

The fluidity of social and ideological projects — as well as these projects' role in creating and strengthening national (self-)identification, not only Philippine, Thai, Indonesian, and Malaysian, but also "foreign" Arab and Chinese — is especially evident in the first 50 years of the twentieth century, when the nation-state was in the process of formation in Southeast Asia. The Sarekat Islam was the first nationalist political organization in Indonesia.[50] Its articulation of nationalism and Islam would branch off into different political paths as Marxism influenced activists such as Haji Misbach and other advocates of "Islamism and Communism."[51] Moreover, Islamic holy sites and travel routes — notably Jerusalem — were sometimes shared with other religions such as Christianity, so that the types of identification enabled by these routes were not necessarily confined to identification with the universal umma or with local Islamic communities, but could accommodate sub-regional, national, and regional identifications as well.[52] Communist movements in Southeast Asia are characterized by the intimate but fraught connection between anti-colonialism, anti-imperialism, nationalism, and internationalism[53] (see the chapters by Onimaru, Hau, and Kasian Tejapira). Anti-colonial nationalist movements in Asia sought in pan-Asianism an ideology and logistical support system that would activate and promote revolution across the region through mutual cooperation and aid (see the chapters by Mojares and Khoo). Recent efforts at institution-building in East Asia (i.e., Southeast and Northeast Asia) continue to highlight the importance of nation-states alongside markets as twin engines of region-making.[54] These contaminations have been productive, not least in the hybrid political imaginaries that they created.

This book looks at nation-making in light of flows and movements of people and ideas. We hope to add historical depth to the current privileging of travel in globalization discourse while also providing correctives to the tendency of globalization discourse to discount the efficacy of nations and states as domains of socio-political and cultural imagination and transformation. Of the ten people featured in this book, eight were born in the late nineteenth to early twentieth centuries and were active at a time when the nation-state was still being imagined and formed in Southeast Asia. Their lives exemplify the fact that flows and movements (or, in the case of the Vietnamese man of letters Vũ Trọng Phụng, discussed by Peter Zinoman in this book, flows without literal movement), and the political, cultural, and intellectual exchanges enabled thereby, were very much a part of life even during the years when earlier phases of globalization were supposedly interrupted by the two world wars. They show that the provenance of political struggles, whether to imagine community or to undermine, defend, or transform it, need not be rooted only in the experiences of displacement and discrimination typical of so-called diasporas, but may be found as well in the experiences of being "thrown together" and displaced that are constitutive of "national" space and time.

Indeed, they question current theories that construct the nation as a bogeyman of cultural stasis and repressive entrapment in order to contrast it to the freedom and transformative agency of cosmopolitan mobility.[55] Political movements are human organizations and networks. They are also techniques of production and circulation of activists, things, ideas, symbols, and knowledge. As such, they have historical breadth and communicative reach, but their scope and influence are unevenly spread and felt across time and space. While their bounds often exceed those of the territorial states, they nevertheless look to and rely in part on nation-states to effect their visions of social, political, economic, and cultural transformation, given the absence of a world order capable of enforcing universal norms and regulations without exceptions on a supranational level. Their visions are often consciously and unconsciously delimited by the assumed boundaries of the nation-state, and by the claims of particularistic communities and belongings that they can neither uncritically embrace nor completely repudiate.[56]

The ten essays in this book also seek to redress the imbalances in current research on travel, which has tended to privilege the unidirectional physical movement of people from the peripheral South to the metropolitan North. While mindful of the ways in which travel is marked by class, gender, race, and culture, discourses of cosmopolitan hybridity often take as their primary example the South-to-North travels (hence their privileging of migrancy and diaspora),[57] which are endowed with the agency of unsettling or undoing the boundaries that cordon off one culture from another. They do not give equal attention to the cosmopolitanism of those who travel between "peripheries" or within a region, those who choose to or were forced to return from their travels rather than settle elsewhere, those who are exiled, those who need to find work abroad, and those who cannot, choose not to, or do not travel physically but who nevertheless lay claim to universalist ideas. In their celebration of the transformative possibilities of "dwelling-in-traveling," they give short shrift to the political implications of traveling-in-dwelling (especially when no physical journey is undertaken), or the ways in which the boundedness of "home" may shape,[58] and be in turn reshaped by, travel experiences.

This book's intention is neither to romanticize travel nor automatically attribute resistance to the act (whether coerced or not) of staying "at home" — indeed, the latter has arguably been a theoretical reaction to, and compensation for, the former — but to pinpoint the political possibilities and, just as important, limits of the kinds of cosmopolitanism and particularism engendered by the historical dialectic between roots and routes in Southeast Asia. It considers travel's embeddedness in specific locations and the political, intellectual, and artistic projects on behalf of which travel is conscripted.

The contributors adopt a biographical approach to illuminate the ways in which the nation is constituted out of concretely embodied flows and movements. Biographies are forms of literary, political, and religious expression that can be productively studied for the ways in which they use narratives to give shape and meaning to particular lives. Biographies are arenas of dispute over meaning, intentions, and agency, rather than simply affirmations or celebrations of them.[59] They offer insights into the historical and cultural processes into which individuals are inserted, while also documenting the agency of individuals who make their histories and cultures.[60] These inscriptions of lives offer pathways for marking out concrete encounters, interactions, and negotiations among individual subjects and between these subjects and the economic, political, cultural, and intellectual structures of authority within and across which they operated. At the same time, though, the "differential specificity" of these lives — that is, the geopolitical and experiential particularities of these personal histories — means that they are not readily assimilable to the larger sociopolitical order and the narratives that they legitimize, and, in the case of marginalized groups, they may even interrogate the assumptions of the general order.[61]

Moreover, as pioneering studies by Craig Reynolds, Anthony Milner, Alfred McCoy, C.W. Watson, and Christoph Giebel have shown, biographies also have political functions. Biographies encode not just forms of organizing societies and the larger world, but are themselves acts of political interpretation that are instrumental in creating, or imagining alternatives to, the larger narratives, usually of nation and history, that interpret and organize political life.[62] In Malaysia, Mohamed Salleh bin Perang of Johor was one of the first Malay authors who, in writing about his travels, postulated the Malay reader of autobiographies.[63] *Hikayat Abdullah*, with its combination of travel and autobiography, was instrumental in creating "Malay" political culture through its redefinition of "Malay" in terms of race rather than rajah-based authority.[64]

Biographies serve as "author functions" that construct and delimit the discourses by which these individuals and their politics are read and interpreted. It is easier for the Thai state to attribute Jit Poumisak's progressive ideas to external "foreign" sources, the better to brand them as alien, rather than consider the likelihood that Jit's political education, along with Marxist discourse, was a home-grown phenomenon mediated by translations that were circulating within Thailand itself.[65] Moreover, as Craig Reynolds has forcefully argued, the activity of piecing together the fragments of Jit Poumisak's life was an incontrovertible means by which the youth movement took shape in Thailand.[66] A more contemporary example of the political uses of biography can be discerned in current studies of Islamic radicalism, which rely on biographical analysis to construct "profiles" of Muslim activists and identify the bonds of kinship and friendship that link one activist to another and to the larger community of believers in the politically loaded language of "terror networks."[67]

For much of the twentieth century, biographies have played a preeminent role in producing and legitimizing national narratives (as well as counter-narratives) that mediate the creation of a collective, whether "public" or "people." Revolutionary biographies in Vietnam offered models for anti-colonial and nationalist self-identification, inspiration, emulation, and action to readers (see the chapter by Paterson).[68] In the Philippines, biographies have been a favored form of elite and middle-class self-expression, with the publicity implied by the graphic display of name and reputation (resonating with the precolonial Malay conventions of nama, name as "reputation") filling in for the absence of "traditional" sources of prestige such as aristocratic titles.[69] In Indonesia, autobiographies offer insights into collective debates about the nation[70] and offer means of making sense of the significant or traumatic periods in Indonesia's history.[71] Focusing on the marginalized and the obscure has been one way of expanding the biographical canon of the nation, producing accounts that expose rather than simply reinforce the foundational fictions of the nation and attest to the irreducible plurality of political projects undertaken in the name of the nation.

The subjects of this book are not exemplary Southeast Asian political travelers such as Jose Rizal, Phan Bội Châu, Tan Malaka, or Tunku Abdul Rahman, nor have they been subjects of full-length biographies, memoirs, or autobiographies.[72] The contributors are not interested in cataloguing the heroic accomplishments of their subjects, nor do they assume that these individuals are autonomous subjects endowed with the will and freedom of thought that automatically resist the strictures of colonial and post-colonial authority. They are more interested in analyzing the possibilities and limits of individual agency; the contingent, historical contexts within which these activists lived; and the conditions of success and failure of their respective political, artistic, and religious projects.

The ten individuals in this book lived in ways that exceed the neat summaries and syntheses of conventional biographies. For one thing, portions of their political or intellectual activities — notably those of Hilaire Noulens — were conducted in secrecy, or, as in the case of Phạm Hồng Thái and Vũ Trọng Phụng, cut short by premature death, thus lending their lives a fragmentary quality that resists intellectual closure and opening their biographies to contestation over interpretation.[73] While some wrote about themselves, others did not or could not. Some took a principled stand on political issues that went against, or would eventually go against, the prevailing politics and political mood and assumptions of the time. All of them worked within, often against, the particular constraints of their historical, social, and cultural locations; and their lives, sensibilities, and work circumvent the easy, celebratory rhetoric of autonomy and cosmopolitanism of current theories of travel. In all ten cases, the tenacity of ideas of home and belonging informed or haunted their activism and travel (see the chapter by Odine de Guzman). Yet their life experiences also challenged and reinvented these ideas in ways that invoked while also exceeding ideas of nation, belonging, and community that organized politics and political life in their time (see the chapter by Yamamoto Hiroyuki).

Though one of the triumvirate of national heroes in the Philippines, Mariano Ponce did not write much about himself, and very little of his correspondence with family and friends is extant. Phạm Hồng Thái became famous for his failed attempt to assassinate the governor of Indochina in Canton in 1924, and for the ways in which his short life and dramatic death provided an exemplary revolutionary biography, at once Vietnamese nationalist and universal figure, through which his readers learned of, and linked themselves to, the anti-colonial nationalist politics of the period.

The voracious reader Vũ Trọng Phụng, who never traveled abroad, acted as the conduit of a "provincial cosmopolitanism" that depended on the selectively filtered circulation, appropriation, and politicization of French and European literary and critical texts and cultural ideas in Vietnam.[74] The Ukrainian Hilaire Noulens, who served as the hub of the Comintern network in Shanghai, made a career out of hiding himself behind numerous aliases, nationalities, addresses, and post-office boxes. The Hakka writer Du Ai, part of the Philippine anti-Japanese movement that incorporated Chinese guerrillas, memorialized the guerrillas' experiences not, as his comrades did, in autobiographies, but in a three-volume novel-epic (the third volume of which was completed by his wife and fellow activist, Lin Bin). The Thai Communist Ruam Wongphan's posthumous reputation underwent political transmutation as it — and the songs and poems that drew on the Party-as-Mother motif he articulated in his farewell letter to his mother — outlived his death and the demise of the Party. James Puthucheary, who joined the Indian National Army, advocated a socialist solution to the issues of poverty, foreign control of economy, and interethnic inequalities in Malaysia that prefigured the New Economic Policy but proved unable to temper the racialist assumptions behind the NEP's affirmative action policies. The Sino-Thai journalist K. Bali contributed to the development of the Malay language and literary culture and to the propagation of a multicultural Sabah nationhood different from the racial politics practiced in other parts of Malaysia. Connie Bragas-Regalado worked as a domestic helper in Hong Kong and eventually headed Migrante International, a progressive organization that has sought Party-list representation in the Philippine Congress as part of its mission to improve the work conditions of Filipino workers abroad.[75] Executed for masterminding the Bali bombings in 2002, Imam Samudra wrote a short autobiography that clearly revealed the influence of active Islamic political networks from Southeast, South, and Central Asia to the Middle East and North Africa on his radical politics.

Resil Mojares tells the life story of Mariano Ponce (1863–1918), a devoted and tireless pioneering publicist and key organizer of the international network of the early Philippine nationalist movement. The least-known and rather modest and reserved among the "great triumvirate" of the Propaganda Movement, which also included Jose Rizal "the apostle" and Marcelo del Pilar "the militant politician," Ponce played "the patient administrator" and constant spokesperson of the movement through its two-decade-long wax and wane, spending more than half his adult life abroad. A proud gentry product of Enlightenment culture and politics sown in a remote overseas corner of the crumbling Spanish empire, he and his cohorts first unsuccessfully pursued a reformist assimilationist politics on behalf of the colonized Philippines in metropolitan Spain. Then, with the outbreak of the nationalist revolution back home, they made a leap of faith and embraced a revolutionary separatist cause. Moving to Hong Kong and Yokohama, Ponce worked hard to procure and arrange the transnational flows of funds and arms, intelligence, and expertise to his comrades-in-arms in the Philippines by joining the Pan-Asianist network of exiled nationalists from various Western colonies and semi-colonies, and thereby won the inter-nationalist solidarity and support as well as personal friendship of such luminaries as Sun Yat-sen. Disheartened by setbacks in his convoluted mission, he gradually reconciled himself to the defeat of the Philippine nationalist revolution under US Occupation and finally returned home to take part in an assimilated regime of self-rule under US tutelage. Mojares ends his chapter with a thoughtful reflection on the self-described "nomadic life" of his subject, who dwelt in turbulent traveling through faraway lands and seas in quest of the best possible political model and order for his nation, and yet managed to stay a remarkably centered and composed, focused, and even course by anchoring himself in a stable sense of "home" as origin and destination.

Taking as her point of departure a single, failed act of anti-colonialist terrorism against the visiting French Governor-General of Indochina by a group of Chinese anarchist-inspired Vietnamese nationalists in semi-colonized Canton, China, in 1924, Lorraine Paterson reconstructs the intricate cultural political afterlife of Phạm Hồng Thái (1893–1924), the drowned icon of patriotic martyrdom, and its contribution to the early formation of modern Vietnamese nationalism, in the transnational context of blurred ethnic/racial, cultural, and political borders and an imported international literary genre of semi-fictional/historical biography. She teases out the many factual contradictions in the various popular and journalistic, archival, and historiographical accounts of Phạm Hồng Thái's heroic/terrorist act (e.g., the concessional space of the attack, the manner of Phạm Hồng Thái's disguise, the number of perpetrator(s), Phạm Hồng Thái's personal and political background, his personal contact with Hồ Chí Minh, and the nature of his demise), with which an anti-national, French concessional space in Canton and Shanghai was posited *vis-à-vis* the sacred national space of Phạm Hồng Thái's prestigious Chinese grave in Canton, and his supposedly self-sacrificing revolutionary martyrdom was represented as a common motif in the imagination and construction of both the Vietnamese national community and the transborder anti-imperialist fraternity of Sino-Vietnamese and other nationalities. Then Paterson proceeds to lay out a complex and multifaceted textual, contextual, and intertextual historical description and analysis of the composition and publication, circulation and prohibition, reception and interpretation, translation and transformation of biographies of foreign and indigenous heroes and heroines, including Phạm Hồng Thái, as "revolutionary romance," which provides the nationalist role models for their Vietnamese readers to emulate. What eventually emerges from her carefully crafted account is the much deeper and wider, intimately intertwined involvement of transnationality in the formation of nationhood in East and Southeast Asia.

Like an archeologist excavating traces of a long-lost and mysterious life underground, Onimaru Takeshi digs up the Shanghai Metropolitan Police's intelligence files and reconstructs the clandestine activities of Hilaire Noulens (1894–1963), the top liaison officer of the Comintern's Far Eastern Bureau in Shanghai in the early 1930s, who had "a lot of aliases, three passports, at least four houses, ten post office boxes, four telegraphic addresses, and eight bank accounts," and whose real name and nationality were never confirmed by his police captors in his lifetime. Taking advantage of the "gray zone" condition of pre-World War II, semi-colonized and cosmopolitan Shanghai with three territorial sections, three administrative bodies, three police forces, a population of around 24 different nationalities, and extraterritoriality, Noulens and a score or so of his multinational comrades, including Hồ Chí Minh and Tan Malaka, turned the port city into the transnational communication hub of the Comintern's regional network that linked together seven national Communist parties in East and Southeast Asia and directed an incessant flow and circulation of agents, funds, instructions, manuals, political statements, propaganda material, and intelligence reports from Moscow via Berlin to Tokyo, Hong Kong, Amoy, Keelung, Manila, Saigon, Haiphong, Yunnan, Bangkok, Singapore, Batavia, Rangoon, and Calcutta. Eschewing conventional biographies that foreground the personalities of their subjects, Onimaru highlights the importance of agency in anonymity, fleshing out the Comintern career of Noulens by palpably invoking the Communist international network in which the political project of socialist revolution overlapped with those of national liberation and took shape within, and evolved out of, the infrastructure and political technologies used by the worldwide colonial empires in the service of predatory capitalism.

By choosing to focus on the complete works of a lesser-known and self-made-in-Vietnam interwar writer, Vũ Trọng Phụng (1912–39), rather than those of his better-known but atypical contemporary compatriots such as Hồ Chí Minh and Phan Bội Châu, who had the uncommon experience of overseas travel and study, Peter Zinoman unearths what he calls "provincial cosmopolitanism" as an arguably dominant and characteristic mode of capture of transnational metropolitan cultural flows in local colonial cultural politics that was probably typical of most colonized intellectuals with narrow parameters of life experience but a sweeping breadth of cultural horizons. He highlights in systematic detail the peculiar character of Vũ Trọng Phụng's reading of modern French literature, which is opportunistic and unsupervised, broad but shallow, eclectic but unsystematic, mottled and diffuse, diverse and selective, decontextualized and ill-defined, idiosyncratic and tendentious, unorthodox and anachronistic, partial and knowingly ignoring, not discriminating between high and low culture, as well as blending various literary genres or styles together all at once, as is evident in Vũ Trọng Phụng's numerous instances of citing, referencing, and translating foreign authors and works. As a self-defined Vietnamese "realist" who neglected most standard French realist writers but aligned himself instead with a host of French naturalists, romanticists, and scandalous writers of obscene works as fraternal "realist" victims of legal persecution and public condemnation, Vũ Trọng Phụng, argues Zinoman, exhibits a characteristic provincial cosmopolitan appropriation of colonial modernity, marked by strategic instrumental localization, selective anachronism, and the temporal abbreviation and collapsing of different historical periods. Made possible by the geographical distance, temporal unevenness, and cultural unfamiliarity between the colonies and the metropolis, his functional transformation of transnational metropolitan literary reputation and categories for local colonial purposes, i.e., to be used as an impressively exotic and intimidatingly aural instrument of strategic and tactical self-defense against critics and enemies, regardless of the larger literary trends and career trajectories that obtained in their original context, warns against any facile imposition of European classificatory system, familiar preconceptions, and putative oppositions of global cultural politics on the study of its national equivalent.

Caroline Hau's subject matter is the role of revolutionary cosmopolitanism in the formation of dual nationalism, Chinese and Philippine, as practiced by overseas Chinese guerrillas. Working together with their local Hukbalahap comrades and various ethnic and tribal people in Japanese-occupied Philippines, these guerrillas were part of a translingual political project that took shape under the historically unique circumstances of inter-imperialist rivalry and war and the international Communist movement from the early twentieth century to World War II. Hau investigates the biographical, organizational, and fictional embodiments of revolutionary cosmopolitanism in the life stories of the authors Du Ai (1914–93) and his wife, Lin Bin (1922–2008), the history of the Wha Chi guerrilla forces, and Du Ai and Lin Bin's co-written novel *Fengyu Taipingyang* (Storm over the Pacific), which shows the deep and intimate entanglements between anti-colonial Chinese nationalism and Philippine radical nationalism, framed by the reach and limits of translation and forged in the community of fate without guarantees, through love and suspicion, friendship and betrayal, kinship and rejection in the difficult and uncertain wartime conditions. Hau sketches the subsequent demise and afterlife of revolutionary cosmopolitanism and dual nationalism in the ideologically hostile and racially exclusivist Philippines after World War II under anti-Communism, post-Communism, and national chauvinism, and their recent partial redemption by the polycentric left in a more inclusive, pluralist, and integrationist manner. Against the grain of erasure by time and popular forgetfulness, her aim is to capture and rediscover that rare and long-lost historical moment of intimacy and intercourse between lovers, comrades, kith, and kin that were the internationalist Chinese Communist flows and the Philippine nation.

The lyrics of a politically innocuous pop song lead Kasian Tejapira to reconstruct the genealogy of the "Party-as-Mother" metaphor in Thailand. Kasian revisits the life, career, and death of Ruam Wongphan (1922–62), a charismatic ethnic Lao Phuan from Suphan Buri province and a student at Thammasat University and Chulalongkorn University who joined the Thai Communist Party and was among the first Thai Communists to be trained in China. After undertaking political and organizational work among ethnic Tais in the Yunnan area of Southern China, Ruam returned to Thailand to work among, educate, and organize the Thai peasants in the countryside. Ruam's work in the countryside was part and process of an important shift in the Thai Communist Party's policy, strategies, and tactics toward ruralization, peasantization and minority ethnicization, militarization, resinicization, and localization. His farewell letter to his mother, written in jail prior to his summary execution by the military government, with its overtones of Party-as-Mother, provided a potent metaphor — in marked contradistinction to the Sarit regime's self-identification with patriarchy — for the nurturing intimacy that the Party sought to create with its members, an intimacy coded in the religious and ideological idioms of conversion, virtue, and incarnation. The survival, but in a substantively apolitical form, of the metaphor parallels the refashioning of Ruam Wongphan's posthumous reputation from committed revolutionary to "democracy" martyr

— both poignant testaments of an "afterlife subsequent to and in spite of (or perhaps precisely because of) the collapse of both the revolution and the Party."

Khoo Boo Teik begins his account of the political life and critical thought of James J. Puthucheary (1922–2000), a leading ethnic Indian left-wing inter-nationalist, democratic socialist, and economic nationalist whose anti-British imperialist struggles spanned colonial India, Singapore, and postcolonial Malaysia during and after World War II, with a breathtakingly sweeping and vertiginous panorama of the complex transnational inflows and outflows as well as internal flows that swirled around and congealed into the historical matrix that was Malaysia. Khoo presents Puthucheary as an embodiment of many of these flows, one who attempted to make history out of them. As an immigrant product of British colonialism-driven mass migration from India to Malaya who grew up in a plural society, an unequal and unevenly developed colonial economy with ethnic division of labor, and a communally segmented cultural, linguistic, and educational environment, Puthucheary fought valiantly and persistently for more than two decades, both armed and unarmed, in jail and at large, for the political and economic independence as well as political and social democracy of India, Malaya, and Malaysia in turn, only to see his hopes dashed, his ideas and projects ending up time and again in defeat, futility, or perversity, be it the INA (Indian National Army), the PAP (People's Action Party), or the NEP (New Economic Policy). His repeated political failures in the face of overwhelming flows notwithstanding, as a public intellectual he never succumbed to the ruling fallacies and consistently mounted a hard-hitting and well-rounded critique of both the deceptive hegemony of the ruling elite and the flawed counter-hegemony of the Communist insurgency with exceptional clarity and sensitivity, reasserting in full the problematique of ethnicity, class, and state that is essential to the understanding of Malaysian chronic communalist antithesis and recurrent political economic dilemma.

Yamamoto Hiroyuki invites us to contemplate the inspiring if disenchanting lifelong search for the best possible *bangsa* or nation of the multilingual migrant Sino-Thai Buddhist Peranakan-turned-Malay Muslim writer, poet, and journalist Tenh Beng Chuan, aka K. Bali (1927–99), an intellectual champion of "bangsa Sabah" and "bahasa Sabah" (Sabah nationhood and Sabah language) among the ethnically diverse, Malay-speaking peoples of North Borneo in postwar Malaysia. Born in Kelantan in 1927 to a Hokkien-speaking Chinese father and a local-born Siamese mother, Kote, as he was called by village folks, grew up a Buddhist among

Malay Muslim children and classmates and dreamed of "bangsa Malaya," a single, unified Malay-speaking nation free from colonial rule where people transcended class and ethnic differences *à la* Indonesian nationalism. When forced instead into a Chinese ethnic minority status and designated school system under "bangsa Melayu" by the rise of UMNO's Malay nationalism and the resulting ethnic polarization after World War II, K. Bali decided to move to the Malay Muslim-majority south of Thailand, so as to convert to and practice Islam as well as to live, work, study, and write as a Malay there. Ousted from Thailand some years later for his political article in a local Malay newspaper, he eventually settled in North Borneo/Sabah, where he devoted his talents for Malay prose and poetry to a collective project of making Sabah his new chosen bangsa and bahasa along with fellow Peranakan journalists and politicians, only to witness again the emergence and enhancement of ethnic awareness and identities in Sabah instead of his dreamt-of trans-ethnic nationhood and identity. Thus, in his 70s, he moved again from Sabah back to his home village in Kelantan to spend the final year of his mobile life. In that sense, K. Bali's life story is an object lesson in nation-building as actually a trans-local or transnational activity, a continuing journey/exile beyond borders of control, an unending attempt at the making and unmaking of the national, in search of the Never-Never Homeland.

Out of a four-decade-long stream of around 10 million overseas Filipino workers (OFWs) from one in every ten middle- and lower-class households in the country to greener pastures around the world, especially in East Asia, the Middle East, North America, and Western Europe, Odine de Guzman reconstructs a sociological portrait of the collective experience of Filipino female domestic workers, through the personal and political itinerary of Connie Bragas-Regalado (1954–), a college-educated government employee-turned-contract domestic worker in Singapore and then Hong Kong as well as single mother of two children, who has become an eminent workers' rights activist and chairperson of the United Filipinos in Hong Kong, the biggest migrant labor union there, and was chosen as a standard-bearer Party-list congressional candidate by the Migrante Sectoral Party, the largest OFW group, in the 2004 Philippine national election. Making use of the Hegelian master-slave dialectics and Marxist-derived feminist standpoint theory, she posits an OFW standpoint of the Filipino female contract domestic workers, overdetermined as it is by class, race, and gender, from which a myriad of complex and superordinately invisible unequal power relationships between them and the taxing and policing states, predatory international capital, and patriarchal family structures both at home and in the host countries can be visualized, understood, and resisted. Thus, despite the deafening official chorus of praise for OFWs' presumed economic heroism and self-sacrifice for the sake of nation and family, what remains unseen or unrecognized is that their hard-earned remittances and taxes have made possible the continuing rule of the masters of the Philippine, Singaporean, Hong Kong, and other host states, that their underpaid and undervalued deskilling domestic work has made possible the lucrative skilled jobs and productive labor of their foreign employers out of the home, that their motherly care and responsibility have allowed their wayward and irresponsible husbands to "move to the next house/life" and leave all family-related burden to them. It was to find ways to break out of this transnational vicious cycle of financially insecure home and overseas contract work, desperate sojourn and unfulfilling return, which has increasingly trapped even their grown-up children, that Connie Bragas-Regalado and her comrades in the Migrante International network brought the force of their political activism home to bear down on the Philippine state as citizen-members of the sovereign nation.

Shiraishi Takashi traces the current transnational flows of radical Islam in Southeast and Central Asia through the life story of Imam Samudra (1972–2008), a captured and executed Indonesian jihadist, member of Jemaah Islamiyah (JI), and "architect" of the Bali terrorist bombings in 2002, as told by himself in his autobiography, interview, and police interrogation. As the young Imam Samudra, taking pride in his deeply pious ulama mujahid Muslim blood, experienced a jolting spiritual awakening, was converted to radical Islam, went to Soviet-occupied Afghanistan on a three-year-long training and fighting jihad mission, and came back to continue proselytizing, organizing, and carrying out terrorist activities in Indonesia and Malaysia, one could see him being gradually sucked down deeper and deeper into the undercurrent of anti-modernist, absolutist, and monolithic Salafism along the underground waterway that was the regional Darul Islam, JI, and al-Qaeda network. Haunted by Internet images of atrocities committed by the Israeli and American "Drakula bin Monster" on helpless Muslims, and enchanted by the "entirely new and very new" and "really, really clean" purist moral community of fellow jihadists in Afghanistan, Imam Samudra led the austere, devoted, and purified life of a mujahid resister that was purged of all fitnah (temptation) *à la* Western modernity, be it the national, the ethnic, the secular, the sexual, the non-religious language and categories, or even social change itself. And yet, while the process of refining culture and self-censorship eventually failed to completely dam the flows of Western modernism as the banished, unholy national categories and even English words seeped into his own language and way of thinking unawares through the back door, it did manage to narrow down his language and understanding of the social world, and resultant scope and choice of action on that world so much so that his itinerary and fateful destiny is almost predetermined.

Anthony Reid reminds us that "timing — when to be absent, when to be actively present, when to be jailed, when to speak out, when to die" is a crucial element in the making of reputations.[76] With the exception of Ponce and Phạm Hồng Thái, almost all of the subjects of this book found themselves at cross purposes with predominant views of the nation and the actually existing nation-state in their respective domiciles, often falling afoul of the authorities that allocated to themselves the right to imagine, speak of, and make the "nation." We began this book with a number of subjects whose lives and careers were shaped by a form of cosmopolitanism engendered by colonialism, imperialism, and regional and global capitalism, and we discussed the efforts of these traveling subjects to imagine and create a nation out of the ideational and material flows that swept through the territories they inhabited and traversed. We end the book with Imam Samudra, a man who came of age in Indonesia, now a nation-state, but spent the better part of his life trying to destroy and replace it with a state organized by a different vision of cosmopolitan community, but one that is nevertheless contaminated by received notions of nation and its territorial boundaries. The reputations of the subjects of this book would undergo the permutations induced by changing times and mores, political and economic contexts, and intellectual trends. But in all cases, their life stories speak across the years to their biographers, whose evolving research agendas have led them to re-interpret, even rewrite, these biographies in ways that necessitate a rethinking of the rules, premises, and conditions by which the subject (in the senses of both topic and person) of the nation is defined, contested, and reinvented.

The chapters show how "travel" and its contingent and uneven processes of translation, circulation, and exchange defined the trajectories of these ten individuals' political thought and action, even as their political inclinations and activism helped set the intellectual and geographical itineraries they would cover in their lifetimes. With these biographies, we highlight the ways in which nation-making is deeply informed by, and in turn shapes, specific patterns and densities of local, regional, and global flows, movements, and networks across modern Southeast Asia. *Traveling Nation-Makers* hopes to illuminate some of the pathways by which people in this region worked, with varying degrees of success, to realize their intellectual, aesthetic, and political visions and projects over the last tumultuous century.

Notes

1 Arjun Appadurai, "Grassroots Globalization and the Research Imagination," in *Globalization*, ed. Appadurai (Durham: Duke University Press, 2001), p. 5. On the idea of "flows," see Scott Lash and John Urry, *Economies of Signs and Space* (London: Sage, 1994), p. 12.

2 For a balanced account, see Susan Strange, *The Retreat of the State: The Diffusion of Power in the World Economy* (Cambridge: Cambridge University Press, 1996).

3 An exemplary formulation is Paul Gilroy, *The Black Atlantic: Modernity and Double Consciousness* (Cambridge: Harvard University Press, 1993), especially chapter 1.

4 On the nation-state's propensity for sweeping ethnic diversities into "fixed and closed sets of cultural categories," see Arjun Appadurai, *Modernity at Large: Cultural Dimensions of Globalization* (Minneapolis: University of Minnesota Press, 1996), pp. 139–57.

5 This is evident in Ulf Hannerz's "global cultural flow chart" in *Cultural Complexity: Studies in the Social Organization of Meaning* (New York: Columbia University Press, 1992), p. 221; and James Clifford's assumption that "discrepant cosmopolitanism" involves displacement and transplantation in his influential essay "Traveling Cultures," in Clifford, *Routes: Travel and Translation in the Late Twentieth Century* (Cambridge: Harvard University Press, 1997), p. 36.

6 Gilles Deleuze and Felix Guattari, *Anti-Oedipus*, vol. 1 of *Capitalism and Schizophrenia*, trans. Robert Hurley, Mark Seem, and Helen R. Lane (London: Athlone, 1984).

7 See, for example, Jonathan Xavier Inda and Renato Rosaldo, eds., *The Anthropology of Globalization: A Reader* (Oxford: Blackwell Publishers, 2002).

8 Jurgen Habermas, *The Postnational Constellation: Political Essays* (Cambridge: MIT Press, 2001).

9 Khachig Tölöyan, "The Nation-State and Its Others: In Lieu of a Preface," *Diaspora* 1, 1 (1991): 3. See also chapters 1 and 2 of *Nations Unbound: Transnational Projects, Postcolonial Predicaments and Deterritorialized Nation-States*, ed. Linda Basch, Nina Glick Schiller, and Cristina Szanton Blanc (New York and London: Routledge, 1993).

10 Harry Kreisler, "Globalization and Islam: A Conversation with Olivier Roy," Institute of International Studies, University of California, Berkeley, 2007, <http://globetrotter.berkeley.edu/people7/Roy/roy07-con5.html>, p. 5. A more nuanced account can be found in Brynjar Lia, *Architect of Global Jihad: The Life of Al-Qaeda Strategist Abu Mus'ab Al-Suri* (New York: Columbia University Press, 2008).

11 On the making of "Southeast Asia" as a "place-name," see Donald K. Emmerson, "'Southeast Asia': What's in a Name?" *Journal of Southeast Asian Studies* 15, 1 (Mar. 1984): 1–21.

12 Anthony Reid, *Southeast Asia in the Age of Commerce, 1450–1680*, vol. 2: *Expansion and Crisis* (New Haven: Yale University Press, 1993), p. 144. See Victor Lieberman, *Strange Parallels: Southeast Asia in Global Context, c. 800–1830. Vol. 1: Integration on the Mainland* (Cambridge: Cambridge University Press, 2003), and *Strange Parallels: Southeast Asia in Global Context, c. 800–1830. Vol. 2: Mainland Mirrors: Europe, Japan, China, South Asia and the Islands* (Cambridge: Cambridge University Press, 2009). See also the essays, especially the introduction, in Laurie Sears, ed., *Knowing Southeast Asian Subjects* (Seattle: University of Washington Press, 2007).

13 For a useful overview and critique of historical writing on early Southeast Asia, see Craig J. Reynolds, "A New Look at Old Southeast Asia," *Journal of Asian Studies* 54, 2 (May 1995): 419–46.

14 Denys Lombard, "Networks and Synchronisms in Southeast Asian History," *Journal of Southeast Asian History* 26, 1 (Mar. 1995): 10–6.

15 See, for example, John Smail, "On the Possibility of an Autonomous History of Modern Southeast Asia," *Journal of Southeast Asian History* 2 (1961): 72–102; and Oliver Wolters, *History, Culture and Region in Southeast Asian Perspectives*, rev. ed. (Ithaca: Southeast Asia Program, Cornell University, 1999). We thank the anonymous reader of this book for this cogent reminder.

16 Devleena Ghosh and Stephen Muecke, "Indian Ocean Stories," *UTS Review Cultural Studies and New Writings* 6, 2 (2000): 25.

17 Fernand Braudel, *The Mediterranean and the Mediterranean World in the Age of Philip II*, 2 vols., trans. Sian Reynolds (Berkeley and London: University of California Press, 1995), originally published in 1949; Immanuel Wallerstein, *The Modern World-System, vol. 1: Capitalist Agriculture and the Origins of the European World-Economy in the Sixteenth Century* (New York and London: Academic Press, 1974), *The Modern World-System, vol. 2: Mercantilism and the Consolidation of the European World-Economy 1600–1750* (New York: Academic Press, 1980), and *The Modern World-System, vol. 3: The Second Great Expansion of the Capitalist World-Economy, 1730–1840* (San Diego: Academic Press, 1989).

18 R. Bin Wong, *China Transformed: Historical Change and the Limits of European Experience* (Ithaca: Cornell University Press, 1997); Andre Gunder Frank, *ReOrient: Global Economy in the Asian Age* (Berkeley: University of California Press, 1998); Kenneth Pomeranz, *The Great Divergence: China, Europe, and the Making of the Modern World Economy* (Princeton and Oxford: Princeton University Press, 2000).

19 See K.N. Chaudhuri, *Trade and Civilization in the Indian Ocean: An Economic History from the Rise of Islam to 1750* (Cambridge: Cambridge University Press, 1985), and *Asia Before Europe: Economy and Civilization of the Indian Ocean from the Rise of Islam to 1750* (Cambridge: Cambridge University Press, 1990); Ashin Das Gupta and M.N. Pearson, eds., *India and the Indian Ocean* (New Delhi: Oxford University Press, 1987); Michael N. Pearson, *The Indian Ocean*

(London: Routledge, 2003), and *The World of the Indian Ocean, 1500–1800: Studies in Social, Economic and Cultural History* (Aldershot: Variorium Collected Studies Series, Ashgate, 2005).

20 See, for example, the essays in Peter J. Katzenstein, ed., *Civilizations in World Politics: Plural and Pluralist Perspectives* (London and New York: Routledge, 2010). Examples include Lynda Shaffer's discussion of the impact of India and Southeast Asia on Chinese economic, cultural, and technological development in "Southernization," *Journal of World History* 5 (1994): 1–21; and Grant Evans, Christopher Hutton, and Khua Khun Eng, eds., *Where China Meets Southeast Asia: Social and Cultural Change in the Border Regions* (Singapore: Institute of Southeast Asian Studies, 2000).

21 Samuel P. Huntington, "Clash of Civilizations?" *Foreign Affairs* 72, 3 (1993): 22–49, and *The Clash of Civilizations and the Remaking of World Order* (New York: Simon & Schuster, 1996).

22 On the Hadhrami diaspora, for example, there is a rich literature: Engseng Ho, "Before Parochialization: Diasporic Arabs Cast in Creole Waters," in *Transcending Borders: Arabs, Politics, Trade and Islam in Southeast Asia*, ed. Huub de Jonge and Nico Kaptein (Leiden: KITLV Press, 2002); Ulrike Freitag and William Clarence-Smith, eds., *Hadhrami Traders, Scholars, and Statesmen in the Indian Ocean, 1750s–1960s* (Leiden: Brill, 1997); Leif Manger, *The Hadrami Diaspora: Community-Building on the Indian Ocean Rim* (Oxford: Berghahn Books, 2010); Huub de Jonge and Nico Kaptein, eds., *Transcending Borders: Arabs, Politics, Trade in Southeast Asia* (Leiden: KITLV Press, 2002). On the Sindhi diaspora, see Claude Markovits, *The Global World of Indian Merchants 1750–1947: Traders of Sind from Bukhara to Panama* (Cambridge: Cambridge University Press, 2000). On the role of the "Chinese" Muslims in the spread of Islam in Southeast Asia, see Tan Ta Sen, *Cheng Ho and Islam in Southeast Asia* (Singapore: Institute of Southeast Asian Studies, 2009).

23 Giovanni Arrighi, Takeshi Hamashita, and Mark Selden, "Introduction: The Rise of East Asia in Regional and World Historical Perspective," in *The Resurgence of East Asia: 500, 150 and 50 Year Perspectives*, ed. Arrighi, Hamashita, and Selden (London: Routledge, 2003), p. 2.

24 Peter J. Katzenstein, *A World of Regions: Asia and Europe in the American Imperium* (Ithaca: Cornell University Press, 2005).

25 Takeshi Hamashita, *China, East Asia and the Global Economy: Regional and Historical Perspectives*, ed. Mark Selden and Linda Grove (London and New York: Routledge, 2008). Another example of a country study that uses a regional lens is Arano Yasunori, Ishii Masatoshi, and Murai Shosuke, *Ajia no naka no Nihon* [Japan in Asia], 6 vols. (Tokyo: Tokyo University Press, 1992–3). Southeast Asia's centrality to region-formation is discussed in Takashi Shiraishi, *Umi no teikoku* [Empire of the Seas: The Making of a Region] (Tokyo: Chuokoron, 2000).

26 An important exception is Vicente L. Rafael, *The Promise of the Foreign: Nationalism and the Technics of Translation in the Spanish Philippines* (Durham: Duke University Press, 2005). For a theoretical clarification of the role of the "contact zone" — in which different nationalities come together in a given space — in mediating the imagination of the nation, see Arif Dirlik, "Transnationalism, the Press, and the National Imaginary," *The China Review* 4, 1 (Spring 2004): 11–25.

27 Anthony Reid and Maria Serena Diokno, "Completing the Circle: Southeast Asian Studies in Southeast Asia," in *Southeast Asian Studies: Pacific Perspectives*, ed. Reid (Tempe: Monograph Series Press, Program for Southeast Asian Studies, Arizona State University, 2003), pp. 96–7.

28 Claudine Salmon, ed., *Récits de voyages des asiatiques: Genres, mentalités, conception de l'espace* (Paris: École Français d'Extrême Orient, 1996), is a pioneering collection of essays dealing with travels to, within, and from Asia.

29 Susan Bayly, *Asian Voices in a Postcolonial Age: Vietnam, India and Beyond* (Cambridge: Cambridge University Press, 2007).

30 Janet Wolff, "On the Road Again: Metaphors of Travel in Cultural Criticism," *Cultural Studies* 7, 1 (1993): 224–39. See also Clifford, "Traveling Cultures," p. 33.

31 Benedict Anderson, *Imagined Communities: Reflections on the Origin and Spread of Nationalism*, rev. ed. (London: Verso, 1991), p. 57.

32 Resil B. Mojares, *Brains of the Nation: Pedro Paterno, T.H. Pardo de Tavera, Isabelo delos Reyes and the Production of Modern Knowledge* (Quezon City: Ateneo de Manila University Press, 2006), illuminates the interactions between the Propagandist Filipinos working in Spain and those in the colony (including Isabelo delos Reyes), showing how the "Enlightenment" was not simply imported, but locally produced.

33 See Prasenjit Duara, "Transnationalism and the Predicament of Sovereignty," *American Historical Review* 102, 4 (1997): 1030–51. See also Caroline S. Hau and Takashi Shiraishi, "Daydreaming about Rizal and Tetchou: On Asianism as Network and Fantasy," *Philippine Studies* 57, 3 (2009): 329–88.

34 Susan Bayly, "Vietnamese Narratives of Tradition, Exchange and Friendship in the Worlds of the Global Socialist Ecumene," in *Enduring Socialism: Explorations of Revolution and Transformation, Restoration and Continuation*, ed. Harry G. West and Parvathi Raman (Oxford: Berghahn Books, 2008), pp. 125–47. See also Bayly, *Asian Voices in a Postcolonial Age*, p. 221.

35 V.I. Lenin, *Imperialism, the Highest Stage of Capitalism* (New York: International Publishers, 1969).

36 Huỳnh Kim Khánh, *Vietnamese Communism 1925–1945* (Ithaca: Cornell University Press, 1982), p. 55. See also Michael Weiner, "Comintern in East Asia, 1919–1939," in Kevin McDermott and Jeremy Agnew, *The Comintern: A History of International Communism from Lenin to Stalin* (Hampshire and London: Macmillan Press, 1996), pp. 158–89, 262–4; and Tim Rees and

Andrew Thorpe, *International Communism and the Communist International 1919–1943* (Manchester: Manchester University Press, 1998), chapters 16–18.

37 On the impact of travel to Shanghai on Tan Malaka's political career and ideas, see Abidin Kusno, "Tan Malaka, Shanghai and the Politics of Geographical Imagining," *Singapore Journal of Tropical Geography* 24, 3 (2003): 327–39. Kusno's account, though insightful, does not address the political imperatives behind Tan Malaka's travel to Shanghai or the relationship between Shanghai and Tan Malaka's role as regional facilitator of the Comintern's Far Eastern Bureau.

38 Christopher E. Goscha, *Thailand and the Southeast Asian Networks of the Vietnamese Revolution, 1885–1954* (Surrey: Curzon, 1999).

39 Robert J. Alexander, *International Maoism in the Developing World* (Westport, CT: Praeger, 1999), p. 26.

40 Dale F. Eickelman and James Piscatori, "Preface" and "Social Theory in the Study of Muslim Societies," in *Muslim Travellers: Pilgrimage, Migration, and the Religious Imagination*, ed. Eickelman and Piscatori (Berkeley: University of California Press, 1990), pp. xii–xxii, 3–25. In Southeast Asian studies, see the pioneering work by Jacob Vredenbregt, "The Haddj: Some of Its Features and Functions in Indonesia," *Bijdragan voor Taal-, Land-, en Volkenkunde* 118, 1 (1962): 91–154; Narifumi Maeda, "The Aftereffects of Hajj and Kaan Buat," *Journal of Southeast Asian Studies* 6, 2 (1975): 178–89; Virginia Matheson Hooker and Anthony Crothers Milner, *Perceptions of the Haj: Five Malay Texts*, Research Notes and Discussion Papers No. 46 (Singapore: Institute of Southeast Asian Studies, 1984); and the essays in Eric Tagliacozzo, ed., *Southeast Asia and the Middle East: Islam, Movement and the* Longue Durée (Stanford: Stanford University Press, 2009).

41 Dale F. Eickelman and James Piscatori, *Muslim Politics* (Princeton: Princeton University Press, 1996), pp. ix–xiv; Robert W. Hefner, "Islam in an Era of Nation-States: Politics and Religious Renewal in Muslim Southeast Asia," in *Islam in an Era of Nation-States: Politics and Religious Renewal in Muslim Southeast Asia*, ed. Hefner and Patricia Horvatich (Honolulu: University of Hawaii Press, 1997), pp. 3–40; Michael F. Laffan, *Islamic Nationhood and Colonial Indonesia: The Umma below the Winds* (London: RoutledgeCurzon, 2003). See also Michael G. Peletz, "'Ordinary Muslims' and Muslim Resurgents in Contemporary Malaysia," in *Islam in an Era of Nation-States: Politics and Religious Renewal in Muslim Southeast Asia*, ed. Robert W. Hefner and Patricia Horvatich (Honolulu: University of Hawaii Press, 1997), pp. 231–73.

42 The classic text on the Islamic revival is Richard P. Mitchell, *The Society of the Muslim Brothers* (Oxford: Oxford University Press, 1993). See also the essays in Barry Rubin, ed., *The Muslim Brotherhood: The Organizations and Policies of a Global Islamist Movement* (New York: Palgrave Macmillan, 2010).

43 Thomas M. McKenna, *Muslim Rulers and Rebels: Everyday Politics and Armed Separation in the Philippines* (Berkeley: University of California Press, 1998);

Patricio N. Abinales, *Making Mindanao: Cotabato and Davao in the Formation of the Philippine Nation-State* (Quezon City: Ateneo de Manila University Press, 2000).

44 Chandra Muzaffar, "Islamic Resurgence: A Global View (With Illustrations from Southeast Asia)," in *Islam and Society in Southeast Asia*, ed. Taufik Abdullah and Sharon Siddique (Singapore: Institute of Southeast Asian Studies, 1986), p. 19; see also Naveed S. Sheikh, *The New Politics of Islam: Pan-Islamic Foreign Policy in a World of States* (London: RoutledgeCurzon, 2003).

45 See Mariam Abou Zahab and Olivier Roy, *Islamist Networks: The Pakistan-Afghan Connection* (London: Hurst, 2003), chapter 5; Quintan Wiktorowicz, *The Management of Islamic Activism: Salafis, the Muslim Brotherhood, and State Power in Jordan* (Buffalo: State University of New York Press, 2001), p. 6; and John Cooley, *Unholy Wars: Afghanistan, America and International Terrorism*, 3rd ed. (London: Pluto Press, 2002).

46 Wiktorowicz, *Management of Islamic Activism*, pp. 111–46.

47 See, for example, Noorhaidi Hasan, *Laskar Jihad: Islam, Militancy and the Quest for Identity in Post-New Order Indonesia* (Ithaca: Southeast Asia Program, Cornell University, 2006); John T. Sidel, *Riots, Pogroms, Jihad: Religious Violence in Indonesia* (Ithaca: Cornell University Press, 2006); and the essays in *Conflict, Community and Criminality in Southeast Asia and Australia: Assessments from the Field*, ed. Arnaud de Brochgrave, Thomas Sanderson, and David Gordon (Washington, DC: Center for Strategic and International Studies, 2009).

48 Kaoru Sugihara, "Introduction," in *Japan, China, and the Growth of the Asian International Economy, 1850–1949*, ed. Kaoru Sugihara, Japan Studies in Economic and Social History, vol. 1. (Oxford and New York: Oxford University Press), p. 1.

49 Ibid., p. 5.

50 Takashi Shiraishi, *An Age in Motion: Popular Radicalism in Java 1912–1926* (Ithaca: Cornell University Press, 1990). On the impact of Indonesian nationalism on, for example, Hadhrami identity, see Natalie Mobini-Kesheh, *The Hadrami Awakening: Community and Identity in the Netherlands East Indies, 1900–1942* (Ithaca: Southeast Asia Program, Cornell University, 1999). For a book-length study of the rise of overseas Chinese nationalism in Indonesia, see Lea E. Williams, *Overseas Chinese Nationalism: The Genesis of the Pan-Chinese Movement in Indonesia, 1900–1916* (Glencoe, IL: The Free Press, 1960).

51 Shiraishi, *Age in Motion*, chapter 7. C.W. Watson discusses two autobiographies by self-identified Muslim Communists, Hasan Raid and H. Achmadi Moestahal, in his *Of Self and Injustice: Autobiography and Repression in Modern Indonesia* (Leiden: KITLV Press, 2006), chapters 1 and 2. See also Hefner, "Islam in an Era of Nation-States," p. 17; and Deliar Noer, *The Modern Muslim Movement in Indonesia, 1900–1942* (Kuala Lumpur: Oxford University Press, 1973). On the ambivalent relationship between nationalism and Islam in Malaysia, see

Ariffin Omar, *Bangsa Melayu: Malay Concepts of Democracy and Community, 1945–1950* (Kuala Lumpur: Oxford University Press, 1993).

52 See, for example, the research by Nelly van Doorn-Harder and Kees de Jong, "The Pilgrimage to Tembayat: Tradition and Revival in Indonesian Islam," *The Muslim World* 91, 3–4 (Sept. 2001): 325–54.

53 Weiner, "Comintern in East Asia," *The Comintern*, p. xviii.

54 Takashi Shiraishi, "Aiming to Build an East Asia Community," *Japan Echo* (Feb. 2006): 58–63.

55 See Pheng Cheah's cogent critique of Clifford and Homi Bhabha's notions of cosmopolitanism in "Given Culture: Rethinking Cosmopolitical Freedom in Transnationalism," in Cheah, *Inhuman Conditions: On Cosmopolitanism and Human Rights* (Cambridge: Harvard University Press, 2006), pp. 82–7, 91–2.

56 See the essays in Cheah, *Inhuman Conditions*.

57 Cheah, "Given Culture," pp. 80–119, 280–5. On globalization's relationship with nationalism and its implications for the concept of "belonging," see Ulf Hedetoft and Mette Hjort, "Introduction," in *The Postnational Self: Belonging and Identity*, ed. Hedetoft and Hjort (Minneapolis: University of Minnesota Press, 2002), pp. xix–xx.

58 Clifford, *Routes*, p. 2.

59 Stanley Fish, "Biography and Intention," in *Contesting the Subject: Essays in the Postmodern Theory and Practice of Biography and Biographical Criticism*, ed. William H. Epstein (West Lafayette: Purdue University Press, 1991), pp. 9–16.

60 Anthony Reid, "On the Importance of Autobiography," *Indonesia* 13 (Apr. 1972): 1–3; Susan Rodgers, ed. and trans., *Telling Lives, Telling History: Autobiography and Historical Imagination in Modern Indonesia* (Berkeley: University of California Press, 1995), p. 8; Alfred W. McCoy, "Introduction: Biography of Lives Obscure, Ordinary and Heroic," in *Lives at the Margin: Biography of Filipinos Obscure, Ordinary, and Heroic*, ed. McCoy (Madison: Center for Southeast Asian Studies, University of Wisconsin-Madison, 2001), p. 2; Mojares, *Brains of the Nation*, p. ix; Roxana Waterson, "Introduction: Analyzing Personal Narratives," in *Southeast Asian Lives: Personal Narratives and Historical Experience*, ed. Waterson (Athens: Ohio University Press, 2007), pp. 1–37.

61 Robert Smith, *Derrida and Autobiography* (Cambridge: Cambridge University Press, 1995), p. 61.

62 See, for example, Christoph Giebel, *Imagined Ancestries of Vietnamese Communism: Ton Duc Thang and the Politics of History & Memory* (Seattle: University of Washington Press, 2004).

63 Amin Sweeney, *Reputations Live On: An Early Malay Autobiography* (Berkeley: University of California Press, 1980), p. 18. See also Benedict R.O'G. Anderson's classic analysis of the Javanese student-activist Soetomo's memoirs, "A Time of Darkness and a Time of Light: Transposition in Early Indonesian Nationalist Thought," in Anderson, *Language and Power: Exploring Political Cultures in Indonesia* (Ithaca: Cornell University Press, 1990), pp. 241–70.

64 Anthony Milner, *The Invention of Politics in Colonial Malaya: Contesting Nationalism and the Expansion of the Public Sphere* (Cambridge: Cambridge University Press, 1995), chapter 2. Also of interest is Milner's critique of Wang Gungwu, ed., *Self and Biography: Essays on the Individual and Society in Asia* (Sydney: Sydney University Press for the Australian Academy of Humanities, 1975), in A.C. Milner, "Post-modern Perspectives on Malay Biography," *Kajian Malaysia* 9, 2 (Dec. 1991): 24–38. For a book-length discussion of auto/biography and politics in the Philippines, see Caroline S. Hau, *On the Subject of the Nation: Filipino Writings from the Margins, 1981–2004* (Quezon City: Ateneo de Manila University Press, 2004).

65 Craig J. Reynolds, "Jit Poumisak in Thai History," in Reynolds, *Thai Radical Discourse: The Real Face of Thai Feudalism Today* (Ithaca: Southeast Asia Program, Cornell University, 1987), pp. 23–5. See also his "The Author-Function and Thai History," *Asian Studies Association of Australia Review* 10, 1 (1986): 22–8. On the circulation and consumption of Marxist texts in Thailand, see Kasian Tejapira, *Commodifying Marxism: The Formation of Modern Thai Radical Culture, 1927–1958* (Kyoto: Kyoto University Press, 2001).

66 Reynolds, *Thai Radical Discourse*, p. 15.

67 On the application of biographical study and "social networks" theory to the study of militant Islam, see Marc Sageman, *Understanding Terror Networks* (Philadelphia: University of Pennsylvania Press, 2004); and *Leaderless Jihad: Terror Networks in the Twenty-first Century* (Philadelphia: University of Pennsylvania Press, 2008).

68 On the importance of auto/biographical practice to representative politics in the modern nation-state, see Betty Joseph, "Representation and Representative Politics: Reading Female Insurgency, Subalternity, and Self-Constitution in the Anti-Colonial Text," *Auto/Biography Studies* 12, 1 (Spring 1997): 52–70.

69 McCoy, "Introduction," *Lives at the Margin*, pp. 7, 18.

70 C.W. Watson, *Of Self and Nation: Autobiography and the Representation of Modern Indonesia* (Honolulu: University of Hawaii Press, 2000), p. 7.

71 Watson, *Of Self and Injustice*, p. 1.

72 Some of these political travelers have written or authorized auto/biographical essays and books. Among the works available in English, see, for example, Jose Rizal, *Reminiscences*, trans. and annotated by Encarnacion Alzona (Manila: Jose Rizal National Centennial Commission, 1961); Phan Bội Châu's "Prison Notes" and Hồ Chí Minh's "Prison Diary," in *Reflections from Captivity*, ed. David G. Marr, trans. Christopher Jenkins, Khanh Tuyet Tran, and Sanh Thong Huynh (Athens: Ohio University Press, 1978); Phan Bội Châu, *Overturned Chariot: The Autobiography of Phan Boi Chau*, trans. Vinh Sinh and Nicholas Wickenden, SHAPS Library of Translations (Honolulu: University of Hawaii Press, 1999); Tan Malaka, *From Jail to Jail*, trans. and annotated by Helen Jarvis, 3 vols., Southeast Asia Series No. 83 (Athens: Ohio University Center for International Studies, 1991); and Ranjit Gill, *Of Political Bondage: An*

Authorized Biography of Tunku Abdul Rahman, Malaysia's First Prime Minister and His Continuing Participation in Contemporary Politics (Singapore: Sterling Corporate Services, 1990).

73 Cf. Reynolds, *Thai Radical Discourse*, pp. 13–8.

74 For an early example of a home-grown intellectual and political actor who laid claim to the ideals of the Enlightenment and the French Revolution, see Cesar Adib Majul's biography of the "Brains of the Philippine Revolution," Apolinario Mabini (1864–1903), *Apolinario Mabini, Revolutionary* (Manila: National Heroes Commission, 1964), and *Mabini and the Philippine Revolution* (Quezon City: University of the Philippines, 1960). Mabini, who was fluent in Spanish and Tagalog and taught himself English, was exiled by the Americans to Guam in 1901, and died shortly after he returned to the Philippines in 1903.

75 For an important corrective to the paucity of biographical narratives of border-crossing women political activists, see Agnes Khoo, ed., *Life as the River Flows: Women in the Malayan Anti-Colonial Struggle* (*An Oral History of Women from Thailand, Malaysia and Singapore*) (Monmouth, Wales: Merlin Press, 2006).

76 We are indebted to Anthony Reid for this quotation and for encouraging us to expand some of the ideas in this paragraph. Anthony Reid, personal communication, 9 Sept. 2009.

CHAPTER 1

The Itineraries of Mariano Ponce

Resil B. Mojares

Bulacan/Manila (Philippines) (1863–87) – Barcelona/Madrid (Spain) (1887–96) – Hong Kong/Yokohama (China, Japan) (1896–1907) – Vietnam/ Cambodia (1906–7) – Manila/Bulacan (1907–18) – Hong Kong (1918)

> *Man is like a dry leaf blown whichever way by Destiny's wind, although for us, Filipinos, it is not just wind but a hurricane.*
>
> — Mariano Ponce to Filipino colleagues, Hong Kong, 22 October 1897

He was the last Propagandist. The steadiest worker of the "Propaganda Movement," the primary vehicle of nineteenth-century Filipino nationalism, he was present at the birth of the movement in Manila in 1880 and its demise in Hong Kong in 1903. Considered one of the movement's "great triumvirate" together with Jose Rizal and Marcelo del Pilar, he survived both and saw the movement shift from the reformist campaign for political assimilation to Greater Spain, to the revolutionary war for independence, and then the accommodation to the nation-building project under US colonial auspices. Through these shifts, no one of his generation was as actively engaged in the international work of the Philippine campaign, writing propaganda, soliciting assistance, and building alliances.

Yet, Mariano Ponce (1863–1918) is barely visible. Modest and reserved, Ponce did not write his biography, and while he wrote a lot, he rarely spoke about himself.[1] The itineraries he took, however, richly illustrate how he positioned himself and the "nation" in the world.

HIS early life followed the familiar trajectory of sons of the landowning gentry in his time, a move from provincial hometown to colonial capital and then (for the most privileged sons) metropolitan Europe. Born in

The "great triumvirate" of the Philippine nationalist movement: (left to right) Jose Rizal, Marcelo del Pilar, and Mariano Ponce

Baliwag, Bulacan, on 23 March 1863, he had his early schooling in Bulacan, attended grammar school in Manila, enrolled in San Juan de Letran, obtained a *bachiller en artes* in 1885, entered Universidad de Santo Tomas in the same year to study medicine, and then left for Europe in 1887 to continue his studies.

He was not an innocent abroad but a young man with a purpose when he arrived in Barcelona in June 1887. He left the Philippines at a time of political ferment, stirred by advancing liberalism in Spain and, in the colony, Enlightenment-inspired reformist activities that began in the mid-nineteenth century. A small but widening formation of propertied and educated Creoles, mestizos, and *indios* agitated for civil rights and the curtailment of the powers of the religious orders.

Ponce was drawn into this ferment early. In 1880, when he was still a secondary-school student in Manila, he and his friends used to gather in a house in the proletarian district of Tondo to listen to Marcelo del Pilar, "our future apostle" (Ponce writes), who instilled in their "virgin minds the germ of new ideas" and in their hearts "the pure love of our fallen country."[2] Del Pilar was Ponce's province mate, 12 years his senior, a lawyer active in both Bulacan and Manila in spreading anti-friar and reformist ideas. Ponce later claimed that the Tondo meetings were the "embryonic" beginnings of what came to be called La Propaganda.[3]

Having left for Spain, Ponce missed out on the events that brought the reformist campaign to a head. There was Jose Rizal's return to Manila from Europe in late 1887, surrounded by the controversy over his recently published anti-colonial novel *Noli me Tangere* (1887). Then there was the unprecedented public demonstration in Manila on 1 March 1888 that called for the suppression of the religious orders, and then the wave of indiscriminate repression that followed.

Ponce was not disconnected from these events. Shortly before he left for Spain, he was part of a group led by del Pilar, called Caja de Jesus, Maria y Jose. Formed ostensibly to raise funds for bright but indigent students, it may have served other purposes as well since it became the nucleus of the Comite de Propaganda, which del Pilar and other leaders formed shortly before del Pilar, fearing arrest, fled to Spain on 31 October 1888. The primary aim of La Propaganda was to pursue the campaign for reforms in the imperial center and the more open environment of Europe. Ponce, therefore, was not in Spain solely to study medicine. He was La Propaganda's "advance party."

The rapid succession of interrelated events indicates that from the time Ponce arrived in Spain there was already a plan to conduct systematic propaganda and create a movement linking reformists in the metropolis and the colony. Within months of his arrival in Barcelona, Ponce was contributing del Pilar's and his own reports on political events in Manila to liberal newspapers in Spain. He corresponded with other Filipinos in Europe and was in communication with the Manila reformists on plans to revive the recently defunct liberal Filipino-Spanish newspaper *España en Filipinas* (1887). When it was decided that a new paper be published instead, Ponce helped organize the Filipino association called La Solidaridad on 1 January 1889, to mobilize support for a new organ. This organ, also called *La Solidaridad*, appeared on 15 February, just a month and a half after del Pilar himself arrived in Barcelona.

From the moment del Pilar arrived in Spain, Ponce and he were already organizing Asociacion Hispano-Filipino as a forum for building alliances with progressive Spanish politicians and intellectuals. (Ponce was the association's secretary until its dissolution in 1896.) In Barcelona, Ponce and del Pilar helped launch the first Masonic Lodge for Filipinos, Revolucion, in April 1889. Within months of del Pilar's arrival — and, in no small part, because of Ponce's preparatory work — they had what were the main instruments of the Propaganda Movement: their own newspaper, the network of Freemasonry and fraternal associations, and, not least, a link to reformists and funding support in the Philippines in the Manila-based Comite.

Ponce and del Pilar did not inaugurate something new. Colonialism draws the colonized into an orbit in which they have to address and contend with a distant source of power. This awareness that there were "other" lands and powers was not new, but the power relations colonialism created were more complex and systemic than sporadic or opportunistic. It was thus that the emergence of Filipino nationalism would be shaped in the interplay of events in widely separated locales, as shown in the repercussions in the colony of the promulgation of the Cadiz Constitution of 1812, the Spanish-American revolutions, and the Glorious Revolution of 1868.

The opening of the Suez Canal in 1869 shortened distances and accelerated politics. The Philippine reform movement widened to include not just Spaniards and Creoles but a broader formation of Chinese mestizos and indigenes (*indios*), and alliances were built between reformers in Manila and liberals and progressives in Spain. This was what men such as del Pilar and Ponce carried forward.

The "Enlightenment" did not dawn on men such as Ponce and del Pilar because of their sojourn in Europe; they carried its seeds with them when they left the Philippines. The argument that colonialism systematically keeps its subject population ignorant and prevents it from having the means (whether it is better education, instruction in Spanish, greater economic and political participation, or a free press) is a central theme in anti-colonial resistance. Yet, in late nineteenth-century Philippines, opportunities existed for a small but significant part of the population to access European learning without going to Europe in the expanding educational system, an increasingly assertive local press, and improving travel and communications.

The confidence with which Rizal and his cohorts claimed "Europe" as their own is quite remarkable. A cogent illustration is the story of Antonio Luna, who arrived in Spain in 1886, barely 20 years old, to continue university studies in pharmacy he began in Manila. It did not take him long to publish his travel impressions of Spain (in *Solidaridad* in 1889), in which he caustically remarked on the squalid conditions and uncouth manners he observed in Madrid.[4] He archly wondered whether he had found himself in the forsaken border regions of northern Morocco instead of the capital of a great European nation. Disappointed, he advised Filipinos at home not to be beguiled by Spain. Its magnificence, he said, was an illusion. Luna's remarks drew the ire of Spanish readers and sparked a debate in the press that ended when Luna, smarting from a personal attack launched by a Spanish editor, challenged the editor to a duel and, when the editor did not respond, tracked him down to a café and spat in his face. (The controversy did not end here. The editor fed police with the report that *Solidaridad*'s office — Ponce's living quarters — was a center of separatist propaganda. The house was raided, materials confiscated, and Ponce briefly detained, but the charges were dropped.)

Rizal joined the fray, criticizing Luna's critics for assuming "Only we Spaniards can be truthful in the descriptions of voyages." Against the charge that Filipinos were just as ignorant of geography as the Spaniards Luna lampooned, Rizal wrote, "Filipinos should not be blamed for it as they are not the ones who have colleges, neither are they the teachers, nor do they make the plan of study, nor can they travel, nor make maps, and so forth." Witheringly, he added: "In the Philippines, all the geography that is taught is reduced to the tiny piece of ground where they [Filipinos] have to kneel down or stretch themselves to be flogged."[5]

Rizal exaggerated. By the 1870s, world geography was taught in Philippine secondary institutes; and it was taught even earlier in Southeast Asia's first university, Manila's Universidad de Santo Tomas, founded in 1611, introducing students to the basic political geography of the world.[6] The "universal" geography and history taught was focused on Europe and Spain and biased in favor of a hierarchic inventory of civilizations and a providential interpretation of history. Within these spatial and temporal frameworks, however, there was latitude for alternative imaginings of the world, since by the late nineteenth century there were sources of new knowledge other than the religious-run schools. Hence the sense of entitlement Filipinos such as Rizal and Luna had as they traveled through Europe. The most cosmopolitan group of Southeast Asians at the time, they could just as well have written, as the Cuban patriot Jose Marti did: "I am a traveler to all parts,/And a newcomer to none."

WITHOUT doubt, Ponce's location in metropolitan Spain deepened his consciousness of self, nation, and the world. After he obtained a medical degree from Universidad de Barcelona in 1889, he devoted himself full-time to political work through his involvement in Freemasonry, Asociacion Hispano-Filipino, and *Solidaridad*. Ponce served as *Solidaridad*'s business manager and, with del Pilar, kept the periodical going for six years and nine months, raising funds from subscriptions and contributions, haggling with printers, soliciting articles, and producing copy.

Published in Spain, *Solidaridad* (1889–95) addressed Filipino, Spanish, and European readers, presenting itself as a liberal organ that had as its core advocacy "assimilation," that is, equal rights for Filipinos with Spaniards, political representation, and reforms in colonial administration. As *Solidaridad* reiterated in its sixth year of publication: "We ask for assimilation. We ask Spain to treat those islands [the Philippines] as eminently Spanish, granting them the rights and liberties that modern democracy has won with so much blood and in accordance with the spirit prevailing in the last years of the XIX century."[7]

Accordingly, the paper engaged in the following editorial moves: it presented itself as the mouthpiece of the colony's "best elements"; staked out an alliance with republican Spaniards and like-minded Europeans; identified with similarly situated Cubans and Puerto Ricans; depicted a "true" picture of Filipinos and their culture; and demonstrated through the act of authorship Filipino intellectual and political capacity.

Ponce was the paper's administrator, the quintessential man Friday. While the major articles were written by del Pilar, Rizal, and the Austrian Filipinist Ferdinand Blumentritt, Ponce produced features, news reports, bibliographical notices, and filler materials. He acted as a liaison with the Spanish press, saying: "We know that for the solution of these problems [of the Philippines], it is necessary to make practical use of the ideas of every party which coincides with our own ideas and points of view."[8] He cultivated contacts with Cubans and Puerto Ricans, such as those working for the Cuban periodical *Patria* and, most prominently, Rafael Ma. de Labra, the Madrid-based Cuban autonomist and member of the Spanish Cortes whose writings on colonial questions were an influence on Filipino émigrés. He corresponded with Jose Marti and the famous Paris-based Puerto Rican intellectual Ramon Betances, whose political writings Ponce followed with interest.[9]

Ponce handled the paper's "international desk" by corresponding with friends in many countries, writing country profiles and biographical sketches of foreign personalities. *Solidaridad* billed its international character by listing "correspondents" not only in the Philippines and Spain but in Paris, London, Austria, New York, Havana, Hong Kong, Saigon, and Borneo. *Solidaridad* engaged in comparative colonialism by publishing reports on German Africa, British Malaya, French Indochina, and the Dutch Indies. These reports were deployed to show Spain as an incompetent and benighted colonial ruler.

Reporting on honors given by the British to the Indian philologist Rajendralal Mitra, Ponce chides Spaniards for putting down colored peoples as an "inferior race of limited intelligence" and denigrating Filipino intellectual achievements as "filibusterism."[10] An article on French Cochinchina (apparently Ponce's) praises French achievements in public services in Cochinchina, saying: "The French have thus shown proofs of their humanity towards their colonials." According to the article, the French respected local customs, allowed political participation, and carried out colonial policies that put Spain to shame. "Our hope," the article concludes, "is that in publishing these articles, they may serve as an example to others."[11]

Ponce imagined a global space in which colonies had a simultaneous, interconnected existence but differed in degrees of progress and assimilation into a "modern" world order. In marking these differences, he privileged the actions of a benevolent imperial power acting in the enlightened spirit of late nineteenth-century modernity. Such a position drew from the location of *Solidaridad* — espousing assimilationist politics in the empire's capital — but it expressed as well the thinking of many in the Propaganda Movement.

It was a position that increasingly became tenuous and untenable. In 1892, La Propaganda unraveled as a network due to financial problems, factionalism, and disenchantment over reformism and *Solidaridad*'s utility. The politics of the movement had begun to shift. There were many (like Rizal) who felt it was futile to wait for Spain to initiate reforms — the work of propaganda had to be brought back to the Philippines.

The final years of the paper were an extremely trying time for del Pilar and Ponce, who between the two of them struggled to keep the paper afloat. Del Pilar was hounded by intrigue, plagued by ill health, and tortured by thoughts of the family he had abandoned in the Philippines. Practically penniless, he and Ponce had to pawn valuables and clothes. There were times when del Pilar had no money even for a postage stamp to write home and was reduced to picking up cigarette butts to smoke and keep warm in winter. Of Ponce himself we have little personal detail except that he stuck it out with his mentor and friend to the end.

Solidaridad's end came with the issue of 14 November 1895, after the Manila Comite advised del Pilar it was terminating support for the paper. Del Pilar and Ponce were told that there was going to be a meeting of the Comite in Hong Kong to discuss the plan to revive *Solidaridad* somewhere outside Spanish jurisdiction. In February 1896, del Pilar and Ponce prepared to leave Barcelona for Hong Kong but missed their boat because del Pilar took ill. They were stranded in Barcelona for several months, practically without money except for their return fare. Suffering from severe tuberculosis, del Pilar died on 4 July 1896 and was buried, with Ponce and a few friends in attendance, in Barcelona's bleak Montjuich cemetery.

Less than two months later, the revolution broke out in the Philippines. Ponce escaped arrest when authorities raided the Barcelona office of Asociacion Hispano-Filipino and arrested some of its members. Government agents caught up with Ponce in Villanueva y Geltru (Catalonia) and brought him back to Barcelona, where he stayed in jail for just a night since the government had decided not to pursue any action against Asociacion Hispano-Filipino. To escape persecution, Ponce fled to Marseilles on 11 October and from there sailed to Hong Kong on 1 November.

IT is difficult to fully document Ponce's thoughts at this time. He did not write articles directly expounding his political views and rarely spoke in his own behalf. His political opinions are to be found inserted into articles on other people and topics. These appear to always conform to the editorial positions of *Solidaridad* itself.

Reviewing a doctoral thesis on colonialism written by a Cuban student, Ponce agreed that "Colonization is a tutelary function." "A nation that colonizes has the primary responsibility of educating and directing properly and effectively the colonized country, for humanity's benefit, to prepare for an independent life." At the same time, he warned against independence "before maturity when its [the colony's] malnourished organisms had not yet acquired the vigor and energy necessary for a life without tutelage." Ponce believed, however, that tutelage was not permanent: "each phase and evolutionary level of the colonial development demands its adequate regime." Without explicitly saying so, he suggested, in saying that "each period [has its] appropriate manner of governing," that independence was logical and desirable.[12]

Even before *Solidaridad* folded up, certain events had put this neat thesis of evolutionary gradualism to a test. Early in 1895, the Cuban insurrection resumed with greater force. In 1894–95, the Sino-Japanese War took place. The Cuban insurrection upset the vision of a "Greater Spain" as a coherent system of plural, autonomous "provinces" by raising the imminent reality of separation and independence. On the other hand, the rise of Japan as a world power relocated the Philippines to a new field of power relations, away from Spain's tributary space (*ultramar*, "overseas") to its geographic location in the "Far East" (*extremo oriente*, *silangang Asya*).

In his last major article in *Solidaridad*, Ponce speaks of the Cuban insurrection — in a characteristic rhetorical move — through an interview with an unnamed Cuban friend he describes (in terms that could well apply to himself) as "an impartial and analytical observer, educated and severe, who despite holding firm to his principles, respects reality and speaks quietly."[13] The Cuban's analysis (which could well be Ponce's) is that the insurrection was to be blamed on Spain's fatal negligence; that many among the colonized, believing independence premature, would have continued under Spain's tutelage if Spain had acted righteously; and that Spain's failure to act had made the insurrection just. Ponce's mediated discourse conveys a persistent ambivalence between the imperatives of reform and revolution and, at the same time, a more pronounced pessimism about the prospects of state-led reform.

Solidaridad devoted a lot of space to the Sino-Japanese War and its implications for Spain and the Philippines. As early as 1893, the paper took up the issue of Japanese expansionism, warning that unless a radical change occurred in the way the Philippines was governed there was the prospect of "national dissolution" in the face of the threat of Japan and Western powers. *Solidaridad*'s editorials on the war demonstrate its keen interest in global politics. Del Pilar used the war to criticize Spain's weakness as a politico-military power to defend its possessions. More important, del Pilar (and Ponce himself) argued that Japan's main threat to Spanish Philippines was not military but ideological. The danger lay not in a military invasion but in Japan's "redemptorist," "Asia for the Asians" policy: "What Spain should fear — it is important to take very good note of this — is the redemptorist policy of that Asian empire." Japan's "redemptorist or emancipationist policy can fertilize the Philippines against Spain." And in fomenting ideas of emancipation, Japan would be more effective than, say, the British or Americans because of "the identity or equality of races between Japanese and Filipinos."[14]

If Spain, del Pilar warned, did not give Filipinos autonomy and justice so as to strengthen their loyalty to Spain, the Philippines would gravitate toward Japan and China in the same way that Cuba and Puerto Rico were being drawn into the orbit of the United States. Hence the urgency of colonial reforms: "Spain is immovable in the Philippines with the Filipinos, but with the Filipinos against her, the Spanish flag cannot survive in the Far East."[15]

There was an increasing shrillness to the call for Spanish reforms, with del Pilar and Ponce still positioned as loyal subjects caught between "two Spains" — the liberal and the reactionary — and their discourse premised on what Spain and other powers, such as Japan, would do rather than what the Filipinos themselves would decide to do. *Solidaridad* is trapped in its discursive location: speaking as "loyal subject" in the empire's capital, unmoored in a movement without power other than "reason."

The outbreak of the revolution in the Philippines in August 1896 rearranged the terms of this discourse.

PONCE arrived in Hong Kong in November 1896 as the revolution raged in the Philippines. In December he joined other Filipinos in the British colony in forming a "revolutionary committee" (later called Comite Central Filipino, or "Hong Kong Junta") to raise international aid for the revolution. As the committee's secretary general, Ponce performed familiar tasks for a new goal, a revolution for independence rather than a campaign for reforms.

When Rizal was executed in December 1896, Ponce issued press releases on the execution; and for the Masonic necrological services held for Rizal in Hong Kong on 14 February 1897, he arranged for the distribution of leaflets containing the poem Rizal wrote on the eve of his execution, "Mi ultimo pensamiento," the first time that the poem saw print.[16] Ponce edited a series of bulletins, *Notas katipunescas* (1897–98), which carried "battlefield reports" of the revolution.[17] He monitored the foreign press and corresponded with sympathizers in many countries, appraising them of the Philippine situation and justifying the revolution. A diligent letter writer, Ponce maintained his contacts in many countries. Among these were Ramon Betances and the Cuban Jose Alberto Izquierdo, a friend from Madrid who had moved to Paris (where he became chancellor of the Cuban Legation in 1909). He also corresponded with Gonzalo de Quesada, Cuba's minister plenipotentiary in Washington, DC, and a friend of Marti, to explore the possibility of arms shipments to the Philippines from the United States or Mexico.

The first flush of revolutionary hostilities ended with the Pact of Biyak-na-Bato. As part of the terms of the pact, Emilio Aguinaldo and 26 other revolutionary leaders arrived in Hong Kong on 29 December 1897 to begin their exile. Ponce acted as Aguinaldo's secretary as the Filipinos plotted the resumption of the revolution. The opportunity to resume hostilities came with the outbreak of the Spanish-American War. Aguinaldo returned to the Philippines to lead the revolution on 17 May 1898, just days after George Dewey's victory over the Spanish armada in Manila Bay. On the eve of Aguinaldo's departure, Ponce prepared for Aguinaldo the draft of a Philippine constitution providing for the establishment of a federal republic, a popularly elected unicameral legislature, and a Bill of Rights guaranteeing civil liberties.[18]

In mid-June 1898, the Hong Kong Junta named Ponce the Philippine representative to Japan. Ponce's mission was to inquire into Japan's foreign policy toward the Philippines, ascertain the possibility of enlisting Japan's support for the Filipino independence struggle, and negotiate for the purchase and shipment to the Philippines of arms and ammunition.[19]

Ponce arrived in Yokohama on 29 June 1898 and set up his base in that port city. Except for brief trips to Hong Kong, he was in Japan from June 1898 to March 1901. Ponce did not know Japanese but knew enough English to communicate with Japanese officials and journalists. An assiduous worker, he quickly established contact with diverse personalities in the network of Japanese "Asianists" both within and outside government.

Ponce interacted with the Japanese at several intersecting levels. On the one hand, he met and corresponded with officials — including Komura Jutaro, the Harvard-educated vice-minister for foreign affairs; Inagaki Manjiro, ambassador to Siam and Asian expert; and, most especially, the former education minister Inukai Ki. Inukai was a member of the Imperial Diet and a close associate of Foreign Minister Okuma Shigenobu, leader of the Progressive Party (Shimpoto). Ponce networked with Japanese journalists, gave interviews, contributed reports to the Japanese press, and attended meetings of the Keizaizashi Kyokai (Economic Society of Tokyo), Shokumin Kyokai (Colonization Society), and Toho Kyokai (Oriental Cooperation Society). Toho Kyokai was founded in 1890 by a group of Japanese intellectuals (who included Prince Konoe Atsumaro, Okuma, and Tsuyoshi) to study conditions in East Asia and foster "Pan-Asianism." Ponce was named an honorary member of this society.

Ponce's stay in Japan brought him into contact with other Asians. He participated in meetings of the "Oriental Young Men's Society," before which he spoke on 23 April 1899. Formed in Tokyo by students from different countries, the association, Ponce wrote, "included Koreans, Chinese, Japanese, Indians, Siamese, and Filipinos, and came to count with a respectable number of members and to gain the patronage of prominent Japanese politicians."[20] At the time, Ponce said, the problems of Korea and the Philippines were the hot topic of discussion.

Japan was a refuge for an assortment of Asian political exiles. Ponce met Prince Pak Yong-hyo, War Minister An Kyong-su, and Home Minister Yu Kil-chun, leaders of the Korean reform movement who had fled from persecution at home to exile in Japan. Ponce also met the Chinese Confucian scholar Kang Youwei, adviser to Emperor Guangxu and leader of the "Hundred Days of Reform" in 1895, who fled to Japan after the empress dowager Cixi took power in a coup d'etat in 1898.

Ponce forged his closest association with Sun Yat-sen. Ponce knew about Sun while he was still in Barcelona, having read newspaper accounts of the "kidnapping" of Sun in London by agents of the Chinese embassy in 1896. He first met Sun in Tokyo in the winter of 1899, when he was invited to dine in Tsuyoshi's house. Generational cohorts, both Western-trained medical doctors, they had much in common. Since they were both based in Yokohama, they saw each other often. "Both of us," Ponce wrote, "each in his own way, pursued the same goal, the happiness of our respective countries — and this united us in mutual sympathy." Sun showed himself to be familiar with the Philippine situation and was interested in the personalities of leaders such as Rizal and del Pilar. Stressing the commonality of Filipino and Chinese interests, he told Ponce: "Let us get to know one another and we will love each other more." For his part, Ponce liked the Chinese leader's austere and serious manner and was impressed by Sun's success in mobilizing international support for his cause, an area in which Ponce had a special interest. He later wrote that he admired the genius of the Chinese in "harnessing together business and propaganda; and through business, propaganda progressed enormously."[21]

Ponce cultivated contacts in the shadowy world of Japanese political adventurers and ultranationalists who operated outside or at the margins of government in promoting Pan-Asianism. He met men such as Hyobei Hirata and Fukushima Yasumasa. Said to be an intermediary for the German-educated Prince Konoe Atsumaro, a leading Pan-Asianist, Hyobei was a Tokyo lawyer who was already talking to Filipino agents as early as 1895. An army colonel, Fukushima was the East Asia Section chief of the Imperial Army General Staff Office and a celebrity of sorts: in 1892–3 he had done a solo horseback crossing of Siberia in the course of an expedition from Berlin to Vladivostok during which he collected intelligence on Russian military capabilities.

In procuring munitions for hard-pressed Filipino forces at home, Ponce had to contend with problems of funds, gun merchants, middlemen, shippers, and changes in the policies and attitudes of Japanese officials. He needed back-channel help, since arms had to be procured covertly because of Japan's official policy of neutrality in the Spanish-American and Filipino-American Wars.

It was Sun Yat-sen, who had been in Japan longer and was the more experienced political operator, who helped provide the first important breakthrough when Sun, at Ponce's instance, asked his Japanese friends Miyazaki Tōten and Hirayama Shu, both former samurais, to help the Filipinos. Upon the advice of Tsuyoshi, the matter was entrusted to

Nakamura Haizan, a member of the Imperial Diet and Tsuyoshi's ally in the Progressive Party. It was Nakamura who arranged for surplus Japanese army munitions to be sold quietly to the Okura Trading Company (Okura-Gumi Shokai, a company that amassed great wealth trading with the military), which in turn sold them to Nakamura through a German middleman. Another broker served as intermediary for Nakamura in the purchase of an old Mitsui tugboat, the *Nunobiki Maru*. When difficulties were encountered in procuring coal for the ship, Uchida Ryohei, another political agent, helped in getting the coal. (In 1901 Uchida formed the Kokuryukai, or "Black Dragon Society," an anti-Western patriotic society, and later he gained renown as the leader of the Japanese Fascist movement.)

On the night of 19 July 1899, the *Nunobiki Maru* sailed from Moji for the Philippines via Formosa. Under the pretence of carrying railroad ties to China, it had a cargo of 10,000 Murata rifles, 6 million cartridges, 10 machine guns, an artillery piece, and assorted military equipment. On board were three Japanese volunteers who were to help provide military training to Filipinos. Six other Japanese volunteers, including Hirayama Shu, were supposed to have been on the boat but had decided to leave earlier for Luzon. Two days later the *Nunobiki Maru* sank in a typhoon in the vicinity of the Saddle Islands, 100 miles from Shanghai. (The Japanese who had left earlier made it to Luzon and found their way to Aguinaldo's headquarters, where they met Aguinaldo and presented to him Inukai Ki's letter of felicitation and gift of a Japanese sword. With the loss of the *Nunobiki Maru*, however, Hirayama and his comrades saw there was no reason for their mission and fled Luzon disguised as fishermen. It was the plan, it is said, for Ponce, Sun, Miyazaki, and other volunteers to sail to the Philippines after the smuggled arms had been successfully landed. The loss of the boat scuttled the plan.)

The loss of the *Nunobiki Maru* so devastated Ponce that he offered to resign as the Filipino envoy to Japan. Sun consoled him with words to the effect that such accidents were part of a revolution and should not dishearten them from continuing their efforts. Thus, in January 1900, another attempt was made to ship arms to the Philippines by the same cast of characters. Nakamura Haizan procured the munitions, but these reportedly could not be moved because of strict government surveillance; around mid-1900 they were still stored in the warehouse of Okura Trading Company. It was at this point that Sun, who was fomenting the uprising that later broke out in Huichow on 8 October 1900, got Ponce and the Hong Kong Junta to agree that the guns be loaned for use in China instead, "since the Philippine effort had failed [and] the weapons were of no further use there." (In mid-1900 Aguinaldo was somewhere deep in northern Luzon, fleeing the advancing US forces.) Miyazaki Tōten quotes Sun saying: "There is neither first nor last in a single cause of great virtue. If our party seizes the opportunity to launch a revolutionary army, it can realize longstanding goals. And if we succeed it should also lead to independence for the Philippines."[22]

It was then that the story of chicanery in the arms deal broke out. Members of the Hong Kong Junta had already raised suspicions that the *Nunobiki Maru* affair was a scam. (Among other allegations, there was talk the boat carried nothing but scrap iron when it sank.) Ponce staunchly defended the integrity of those he had dealt with. This time, however, it was discovered that the second shipment Sun wanted diverted to China could not be released because of conflicts over payments. Nakamura Haizan had pocketed part of the money and forged bills, and the weapons in the Okura warehouse were either defective or useless. Many Japanese sympathizers were indignant and blamed the fiasco for the defeat of the revolutionaries in China and the Philippines. There was not much, however, that could be done to repair the damage. Sun and the Filipinos were resigned, but a furious Miyazaki said: "When I think of this, I could not quiet myself even if I were permitted to eat Nakamura's flesh and drink his blood."[23]

Despite the arms fiasco, Ponce's sojourn in Japan was not unproductive. In letters and interviews with the Japanese press, Ponce clarified the Philippine situation and explained the justice of the Filipino cause. On the other hand, he dutifully sent back to the Hong Kong Junta intelligence on Japanese politics and foreign policy and reports on his activities.

His most substantial piece of writing was *Cuestion Filipina: Una exposicion historico-critica de hechos relativos a la guerra de la independencia*. First serialized in *Keikora Nippo*, it was published as a book in Tokyo in February 1901 in a Japanese translation by Miyamoto Heikuro and Fujita Suetaka, under the title *Nan'yo no Fuun: Firipin Dokuritsu Mondai no Shinso* (Social Unrest in the South Seas: The Truth about the Issue of Philippine Independence). The book concentrates on the anti-Spanish part of the revolution, perhaps because Ponce, at this time, did not want to jeopardize the possibility of a settlement with the United States. Here Ponce argued that the Filipino war for independence was a just war, that Filipinos had the capacity to form a nation-state, and that this was demonstrated in the achievements of their leaders and the Aguinaldo republic.

Translated into Chinese under the title *Feilubin duli zhanshi*, published in Shanghai in 1902 and reissued in 1913, it was, according to Rebecca Karl, "perhaps the single most influential text for post-1902

Chinese interpretations of the global and Chinese significance of the Philippine revolution."[24]

PONCE was a studious traveler, genuinely interested in the countries he visited. A friend provides the following description:

> In his travels, [Ponce] lived the intimate life of the inhabitants of places visited, accepting local idiosyncracies without prejudice; always studious. In Japan, he lived far from the European concessions, in a genuine Japanese house, dressed up and ate as a Japanese, identified with their sorrows and aspirations; thus learned what moved Japanese nationalism. His studies and travel gave him amplitude of criterion and tolerance unlike "globetrotters" with their biased, hasty judgments after briefly passing through a country.[25]

Japan enchanted Ponce. Writing to Blumentritt on 8 July 1898, he enthused over Japan's lovely landscapes (he said the sky seemed fastened to nearby mountains), its bright colors and quaint rural customs, and its "unintelligible language that seems like birdsong, surprising one with its power to express something that has meaning, and above all that thoughts can be transmitted in this cumulation of sounds."

> Everything appears to me full of enchantment such that all seems enveloped in mysteries. Loti is right. The experience destroys all notions we have acquired in Europe since all these reveal an unknown world, completely foreign and exotic to all that one can imagine before one has seen it. For this reason it has inspired in me great curiosity.[26]

Sojourning in Japan, Ponce bought books on Japan and, telling a Japanese friend that he had just acquired a copy of B.H. Chamberlain's English translation of *Kajiki*, lamented that because he did not know Japanese he could not read such classics as the chronicles *Nihongi* and *Nihon Gwaishi* and the poetry collections *Manyoshu* and *Hyaku-ninshu*.

Ponce married a Japanese woman, Udagawa Okiyo, said to have been the daughter of a samurai, in whose parents' house in Yokohama Ponce had taken up lodgings. (They had a child born in Yokohama, another in Hong Kong, and two more in the Philippines.) Photographs of Ponce in Yokohama show him in Japanese kimono and sandals beside Sun Yat-sen dressed in a Western suit, or in his cramped office decorated with framed photographs of Aguinaldo and other revolutionary leaders, a desk with books and papers, and copies of *La Independencia*, the organ of the Philippine Republic, pinned to a wall.

Mariano Ponce (in kimono) with Sun Yat-sen in Yokohama, *circa* 1900

For Ponce, Japan was a usable model. He saw in Japan a nation that desired to join a modern world but adapted to this world and changed without imprudent haste, leaving behind traditions contrary to modern progress but adopting the new with discretion and intelligence. Ponce believed there was much Filipinos could learn from how the Japanese combined and harmonized new institutions with old ones, incorporating into their own system what was good in the world, including, Ponce said, the "democratic" spirit he observed in Japanese political life. He told a Japanese friend that he wanted to "make the knowledge of Japan popular in my country" in order to give "a model for the rising institutions of my country and to fortify more and more the ties of sympathy that already unite Japan and the Philippines."[27]

On suspicions of Japanese expansionism, Ponce wrote: "In the short time that I have studied this [Japanese] government, I can say that what has been said about their need to be a colonizer is not true."[28] He added that the Japanese did not wish to be embroiled in the kind of problems they had in Formosa. (This was a view *Solidaridad* had already expressed in 1894, citing the example of Korea, where Japan was, it said, pursuing a "redemptorist" policy in supporting Korean independence from Chinese influence.) On Japanese aid to Filipino revolutionaries, Ponce understood why the government was not forthcoming. Japan was cautiously assessing the Filipino revolutionaries' chances of success and did not wish to come into open conflict with the United States. He wrote to the Hong Kong Junta on 11 January 1899: "In sum, we are treated by a woman who has told us she loves us and has given us her *yes* but refuses to fall into our arms for fear of the consequences."[29]

Ponce took a benign, romanticized view of Oriental solidarity. Among Filipinos and Japanese, he said, affinities of geography and race authorized bonds of friendship and underwrote similar interests *vis-à-vis* Europeans and Americans. In this he echoed the current of Pan-Asianism in Japan at the time. He imagined a mutuality of interests in which both nations were engaged in shared "civilizational" work in which Japan took the lead but did not dominate.

"Asianism" was a theme in Filipino thought even before Ponce arrived in Japan.[30] Intellectuals such as Rizal and Pedro Paterno located the Philippines in a "Malay" cultural world and drew racial and cultural affinities that connected the Philippines to *Malasia* (roughly, insular Southeast Asia) as well as mainland Southeast Asia and much of Asia and Oceania. This discourse on racial, linguistic, and historical filiations was an anti-colonial, universalizing move that claimed for Filipinos a high and distinct culture connected to "world civilizations" and thus deserving of the benefits of autonomy *within* the Spanish imperial order. It did not become an argument for separatism until the revolution. Moreover, this Asianism was a fluid, indeterminate construct that depended not only on categories of comparison but on the political utility of these categories. Hence the discourse on affinities of race and territory between Filipinos and Japanese, on the one hand, and the view of the revolution's leaders that they were opening the way for the emancipation of the colonized peoples of *Malasia*.

While Ponce may have idealized Asian solidarity, the Philippines was always his point of reference. Ponce declared he was a realist. Writing to a friend in Spain on 5 August 1898, he said that no society was unaffected by the modern currents of "positivism": "There is no nation today that moves unless driven by its own interests." The United States, for instance, could not be expected to be benevolent simply because it was already rich. Its ambition would not allow it to rest until it became "arbiter of the world, director of human affairs" and held "supremacy in the Globe."

Thus, Ponce wrote:

> ... if we do not want our own distinct human personality (*nuestra personalidad humana*) to be erased in the future ... if we want to develop

> out of our own faculties, by our own means, conserving our distinct character (*caracter tipico*), even as we associate with other peoples, I believe it is the better way not to admit external influences except those that are really necessary.[31]

At the same time, however, he was ready to set limits on "realism." In another letter (3 February 1899), days before the start of Filipino-American hostilities, he said: "I have tried to be as practical as possible in life and not be carried away by illusions; but on the question of my country, whatever the course of events, with or without illusions, we must now firmly embrace the cause of independence."[32]

IN 1901 Ponce was recalled from Japan. The Hong Kong Junta decided that nothing more could be expected from Japan. The war in the Philippines was winding down. The severely weakened Junta continued after Aguinaldo's capture on 23 March 1901 and the surrender of his successor, Miguel Malvar, on 16 April the following year. On 31 July 1903 the Junta was dissolved. Its remaining funds and properties, including its archives and library, were placed under Ponce's care. Though there were efforts in the years that followed to revive the Junta and continue the war for independence, Ponce stayed out of what he must have seen as futile attempts to revive the war.

With his young family, Ponce stayed on in Hong Kong. He continued to write, contributing articles to Manila papers, mostly memorializing pieces on leaders such as Rizal and del Pilar.[33] In 1906 he saw Sun Yat-sen for the last time. Sun had written from Japan that he was passing by Hong Kong on his way to Guangxi by way of Saigon. (Sun was on one of his visits to French Indochina, where he was building a base in Hanoi to foment border insurrections in China with French support.) Since the British prohibited Sun from setting foot in Hong Kong, Ponce saw his friend aboard the French vessel that carried Sun as it docked in the city. Ponce wrote: "I found him more spirited than ever. He told me about his plan to enter Kwangsi through the frontier of Indochina. His career was moving like a sail to the wind."[34]

Ponce, for his part, was hauling down his sail. In December 1906 he took the steamer from Hong Kong to Saigon, and he traveled through Indochina until early 1907. His itinerary is not clear, but the places he visited may have included Bien Hoa, Phan Rang, Cam Ranh, and Nha Trang in Annam (southern Vietnam); he may have gone as far as Siem Reap and Battambang in Cambodia and, possibly, Thailand. In Annam,

Ponce said, he heard of Sun's passage "here and there and that he had gone to Tonkin to enter Kwangsi."[35] It is not clear what Ponce's motives were for the trip (he apparently also took trips to Shanghai, Canton, and Hangkow during his time in Hong Kong). He says little about himself, his travel companions, or the specific itineraries he followed.

The travel reports he published in the Manila press indicate the Indochina trip was nothing more than a learning journey. In these reports, he showed particular interest in Filipino-Vietnamese historical connections and the presence of Filipinos in Indochina, mostly those who stayed in the region after service in the French army and those employed in the court of King Norodom I of Cambodia (court musicians, palace guards) after the King's spectacular visit to the Philippines in 1872. Ponce drew attention to the largely forgotten participation of more than 1,000 Filipinos in the French occupation of Vietnam in 1858–62, either as recruits of the French navy or as soldiers in the Spanish expeditionary force that fought with the French. Ponce talked with pride about Filipino bravery in the war, saying, "the triumph of the French in Cochinchina is due in large part to the Tagalogs."[36] Yet, he was not blind to the irony of Filipinos fighting for the French. He recounted one of these Filipino soldiers confessing to him that it was only when the Filipinos staged their revolution in 1896 that he realized "the great error and absurdity" of their helping the French against the Annamese, who were trying to defend their own country. This realization, the former soldier said, deepened his affection for the Annamese.

Ponce was curious about Indochina. He was an educated traveler, citing as sources Francis Garnier (who published *Voyage d'exploration en Indo-Chine* in 1873) and the Vietnamese Francophile Truong Vinh Ky. In a short monograph Ponce subsequently wrote, *Indo-China* (1914), he showed himself conversant with the region's history and cultures, recommending the importance of its study for Filipinos because there are "many points of contact" between Indochina and the Philippines, shared "Malay" elements in race and language, and lessons on development one nation can learn from the experiences of the other.[37] Remarking on the region's magnificent ancient relics, Ponce said there was much to be learned on the causes that led to the decline of these civilizations as well as the processes by which Vietnamese and Cambodians had so admirably conserved their "social autonomy, traditions, customs, religion" — the "force of ethnic resistance" (*fuerza de resistencia etnica*) — despite the loss of political autonomy and dispersal of the population.

Indo-China is important because it is one of the rare times that Ponce — now freed from his role as publicist — spoke for himself rather than a movement or government. He scathingly criticized colonialism as a "politics of brutalization" (*politica de embrutecimiento*). "It is the colonizers' deliberate politics not to give much light to minds that are open." The colonized were reduced to mere servants and petty functionaries so that they would "acquire the habits of servitude and not aspire for their social improvement." He cited French restrictions on the Vietnamese traveling to Europe and Japan, and recounted the trouble he had with local officials who took him to be Japanese and subjected him to interrogations at local government stations, and inconveniences in getting permits to hire conveyances and porters needed for travel in the interior. He wrote that the "politics of absorption, intolerance, and exploitation" only produced "the general desire to be free of the yoke" of colonial rule. He talked to many ordinary Vietnamese, he said, and found them "an intelligent race, devoted to their history and traditions, and open in the proper time to the change of progress in each epoch." "In the same way that they assimilated much of Chinese civilization, they will assimilate that of Occidental civilization that do not conflict with their natural way of knowledge and their venerated traditions, beliefs, and customs."[38]

Ponce stressed, however, that "the only way towards redemption" for Cambodians and Vietnamese lay beyond what was exclusivist and retrograde in local culture. He believed that "if their natural powers and energies do not receive aid and reinforcement from outside, in the form of instruction of the great knowledge of the world and its affairs, suitable for assimilating the modern advances of progress, their natural powers and energies, we repeat, will end up being annihilated and annulled."[39]

This was a view espoused by anti-colonial Vietnamese intellectuals at the time, but it does not appear that Ponce made contact with these intellectuals during his visit; and he makes no reference to the anti-colonial movement in Indochina at the time. It does not appear that he knew of Phan Bội Châu, the leading Vietnamese nationalist, who, at the time Ponce was in Hong Kong and Indochina, circulated in the same political space (Hong Kong, China, Japan, Vietnam) and carried out the same political tasks as Ponce, enlisting Chinese and Japanese support for Vietnamese anti-colonial efforts, procuring weapons.[40] There was a lag in time, however: Phan was at the beginning of his struggle, while Ponce was at the end of his.

Ponce's stress on self-renewal indicates that, aware of what was happening in the Philippines, Ponce had already abandoned hope of "immediate" independence through revolutionary action. By 1907, the "altruistic" form of pan-Asianism in Japan had been eclipsed by the shift to a more self-interested, imperialistic posture by Japanese officialdom in the wake of the Russo-Japanese War of 1904–5, when Japan entered into treaties and agreements that committed Japan to recognizing the claims of Western powers in the region at the same time that they assured for Japan certain prerogatives as an accepted member of the imperialist club in Asia.

ON 21 December 1907 Ponce returned to the Philippines with his wife and children. He had been away for 20 years. He was ill at the time and was vague about his plans, saying he might stay only a few months. He and his family proceeded directly to Baliwag, but he was back in Manila to give a speech at festivities marking Rizal Day on 30 December and was honored as a returning hero in a banquet in Malolos, Bulacan, on 26 January 1908.[41]

The year 1907 was pivotal in the US occupation of the Philippines. Concerted US efforts to transition to a form of self-government in the Philippines defused the revolution and won over virtually the entire Filipino leadership. In extending the US Bill of Rights to Filipinos, providing for an elective national assembly, allowing the formation of political parties, and "Filipinizing" the bureaucracy, the Americans provided the Filipino elite what they had campaigned for before the Revolution. A symbolic climax was reached when an all-Filipino national assembly was inaugurated on 16 October 1907.

Ponce took his place in the new order. He joined the country's leading newspaper, *El Renacimiento*, as one of its editors (1908–9) and helped establish *El Ideal* (1910–8), the organ of the ruling Nacionalista Party. A member of the party's executive committee, he was elected to the Philippine Assembly, representing the second district of Bulacan (1910–2). It does not appear, however, that political office particularly appealed to him. After leaving the assembly, he was quoted as saying it was his aim "to enlighten my countrymen as to the future needs of the Islands along the path marked out by education and industry, and to propagate intellectual fire and light."[42]

He devoted himself to scholarly pursuits. In the main, he was continuing the role of publicist that he played in the Propaganda Movement, although this time his work had a retrospective character. He preserved numerous documents (including Rizal's manuscripts) later acquired by the Philippine Library and Museum, which conferred on him an appointment as "historical investigator." He produced documentary chronicles and bibliographies on Rizal, del Pilar, and such topics as the Revolution.[43]

Around 1916 Ponce helped establish Sociedad Historico-Geografica de Filipinas, which organized lectures and published a *Boletin*. In collaboration with Jaime de Veyra, Ponce published *Efemerides Filipinas*, a series of articles on Philippine history that he started in *Solidaridad*, continued in *El Ideal* (1910–2), and issued as a book in 1914. His other writings included articles in *Hojas Sueltas*, a Masonic monthly launched in Manila in 1914; a history of his home province, *La Provincia de Bulacan* (1917); and a Tagalog treatise on language and race, *Ang Wika at Lahi* (1917).[44]

Ponce pursued his interest in Asia. He wrote on his Indochina experience: *En el pais Indo-Chino* (1907) and *Indo-China* (1914). In 1912 he published an admiring biography of Sun Yat-sen — cited by Teodoro Kalaw as "the first book by a Filipino on China" — serialized in *Renacimiento Filipino* three months after Sun assumed his short-lived role as President of the Republic of China. In 1915, Ponce founded Sociedad Orientalista de Filipinas and acted as its secretary general. With around 100 members, it aimed to promote an informed knowledge of the region (East and Southeast Asia) through research, publications, conferences, linkages with similar societies elsewhere in Asia, and the creation of a library of Asian materials. In January 1918 the society launched a monthly journal of Asian affairs, *Boletin de la Sociedad Orientalista de Filipinas* (at least ten issues came out), under the editorship of Jose Alejandrino, the society's president. Like Ponce, Alejandrino, a Belgian-educated engineer, was involved in the Hong Kong Junta and efforts to procure arms in Japan in 1896–8.

"Asianism" inspired the society and its journal. In a maiden-issue article, Alejandrino published a lecture on "pan-Orientalism" he gave in Manila's Club Democrata on 23 March 1917, in which he traced the development in Japan of the "noble and altruistic aspiration to regenerate the old nations of the Orient and emancipate them from the tyrannical tutelage of the Occident." While he lamented that pan-Orientalism had taken an aggressive and imperialist form in Japan, he believed that the original, emancipative spirit of the idea must be promoted by Asians.[45]

Ponce had settled down with his family in his hometown of Baliwag. His wife's story is remarkable in itself. Okiyo raised four children, became a Catholic, took a Filipino name, learned Tagalog, and was well loved in the town. Stories are told about how she protected town residents from abuses by Japanese soldiers during the Japanese Occupation. She survived Ponce by many years (she died in Baliwag on 27 May 1942), and a family photograph shows her as the venerable matriarch dressed in traditional Philippine dress.[46]

In April 1918, Ponce embarked on a journey to visit Sun Yat-sen in Canton and from there proceed to Japan to see old friends and update himself on the country's situation. He never made it to Canton. Transiting in Hong Kong, Ponce took ill and died in the Crown Colony's Civil Hospital on 23 May 1918. His remains were brought back to the Philippines, buried in Manila's North Cemetery, and in 1942 transferred to the family mausoleum in Baliwag.[47]

A friend lamented his death as "a real national misfortune," saying that at a time when Asian solidarity was needed Ponce's experience and expertise in Asian affairs would have been invaluable to the country's political leaders. "Few among us have achieved a conception as clear of the Far East and its leaders as M. Ponce."[48] Yet, despite the eulogies, it was clear that Ponce had receded into an icon of the past. This was occasioned by the changed times. The transition to US rule had radically altered political geography for Filipinos, orienting them to a new center of power, the United States, instead of the worlds of Europe and Asia that Ponce knew well. Then there was the man's character. Reticent and modest, he was remembered as one who never claimed the limelight or imposed his ideas on others, always striving for a consensus with interlocutors. He did not leave behind memoirs that would have allowed others (a colleague writes) to inquire into his "secret thoughts and personal judgments."[49]

WHEN they started corresponding in 1888, Rizal asked Ponce why he did not publish. Ponce replied he did not have the talent for it and sent Rizal "little articles" he had published in Barcelona "to demonstrate this truth." Ponce said, "Not all who wish to write can."[50] Yet, Ponce was not without talent. He was fluent in Tagalog and Spanish, apparently competent in English and French, and studious and eclectic in his interests (as suggested by his allusions to Emile Zola, Pierre Loti, and Jose Marti). He was not, however, an intellectual of the caliber or type of Jose Rizal or Marcelo del Pilar. Cautious and self-effacing, he did not have Rizal's originality or del Pilar's boldness.

He played the role of spokesperson for a movement, government, or nation. Much of his writing was impelled by the need to propagandize for a cause. Writing in a clear, discreet, and unadorned style, he defended the character and achievements of his people; explained and justified their struggle for independence; and, in his final years, devoted himself to building an archive of his generation. One who did not draw attention to himself or his personal views and, at the same time, a genuine believer in what he saw to be the goals of the movement, he was perfectly comfortable with the role and eminently suited to it.

Epifanio de los Santos wrote that what stood out in Ponce was "the generosity of his character and his disinterested love for the country … elevated in him to a habit and virtue, in *constans et perpetua voluntas*, through continual acts in the private life as in the public."[51] He did not cut a "brilliant figure," *El Ideal* eulogized on his death, "a friend of quiet and solitude, he was never charismatic to the masses but his silent labor was not, for all this, less effective."[52] Of the triumvirate of the Propaganda Movement, Teodoro Kalaw wrote:

> Rizal was the apostle, the historical incarnation of the Native Land, the soul of nascent and combative nationalism, a superior spirit full of honesty and respectability; del Pilar was the militant politician, the fighting journalist, the peerless lawyer in defending in the daily breach a great people and a Grand Cause; and Ponce, quieter, more retiring, was the patient administrator, the useful collaborator, the confidant without equal; in a word, the one who attended to the thousand details of the campaign with the veritable industry of the ant.[53]

Ponce's constancy is impressive. From the time he was 17, when "the germ of new ideas" stirred his "virgin" mind, he was entirely devoted to the work of the "nation." (I have found no reference, for instance, to his having practiced as a physician.) Writing from Hong Kong, he complained to Epifanio de los Santos that his books and papers had been scattered because of "the nomadic life" (*vida nomada*) of one who (he quotes from a poem) "does not know at the beginning of his days/in what desert he will pitch his tent."[54] Yet, his travels were not nomadic; there was always a purpose to his moves, and these were always anchored in a stable sense of "home" as origin and destination.

In 1906, when he was already preparing to return home, he mused about how the exile's desire for the homeland was such that "all that the eyes see take on the hue and scent of the native land, named by the names one first learned from a mother's lips." All flowers evoke the native *sampaga* or *kampupot*; all mountains become Sinukuan, Mayon, or Makiling; the rivers Seine, Thames, or Kamogawa take on the appearance of the Pasig.[55]

Ponce witnessed the death of friends away from home — del Pilar in a poor man's hospital in Barcelona, Juan Luna in Ponce's own lodgings in Hong Kong. His own family had its share of tragedy. While Ponce was abroad, his cousins — the brothers Francisco, Vicente, and Damaso — were exiled to Iligan in Mindanao after they had a street fight with the Spanish parish priest of Baliwag, who caned them when they failed or refused to kiss his hand. Only Francisco survived the exile to return home. In one of his letters, Ponce briefly mentions that Damaso was shot and his other cousins imprisoned. Ponce could be quite moving in his tributes to dead friends, but he did not dwell on his own private misfortunes.[56]

Writing to Filipino colleagues from Hong Kong in 1897, he said: "Man is like a dry leaf blown whichever way by Destiny's wind, although for us, Filipinos, it is not just wind but a hurricane."[57] He was thinking of how injustice at home had scattered Filipinos across the globe — and in ways not merely geographic. It is amazing how Mariano Ponce managed to keep to a still center and stay, despite the turbulence, on such an even keel.

THAT Ponce stayed remarkably centered and composed is to be explained by variables of personality, education, the spaces abroad he chose to inhabit, and — most important — the historical context of his departure and imagined destination.

It has to do with how he traveled. There were shifts in Ponce's politico-spatial orientation as he journeyed (from an assimilationist politics in the context of Greater Spain, to a separatist position in an "Asian" frame, to a distanced accommodation to US rule), but these shifts were not as sudden or radical as they seem. Like many of the early nationalists, Ponce had always conceived the Philippine problem as a global problem in the light of Enlightenment thought. His peregrinations in the world traced a series of political positionings in which each new position was prefigured in an earlier one.

He was a Kantian traveler, educated in geography and history prior to his departure for Europe, studious and purposeful, driven by a plan and goal that the experience of travel was meant to serve. Writing on travel, Rizal stressed the dynamisms of movement, contact, and exchange in the encounters of cultures and societies. His view may have been more expansive than Ponce's, but he, too, conceived of travel in organic terms as an experience homologous to nature's ceaseless evolutionary change and the inexorable advance of human knowledge.[58]

Current studies on travel have emphasized the experience of rupture, dislocation, and difference. We need to look at certain forms and styles of travel that account for the tenacities of ideas of home and nation.

It can be said that a certain blindness underwrites the logic and consistency of Ponce's moves. His serene detachment and faith in the inexorable force of reason and evolution explain why he could move with seeming mental ease from one position to another (except perhaps for his one "leap of faith" when he embraced, albeit from "abroad," the revolution), or why, after condemning colonialism as a "politics of brutalization," he would accede to US exceptionalism and accept its "tutelary" rule in the Philippines.

Ponce had an untroubled vision of the nation he spoke for. *Cuestion Filipina* has been criticized for its "suppression of the heterogeneity of Filipino society" and of the class conflicts within the revolution.[59] It should be noted, however, that while Ponce dressed up his account as a "historico-critical exposition," it was intended as publicity for the independence struggle and as such had to present the coherent, unitary face of this struggle to the world. Moreover, it is not certain that Ponce knew about Andres Bonifacio and the factional conflicts within the revolution given his location and sources of information. (I have found no reference to Bonifacio in his extant correspondence.) And even if he was aware of the internal contradictions, he spoke out of what, for many in his generation, were intellectual givens about the role of educated elites in directing nations. Thus the prominence he gave to reciting the achievements of the country's writers, scientists, artists, and political leaders in his brief on Filipino "capacity" for fully participating in the modern world. This is echoed in an article he published in 1913.[60] Tracing the genealogy of Filipino nationalism back to early nineteenth-century reformers such as Luis Rodriguez Varela, Jose Ma. Jugo, and Domingo Roxas, he inscribed (as did contemporaries such as T.H. Pardo de Tavera and Manuel Artigas) what later historians would malign as an elite version of Philippine history.

Ponce intellectualized the "nation" in the grid of Enlightenment-inspired modernity and remained devoted to this vision throughout his life. He had limited practical knowledge of the country, having spent more than half his adult life abroad. The ambit of his foreign travels was wide, yet — like most of the time's leading nationalists — the domestic social and territorial space he circulated in was quite narrow.

It may be of the moment to note that his first published piece of writing was a compilation of the folklore of his home province, *El Folk-Lore Bulaqueño*, which appeared in *La Oceania Española* in 1885, prior to his departure for Spain. It was meant as a contribution to Isabelo de los Reyes' *Folk-Lore Filipino* project, a radical and ambitious attempt to build an archive of local knowledge as an intellectual resource out of which the nation could be imagined as well as an epistemic site from which the "Filipino" could relate with the world.[61] It is interesting that among Ponce's last writings were a history of his province and a piece in Tagalog on language and race. He had spent much of his life abroad, addressing others about his land. He was now home, speaking to his own countrymen.

One is beguiled by the thought that Ponce, after roaming the world, had returned to the place where he started — perhaps to know the place "for the first time." Yet, the act is neither clarified nor completed. Ever reticent, Ponce did not declare what his final itinerary was.

Notes

I wish to acknowledge the kind help of Shiraishi Takashi and Caroline Hau in the preparation of this chapter.

Ponce's personal papers were lost in the destruction of National Library collections during World War II and in a fire that gutted the Ponce residence in Baliwag in 1962. His published correspondence, selected by Teodoro Kalaw, is limited to the years 1897–1900 and does not include family letters. It is ironic that while Ponce preserved the manuscripts of colleagues such as Rizal and del Pilar, he left behind few personal records of his own.

1 Ponce was the eldest of seven children of Mariano Ponce and Maria Collantes de los Santos. As early as the eighteenth century, members of the de los Santos family were *capitanes* and *gobernadorcillos* in Baliwag. Oral sources claim that Ponce's grandfather was a Spanish friar and that the family had large landholdings in Bulacan and other provinces. Interview with Vicente C. Ponce, 81 years old, nephew of Mariano Ponce, Metro Manila, 31 Aug. 2006.

For biographical sketches, see "Hon. Mariano Ponce," *Renacimiento Filipino* (7 Apr. 1911), pp. 18–9; M.M. Norton, *Builders of a Nation* (Manila: E.C. McCullough, 1914), pp. 103–8; Manuel Artigas, "Un esforzado obrero de la Log. 'Sinukuan,'" *Acacia* 1, 16 (30 Nov. 1920): 525–48; Rolando E. Villacorte, "Ponce; The Scholar as Patriot," *Philippines Free Press* (19 May 1951), pp. 20–1; Rolando E. Villacorte, *Baliwag: Then and Now* (Caloocan: The Author, 1970), pp. 269–70; A.F. Paredes, "Mariano Ponce," *This Week* (1 July 1956), pp. 32–3; Gabriel F. Fabella, "Mariano Ponce: Propagandist and Scholar," *Philippines Free Press* (9 Feb. 1957), pp. 18–9, 46; Gregorio F. Zaide, *Great Filipinos in History* (Manila: Verde Book Store, 1970), pp. 418–21.

2 Mariano Ponce, "Septimo aniversario de la muerte de Plaridel," in Magno S. Gatmaitan, *Marcelo H. del Pilar, 1850–1896* (Quezon City: The Author, 1965), pp. 46–53. Reprinted from *El Renacimiento* (3 July 1903).

3 The classic study of the Philippine nationalist movement is John N. Schumacher, *The Propaganda Movement: 1880–1895* (Manila: Solidaridad Publishing House, 1973). Also see Resil B. Mojares, *Brains of the Nation: Pedro Paterno, T.H. Pardo de Tavera, Isabelo de los Reyes and the Production of Modern Knowledge* (Quezon City: Ateneo de Manila University Press, 2006).

4 Antonio Luna (pseud., Taga-Ilog), "Impresiones Madrileñas de un Filipino," *La Solidaridad*, trans. G.F. Ganzon and L. Maneru (Metro Manila: Fundacion Santiago, 1996), 1, 18 (31 Oct. 1889): 682–7; 1, 19 (15 Nov. 1889): 712–7; 1, 21 (15 Dec. 1889): 794–8.

5 Jose Rizal, *Political and Historical Writings* (Manila: National Historical Commission, 1972), pp. 168–9.

6 Encarnacion Alzona, *A History of Education in the Philippines, 1565–1930* (Manila: University of the Philippines Press, 1932), p. 128; Evergisto Bazaco, O.P., *History of Education in the Philippines* (Manila: University of Santo Tomas, 1953), pp. 337–8.

7 "We Continue Our Mission," *Solidaridad* 6, 119 (15 Jan. 1894): 5.

8 Mariano Ponce (pseud., Naning), "El nuevo regimen," *Solidaridad* 3, 48 (31 Jan. 1891): 31.

9 The reference must be to the New York-based *Patria* (1892–98), founded by Jose Marti. That Ponce corresponded with Marti is mentioned in his letter to Gonzalo de Quezada, 8 Sept. 1898, in Mariano Ponce, *Cartas Sobre la Revolucion, 1897–1900* (Manila: Bureau of Printing, 1932). It does not appear likely that he actually met the Paris-based Betances or Marti, who was based in New York from 1880 to 1895, just prior to his death.

A fascinating account of transnational political networks at the time is given in Benedict Anderson, *Under Three Flags: Anarchism and the Anti-Colonial Imagination* (Metro Manila: Anvil Publishing, 2006).

10 Mariano Ponce (pseud., N.), "Rajendralal Mitra," *Solidaridad* 3, 65 (15 Sept. 1891): 446–9.

11 "News about the French Colonies: Cochinchina," *Solidaridad* 5, 80 (31 May 1892): 253–61.

12 Mariano Ponce (pseud., Kalipulako), "Regimes of the Colonial Government," *Solidaridad* 6, 126 (30 Apr. 1894): 192–5.

13 Mariano Ponce (pseud., Tigbalang), "About Cuba," *Solidaridad* 7, 149 (15 Apr. 1895): 160–9.

14 M.H. del Pilar, "Hispano-Japanese Treaty," *Solidaridad* 6, 138 (31 Oct. 1894): 475–81. Other articles by del Pilar on the Sino-Japanese War are in the issues of 15 Apr. 1893, 15 Aug. 1894, 30 Sept. 1894, 15 Nov. 1894–15 Feb. 1895, 15 Jan. 1895, 30 Apr. 1895, and 15 May 1895.

15 M.H. del Pilar, "Spain and Japan in the Philippines," *Solidaridad* (31 Dec. 1894): 575.

16 Ambeth R. Ocampo, *A Calendar of Rizaliana in the Vault of the Philippine National Library* (Metro Manila: Anvil Publishing, 1993), nos. 304, 310; *Pensamientos de Rizal* (Manila: Comision Nacional del Centenario de Jose Rizal, 1962), p. 49.

17 Manuel Artigas ("Un esforzado obrero") says that ten numbers were issued from 15 October 1897 to 15 February 1898. Also Teodoro M. Kalaw, *The Philippine Revolution* (Mandaluyong: Jorge B. Vargas Filipiniana Foundation, 1969).

18 Gregorio F. Zaide, *Philippine Constitutional History* (Manila: Modern Book, 1970), pp. 17–9, 131–5.

19 Efforts to secure Japanese military assistance began as early as 1895 and involved diverse personalities. See W.E. Retana, *Archivo del Bibliofilo Filipino* (Madrid: Viuda de M. Minuesa de los Rios, 1897) 3, nos. 43, 53; Jose Alejandrino, *The Price of Freedom* (Manila: M. Colcol, 1949; original Spanish ed., 1933), pp. 64–74; Grant K. Goodman, "Filipino Secret Agents, 1896–1910," *Philippine Studies* 46, 3 (1998): 376–87. For the context, see Josefa M. Saniel, *Japan and the Philippines, 1868–1898* (Quezon City: University of the Philippines Press, 1969); Ikehata Setsuho, "Firipin Kakumei to Nihon" [The Philippine Revolution and Japan], in *AAken Tonan-Ajia kenkyu dai-ichi-kan: Seikitenkan-ki ni okeru Nihon Firipin kanke* [Asia-Africa Institute, Southeast Asian Studies, vol. I: Japan-Philippine Relations at the Turn of the Century] (Tokyo: Tokyo University of Forcign Languages, 1989), pp. 1–36; Suguru Hatano, "Firipin Dokuritsu Undo to Nihon no Taio" [Philippine Independence Movement and Japanese Response], *Ajia Kenkyu* 34, 4 (1988): 69–95. I owe the English translation of the Japanese sources to Caroline Hau and Shiraishi Takashi.

20 Mariano Ponce, *Sun Yat-sen: The Founder of the Republic of China*, trans. N. Joaquin (Manila: Filipino-Chinese Cultural Foundation, 1965), pp. 29, 40. Originally published in Spanish in *Renacimiento Filipino* (28 Mar.–21 May 1912).

21 Ponce, *Sun Yat-sen*, 1–3, 11, 40. For a context to Ponce's hagiographic portrait of Sun, see Marie-Claire Bergere, *Sun Yat-sen*, trans. J. Lloyd (Stanford: Stanford University Press, 1998).

22 Miyazaki Tōten, *My Thirty-Three Years' Dream*, trans. Eto Shinkichi and M.B. Jansen (Princeton: Princeton University Press, 1982; original Japanese edition, 1902), p. 196. For a report on the *Nunobiki Maru* affair, see "Filipinos Look for Aid," *New York Times* (24 Sept. 1899).

23 Quoted in Li Yun-han, "Dr. Sun Yat-sen and the Independence Movement of the Philippines (1898–1900)," *China Forum* 1, 2 (July 1974): 224.

24 Rebecca E. Karl, *Staging the World: Chinese Nationalism at the Turn of the Twentieth Century* (Durham: Duke University Press, 2002), pp. 103, 247. Also see Anderson, *Under Three Flags*, pp. 213–5.

25 "Necrologia. Mariano Ponce," *Boletin de la Sociedad Orientalista de Filipinas* 1, 7 (July 1918): 11–2.

26 Ponce, *Cartas*, p. 125.

27 Ibid., p. 230.

28 Ibid., p. 248. On the history of Pan-Asianism in Japan, see Sven Saaler and J. Victor Koschmann, eds., *Pan-Asianism in Modern Japanese History: Colonialism, Regionalism and Borders* (London: Routledge, 2007).

29 Ponce, *Cartas*, p. 257.

30 See Resil B. Mojares, "Claiming 'Malayness': Civilizational Discourse in Colonial Philippines," in *More Hispanic than We Admit*, ed. I. Donoso

(Quezon City: Vibal Foundation, 2008), pp. 303–25; Resil B. Mojares, "Early Asianism in the Philippines," *Ideya: Journal of the Humanities* 11, 1 (2009).

31 Ponce, *Cartas*, p. 137.

32 Ibid., p. 271.

33 His writings at this time included an article on Rizal's Tagalog translation of Schiller's *Wilhelm Tell*: "Salita sa dula ni Schiller na tinagalog ni Rizal" (Hong Kong, Kowloon: s.n., 1906), 17 leaves (University of the Philippines Library); "Paunang salita," in Friedrich von Schiller, *Guillermo Tell (Wilhelm Tell)*, trans. Jose Rizal (Maynila: Pambansang Komisyon ng Ikasandaang Taon ni Jose Rizal, 1961; first published in 1908), pp. vii–xiv.

34 Ponce, *Sun Yat-sen*, p. 22.

35 Ibid.

36 Mariano Ponce, "Ang mga Pilipino sa Indo-Tsina," in *Sa Labas ng Tahanan at sa Lilim ng Ibang Langit* (Maynila: Limb. ng "La Vanguardia" at "Taliba," 1916), p. 68.

On Filipino participation in the French occupation of Vietnam, see Eulogio B. Rodriguez, *The Services of Filipino Soldiers in Foreign Lands during the Spanish Regime* (Manila: General Printing Press, 1929); Domingo Abella, "When Filipino Colonial Troops Fought in Viet-Nam in 1858," in Abella, *From Indio to Filipino* (Manila: Milagros Romualdez-Abella, n.d.), pp. 167–80. On Norodom's Philippine visit, see Felix Roxas, "Norodom I of Cambodia," in Roxas, *The World of Felix Roxas* (Manila: Filipiniana Book Guild, 1970), pp. 10–2.

37 Mariano Ponce, "Indo-China," *Cultura Filipina* 5, 3 (Dec. 1914): 220.

38 Ibid., pp. 231–3.

39 Ibid., p. 250.

40 At the time of Ponce's visit, Vietnamese intellectuals were already engaged in reformist activities. The principal figure in this movement was Phan Bội Châu (1867–1940), who — in 1905–7, when Ponce was still based in Hong Kong — was on the move in places such as Hong Kong, China, and Japan and was engaged, like Ponce, in trying to procure arms and enlist Japanese and Chinese support for the Vietnamese cause. In Japan, Phan linked up with the same personalities Ponce had met a few years earlier. Recalling Ponce's experience, Phan procured a quantity of arms, had difficulty shipping them to Vietnam, and later decided to "loan" the arms to Sun Yat-sen for use in China.

See Vinh Sinh and Nicholas Wickenden, trans., *Overturned Chariot: The Autobiography of Phan Bội Châu* (Honolulu: University of Hawaii Press, 1999); David G. Marr, *Vietnamese Anticolonialism, 1885–1925* (Berkeley: University of California Press, 1971), pp. 98–184; Christopher E. Goscha, *Thailand and the Southeast Asian Networks of the Vietnamese Revolution, 1885–1954* (Surrey: Curzon Press, 1999), pp. 28–43.

41 "La llegada de Ponce," *El Renacimiento* (23 Dec. 1907), p. 3; "Ang pagdating ni G. Ponce," *Muling Pagsilang* (23 Dec. 1907), p. 3; "En honor a Ponce," *El Renacimiento* (27 Dec. 1907), p. 4; Ponce's Rizal Day speech: "La infancia de Rizal," *El Renacimiento* (31 Dec. 1907), p. 3.

42 Quoted in Norton, *Builders of a Nation*, p. 107.

43 Ponce's works include *Bibliografia Rizalina* (which he prepared while he was in Hong Kong and Annam), published in *El Renacimiento* in 1906; *Bibliografia Plaridelina* (on del Pilar's writings; compiled in Hong Kong in 1906), published in *Plaridel* in 1907; *Bibliografia Revolucionaria*, published in *Revista Historica de Filipinas* in 1906 but uncompleted because the journal ceased publication; *Bibliografia Parlamentaria* (1910), which he did as chairman of the Philippine Assembly's Committee on Libraries; and *Biblioteca Filipina: Parte referente a la revolucion Filipina y ocupacion Americana*, an undated manuscript in the University of the Philippines Library. He collaborated with Teodoro Kalaw in producing the unfinished *Documentos Constitucionales de Filipinas*, a project aimed at recording the evolution of Filipino political thought.

44 See *Numero extraordinario de "Hojas Sueltas" en su V aniversario* (Manila: Logia Nilad no. 12, 1918). I have not seen copies of *La Provincia de Bulacan* and *Ang Wika at Lahi*.

45 Jose Alejandrino, "Conferencia acerca del pan-orientalismo celebrada en el 'Club Democrata' el 23 de Marzo de 1917," *Boletin de la Socidad Orientalista de Filipinas* 1, 1 (Jan. 1918): 17–41. Also see "Oriental Association," *The Independent* 1, 6 (15 May 1915): 8; Mariano Ponce, "Acontecimiento politico Chino," *Boletin de la Sociedad Orientalismo de Filipinas* 1, 4 (Apr. 1918): 19–22.

46 Villacorte, "Kiyo-San," *Baliwag*, pp. 272–3.

47 "El entierro de Mariano Ponce sera una manifestacion de duelo nacional," *El Ideal* (27 May 1918), p. 1.

48 "Mariano Ponce," *El Ideal* (25 May 1918), p. 8.

49 "Necrologia. Mariano Ponce," pp. 10–1.

50 *Cartas Entre Rizal y sus Colegas de la Propaganda* (Manila: Comision Nacional del Centenario de Jose Rizal, 1961), p. 176.

51 Epifanio de los Santos, "Mariano Ponce," *Filipinos y Filipinistas* (Madrid: Libreria General de Victoriano Suarez, 1909), p. 26, first published in *Plaridel* (29 Jan. and 1 Feb. 1908).

52 "Un buen patriota muerto," *El Ideal* (25 May 1918), p. 4.

53 Teodoro M. Kalaw, "Prologo," in Ponce, *Cartas*, v.

54 De los Santos, "Mariano Ponce," p. 28.

55 Ponce, "Paunang salita," pp. vii–xiv.

56 Ponce, *Cartas*, p. 20; Villacorte, *Baliwag*, p. 6.

57 Ponce, *Cartas*, p. 57. This recalls the lines from Rizal's *Canto del Viajero*: "Dry leaf that flies at random/Till it's seized by a wind from above:/

So lives on earth the wanderer,/Without north, without soul, without country or love." Ponce preserved the manuscript of this poem and arranged for it to be published in *El Renacimiento* (29 Dec. 1903); also in *Dia Filipino* 5, 6 (19 June 1918), unpaginated.

58 Jose Rizal (pseud., Laong Laan), "Travels," *Solidaridad* 1, 7 (15 May 1889): 156–61.

59 Karl, *Staging the World*, p. 103; Ikehata Setsuho, "Japan and the Philippines, 1885–1905: Mutual Images and Interests," in *Philippines-Japan Relations*, ed. Ikehata Setsuho and L.N. Yu Jose (Quezon City: Ateneo de Manila University Press, 2003), pp. 19–46.

60 Mariano Ponce, "Sobre Filipinas," in Norton, *Builders of a Nation*, pp. 17–52.

61 See Isabelo de los Reyes, *El Folk-Lore Filipino*, vol. 2 (Manila: Tipo-Litografia de Chofre y Cia., 1889), pp. 40–80.

CHAPTER 2

A Vietnamese Icon in Canton: Biographical Borders and Revolutionary Romance in 1920s Vietnam

Lorraine M. Paterson

> *Canton! The city every young Vietnamese dreams about! Canton, the site of the tomb of Phạm Hồng Thái, a young revolutionary who in June 1924 had thrown a bomb at the Governor General Merlin and had become a hero. Canton! City of Vietnamese dreams.*
>
> — Louis Roubaud, *Viet-Nam La Tragédie Indo-chinoise* (1931)[1]

During the French administration of Vietnam, China remained an unstable and contested territory: a site where deals could be struck or thwarted, revolutionaries apprehended or aided, and the reach of the French Sûreté extended or undermined.[2] This was particularly true of the French concessionary areas in Guangzhou (Canton) and Shanghai in the first decades of the twentieth century. The French Concessions in southern China complicate Vietnamese notions of travel, nationalism, and national boundaries in fascinating and virtually un-researched ways. Guangzhou was the site of one of the most famous Vietnamese nationalist incidents of the 1920s: the attempted assassination of the Governor-General of Indochina. This chapter will begin by exploring the biography of his would-be assassin, Phạm Hồng Thái, written by one of the most renowned Vietnamese nationalists of the early twentieth century, Phan Bội Châu. It will explore how this particular biography depicted an idea of romantic political biographies that became increasingly popular in 1920s Vietnam. This genre was developed in Japan at the turn of the century but had trans-Asian translation links; it came to Vietnam via Chinese reformers in Yokohama, Japan.

Phạm Hồng Thái

Phạm Hồng Thái's grave in Guangzhou, China

As the epigraph suggests, Phạm Hồng Thái was eulogized because of his attempt to assassinate the Governor-General of Indochina, Martial Merlin, during the latter's official visit to Guangzhou (Canton) in June 1924. Thái's attack and his attempt to escape both failed, and he drowned in the Pearl River, which flows through Guangzhou. Thái's Chinese grave became a place of pilgrimage for many expatriate Vietnamese; exiles and students visited his tomb to ritually dedicate themselves to Vietnamese independence, making it in effect a sort of sacred national space. When Hồ Chí Minh established the Thanh Niên (Youth League), in 1926, all of its members had to pledge allegiance to the League in front of the tomb of Phạm Hồng Thái. As William Duiker points out, they had to "make a solemn and moving oath to bring about the deceased patriot's dream of a united free Vietnam."[3] They were taught to keep his spirit alive and emulate his nationalistic spirit.[4]

In 1931, the French journalist Louis Roubaud described assemblies at Phạm Hồng Thái's tomb every June, further emphasizing its role as a scene of pilgrimage for Vietnamese.

> Each year on June 19th in a suburb of Canton, there is a gathering to commemorate an incident when an Annamite student[5] killed five French people. Is this to commemorate our poor fallen compatriots? No, it is to commemorate their assassin. This is the tomb of Phạm Hồng Thái, which is oriented towards the Southwest, in order that his soul is eternally facing his native soil.[6]

Phạm Hồng Thái's fame eventually spread to Vietnam, even amongst those imprisoned by the French. In the notorious Hanoi prison Hỏa Lò, 1930s inmates were introduced to the actions of Phạm Hồng Thái. Although the French were concerned with politically instructive theatrical performances in their prisons, they usually tolerated them, albeit under "strict surveillance."[7] Due to this attitude, Vietnamese prisoners were able to enjoy a biographical drama titled *The Bombs of Phạm Hồng Thái*.[8] This was only one way in which a romanticized tale of Phạm Hồng Thái was adopted and adapted in varying contexts. This chapter discusses the historical circumstances in which this narrative was constructed and some tentative ideas that can be derived from it, as well as placing it within the biographical milieu of late-1920s Vietnamese publishing.

Competing Cartographies of a Crime

Much of Phạm Hồng Thái's posthumous fame derived from a biography published by Phan Bội Châu in Guangzhou just two months after his death.[9] The text, *Truyện Phạm Hồng Thái* (The Story of Phạm Hồng Thái), raises many fascinating issues of how a Vietnamese is depicted in "nationalist" acts, carried out with the territorial boundaries of Indochina.

French authorities had long regarded the sphere of southern China with trepidation, especially after the Chinese revolution in 1911. The revolution highlighted French difficulty in the surveillance of populated centers within and outside the colony: Vietnamese revolutionaries could all too easily blend into the "swarming masses." As the Resident Superior of Tonkin reported in 1912:

> The difficulty of finding, amongst the swarming Indochinese native towns, the envoy sent by the revolutionary party, is equal to the difficulty of putting your hand on the heads of the party, outside Indochina. In the populous towns of Canton, Shanghai, Hong Kong and Bangkok, ever since the Chinese revolution, there are all kinds of indistinguishable ethnic elements. The Chinese police and the local authorities, without taking the part of the Annamite refugees officially, do so basically by their listlessness and the way in which they do not press forward the requests of our representatives.[10]

This difficulty of finding the Vietnamese amongst "indistinguishable ethnic elements" is paralleled by the ways in which revolutionary Vietnamese were able to vanish within Vietnam itself. It is clear that Phan Bội Châu, as well as many of his nationalist colleagues, often disguised themselves as Chinese peddlers, blending in with the Chinese as they moved in and out of the boundaries of Indochina. It is doubtful that this charade would have fooled the experienced eye of a native Vietnamese or an ethnic Chinese, but this method was often successful in tricking the colonial surveillance apparatus. As the Resident's report colorfully continued:

> They are in humble villages, forests of bamboo and also in the suburban centers of Hanoi and Saigon, where the revolutionaries perhaps look for shelter in the heart of the immigrant population who assemble in certain quarters. The Indochinese capitals are therefore, sadly, like the others in Europe, with their external boulevards and where thieves, assassins and Asiatics [that is, Chinese] inflamed with vice constitute the volunteers for crime and where Phan Bội Châu recruits his accomplices. In vigorous cleansings of these areas, accomplished by the police, it is possible to periodically break up these groups but one cannot prevent them from re-forming, this kind of patience and obstinate slyness is the character of the Asian.[11]

A report by a French lieutenant, Coulon, who went by land from Hong Kong to Hanoi in January 1913, collecting information for the Ministry of Colonies along the way, attests:

> Someone who has never visited Canton cannot imagine what a labyrinth it is. In the immense crowds swarming the streets, everyone looks alike, and any attempt at investigation would therefore be doomed to failure, unless the investigator had a strong police force at his disposal.[12]

In a sea of similar faces and potential assassins, Coulon suggests that the only French advantage is the Vietnamese love of gossip. Coulon notes:

> In order to trace all the cases of agitation caused by Annamite activists based in Canton, a special agency would have to be established in this Chinese city, modeled along the lines of the espionage network organized by the Japanese in Indochina around 1904.[13] The population at large would have to be lured into a number of shops kept by Annamite agents, where they could satisfy their natural urge to communicate and their irresistible compulsion for careless talk.

Interestingly enough, Coulon mentions that Guangzhou was an easy area for the Vietnamese to move around in, because by 1913 the Qing-mandated hair queues of the Chinese had been cut off in that area.

> This area had the advantage that, since the pigtails were cut off, they [the Vietnamese] could remain there unnoticed, while at the same time being close to the border where letters and sums of money could change hands.[14]

What is striking about this quotation is that prior to 1913 Vietnamese men could easily have put their long hair into Chinese queues, shaved the front of their foreheads, and passed as ethnic Chinese anyway, just as numerous nationalist accounts mention.[15] However, what Coulon's observation also hints at is the erroneous French idea that the queue was somehow a distinguishing marker between Chinese and Vietnamese ethnicity.

By the early 1920s, Guangzhou had become something of an "anti-imperialist Mecca," with large numbers of dissidents arriving from all over East and Southeast Asia.[16] Among them, Vietnamese may well have been the most numerous émigré group.[17] In 1923, some Vietnamese nationalists formed an organization called the Tâm Tâm Xã (Society of Like Hearts), inspired by Chinese anarchism.[18] Like the former Vietnamese Restoration League, it made "use of direct action as a means of destabilizing the colonial regime, gaining publicity and mobilizing popular opinion."[19] In 1924 it was this society that resolved to assassinate Merlin in China while he was visiting, amongst other places, the French Concession on Shameen Island. France had had a relatively small concession on Shameen Island since 1861: the larger, western area of the island was a British Concession, and it was there that the group planned to strike, on 19 June 1924.

Before discussing subsequent portrayals of the assassination attempt, it is important to establish, inasmuch as possible, an accurate sequence of events. A standard historical version of what happened on 19 June 1924 is the account of the historian William Duiker in *The Rise of Vietnamese Nationalism*:

> Failing to achieve their goal in Japan because of tight security precautions, they [the Society of Like Hearts] were finally able to make a bombing attempt on June 19, 1924, while Merlin was attending a state banquet at the Hotel Victoria in the French concessional area of Canton. Although their attempt on the official's life was unsuccessful, the explosion mortally wounded five other French citizens attending the dinner and Pham died by drowning while trying to escape.[20]

However, primary sources in French, English, and Vietnamese, and in the Chinese press, exhibit discrepancies. The major contradictions concern the precise location of the attack and the manner of Phạm Hồng Thái's approach to the site. After examining these two issues, this chapter will consider what the contradictions reveal about Vietnamese concerns in the biographical memorialization of Phạm Hồng Thái and examine its links to the biographical genre of late-1920s Vietnam.

The first discrepancy is a fairly simple one: in what concessional space did the incident actually occur? Without poring over maps of Shameen Island, the very name of the hotel indicates in which concession it occurred: The Hotel Victoria lay squarely within the British settlement. Chinese authorities at the time were under no illusion as to where this incident had occurred, as the following dispatch clearly shows. Sun Yatsen, who was then head of the Supreme Military Council in Guangzhou, sent a telegraph to the Society of Foreign-Chinese Affairs in Hải Phòng:[21]

> This tragic drama unwound in the British concession, therefore the British authorities have the full responsibility of finding out who was responsible for this attack and they should decide what measures to take to catch these people entering into the concession at Shameen.[22]

However, the idea that the attempt occurred within the French Concession is remarkably pervasive. As noted above, Duiker never doubted that it occurred in the French Concession. This persists not only in Duiker's account but also in the excellent groundbreaking book *Ho Chi Minh: The Missing Years 1919–1941*. In her narrative of this incident, Sophie Quinn-Judge recounts that "the recent émigré Phạm Hồng Thái, posing as a photographer," deposited a suitcase bomb "at a reception in the French enclave of Shameen."[23]

This misconception about where the assassination attempt actually occurred seems to have arisen from factually incorrect Vietnamese accounts at the time. The most influential such account was the heroic biography written by Phan Bội Châu. Phan wrote:

> Pham decided to kill Meclánh [Merlin] on French colonial soil [lit. the French colonial earth] but not to hurt people from other countries. Pham considered the people of Quảng Đông [Guangdong] to be the same as Vietnamese. If Meclánh was not bombed with care, it would cause a catastrophe for the people of Quảng Đông .[24]

Returning to this incident in his later autobiography, Phan Bội Châu laid great emphasis on its occurrence being on French soil.

> The Chinese and Western newspapers all praised the act of Phạm Hồng Thái for its courage and perceptiveness. The explosion did not occur at the reception by Chinese officials nor at the party attended by other foreigners, but rather at the time when Governor-General Merlin was having dinner with the French residents. This was appropriate because the place where the explosion occurred was in the French concession and the target was exclusively French.[25]

This construction of space involved an insistence that the concession was demarcated as French territory; for the ways that Vietnamese later positioned Phạm Hồng Thái's legacy, it was important to assert that he died on French colonial soil.

The second and greater contradiction in the different historical accounts concerns how Phạm Hồng Thái actually carried out the attack, namely, issues of "dress and access." On this point, sources all suggest that Phạm Hồng Thái wore European dress; yet as to how Phạm Hồng Thái executed the attack, Vietnamese and French sources do not agree.

First, what was the would-be assassin disguised as? A banquet guest, hotel worker, member of the press, or some other respectable member of the concessional community? Although Duiker skims over the method by which Thái accessed the banquet hall, most English-language accounts state that Phạm Hồng Thái posed as a photographer from a Cantonese newspaper. As Hue Tam Ho-Tai suggests: "Posing as a reporter, Thái hid the bomb inside a camera and threw it at the gubernatorial party as it settled down to dinner at the Victoria Hotel."[26] This idea seems to have arisen from an erroneous article in the *South China Morning Post*, asserting that Thái was presumed to be a photographer by the British and French guards.[27] Yet neither the French nor the Vietnamese reports from the year 1924 suggest this was the case. However, the idea that Phạm Hồng Thái gained admittance to the banquet hall not as a guest but as a photographer passed into the historical record as fact. However, if he was not disguised as a photographer, how did he gain access to the room?

Governor-General Merlin's own report at the time suggests Thái didn't enter the room at all, and that the attack actually took place from outside the reception room:

> On 19 June, the day before my arrival in Canton, the conspirators had installed themselves close to Shameen in two neighboring hotels. But, while walking around in the afternoon Pham Thanh Tich[28] went on a tour of Shameen. He saw that the banquet at the Victoria Hotel would offer the best possibility of an attack. He decided to wait for the moment of the banquet and went to a restaurant in the Chinese city close to the British concession. At the English bridge the guard on patrol did not ask to see inside the briefcases as he should have done. At half past eight I returned to the Hotel Victoria: some of the policemen were standing at the windows of the dining room. At 8.45pm, the bomb ... the massacre! Three killed, two dying, and ten injured.[29]

Here, Merlin's own (rather vague) report seems to imply that the bombs were hurled in from outside the window. He blames the assassin's access to the island on the failings of the British guard at the "English bridge." But then, elsewhere in his report, Merlin also describes arriving at the hotel's pier and receiving a salute from the police in the gardens at the back of the hotel. Fifty guards from the British and French Concessions were guarding these gardens, his point of access from the small pier. Such a heavily guarded outside area does not seem a plausible location for Phạm Hồng Thái to have launched his bomb.

So, how else might Phạm Hồng Thái have gained access to the banquet hall? Due to his Western dress was he perhaps mistaken for a French *métis*, a Sino-French businessman?

Certainly, French colonial reports stress in great detail how Phạm Hồng Thái and his co-conspirators passed themselves off in Western outfits.

> He [Phạm Hồng Thái] came from Thailand, with a Chinese costume under his Western clothes, into the enclosure of the concessions. Towards the 15th or 16th of June, Hoang bought Phạm Hồng Thái a French traveler's outfit: flannel trousers and a straw hat. He also gave him a shirt, a tie, a belt, socks and cloth shoes.[30]

Phan Bội Châu's biography asserts that Phạm Hồng Thái was able to gain access to the room simply because he looked French:

> Phạm Hồng Thái was dressed in western clothes, wearing western shoes, and carrying a western cane in his hand. From the bridge gate, he walked with an assured air straight to the door. The French military police who were guarding the door on both sides all thought he was a French guest at the reception because his outfit and deportment looked like those of a Frenchman, so that they suspected nothing.[31]

From this account it appears that he simply wore Western clothes, but no professional disguise. Interestingly enough, French colonial sources often reflect concern over an ability to racially distinguish; archival documents include repeated requests for photographs of Vietnamese nationalists in Western dress, rather than only in Asian dress.[32] Nationalists played on this, creating a situation where it would have been difficult to pinpoint the Vietnamese amongst the multiracial anti-colonial opposition that was emerging out of what French authorities often perceived as the aforementioned "indistinguishable ethnic elements."

Another interesting contradiction between what actually happened and how it was later depicted is that many of these accounts proclaim Thái acted alone. The figure of the lone assassin had two faces: celebrated by radicals and equally the source of particular fear and terror to colonial authorities. Lê Hồng Sơn later admitted in 1927 to the Sûreté that a leading role in this attack was played by a former student of the Study East education movement who had joined Phan Bội Châu in Japan in 1905.[33] Approached by an anarchist Chinese, a fellow officer in the Yunnan army stationed in Guangzhou, this Chinese officer offered to help him construct two briefcase bombs.[34]

Phan's biography of Phạm Hồng Thái made an important contribution to ideas about revolutionary romanticism. André Malraux, later French Minister of Culture, but at the time the owner of the Cochinchinese newspaper *Indochine*, records how in 1925 one of his staff, called Hien, decided to assassinate the governor of Cochinchina, Maurice Cognacq, after being "constantly harassed by the Suretė."[35] The proposed details of the plot were identical to Phan Bôi Châu's depiction of the attempted assassination of Merlin: the same kind of event, the same kind of bomb, even the same erroneous method of getting close to the proposed victim while posing as a photographer. In the end, however, after vain attempts by the staff at *Indochine* to dissuade their colleague, Cognacq's itinerary changed and Hien's plot was abandoned.[36]

Phạm Hồng Thái's actual antecedents are difficult to surmise, such is the nationalist mythology that surrounds him. Stories of his life may be somewhat exaggerated or apocryphal. It appears certain that he was born in 1893 and that his father had been involved in the *Cần Vương* — Save the King — uprisings of the 1880s. Beyond these details, it is difficult to say that his life story can be substantiated from reliable sources.

Within months of his death, admirers moved Phạm Hồng Thái's body from the original burial site to one of the most prestigious revolutionary burial sites in China. In December 1924, the Chinese nationalist Wang Jingwei had Pham's coffin placed beside the monument to the 72 "martyrs" of the 1911 Wuhan uprising.[37] Hu Han-Min, then governor of Guangdong, wrote the calligraphy for the inscription on the tomb. Now, Phạm Hồng Thái's past developed a distinctly socialist tone.[38] The Phạm Hồng Thái of this inscription was a child of the Confucian elite who had been upset by French educational policies and left his studies to work in a factory, where he had risen to be a foreman.[39] He had first wanted to mobilize colonial troops to mutiny but had come to realize that only an anarchist act could really be effective.[40] On Hu Han-Min's graveside stele, Phạm Hồng Thái's past is eulogized in much the same way as that of the revolutionary icon Sofya Perovaskaya.[41] A heroine of Czarist Russia, she too had left a privileged family to work among the downtrodden masses, only to end up dying as the result of an assassination attempt (in her case a successful one).

The Story of Phạm Hồng Thái narrates the story of Thái's formative heroic experiences with many of the psychological nuances that Phan Bội Châu first manifested in his own memoir, *Prison Notes*.[42] But Phan Bội Châu also invents a conversation between Phạm Hồng Thái and Hồ Chí Minh in which the latter turns Thái from peaceful methods to a resolute adherence to the need for violence and social revolution.[43] In fact, Hồ Chí Minh arrived in Guangzhou only in November 1924, five months after the death of Phạm Hồng Thái, and it is clear that they never met. According to Phan's account, however, Phạm Hồng Thái even derived class awareness from his contacts with Hồ Chí Minh, in contradiction to the epitaph on the graveside stele. The biography concludes with Phan approvingly quoting Hồ Chí Minh's thesis on the need for a fundamental social revolution in Vietnam[44] and overtly stating that individual acts of heroic violence, like that of Phạm Hồng Thái, could "serve to awaken thousands to the possibilities of organizing violence against the colonial system."[45]

Besides invented conversations with Hồ Chí Minh, different themes emerge in the various renditions of Phạm Hồng Thái's martyrdom. Another inscription at his tomb invoked the image of the lone assassin, the traveling knight errant of East Asian stories, by claiming "he had followed Merlin to Japan and Shanghai with the aim of assassinating him. But it was in vain because of police vigilance."[46] Yet another story echoes Vietnamese myths of how new political orders (in this case a dynastic order) could be created through heroic self-sacrifice:

> The Europeans of Canton believe that he just drowned while swimming away but for the Vietnamese it was suicide and not an accident. The legend is that a young man of beautiful appearance would sacrifice his life outside his country in order to accomplish the grand destiny of the fisherman Le, founder of the Le dynasty.[47]

The Lone Assassin

Along with Phan Bội Châu's biographical text, another pamphlet about Phạm Hồng Thái was reputed to circulate clandestinely "in schools, high schools, workshops and among young people."[48] Colonial authorities discovered a small book with reproductions of the tomb, the briefcase in which the bomb was hidden, and also a picture of the room in which the explosion occurred. A concerned governor general noted: "It is these brochures that circulate from Hanoi to Guangzhou and back again which rouse revolutionary support."[49]

Revolutionary accounts contain examples of people being taken to swear allegiance to the nationalist cause at the tomb in Guangzhou.[50] By 1931, the French Sûreté felt compelled to warn local officials in Vietnam to be particularly vigilant on 27 days of the calendar year, among them the anniversary of Phạm Hồng Thái's death.[51] Phạm Hồng Thái was used as a pan-Asian symbol of martyrdom against imperialism, with one archival document describing celebrations at the Whampoa military academy among Chinese and other students:

> In Canton on 18th June, students of different nationalities of the Whampoa military school, numbering about 3000 celebrated the anniversary of the death of the revolutionary martyr Phạm Hồng Thái. During the ceremony they swear fidelity between themselves and the Annamites.[52]

French authorities fumed at such heroic treatment being given to a foiled assassin. The French consul in Guangzhou composed a very stern letter of protest to the Chinese Nationalist Party.[53] Worse, such gestures and stories circulated across what French authorities preferred to consider discrete colonial boundaries — political, cultural, and geographical. After all, his martyrdom might not have become as widely cited had the Chinese nationalists not allowed Phạm Hồng Thái's grave to be placed in such a prestigious location.

As Hue-Tam Ho Tai points out, this veneration also encouraged Phan Bội Châu to want to open a Vietnamese academy similar to Whampoa; he traveled to Beijing, where he was introduced to two Comintern agents.[54] However, the Comintern were more interested in Hồ Chí Minh himself, who had just arrived from Moscow with Mikhail Borodin. The links between Vietnamese nationalists and the wider Comintern movement were to become stronger through Hồ Chí Minh and his contacts rather than Phan Bội Châu and his attempts to forge contacts through Chinese intermediaries.

Shanghai Spaces

Such drama in Guangzhou also made French authorities feel concerned for the vulnerability of their Shanghai concession. Racial demarcation of space seemed undermined by the increasingly crossed, or even blurred, cultural and political boundaries suggested by the accounts above. Yet, for those present in the concessionary areas there was, at times, no blurring of the physical borders. Vietnamese who were in Shanghai in the 1910s, for instance, left accounts that illustrate how clearly they understood the need to avoid addresses within the French Concession, as well as an awareness of the territorial boundaries of the International Settlement, which was controlled by the British.

One particular incident highlights this. When Vietnamese students in Shanghai wanted to go to the city's most famous amusement venue, which unfortunately lay just over the concessionary border:

> The Chinese informer told the Consul General [of Shanghai] that the Annamites are taking classes at the Ecole Militaire in Pao Ting Fou.[55] They were staying in a hotel in the international concession. They originally wanted to go to the "Grand Monde" [Great World] the amusement centre in the French Concession but then they changed their minds out of fear because this famous amusement hall lay in the French concession.[56]

At this time the Great World was the largest entertainment venue in Shanghai. It had been formally opened to the public on 14 July 1917, France's National Day, when the French Concession was festooned with flags and lamps. Its myriad delights were evoked as follows:

> … customers moved from floor to floor, shopping from one layer of entertainment to the next: theaters, puppet shows, wrestling, sing-song girls, food shops, and games of chance …[57]

For the Vietnamese, crossing into French concessional space might have particular repercussions, ones they were not willing to risk, even though the Great World was literally just a few feet inside the boundaries of the French Concession, and hence tantalizingly accessible.

What is ironic about this, however, is that despite Vietnamese perceptions, the supposedly French space of the Concession was barely under French control at all. Although the French sought to use their concession in Shanghai as a power base from which to implement surveillance policies, by the mid-1920s the actual organization and policing of the concession was in significant disarray. A deal with the Shanghai crime organization the Green Gang meant the security of the French Concession was bartered for an opium monopoly.

Ironically, the deal between the French and the Green Gang ultimately had very serious repercussions for the ability of the French consuls to administer their own concessional space.[58] Rather than being bolstered, their power was slowly eroded by a developing Green Gang power monopoly. However, before the local balance of power had shifted so decisively to the Green Gang, there were several ways in which the Sûreté seems to have benefited from this rather sordid association.[59]

One of them was the spectacular capture of Phan Bội Châu himself on Chinese soil in July 1925. While walking out of the north Shanghai train station (in the Chinese section of Shanghai), on his way to catch a boat to Guangzhou, Phan was kidnapped by four men and taken into the French Concession. Ironically enough, this time it was Phan's own inability to racially distinguish foreigners in cosmopolitan Shanghai that left him vulnerable to French kidnapping:

> As soon as I came out of the train station, I saw a rather luxurious automobile and four Westerners standing by it. I did not realize that they were French, because in Shanghai there was a great mixture of Westerners and there were swarms of foreign guests.[60]

Once he had been forced into the car, Phan and his four assailants entered the French Concession "in no time."[61] As the Concession was considered French territory, subject to French jurisdiction, no formal extradition procedures were required. Despite numerous later protests from Chinese nationalists over issues of Chinese sovereignty and this open violation of Chinese territory, Phan was kept overnight and then forcibly taken by boat to Hải Phòng.[62]

A Vietnamese Martyr in French Shanghai?

What do we know about the circumstances surrounding this event? Archival records contain no specific sum, although it can be surmised that Phan's movements were revealed to the Sûreté for a large price. Great historical controversy still surrounds the identity of the informer. Some historians have suggested the revolutionary figure who invited Phan to travel to Guangzhou (i.e., Hồ Chí Minh) was the person who could most easily have betrayed Phan. However, it seems unlikely that Hồ Chí Minh would have betrayed an older colleague either for a large sum of money to replenish revolutionary funds or to gain a martyr for the cause.[63]

Regardless of the mystery that surrounds the characters involved, in reviewing the historiography of these events we find a very strong sense that the demarcation between French and Chinese/international space was vitally important. In several of the depictions that assume Hồ Chí Minh's duplicitous involvement, the traitor's crucial challenge is presented as luring Phan Bội Châu over the borders of the French Concession. Thus, Hoang Van Chi, a writer anxious to find Hồ Chí Minh culpable, claimed:

> In June 1925, Phan Bội Châu was tricked by communist leader Nguyen Ai Quoc (now known as Ho Chi Minh) who had arranged to betray him to Sûreté for the sum of 100,000 piasters (a buffalo cost five piasters at the time). Having complete confidence in Nguyen Ai Quoc, who he knew as a communist but refused to consider as a rival, Phan was persuaded to go to an address in Shanghai, not realizing it was just inside the French Concession. He was at once arrested by the French police and sent back to Vietnam.[64]

Phan as an unwitting victim, lured to an address within the French Concession, is a powerful image, and one that highlights the non-negotiability of the territorial borders in question. Despite many similarly partisan depictions of his kidnapping that claimed it took place in the French Concession, in fact Phan was actually taken prisoner on Chinese territory. We find here an interesting echo of the popular insistence of a

French concessionary location for Phạm Hồng Thái's deed, which nevertheless clearly occurred in the British Concession. Neither Phạm Hồng Thái's attempted assassination nor Phan Bội Châu's kidnapping, both regarded "martyrdoms" for the nationalist cause, actually took place on French concessionary soil, notwithstanding that, in the former case, such an enclave was located nearby, and in the Shanghai case one was even implicated in the string of events. The reason for these misconceptions passing into historical fact lies, in my view, in the narrative necessity for these events to have occurred on "French soil" in later accounts of them. These post hoc depictions required these areas of anti-colonial sacrifice to become extensions of a Vietnamese space, a place where a "nationalist" sacrifice could be depicted as occurring on French territory.

Arriving in Vietnam, Phan Bội Châu was immediately put on trial and received a life sentence of hard labor. However, the storm of protests within Vietnam, and by French liberals in Paris, proved too much for newly installed Socialist Party Governor-General Alexander Varenne, and he commuted the sentence to house arrest. Phan lived in Hue until his death in 1940, his last years spent in virtual isolation while the local Sûreté spent their days "harassing his guests."[65] Phan Bội Châu returned to house arrest in a cultural milieu in which the genre he had helped develop, the romantic revolutionary biography, had become more popular in Vietnamese publishing. However, if territorial sites had to be national, the biographical icons that appeared within them could be resolutely international.

Icons to Emulate

In his annual report on the indigenous press in 1922, Monsieur Vinay, the head of censorship for the Sûreté in Tonkin, warned that "without cease, like in court poems, the press likes to discuss their glorious country and never neglects to cite the amazing deeds of great men who, after having expelled foreign powers, organized themselves."[66] Vinay was evidently concerned about the effect that these ideas might have on the growing literate population. Throughout the 1920s, these stories of great heroes who after expelling foreign powers organized themselves (many of them were heroes to the Vietnamese rather than actually being Vietnamese themselves) continued to be published, just as numerous turn-of-the-century biographies were republished.

In his seminal work *Vietnamese Tradition on Trial*, David Marr asks: "why [by the end of the 1920s] were biographies so popular? Undoubtedly one factor was Chinese attention to biography from which traditional Vietnamese had developed their own genre."[67] However, in first linking these biographies back to a fourteenth-century text, *Việt Điện U Linh* (Vietnamese Palace Spirits), Marr underemphasizes the societal context in which the new biographies were printed; biography had become a didactic tool in increasingly politically charged ways. Marr elaborated his thoughts on biography in a later article:

> Individual heroism fascinated young Vietnamese intellectuals of the 1920s. Among the hundred or so biographies and biographical dramas published during this period, almost all emphasized personal courage, fortitude and charisma. It was a calling up of souls, Vietnamese or foreign who could serve as role models and sources of inspiration for future action. Precisely because these persons were paragons, however, almost no attention was devoted to emotional nuances or contradictions of character.[68]

Marr seems overly harsh in considering these works to be devoid of emotional nuance; many of the biographies published at this time in fact display fascinating ideas about the role of the individual psyche at a time of societal upheaval.

Irrespective of whether these heroic biographies were the embodiment of hyperbole and overly sentimental fiction, their popularity in the 1920s indicates they had roused the interest of the literate Vietnamese population, in part at least because their history — as specific texts and as a genre — was both deeper and wider than commonly acknowledged. Many historians assume that these biographies originated in the late 1920s. However, many of the texts that were published during the late 1920s were actually reprints of turn-of-the-century texts that had circulated in Vietnam since 1900 through institutions such as the Đông Kinh Nghĩa Thục, usually translated as the "Tonkin Free School." These texts were often romanized texts of previously circulated Chinese texts. The cultural thread continued from the turn of the century until the late 1920s.[69]

Publishing houses were founded that specialized in publishing these biographies, including in Hanoi the Giấc Quan Thư Xã, the Awakening Publishing House, and the Cường Học Thư Xã, the Strengthening Study Society. Just as in turn-of-the-century publications, they evoked foreign icons center stage along with Vietnamese heroes: Lord Nelson rubbed shoulders with Peter the Great, Louis Kossuth, The Three Italian Heroes, Columbus, George Washington, and several others.[70] If territorial space had to be definitely defined as French, then the icons moving through "national" space could be universal figures. Why was this the case? Perhaps a partial answer lies in a parallel Chinese preoccupation.[71] Hu Ying suggests for the Chinese context that this is about an encountering of the modern: "The gradual transformation of these imported figures narrates the complex relationship between imagining a foreign other and re-imagining the self amid the interplay of local and global forces."[72] There are many links between an interest in these foreign figures and a similar Chinese preoccupation with them, largely through the writings of turn-of-the century figures such as the Chinese reformer Liang Qichao.

Indeed, Trần Huy Liệu, the young journalist who founded the Strengthening Study Society, acknowledged the Society was modeled on Liang Qichao's Society for Promoting Learning.[73] Set up after the Treaty of Shimonoseki in 1895 by Liang Qichao and fellow reformer Kang Youwei, the Society boasted a library and showroom of modern maps and instruments.[74] Furthermore, Liệu states that the Society's published books "generally originated from the works of Yên Sĩ Phi Lý Thuần," using the transliterated word for "inspiration" in place of Liang Qichao's name. As Trần Huy Liệu's memoirs later explain, "in spite of a three-decade lapse from the appearance of the publication of Liang's original works, these works were still very enthusiastically received by the [Vietnamese] public in the late 1920s."[75] Vietnamese and Chinese reformists' interest in biography intersected with their desire to promote nationalism, although arguably that was not their exclusive appeal to the reader.

Prior to running the Strengthening Study Society, Trần Huy Liệu had been a very active journalist; he was editor of the *Đông Pháp Thời Báo* (Indochina Times), which owed much of its reputation to him.[76] As Philippe Peycam points out: "behind his [Trần Huy Liệu's] numerous articles lay a clear agenda: cultural renovation was a prerequisite to political change."[77] Such ideas were undoubtedly taken from Liang Qichao's writings. This Chinese intellectual's influence on Trần Huy Liệu's thought is also shown in an essay the latter wrote about Liang Qichao in 1950.

> In the development of my thoughts the one writer who came to me very early and stayed with me for a long time was Liang Qichao. As a matter of fact, from the early years of the twentieth century to the First World War, among thoughtful Vietnamese intellectuals, who could not have received an impact from Liang Qichao?[78]

Later, as minister of propaganda for Hồ Chí Minh's Việt Minh, and a leading north Vietnamese intellectual, Liệu had to qualify his earlier praise for a Chinese intellectual who did not understand the primacy of socialist thought. In the 1970s, during a period of tension with China, Trần Huy Liệu described his early intellectual trajectory as "narrow minded" and "lacking in focus,"[79] something best interpreted as a rather vague genuflection to the fact he should have focused more clearly on Marxist-Leninist thought at the time. However, Liệu's interest in Liang Qichao remained clear, not only through his translations of many of Liang's biographies but also through a book that he published on Liang titled *Tiểu Sử và Tập Diễn Văn Lương Khải Siêu* (Biography and Speeches of Liang Qichao).[80] In this work, Liêu compiled several of Liang's key speeches, coupled with a short biography of Liang. Its significance did not escape the Resident Superior of Tonkin at the time, who informed the Sûreté that "by writing a biography of this patriotic Chinese Lương Khải Siêu, the translator Trần Huy Liệu is proposing to make a political education for his compatriots."[81]

If much of what Trần Huy Liệu's Society and the other publishing houses produced were biographies, most of them used a very particular structure. For example, the cover of each volume published by the Strengthening Study Society had a picture of the featured hero on the front and above it the words: *Giữ Đạo Đức, Mở Trí Thức, Chấn Tinh Thần* (Guide Virtue, Open Minds to Knowledge, and Correct Self-Control). Many of the biographies had a quotation from Mencius on the cover: "to understand a person one must examine the times in which they lived," hence the placing of each biographical figure within societal context.[82] There were editorial comments positioned throughout, and then a direct plea to the reader in the concluding paragraphs. Most of these arguments were expressed in rhetoric that questioned what the reader would be prepared to sacrifice on behalf of her or his country, especially asking whether they would be willing to emulate the protagonists. Even romantic love was, on occasion, evoked: "just as people fall in love, the reader must fall in love with the story of our people."[83]

Explicit admonitions to act were often within a section referred to as *Lời Phê Bình*, which can be translated as "Critical Words" or "Words of Review." In one biography of Sun Yat-sen titled *Anh Hùng Cưu Quốc* (A Hero Who Saved His Country), for example, the notion of reader identification with the biographical protagonist is summed up thus:

> Who reads this and does not feel something in their conscience? The story of this man is an example of someone who loves his country in a very clear and direct way. He is a vexed genius. Surely the soul of China and the soul of Vietnam have some likeness between them? Our citizens need to have clear souls.[84]

The land might have to be French, but the heroes could be (inter) national. Calls to anti-colonial action were often voiced in the prefaces and conclusions of these biographies, and the heroic models that they depicted often led to the emulation of revolutionary violence rather than a concept of greater moral fortitude. For example, the conclusion to the biography of the Chinese nationalist Huang Xing,[85] titled *A Great Man Who Founded a Nation*, read:

> Brothers and sisters, this is the voice of the scholar-commander. Brothers and sisters, try to see there's nothing like the salvation of the nation. Please engrave the need for salvation on your hearts and ask yourselves what you would do to achieve that salvation. It must be possible to strive for the revolution of the masses.[86]

Individual and societal transformations are here conflated; they become a single process, informed by what I call a context of "revolutionary romance" that had matured by the mid-1920s from its turn-of-the-century antecedents. By the "romance" of revolution, I do not mean to imply a specific format or narrative convention, but rather a complex of representational practices that attained their power, and the circuits of circulation and interpretation of such works, as they created particular links to the political during this period. In so doing, they drew on a variety of conventions from within Vietnam and beyond. Thus we see, for example, in the incitement to individual action in the introduction to *A Great Man Who Founded a Nation*,[87] there are clear Social Darwinian overtones: "In this period of competition, when strong countries oppress weak ones, and others are like a piece of meat in between … who was this Chinese person who saved the nation?"[88]

Similarly, in consciously evoking the actions of figures such as Phạm Hồng Thái, the biography of Huang Xing concludes: "Brothers and Sisters! We today are the officers of the nation and the revolutionary people. When there is a struggle many people have to say that they will die."[89] This desire to have the utterance of martyrdom runs throughout many of these biographies. The temporal emotiveness of the translation is apparent: "today, this day, we copy and transcribe this story of Huang Xing to pay homage to a man."[90]

The translator's comments on these biographies often fed this atmosphere by stressing a sense of immediacy linking the subject and the reading self. In the biography of Louis Kossuth, *Hiến Thân Cho Nước* (Dedication to One's Country), the translator thus reflects on his task:

> I finished translating the story of Mr Kossuth and it made me think: Oh heavens! the condition of the country of Hungary was formerly like that and now it is made anew. So let it be the same for our country![91]

Liang Qichao's biography, *The Three Italians*, was renamed *Gương Phục Quốc: Ý Đại Lợi Tam Kiệt* (Mirror of National Strength: Three Famous Italians) and translated by Trần Huy Liệu. Liêu introduces the books with these words:

> This is the time for my pen to descend to applaud these episodes. On reading the episodes of these lives, my heart heaves. We study the narrative of these stories of foreign countries so we know that it is not impossible to have the same story in our country, to perceive that the things we wrestle with are not impossible. Through this examination of these foreign figures we can find a very personal compassion. Such slender pieces of knowledge have such importance! The country of Italy was able to create a new nationalism, a new freedom that is constitutional.[92]

The translator's comments at the end are imbued with emotion:

> As I was translating the *History of the Three Italians* my heart was palpitating, my hands trembled with emotion more than one time. I struck my hands on the table and cried: "Beautiful! Beautiful! What happiness! What happiness!" It is for you to also feel this emotion.[93]

A further theme of real importance to these translators was addressed directly through an otherwise stumbling comparison between Mazzini and Cavour. If Mazzini was best loved in Asia, this translator asserted, it was because his motives, uncontaminated by a desire for power, were purer, as a hero's had to be.

> According to the ideology of Eastern people, they are usually the fondest of Mr Mazzini. According to the ideology of Western people they like Mr Cavour better. Eastern people care for faith and reliability whereas Western people look for authority and power. In spite of these notions we know that Cavour was still very faithful to his country. Individuals that are scoundrels love to use power for their personal gain, but Cavour only used his power in order to work for his country; the artifices and tricks of power are not used by him in any way. In so far as the virtue or good conduct of these men is important. Lương Khải Siêu [Liang Qichao] also said that we must resist pretence and only speak our true desires and state how we want to save our country. They are the heroes that we stumble towards. These are the models of patriotism, virtue, peacefulness.[94]

Looking around in mid-1920s Vietnam, Trần Huy Liệu applied these Italian "models of patriotism" in the local context when he idealized a short-lived political group, the Jeune Annam (Young Annam), as a potential Vietnamese version of the nineteenth-century Young Italy party. The Young Annam movement had originally been part of the liberal, reformist Constitutionalist Party of Cochinchina, with its name taken from Gandhi's Young India party. But by 1925 a group of young urban radicals, mostly students, had taken Jeune Annam with them when they split from the rest of the Constitutionalist Party.[95] It was then linked to an anti-colonialist newspaper, published in Saigon in 1926 and banned shortly thereafter. By then, it was not to Young India but Young Italy that Liệu exhorted young Vietnamese to look for inspiration: "It is for you, readers to experience yourself the great impressions on their history. In reading the history of other countries … In the party of Young Italy there was a free, unified and independent Italy. What about Young Annam?"[96]

Mirror of National Strength: Three Famous Italians attracted the Sûreté's attention fairly rapidly. As with numerous other such biographies, it was "the public outpouring of enthusiastic interest with which such publications are greeted"[97] that most concerned the police. But it was not only a matter of biographies obviously designed to inflame patriotic feelings. Other seemingly innocuous ones could also appear subversive to colonial eyes in Vietnam. One such text was a biography of Lord Nelson that caused a furor among French administrators in Saigon. This 1927 biography, titled *Anh Hùng Yêu Nước* (A Hero Who Loves His Country), translated from the Chinese original into *quốc ngữ*, appeared in Saigon, where it was promptly prohibited.[98] Presumably it was the country against which Nelson had fought that elicited the ban on an otherwise fairly innocuous biography.

Biographies authored by women emerged at this time as well. In September 1928, the Resident Superior of Tonkin contacted the director of the Sûreté about the need to suppress a publication titled *Gương Nữ Kiệt* (Mirror of Women to Emulate or Mirror of Remarkable Women) by Phân Thị Bạch Văn, a member of a women's society in Gò Công, Cochinchina.[99] The reason was, as the letter pointed out, that "the first section compares Madame Roland to the two Trưng sisters and then incites compatriots to follow their example.[100] The second part is an analysis of the role played by Madame Roland *vis-à-vis* the French Revolution."[101] The letter goes on to quote one of the most egregious passages:

> The immortal heart of Madame Roland knows the grief that is written in the pages of history. The people here have not lost their hope of not

> being the victims of injustice. It might happen one day that Annam will be like France where the nobles were massacred and floating in a sea of blood, littered with thousands of bodies.[102]

As we see here, although early twentieth-century readers were often left to deduce from the text what comparisons could or should be made with contemporaneous contexts, by the late 1920s explicit links were being drawn between them. This is also suggested by the use of the word *gương*, which appeared here and in several other titles of contemporaneous translated biographies. *Gương*, meaning "mirror" or "model" in both Chinese and Vietnamese, had been used throughout Vietnamese literary history to indicate books of examples. But by the later 1920s, due to its new use by journalists, this mirror became one in which people were meant to see themselves and their own situation, in other words, to become more self-aware.[103]

Historians generally refer to these biographies as marking a radical shift in the 1920s from the ideas of the "reform generation."

> The biographical literature of the 1920s provided the most forceful articulation of a radical shift in focus from the reform generation's efforts to cultivate a new set of elite values for Confucian superior men, to calls for a revolutionary transformation of individual thought and behavior at all levels of society.[104]

However, despite the fascinating contextualization of these biographies that occurred in the late 1920s, many excerpts of biographical texts of the 1920s had already been circulating in Vietnam since 1904–5, admittedly in abbreviated form to a limited audience. Second, in my analysis these texts were not merely or mainly concerned with traditional elitist ideas. While the connection between politics and morality was still apparent, it was mediated through new ideas of modern, awakened individuals who emulated acts of heroic romanticism. These ideas were bolstered by the increased production of romanized versions of the works in question, and by increased circulation of texts in general. In terms of circulation, most of these biographies had a print run of 3,000 copies, standard at that time, which sometimes went to a second or third printing if not banned first.[105]

Popular Tastes and Literary Despair

The legacy of a Chinese intellectual such as Liang Qichao's thought can be seen elsewhere in 1920s intellectual life, not simply in the genre of biographies. His ideas about the nature of literature, for instance, were also being translated and modified, as is shown by an examination of another key text that was translated into romanized Vietnamese, "The Relationship between Fiction and the Poetics of the Public,"[106] based on Liang Qichao's seminal 1902 essay on fiction titled "On the Relationship between Fiction and the Government of the People."[107] It was contained in a collection titled *Thời Bệnh Luận* (Discussion of the Sickness of Our Times). In his introduction the translator, Thiên Túng, mentions that "a lot of people criticize the group of new learning (*tân học*) but we are just trying to raise the capacity for learning. At this time, the kind of novels most in vogue in our national literature are those from olden times, but we need to learn from new horizons."[108]

Liang Qichao's famous opening line — "if one intends to renovate the people of a nation, one must first renovate its fiction"[109] — is here rendered as "national salvation depends on the novels that people read."[110] Similarly with Liang's statement: "Since fiction as a genre has such power to penetrate the reader's mind and move him, the universal fondness for fiction above other kinds of writing is in fact a spontaneous psychological phenomenon beyond human control."[111] The more assertive Vietnamese version reads: "The fiction movement spreads and becomes stronger all the time. People are so fond of fiction but instead of literature that will save the country, literature has become like a lullaby, beyond the control of humans. This must be changed."[112]

This sentiment of despair over the kinds of fiction the populace wanted to read was expressed by Liang in Japan in 1902, but also in Vietnam in 1929. The Vietnamese conclusion is more faithful to the original. The Vietnamese term *tiềm lực*, meaning "latent force," is often used, indicating the power that fiction can have. Although this is part of Liang's message as well, his overall tone is more pessimistic. The Vietnamese conclusion reads: "Although fiction has trapped the masses in love stories and mindless thought there is still hope. The trend of society might be to aim for fame in fiction but there is still a chance to develop the destiny of our country and the minds of our people. The reforming of the people is still possible."[113]

Liang's legacy also contains elements of motivational projects of transformation and of despair over the literary tastes of most readers. In "Fiction Seen in Relation to the Guidance of Society," Liang concludes:

> Alas! If this situation is allowed to continue, there is no question that the future of our nation is doomed! Therefore, the reformation of the government of the people must begin with a revolution in fiction, and the renovation of the people must begin with the renovation of literature.[114]

Such a view contained rather more despair than the later Vietnamese modification.

Publishing Constraints

It is important to realize that unlike the early years of the twentieth century, when reformist papers such as *Nông Cổ Minh Đàm* (News of the Old Agricultural People) could exist without proper registration, by the end of the 1920s the surveillance of the French administration, through the Sûreté, became more sophisticated.[115] In June 1917, the service was overhauled and all the security archives were moved to the new head of the Sûreté. Better communication links were also established with the heads of provinces.[116] As Shawn McHale asserts about the Sûreté: "its reports from the early 1920s are sketchy but they improve in analytical depth, comprehensiveness, and accuracy from the mid-1920s onwards."[117] To collect this information, the French sent agents to political rallies, infiltrated political parties, opened mail, and investigated the personal lives of suspects.[118] The reputation of the Sûreté amongst the Vietnamese general public became even worse. They complained of brutality and torture, and there was little freedom of press or assembly. Indeed, in 1927 Trần Huy Liệu was given a six-month prison sentence for political activities and in the 1930s a six-year sentence.[119]

However, the Sûreté was hardly the all-seeing eye of the colonial state. The fact that such biographies could be published at all shows legal loopholes existed. *Arrêtés*, or stays of publication, occurred *after* materials had begun to circulate, not prior to sale. Furthermore, recalling publications was time-consuming and difficult. Different legal systems between the three colonial regions of Vietnam also meant that a brochure or pamphlet might be published in one of the three regions but not immediately banned in another, or there would at least be a time lag between the different stays of publication being issued.[120] The French hope was that publishing houses would become worried about their publications being seized and destroyed, and the resulting financial loss would lead to self-censorship; prohibitions were applied only if other forms of pressure failed.

Conclusion

In the 1920s, as censorship of overtly political materials became more stringent, semi-fictional or historical literature seemed a possible conduit to express partly occluded political opinions. Biographies in particular had the potential to exert a strong influence over a broad cross section of Vietnamese society while circumventing censorship laws. The rigid geographical boundaries of the French Concessions in China contrast with the blurred (inter)national cultural/racial boundaries that are in evidence throughout this chapter. Biographies embody aspects of the processes of translation, circulation, and intellectual exchange that gave rise to such blurred spatial and social boundaries. By the end of the 1920s the French colonial government decided to try to undermine the influence of heroic biographies. In 1929, the year of Liang Qichao's death and the fourth year of Phan Bôi Châu's house arrest in Hue, the Resident Superior of Tonkin officially banned 30 biographies and set up stricter procedures for their overall publication.[121]

Under house arrest in Hue for 15 years, Phan Bội Châu often referred to himself as a political failure. In some ways that is correct. Yet, the cultural imaginaries created by his promotion of heroic models, embodied by the biography of Phạm Hồng Thái, had resonance through the flourishing of literary groups, and their publications, in this seminal period of modern Vietnamese literary and intellectual history.

Abbreviations of Archival Holdings

Centre des Archives d'Outre Mer, Aix en Provence (*CAOM*)
Series Geographiques, Indochine (SG/Indo)
Fonds Gouvernement-Général (GGI)
Résident Supérieure du Tonkin, Nouveau Fonds (RSTNF)
Service de Liaison des Originaries des Territoires Français d'Outre Mer (SLOTFOM)
Vietnamese National Archives
Trung Tâm Lưu Trữ Quốc Gia – I – TTLTQG (National Archives of Vietnam, Archive I, Hanoi)
Bibliothèque Nationale de France (*BNF*)

Microfilm Holdings

Journals

Nghiên Cứu Lịch Sử (NCLS) [Journal of Historical Research]

Notes

1 Louis Roubaud, *La Tragédie Indochinoise* (Paris: Valois. 1931), p. 32.

2 The French police will be referred to as the Sûreté throughout this article.

3 See William J. Duiker, *The Communist Road to Power in Vietnam* (Boulder, CO: Westview Press, 1981), p. 19. Duiker states that 1925 was the year that

the Thanh Niên was established, which is the conventional date previously used by many historians. However, Sophie Quinn-Judge's new research points out that "this grouping did not come to exist as a real political party until sometime in 1926, to judge by the available evidence." See Sophie Quinn-Judge, *Ho Chi Minh: The Missing Years, 1919–1941* (Berkeley: University of California Press, 2002), p. 84. Depictions of these dedication ceremonies are contained in Huynh Kim Khanh, *Vietnamese Communism: 1925–1945* (Ithaca: Cornell University Press, 1982), p. 75; and Hue-Tam Ho Tai, *Vietnamese Radicalism and the Origins of the Vietnamese Revolution* (Cambridge: Harvard University Press, 1992), p. 177. The full title of the Youth League is Việt Nam Thanh Niên Cách Mạng Đồng Chí Hội, the Vietnamese Revolutionary Youth Organization.

4 A wonderfully full description of the ceremony is given in Hue-Tam Ho Tai's recent biography of her aunt: *Passion, Betrayal and Revolution in Colonial Saigon: The Memoirs of Bao Luong* (Berkeley: University of California Press, 2010), p. 50.

5 "Annamite" was the term used to describe all Vietnamese, not just those originating from the French protectorate of Annam.

6 Louis Roubaud, *La Tragedie Indochinoise*, p. 34.

7 See Peter Zinoman, *The Colonial Bastille: A Social History of Imprisonment in Colonial Viet Nam 1862–1940* (Berkeley: University of California Press, 2001), p. 224.

8 Ibid.

9 *Truyện Phạm Hồng Thái*, Phan Bội Châu Toàn Tập [Phan Bội Châu Collected Works] (Huế: Nhà Xuất Bàn Thuận Hóa), vol. 5, pp. 250–95. This particular text has been republished in many different editions.

10 CAOM: Indo/NF-605 – Governor-General of Indochina (GGI) to the Minister of Colonies, April 1913 (day illegible).

11 Ibid.

12 Trung Tâm Lưu Trữ Quốc Gia I [National Archives of Vietnam I, Hanoi] (TTLTQG) GGI F5-2205. Coulon to Minister of Colonies, copied to GGI, 5 Jan. 1912.

13 This was widely rumored.

14 TTLTQG – I: GGI F5-2205 – Coulon to Minister of Colonies, copied to GGI, 5 Jan. 1912.

15 Generally, traditional Vietnamese men kept their hair in a bun on the top of their heads. This was in accordance with the Confucian idea that keeping the hair long denoted filial piety.

16 David Marr, *Vietnamese Anticolonialism 1885–1925* (Berkeley: University of California Press, 1971), p. 260.

17 Ibid.

18 For more explanation on the origins and background of the group, see Trưng Chính "Tâm Tâm Xã Là Gì" [What Is the Society of Like Hearts?],

Nghiên Cứu Lịch Sử (NCLS) [Journal of Historical Research] 34 (Sept.–Oct. 1970): 5–6. Phan Bội Châu was not directly involved in the establishment of this group.

19 Tai, *Vietnamese Radicalism*, p. 66; Hy Sinh, *Phạm Hông Thái Mưu Giết Merlin* [Phạm Hồng Thái's Murder Plot of Merlin] (Hà Nội: Minh Hai, 1954), p. 12.

20 Duiker, *Rise of Vietnamese Nationalism* (Ithaca: Cornell University Press, 1976), p. 83. In this description Duiker calls it the "Secret Heart Society," which is inaccurate. It is the "Same Heart Society" or "Society of Like Hearts."

21 Hải Phòng is a Vietnamese port city north of Hanoi.

22 CAOM: RSTNF-06775. Sun Yat-sen to the Society of Chinese Affairs, Hải Phòng, 28 June 1924.

23 Quinn-Judge, *Ho Chi Minh: The Missing Years*, p. 73.

24 Phan Bội Châu, *Truyện Phạm Hồng Thái*, in *Phạm Hồng Thái và Tiếng Bom Sa Diện*, ed. Chương Thâu [Phạm Hồng Thái and the Noise of Bombs in Sa Diện] (Nghệ An: Nhà Xuất Bản Nghệ An, 2003), p. 134. Merlin's name is also sometimes transliterated as "Mác-lanh."

25 Phan Bội Châu, *Overturned Chariot: The Autobiography of Phan Bội Châu*, trans. Vinh Sinh and Nicholas Wickenden (Honolulu: University of Hawaii Press, 1999), p. 52. Vĩnh Sính, "Đóng góp vào việc tìm hiểu them Phạm Hồng Thái và Tiếng Bom Sa Diện" [Further Contribution to Study about Phạm Hồng Thái and the Bomb Explosion of Sa Diện], *NCLS* 291, 2 (1997): 7–15. In this article, the Vietnamese-Canadian writer Vĩnh Sính does mention that the Hotel Victoria is in the British Concession. However, this does not stop subsequent Vietnamese articles and books from repeating the French soil myth. See Chương Thâu, "Introduction," in *Phạm Hồng Thái và Tiếng Bom Sa Diện*, ed. Chương Thâu [Phạm Hồng Thái and the Noise of Bombs in Sa Diện] (Nghệ An: Nhà Xuất Bản Nghệ An, 2003), p. 14.

26 Tai, *Vietnamese Radicalism*, p. 66.

27 The passage in the *South China Morning Post* is quoted in a footnote of the French translation of Phan Bội Châu's memoirs, *Mémoires de Phan Bội Châu*, trans. Georges Boudarel, p. 191. One of the problems with these memoirs is that Boudarel used Sûreté files to edit the text and compile his footnotes. There are many potential pitfalls in taking such an approach.

28 Pham Thanh Tich was an alias of Phạm Hồng Thái.

29 CAOM: RSTNF-87221 – GGI Merlin to the Minister of Colonies, 8 July 1924.

30 CAOM: SLOTFOM 3/115 – GGI to Minister of Colonies, 18 July 1924. Hoang Chi Nguyen was one of his accomplices.

31 Phan Bội Châu, *Niên Biểu*, p. 206.

32 For one example, see CAOM: RSTNF-06661. Letter from the GGI to the French ambassador in Tokyo requesting photos of Phan Bội Châu and Mai Lão Bạng in both Vietnamese and Western dress, 13 Sept. 1908. There are numerous other requests like this one. According to Nguyễn Văn Ký, Phan Chu Trinh was one of the first renowned Vietnamese nationalists to adopt

European dress around 1907–8. Nguyễn Văn Ký, *La Société Vietnamienne Face à la Modernité*: *Le Tonkin de la fin du 19th Siecle à la Seconde Guerre Mondiale* [Vietnamese Society Facing Modernity: Tonkin from the End of the Nineteenth Century to the Second World War] (Paris: L'Harmattan, 1995), p. 245.

33 Sophie Quinn-Judge, *Ho Chi Minh: The Missing Years*, p. 72.

34 CAOM: GGI- File 90014. GGI to Minister of Colonies, 5 July 1924.

35 Tai, *Vietnamese Radicalism*, p. 136.

36 Ibid. Tai notes that rather ironically, "although thwarted in his desire to emulate Phạm Hồng Thái, Hien would later achieve a different kind of immortality." This was by becoming the model for the character Chen in Malraux's celebrated novel set in Shanghai, *La Condition Humaine* (Man's Fate).

37 Tai, *Vietnamese Radicalism*, p. 66. The Wuhan uprising had been at the center of the 1911 Chinese revolution.

38 Duiker also makes reference to this in *Rise of Vietnamese Nationalism*, p. 82.

39 See Tai, *Vietnamese Radicalism*, p. 66.

40 Roubaud, *La Tragedie Indochinoise*, pp. 50–1; Tai, *Vietnamese Radicalism*, p. 66. This is a reference to the fact that many of the troops used by the French government in concessionary areas were actually Vietnamese.

41 She seems appropriate to mention, given the popularity of Chinese biographies written about her.

42 This was an autobiography written by Phan Bội Châu while he was in prison in China.

43 Phan Bội Châu, *Truyện Phạm Hồng Thái*, pp. 116–7. Hồ Chí Minh's writings had been distributed in Marseilles since 1920, something that the French authorities in Indochina took careful note of. See CAOM: Indo/NF-6.

44 In his own writings, Hồ Chí Minh acknowledges his "spiritual debt" to Phan Bội Châu. See Marr, *Vietnamese Anticolonialism*, p. 209.

45 Phan Bội Châu, *Truyện Phạm Hồng Thái*, p. 117. Although Phạm Hồng Thái hadn't met Hồ Chí Minh, Phan Bội Châu had known him since he was a child as he was a friend of his father's.

46 Chương Thâu, *Phạm Hồng Thái và Tiếng Bom Sa Diện*, p. 178.

47 Roubaud, *Le Tragedie Indochinoise*, p. 34.

48 Ibid.

49 CAOM: SLOTFOM 3/115. GGI to Minister of Colonies, 18 July 1924. No publication details are mentioned for the pamphlet.

50 For an account of one individual (Nguyen Luong Bang) being taken to Phạm Hồng Thái's tomb to ascertain his anti-French sentiments, see Tai, *Vietnamese Radicalism*, p.177.

51 David Marr, *Vietnamese Tradition on Trial 1920–1945* (Berkeley: University of California Press, 1981), p. 283.

52 CAOM-RSTNF: 06649. Resident Superior of Tonkin (RST) to the GGI, 20 June 1930.

53 Ibid.

[54] Marr mentions that Phan Bội Châu later wanted to lay his hands on anything Russian he could get.

[55] This military school was near Beijing, in northern China, and so the students must have been on holiday in Shanghai.

[56] CAOM: Indo/NF28-4 No. 13. Wilden, French Consul in Shanghai, to Sarraut, GGI of Indochina Shanghai, 3 March 1918.

[57] Frederic Wakeman, *Policing Shanghai: 1927–1937* (Berkeley: University of California Press, 1995), p. 105.

[58] Many parallels can be drawn between this and nineteenth-century Singapore, where the state also sold some of its policing and revenue-raising powers (especially) over opium to consortia with their own armed gangs of enforcers who collected the revenue, at a profit of course.

[59] For a more detailed account of the interactions between the French and the Green Gang, see Brian Martin, *The Shanghai Green Gang: Politics and Organized Crime, 1919–1937* (Berkeley: University of California Press, 1996).

[60] Phan Bội Châu, *Overturned Chariot*, p. 262.

[61] Ibid.

[62] See Kim J. Munholland, "The French Response to the Vietnamese Nationalist Movement 1905–1914," *Journal of Modern History* 47, 4 (Dec. 1975): 659.

[63] For example, see Joseph Buttinger, *Viet-Nam: A Dragon Embattled Volume I: From Colonialism to the Vietminh* (New York: Praeger, 1968), p. 159. Sophie Quinn-Judge writes, based on archival evidence, "it appears unlikely that Hồ was involved in turning over Phan to the Sûreté." See *Hồ Chí Minh: The Missing Years*, p. 75. As Duiker also points out, "Phan could not possibly have been a danger to him [Hồ] — indeed, the old revolutionary was apparently just preparing to reorganize his party along lines desired by Hồ himself," *Rise of Vietnamese Nationalism*, p. 86. Lam Duc Thu, a close associate of Phan and French informer since at least 1924, is the most likely candidate. Phan suggests in his autobiography that his own secretary and protégé, Nguyễn Thượng Huyền, had betrayed him, which is almost certainly wrong.

[64] Hoang Van Chi, *From Colonialism to Communism: A Case History of North Vietnam* (New York: Praeger, 1964), p. 18.

[65] Marr, *Vietnamese Anticolonialism*, p. 267.

[66] CAOM: RSTNF-36411. Report on the Indigenous Press. Vinay, Head of Censorship, to RST, 20 Dec. 1922.

[67] Marr, *Vietnamese Tradition on Trial*, p. 263. *Việt Điện U Linh* was by Lý Tế Xuyên.

[68] David G. Marr, "Concepts of 'Individual' and 'Self' in Twentieth-Century Vietnam," *Modern Asian Studies* 34, 4 (2000): 781.

[69] Arguably, the main difference between earlier foreign biographies (from 1905 to say 1910) and those from the end of the 1920s was the number on Sun Yat-sen (Tôn Dật Tiên in Vietnamese), about whom six biographies appeared in the late 1920s.

70 The Vietnamese heroes evoked include Lê Lời, founder of the Lê dynasty and victor over the Ming as well as Phan Chu Trinh. Indeed, three biographies of Phan Chu Trinh were published shortly after his death in 1926. See Marr, *Vietnamese Tradition on Trial*, p. 263.

71 For a brief description of this phenomenon, see D.E. Pollard, "Foreigners to Admire in Late-Qing China," *CUHK Journal of Humanities* 1 (1997): 30–8.

72 Hu Ying, *Tales of Translation: Composing the New Woman in China, 1899–1918* (Stanford: Stanford University Press, 2000), p. 5.

73 Trần Huy Liệu, *Hội Ký* [Memoirs] (Hà Nội: Khoa Học Xã Hội, 1991), p. 30.

74 Philip Huang, *Liang Chi-chao and Modern Chinese Liberalism* (Seattle: University of Washington Press, 1972), p. 24. The Treaty of Shimonoseki marked the end of the Sino-Japanese War in a defeat for the Chinese.

75 Trần Huy Liệu, *Hội Ký*, p. 152.

76 It was published in 1923 in both French and *quốc ngữ*.

77 Philippe Peycam, "Intellectuals and Political Commitment in Vietnam: The Emergence of a Public Sphere in Colonial Saigon, 1916–1928," PhD dissertation, University of London, 1999, p. 197.

78 Trần Huy Liệu, *Hội Ký*, p. 31.

79 Trần Văn Giàu, "Chủ nghĩa Dân tọc Cách mạng ở Việt Nam và Sự biên chuyển của nó trong giai đoàn lịch sử giữa hai cuộc Chiến Tranh Thế Giới" [Revolutionary People's Democracy in Vietnam and the Sudden Change of It within the Historical Period until the Second World War], *NCLS* 151, no. 7-151, no. 8 (1973/4): 6–25. Trần Huy Liệu is quoted in this article, pp. 9–10.

80 BNF: *Tiểu Sử và Tập Diễn Văn Lương Khải Siêu* [Biography and Speeches of Liang Qichao] (Saigon: In Tại Nhà in thạnh thi Mau, 1927).

81 CAOM: RSTNF-578. RST to GGI, 7 Apr. 1928.

82 All texts published by the Strengthening Study Society had this quotation by Mencius on the cover.

83 BNF: Lương Khải Siêu [Liang Qichao], *Hiến Thân Cho Nước* [Dedication to One's Country: Truyện Ông Cát Tô Sĩ, Louis Kossuth], trans. Trần Huy Liệu (Saigon: Imprimerie Thạnh Thị Mau, 1928), p. 22.

84 BNF: *Anh Hùng Cưu Quốc* (Saigon: Imprimerie Commerciale Ardin, 1927), p. 43.

85 He was a colleague of Sun Yat-sen and the military leader of the 1911 revolution.

86 BNF: Dao Khắc Hưng, *Khai Quốc Vĩ Nhân* [A Great Man Who Founded a Nation], Cường Học Thư Xã (Saigon: Impr. C, Ardin, 1928), pp. 42–3.

87 BNF: Dao Khắc Hưng, *Khai Quốc Vĩ Nhân*.

88 Ibid., p. 1.

89 Ibid.

90 CAOM: RSTNF-578. This pamphlet had many interesting ways of clandestine circulation and distribution. As a Sûreté report mentioned, "Nguyễn Văn Minh, secretary of the Indochina Bank in Hải Phòng has been distributing for free

the brochure *Khai Quốc Vĩ Nhân* (*A Great Man Who Founded a Nation*)." The report went on to link this to Minh's desire to launch his own small review that would contain articles on "hygiene and gymnastics with a view to making strong and robust men." In terms of this sort of clandestine circulation, Shawn McHale mentions pharmacies involved in the distribution of anti-French tracts even as late as 1935. See Shawn Frederick McHale, *Print and Power: Confucianism, Communism and Buddhism in the Making of Modern Vietnam* (Honolulu: University of Hawaii Press, 2004), p. 198, n. 55.

91 BNF: Lương Khải Siêu [Liang Qichao], *Hiến Thân Cho Nước* [Dedication to One's Country: Truyện Ông Cát Tô Sĩ, Louis Kossuth], trans. Trần Huy Liệu (Saigon: Imprimerie Thạnh Thị Mau, 1928), p. 25.

92 Ibid., p. 3.

93 BNF: Lương Khải Siêu [Liang Qichao], *Gương Phục Quốc: Ý Đại Lợi Tam Kiệt* [Mirror of National Strength: Three Famous Italians], trans. Trần Huy Liệu (Saigon: Imprimerie Thạnh Thị Mau, 1928), p. 80. The "Translator's Comments" are in a separate section headed by the phrase "Lời Bàn them của người dịch."

94 Ibid.

95 Tai, *Vietnamese Radicalism*, p. 139.

96 Liang Qichao, *Ý Đại Lợi Tam Kiệt*, p. 81.

97 CAOM: RSTNF-578.

98 BNF: Lâm Vạn Lý, *Anh Hùng Yêu Nước: Ông Nạp Nhi Ton* [A Hero Who Loves His Country: Mr Nelson], trans. Trần Huy Liệu (Saigon: Imp. Duc Luu Phuong). The date of publication is illegible, but from the police report it would appear to be 1927.

99 CAOM: RSTNF-587. Letter from the RST to Director of the Sûreté, 8 Sept. 1928. Phân Thị Bạch Văn was eventually taken to court for "disrupting peace and security in the region by means of literature and ideas." She was fined 250 francs, and the publishing house had to be disbanded. See Marr, *Vietnamese Tradition on Trial*, p. 220.

100 According to Vietnamese legend, the two Trưng sisters were daughters of an early northern warlord; in AD 40, they led a rebellion against the Chinese governor and formed their own kingdom based in Mê Linh. They were defeated three years later by the Chinese general Ma Yuan and ended up killing themselves. Keith Weller Taylor, *The Birth of Vietnam* (Berkeley: University of California Press, 1983), p. 328.

101 CAOM: RSTNF-587. Letter from the RST to Director of the Sûreté, 8 Sept. 1928.

102 CAOM: RSTNF-587. Letter from the RST to Director of the Sûreté, 8 Sept. 1928. BNF: *Gương Nữ Kiệt* [Mirror of Women to Emulate] (Saigon: Imprimerie Bao Ton, 1928). The file makes special mention that the publicaation was sponsored by a women's society in Gò Công.

103 Greg Lockhart, *The Light of the Capital: Three Modern Vietnamese Classics* (Kuala Lumpur: Oxford University Press, 1996), p. 5.

104 Mark Bradley, "Becoming Van Minh: Civilizational Discourse and Visions of the Self in Twentieth-Century Vietnam," *Journal of World History* 15, 1 (2004): 78.

105 Trần Huy Liệu, *Hội Ký*, p. 76.

106 Liang Qichao, "Sự quan hệ của Tiều Thuyết đói với chính trị nhân quần" [On the Relationship between Novels and the Politics of the People], *Thời Bệnh Luận* [Discussion of the Sickness of Our times], trans. Thiên Túng (Hanoi: Ỉmp. Long Quang, 1929).

107 This was first published in 1902 in the Chinese magazine *New Fiction*, which was published in Japan. I did not find any explicit evidence of it circulating in Vietnam prior to this *quốc ngữ* version in 1929.

108 Ibid., p. 1.

109 Liang Qichao, "On the Relationship between Fiction and the Government of the People," in *Modern Chinese Thought: Writings on Literature 1893–1945*, trans. Gek Nai Cheng, ed. Kirk A. Denton (Stanford: Stanford University Press, 1996), p. 74.

110 Liang Qichao, *Thời Bệnh Luận*, p. 24.

111 Liang Qichao, "On the Relationship between Fiction and the Government of the People," p. 78.

112 Liang Qichao, *Thời Bệnh Luận*, p. 23.

113 Ibid., p. 27.

114 Liang Qichao, "On the Relationship between Fiction and the Government of the People," p. 81.

115 It was not until a trial involving materials published in it that French authorities realized the paper was not registered properly.

116 CAOM: RSTNF-02030. This is a large file on the expansion of the Sûreté. The order for reorganization was given on 29 June 1917, and the new head of the agency was M. Janbreau. CAOM: RSTNF-36405. A report on this from the RST to the GGI dated 20 January 1920 discusses sending Sûreté agents into the provinces.

117 McHale, *Print and Power*, p. 45. According to Nola Cooke, surveillance was more extensive in Tonkin and Cochinchina than in Annam. See "Colonial Political Myth and the Problem of the Other: French and Vietnamese in the Protectorate of Annam," PhD dissertation, Australian National University, 1991, pp. 252–4, chapter 6.

118 Information on the sending of Sûreté agents into the provinces is contained in CAOM: RSTNF-36405.

119 Zinoman, *Colonial Bastille*, pp. 110–1. Trần Huy Liệu commented on how by the time of his second incarceration "conditions for political prisoners had deteriorated." Ibid.

120 McHale calls banning a "cumbersome process" and the formal stay of publication "a poor weapon," *Print and Power*, p. 50.

121 CAOM: RSTNF-22512. RST Publication Note, 8 Aug. 1929.

CHAPTER 3

Living "Underground" in Shanghai: Noulens and the Shanghai Comintern Network

Onimaru Takeshi

In the 1920s and 1930s, Communism was one of the major political thoughts that fueled anti-colonial movements in Southeast Asia. Communists tried to mobilize people for overthrowing colonial regimes by establishing Communist parties, youth organizations, labor unions, and other communistic organizations. For colonial authorities, such movements were a major threat to their regimes, so they suppressed Communist movements by banning Communist parties and other Communist-led organizations; monitoring Communists' activities; and arresting, imprisoning, and deporting Communists. Under these repressive conditions, many Communists went underground or abroad to escape detection and continue their revolutionary activities.

Many anti-colonial revolutionaries, not only Communists but also nationalists, have had the experience of going underground or going into exile during their career. It is not easy, therefore, to write a biography of those revolutionaries or agents who spent most of their career underground, because underground activity by definition requires secrecy, and so available sources to reconstruct their lives underground are basically scarce. In the case of celebrated revolutionaries or agents such as Ho Chi Minh (before World War II he was known by the name Nguyen Ai Quoc) and Zhou Enlai, their lives are relatively well documented, and we know of their underground activities from several biographies on them.[1] Some revolutionaries wrote their own memoirs, and these memoirs themselves are important firsthand sources for details on their underground lives.[2] These biographies and memoirs sometimes refer to the kind of tasks

Hilaire Noulens

underground revolutionaries conducted, but they rarely mention how they went about doing so. What kinds of strategies, skills, abilities, and techniques did they apply to their own revolutionary plotting? In order to understand the lives of revolutionaries or agents underground, it is essential to focus on the tasks they carried out as well as the strategies, skills, abilities, and techniques they employed to conduct them.

This chapter focuses on the strategies and techniques utilized by a key liaison officer of the Third International (the Comintern), who was sent to Shanghai. His name was Hilaire Noulens, and he was in charge of maintaining and managing liaisons between the Comintern headquarters in Moscow and Communist parties, labor unions, Communist youth organizations, and other communistic organizations in East and Southeast Asia. He was arrested, along with his wife, by the Shanghai Municipal Police (SMP) on 15 June 1931. After his arrest, it was revealed that he had a number of aliases, three passports, four or five residential addresses, ten post-office boxes, eight telegraphic addresses, and eight bank accounts. All of these were clearly utilized by Noulens to hide his existence from police eyes and to cover the tracks of his liaison work. His efforts were so successful that the SMP failed to discover his real identity.

The Noulens Case (or Pan-Pacific Trade Union Secretariat[3] Case) is mentioned in several studies on Shanghai and the Communist movements and political police activities against these in East and Southeast Asia in the 1920s and 1930s,[4] but there is only one study that focuses on Noulens himself. Frederick Litten's paper reveals that Noulens' real name was Yakov Matveevich Rudnik and that he was Ukrainian.[5] Litten describes the arrest and judicial procedure involving the Noulens couple, the activities of the Comintern apparatus in Shanghai, and short biographies of the couple, but he only briefly mentions the strategies and techniques employed — such as nationalities, aliases, residences, postal and telegraphic addresses — and does not discuss how these strategies and techniques were utilized for both Noulens' tasks and his life underground.

This chapter departs from conventional biography by offering a portrait of Noulens not as an individual, but as a liaison officer of the Comintern's Far Eastern Bureau. Noulens had a life beyond his Comintern career: although he was initially sentenced to death following his arrest in 1931, his sentence was commuted to life imprisonment. He (along with his wife) was quietly released in 1937 and left China for the USSR in 1939. Nearly a quarter of a century would pass before Noulens' death in 1963, followed by that of his wife a year later.[6] This chapter does not offer a full account of Noulens' life; it offers, instead, a slice of that life, one that was peculiarly defined by the imperative for secrecy and self-effacement — a life that, for the time in which it was lived underground, can only be gleaned from, and understood in terms of, the organizational form, the Far Eastern Bureau, in and through which Noulens operated. This episode in Noulens' career is one of crucial importance to the development of a regional network of Communist and anti-colonial activists in Asia, but the irony is that the man who acted as the hub of that network can only be fleshed out in terms of the strategies and techniques of anonymity that he deployed to conceal his existence and identity as part of his mission to maintain and manage the liaison network in East and Southeast Asia. In other words, these strategies, skills, abilities, and techniques were essential to Noulens' ability, as liaison officer, *not* to foreground himself, but rather to serve as the unknowable contact who linked one set of activists to another across space. Noulens devoted himself to underground activities. To understand Noulens' life as an agent requires that we understand his missions and how he conducted them. The chapter also argues that the specificity of Noulens' tasks may be better understood through a comparison of Noulens with other (visible and better-known) revolutionaries and agents.

Communist Movements in East and Southeast Asia in the 1920s and 1930s

In the 1920s and 1930s, Communism provided a major source of inspiration to revolutionary movements all over the world. The success of the Russian Revolution in 1917 was so impressive that those who were inspired by this first successful Communist revolution tried to create their own revolutions in their countries. In East and Southeast Asia, Communism was received with enthusiasm by young intellectuals who wanted to liberate their countries from colonial rule or tried to solve social and economic inequalities by way of Communist revolutions.[7] Communist thought was disseminated among laborers and peasants at night schools or by the distribution of leaflets, and organization work and mobilization for strikes and demonstrations were undertaken. Labor unions, peasant associations, and Communist institutions were established. The first Communist party in East and Southeast Asia was the Communist Association of the Indies, which was established in the Dutch East Indies in 1920 (and renamed the Communist Party of Indonesia in 1924). The next year the Chinese Communist Party was established, followed in 1922 by the Japanese Communist Party. In 1930 four Communist parties were established in Southeast Asia: the Indochinese Communist Party, the Siamese Communist Party, the Malayan Communist Party, and the Philippine Communist Party.

Local Communist movements in East and Southeast Asia were led by these Communist parties, labor unions, and peasants associations, but there was another important dimension to the Communist movements in the 1920s and 1930s: the regional reach and connectedness of these Communist movements. Regional Communist movements were promoted by local Southeast Asian Communists, Chinese Communists, Japanese Communists, and comrades dispatched by the Comintern. Local Communists in Southeast Asia who engaged in regional Communist movements were mainly Indonesians and Indochinese who had escaped from severe police suppression in the Dutch East Indies and French Indochina.[8] Indonesians tried to spread Communism among Malays in British Malaya, and Indochinese also tried to spread Communism in Siam.[9]

Chinese Communists were the most important regional promoters of Communist movements in Southeast Asia in the 1920s and 1930s. The Chinese Communist Party tried to spread Communism through linkages among overseas Chinese in the Philippines, British Malaya, French Indochina, and Siam. Especially after 1927, when the alliance between the Chinese Communist Party and the Kuomintang broke up, many Chinese

Communists left China for Southeast Asia in order to escape severe suppression there, and they not only continued their revolutionary activities for China but also became regional promoters of Communist movements.[10] As for Japanese Communists, some of them devoted themselves to revolutionary movements in China, but none of them appear to have successfully established linkages with Communists in Southeast Asia in the 1920s and 1930s.[11]

Finally, regional promoters in East and Southeast Asia were agents dispatched by or working together with the Comintern. These agents or couriers were in charge of establishing liaisons between Communist movements in East and Southeast Asia and the Comintern Central in Moscow, distributing funds and directives, and gathering information in the region. But making and maintaining liaisons between Moscow and East and Southeast Asia were not easy because of their distance. How did the Comintern try to solve this problem?

The Comintern and Its Regional Headquarters in Shanghai

The Third International (the Comintern) was established in Moscow in 1919, two years after the Russian Revolution. As "the International Communist Party," the Comintern tried to supervise Communist movements all over the world. Supervision meant recognition of the establishment of a Communist party in each country, approval of personnel appointments in each Communist party, allocation of funds for Communist movements, dispatching of agents, distribution of directives, receiving and training of Communists from other countries, and so on.[12]

The "supervising" activities were conducted through liaisons between Moscow and Communist movements in each country, and the organization that constructed, operated and maintained these liaisons was the OMS (Otdel mezhdunarodnykh svyazey: the Department of International Communication), established within the Comintern in 1921. The OMS "conducted the clandestine activities of the Comintern abroad, including the distribution of confidential directives and propaganda material, the forging of passports and identity papers for overseas agents and the implementation of espionage operations."[13] The activities of the Comintern, especially clandestine activities abroad, were heavily dependent on liaisons operated and maintained by the OMS, but it was not easy to maintain liaisons between Moscow and distant places such as East and Southeast Asia.

To solve this problem of distance, a regional headquarters, the Far Eastern Bureau of the Comintern, was established in Shanghai. The Far Eastern Bureau was set up in 1926, and its original mission was to supervise Communist movements in China, Japan, and Korea. But by 1930 its jurisdiction had expanded to Taiwan, French Indochina, the Dutch East Indies, British Malaya, and the Philippine islands.[14] There was another organization in Shanghai that was also in charge of supervising Communist movements in East and Southeast Asia. This was the Pan-Pacific Trade Union Secretariat, established in 1927. The mission of the Pan-Pacific Trade Union Secretariat was to support and promote labor union movements in China, Japan, Korea, India, and Southeast Asia.[15]

These two organizations were formally distinct and separate, but most of their personnel and activities overlapped, so that the regional headquarters in Shanghai in fact mediated the activities of both organizations.[16] Liaisons were constructed from the regional headquarters in Shanghai both to Communist movements in East and Southeast Asia and to the Comintern Central in Moscow, and thus Shanghai became the liaison center of regional Communist movements in East and Southeast Asia. But why Shanghai?

Shanghai as Liaison Center

David McKnight points out three reasons for why Shanghai was chosen as the location of the Far Eastern Bureau. The first was the availability of legal protection, the second was that Shanghai was equipped with modern communication systems, and the third was the existence of a large international community.[17]

The first point, the availability of legal protection, was the existence of extraterritoriality. During the 1920s and 1930s, 14 states could exercise this right in Shanghai: Britain, the United States, Belgium, Brazil, Denmark, France, Italy, Japan, the Netherlands, Norway, Portugal, Spain, Sweden, and Switzerland.[18] This extraterritoriality was crucial for comrades who had Western nationalities, because if they failed to exercise this legal privilege when they were arrested, they were tried by the Chinese courts and were likely to be sentenced to death or life imprisonment.

Regarding the second point, modern communication systems, Shanghai in the 1920s and 1930s was already well equipped not only with modern communication systems, such as radio and cable communications, and postal services, but also with other forms of infrastructure such as gas and gas lighting, electricity, waterworks, and public transportation. Foreign and Chinese banks had offices in Shanghai, and international bank transfers as well as remittances to and from East and Southeast Asia through Chinese "local" banks and money changers were possible.[19] All this infrastructure promoted economic activities in Shanghai and made

Table 3.1 Principal Foreign Groups in Shanghai (1930 Census)

Nationality	*International settlements*	*External roads area*	*French Concession*	*Total*
Japanese	12,788	5,690	318	18,796
British	4,606	1,615	2,228	8,449
Russian	3,113	374	3,879	7,366
American	1,145	463	1,541	3,149
Indian (British)	1,758	84	–	1,842
Portuguese	847	485	267	1,599
German	524	309	597	1,430
French	159	39	1,208	1,406
Tonkinese (French)	–	–	941	941
Filipino	356	31	–	387
Danish	143	43	164	350
Polish	159	28	156	343
Italian	168	29	123	320
Spanish	116	32	73	221
Swiss	93	32	81	206
Dutch	42	40	108	190
Greek	109	12	64	185
Norwegian	84	20	69	173
Korean	139	12	–	151
Czecho-Slovakian	88	12	39	139
Austrian	64	24	44	132
Swedish	44	43	31	118
Belgian	25	2	61	88

Source: *All About Shanghai: A Standard Guidebook* (first published 1934–5 by the University Press, Shanghai; reprinted 1983 by Oxford University Press), p. 35.

life in Shanghai "modern" and comfortable. Communists fully utilized these conveniences and the metropolitan character of Shanghai for their activities.

Regarding the third point referred to above, the cosmopolitan character of Shanghai, the total population of the city in 1930 was 3,144,805,[20] of which foreigners totaled 58,607.[21] Shanghai was the sixth-largest city in the world at that time. As shown in Table 3.1, the ethnic composition of foreigners was diverse, and this variety was useful for Communists because those who engaged in Communist movements in East and Southeast Asia were also a heterogeneous lot: Chinese, Japanese, Tonkinese, Annamese, Cochinchinese, Javanese, Filipino, Korean, Taiwanese, Indian, as well as Russian, Ukrainian, American, French, British, German, and other "Westerners." The ethnic diversity and cosmopolitanism of Shanghai made the city a suitable place to conduct underground revolutionary activities not only for Western staff in the Comintern regional headquarters but also for local Communists from East and Southeast Asia.

These three points highlighted by McKnight were key factors in making Shanghai the liaison center of regional Communist movements. However, these factors, except extraterritoriality, were also true for the largest city in Asia in 1930 — Tokyo. Tokyo was also equipped with modern communication systems and other infrastructure; and its total population in 1930 was 5,408,678, including 50,934 foreigners.[22] There is no extant data on the ethnic composition of foreign residents in Tokyo in 1930, but the ethnic composition of Tokyo should not have been far less heterogeneous than Shanghai's.

Even though Shanghai and Tokyo shared, except for extraterritoriality, similar characteristics that qualified them to serve as liaison centers of underground regional Communist movements, there were two more crucial factors that made Shanghai the far more germane choice. These were: accessibility to other places, and the division of administration.

Accessibility to other places in East and Southeast Asia was far more convenient from Shanghai than from Tokyo. Tokyo, or more precisely Yokohama, was an important port of international steamship lines, especially from East Asia to the United States, but Shanghai was far more frequently and conveniently connected with various ports in East and Southeast Asia and beyond by steamship. A guidebook published in 1934–5 showed this accessibility of Shanghai as follows.

> Where next? To the traveler, Shanghai offers a unique advantage; the entire world, literally, is open for his selection. He can go to Europe by going West, or he can go to Europe by going East, with distances, time, and cost showing but slight variation. It may be an exaggeration to call Shanghai the "center of world" but it looks very much like it on a travel map.[23]

This accessibility from Shanghai not only to East and Southeast Asia, but also to Europe, the United States, and Moscow, was essential to establish and maintain liaisons, because basically these liaisons were sustained by couriers, agents, and local Communists who made contact with each other in Shanghai or in the region.

The division of administration was a direct by-product of Shanghai's semi-colonial status in the 1920s and 1930s. In this era, Shanghai was administratively divided into three sections: the International Settlement, the French Concession, and the Chinese Municipality. Each section had its own police force and surveillance apparatus, and their jurisdictions were also divided along administrative lines. Even though administrations were divided into three, there were no restrictions on movements between these administrations. This combination of the division of police territories and the freedom of passage generated "gray zones" in Shanghai. A gray zone was a place where a certain degree of ambiguity existed in law enforcement and administrative control. The existence of gray zones was an obstacle for policing and surveillance, but it was a boon for political underground activities in Shanghai.

And this existence of gray zones was the crucial differentiating factor that favored Shanghai over Tokyo. Tokyo had no division of administration and was policed by the Tokyo Metropolitan Police. Policing against criminals in Tokyo was tightened from the late nineteenth century. From 1876, police conducted regular censuses in Tokyo to identify "criminals." The Special Branch, established in 1906, was in charge of monitoring and suppressing political movements, conducting censorship, and monitoring foreigners. Communist movements were the main target of the Special Branch. During the 1920s and 1930s the Communist Party of Japan was severely suppressed by the Special Branch, and it finally collapsed in 1935. Foreigners, especially Russians and Jews, were monitored and censored, and organizations suspected to have a relationship with Russia, the Russian Communist Party, or the Comintern were closely monitored by the Special Branch.[24]

Communist movements were monitored and suppressed also in Shanghai, but Communists could utilize the gray zones fully and could continue their activities there. The well-known Soviet agent Richard Sorge, who conducted underground activities in both Shanghai and Tokyo, described early 1930s Shanghai as a "relatively safe place for underground works" in his memoir, which he wrote after his arrest in Tokyo.[25]

With its extraterritoriality, modern infrastructure, international communities, convenience, accessibility to and from other places, and gray zones, Shanghai was an eminently suitable place in and through which to conduct political underground activities, and it was the natural choice for the site of the regional headquarters of the Comintern.

Maintaining and Managing the Liaison Network

Noulens arrived in Shanghai in March 1930,[26] and as the head of the OMS in Shanghai he was in charge of maintaining and managing the liaison network from Shanghai to East and Southeast Asia, and Moscow.

Figure 3.1 The Comintern Network in Asia connected by Couriers

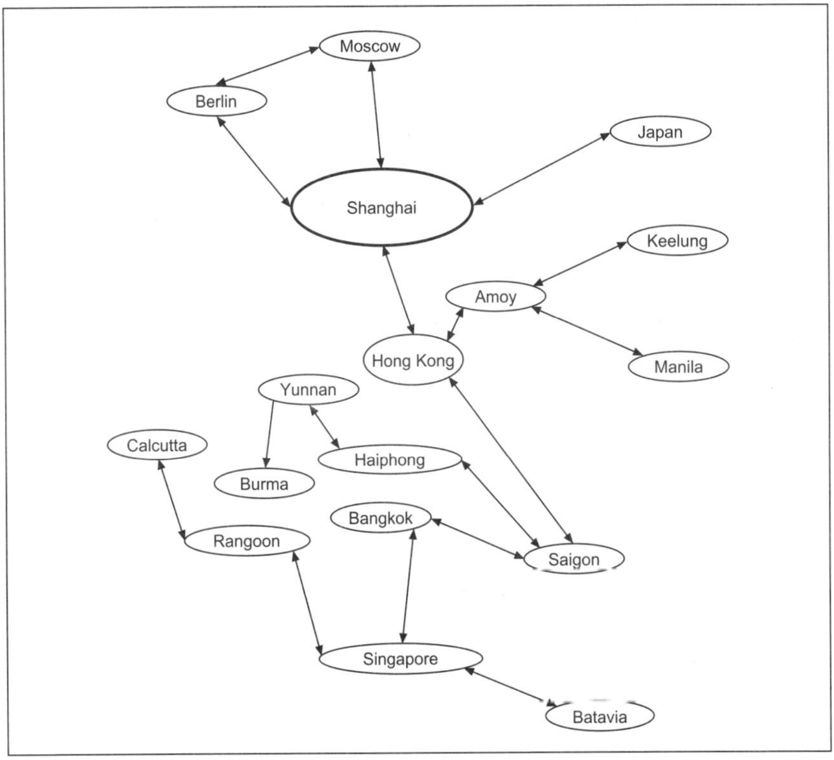

Note: Courier service between Berlin and Shanghai was basically via Marseilles (from there by ship) or via Moscow (by Trans-Siberian Railway).

Source: SMP Files D2527/45.

Liaison-making was not a unidirectional activity that radiated only from Shanghai. Communist parties, labor unions, and other communistic organizations in East and Southeast Asia that wanted to establish contact with Moscow for the purpose of getting directives, obtaining approval of appointed personnel and party missions, and gaining access to funds also actively sought liaisons with Shanghai. Initial contacts with the regional headquarters in Shanghai or with Communist organizations in the region were undertaken by agents dispatched from Shanghai to Communist organizations in East and Southeast Asia or vice versa. Once contacts were made and liaisons were established, they were maintained by agents and couriers who were dispatched from and to Shanghai, and by means of mail and telegraph (see Figure 3.1). Noulens' roles as head OMS officer in

Shanghai consisted of the following: offering safe houses for couriers and agents, managing post-office boxes and telegraphic addresses for communications, and maintaining bank accounts for storing funds sent from Moscow.[27]

He undertook these tasks by utilizing various strategies and techniques. Safe houses were essential for couriers and agents to hide themselves from police surveillance and to carry out their work safely. When Noulens was arrested, it was revealed that he had kept at least 14 or 15 houses, rooms, and offices in Shanghai. All of these, except four houses and rooms that he used himself, were used as safe houses for couriers, agents, students going to or returning from Moscow, and staff in the regional headquarters in Shanghai; as meeting places; and as cover addresses for postal and telegraphic addresses. Each of these houses and rooms was leased under different names to avoid disclosure, and was frequently changed "for Police reasons."[28] The monthly average expenditure for renting them was about 260 pounds.[29]

Correspondence by way of mail and telegraph was an important component of the liaison network. Ten post-office boxes and eight telegraphic addresses were managed by Noulens at the time of his arrest (see Tables 3.2 and 3.3). PO boxes were used for receiving newspapers, journals, printed matter, and ciphered letters from Europe, China, Japan,

Table 3.2 PO Boxes Used by Noulens

No.	*Name of holder*	*Cover address*	*Date obtained*	*Number of mails cleared by SMP*
206	Hilaire Noulens	107/9 Szechuen Road	24 Mar. 1930	17
407	The Sincere Co.	560 Nanking Road	21 Jan. 1929	–
883	H. Vanutsen	92 Wutting Road	1 Mar. 1931	49
1077	Bemhard Schreiber	210 Bubbling Well Road	1 July 1929	30
1085	Gerhart Eisler	Hotel Burlington	9 Mar. 1929	6
1265	Renaat Dillen	280 Yu Yuen Road	13 Feb. 1929	33
1382	Albert E. Stewart	Room 512 Hotel Plaza	16 Feb. 1931	–
1518	Serge N. Lefranc	Room 215 Palace Hotel	23 Feb. 1931	64
1532	Mrs. Adele Ruck	142 Szechuen Road, 3rd Floor	15 Jan. 1931	7
1941	H. Noulens	–	–	–

Source: SMP files, D2527/41, D2527/43.

Table 3.3 Telegraphic Addresses Used by Noulens

Telegraphic address	*Name of holder*	*Registered address*
"Hilanoul"	Hilaire Noulens	235 Szechuen Road
"Arcered"	Edward Briggs	Room 30-C Central Arcade, 49 Nanking Road
"Mamoeng"	Marcel Motte	74 West End Garden, Yu Yuen Road
"Saneselus"	Samuel Herssens	66 Hart Road
"Beremdo"	Rudolf Bergmann	168 Szechuen Road

Source: SMP files, D2527/42.

and Southeast Asia. All of these PO boxes were not obtained by Noulens. Some of them were obtained by other staff members in the regional headquarters in Shanghai or agents who came there. Noulens inherited these and utilized them for his liaison work. He himself used mainly seven PO boxes (206, 883, 1077, 1085, 1265, 1518, and 1532) and differentiated these according to the contents of correspondence.[30] For example, Nos. 1077 and 1085 were used mainly for correspondence from Japan, and No. 1518 was stuffed with French journals and newspapers.[31]

Telegraphic addresses were registered at two companies in Shanghai,[32] and telegraphs were utilized mainly for communicating with Berlin. Long messages were separated and sent to different telegraphic addresses. For example, a ciphered message from Moscow was sent to Shanghai via Berlin by separating it into four and sending the divided parts on two different days — 17 and 18 June 1931. The first portion was sent to "Arcered" on 18 June, and the second to "Saneselus" on 17 June. The third one was sent to "Mamoeng" on 18 June, and the last one to "Saneselus" on 18 June. These separated messages were decoded and reconstructed in Shanghai.[33] Different cipher systems were applied to postal and telegraphic communications, and these cipher systems "combined a reasonable maximum of security with the minimum of compromising books."[34]

Finally, receiving, storing, and sending funds was the most crucial part of Noulens' task in Shanghai. Noulens possessed eight bank accounts in seven Chinese banks under six Chinese names. The total balance of these eight accounts was 47,500 dollars (see Table 3.4).[35] He also had about 103 dollars with him when he was arrested; and 1,323 dollars, 152.97 Japanese yen, 2 Shanghai taels, 2.13 Reichsmarks, 6.84 Mexican dollars, and 189.04 rubles were found on the premises.[36] Apparently, all of these denominations were not only used for underground activities by staff in

Table 3.4 Bank Accounts Maintained by Noulens

Name of depositor	*Passbook number*	*Name of bank*	*Account balance*
Chow Zing (周静)	1610 (fixed deposit)	Day & Night Bank, Chekiang Rd. Branch	$2,500.00
Chow Zing	6889 (fixed deposit)	The Ningpo Commercial and Saving Bank	$3,000.00
Wong Sz Zung (王思慎)	1579 (current accounts)	Bank of Communications	$10,000.00
Zao Yoong Ying (趙雲影)	1362 (current accounts)	The Continental Bank	$9,000.00
Zao Yoong Ying	Deposit book	The China & South Sea Bank	30 Jan. 1931, deposited 2 Bank of China cheques, Nos. 142 and 137, for $9,000.00
Chi Wei Nan (齎味南)	223 Commercial Bank	Yien Yieh	$4,000.00
Wong Dih Zung (王滌塵)	387	The Bank of China	$5,000.00
Zung Tien Sz (鄭退思)	347	The Bank of China	$5,000.00

Source: SMP files, D2510/13.

the regional headquarters in Shanghai, couriers, and agents, but were also allocated for Communist and labor movements in East and Southeast Asia.[37]

These funds were sent from Moscow via Berlin to Shanghai by international bank transfers. In Shanghai, a staff member in charge of budgets withdrew transferred funds from banks, separated them into small amounts, and handed these to Noulens at night. Noulens stored these funds in eight bank accounts and used them for renting houses and rooms; salaries of staff in the regional headquarters; underground activities by staff, couriers, and agents; and budgets allocated to Communist and labor movements in East and Southeast Asia. For example, monthly budgets allocated to the movements in China, Japan, Korea, and Indochina in early 1931 were 14,530; 427; 500; and 213 dollars respectively.[38]

As mentioned above, funds were sent from Moscow via Berlin to Shanghai by international bank transfers, but this raises the question of how the allocated budgets were sent to the Communist movements in the region. For the movements in China it was easy, because the Central Committee of the Chinese Communist Party was also in Shanghai.[39] But for movements other than in China, funds had to be delivered by couriers or agents, or handed over to comrades dispatched from the region to Shanghai. For example, budgets allocated to the movements in Japan were brought by agents in February 1931.[40]

Liaisons from Shanghai to Moscow, Europe, and East and Southeast Asia were maintained and managed by Noulens through strategies and techniques such as offering houses and rooms to couriers and agents; communicating by post and telegram; and receiving, storing, and distributing funds. But in order to maintain liaisons, Noulens had to be skilful as well in other important matters: hiding his existence and identity.

Concealing Existence and Identity

In order to carry out his liaison work effectively, Noulens needed not only to cover the tracks of couriers and agents, but to hide the paper trail of correspondence, papers, documents, bank accounts, and funds, and also conceal his identity and existence in Shanghai, because his discovery by the police would lead to exposure of the liaison network. (This, in fact, happened following his arrest in 1931.) So he tried to hide himself behind various passports and aliases, and by rotating among different residences.

When Noulens was arrested, he had three passports and his wife had two (see Table 3.5). Even though he had three passports, he seemed to have used only one — a Belgian passport under the name of Samuel Herssens, which he used for his trip from Europe to Shanghai in 1930. We know of his itinerary from the stamps in this passport. He entered Germany from Belgium on 23 February, and from Germany he went on to Poland on 26 February. He entered the USSR on 27 February and departed for Changshun, in Manchuria, on 10 March.[41]

From his passport, we can trace his tracks from Belgium to Changshun. A report made by the Special Branch of the SMP takes up the story by tracing his itinerary from Changshun to Shanghai:

> On December 4, 1929, under the name of Samuel Herssens, Hilaire Noulens obtained in Brussels Belgian Passport No. 64618/19534F to enable him to travel to the Far East. It will be remembered that Noulens, still under the name of Herssens, was in Germany and Russia during February of 1930 and in Manchuria in the following month, arriving

Table 3.5 Passports Possessed by Noulens Couple

	Name	*Number*	*Nationality*	*Occupation*	*Place of birth*	*Date of birth*	*Expiration date*	*Place and date of issue*
1	Samuel Herssens	64618/19534F	Belgian by birth	Merchant	Brussels	8 Mar. 1895	4 Dec. 1931	Brussels, 4 Dec. 1929
2	Fernand Vandercruyssen	B10771/23182F	Belgian by birth	Business	St. Gilles	24 Dec. 1894	6 May 1932	6 May 1930
3	Donat Boulanger	102573	Canadian	Journalist	Quebec	12 May 1894	_	10 June 1930
4	Sophie Louise Herbet, nee Lorent	55833/16862F	Belgian	"Proprietaire"	Anvers	15 Dec. 1894	17 Aug. 1931	Brussels, 17 Aug. 1929
5	Marie Vandercruyssen, nee Dunson	B10772/23183F	Belgian by birth	"Proprietaire"	Alseonberg	14 May 1894	6 May 1932	6 May 1930

Source: SMP files, D2527/41.

Table 3.6 Aliases Relating to Noulens in Shanghai

	Name	*Residence*	*PO box*	*Mailing address*
1	Hilaire Noulens	O	O	O
2	Samuel Herssens	O		O
3	Charles Alison	O		
4	Marcel Motte	O		
5	Edward Briggs	O		O
6	A. Ruck	O	O	O
7	H. Vanutsen		O	O
8	Alfred Julien		O	O
9	Mr. Dillen (Dilan)		O	O
10	Mr. Schreiber		O	O
11	Gerhart Eisler		O	O
12	Rudolf Bergmann			O
13	Mr. C.H. Smith			O
14	Mr. V. Midler			O
15	Dr. W. O'Nell			O
16	Dr. J.H. Stimson			O

Source: SMP files, D2510/2, D2527/41.

> at Tientsin on March 12, 1930. He stopped there for a day at the Hotel Moderne, and made his way to Shanghai by the s.s. "Tungchow," putting up at the Plaza Hotel, Rue Montauban, where he continued to employ the name of Herssens.[42]

After his arrival in Shanghai, he did not need to use his passports until his arrest in June 1931. When he was arrested, he claimed that he was Belgian. His wife claimed to be French, and then Belgian, and carried a passport under the name of Marie Vandercruyssen. Noulens was known as Fernand Vandercruyssen, but the Noulens couple's claim to Belgian citizenship was rejected by the Belgian consul-general. Thereafter they claimed to be Swiss citizens without any certificates, but this time their claim was rejected by the Swiss consul-general.[43]

The reason they claimed French, Belgian, and Swiss nationalities was that they were trying to take advantage of extraterritoriality; but since their attempts failed, they were brought to trial in Nanjing. Noulens was sentenced to death, and his wife was sentenced to life imprisonment.[44] Noulens and his wife may have failed to prove their claim to various nationalities, but the SMP also failed to uncover their Ukrainian citizenship.

The second technique Noulens used to hide his identity was aliases. Table 3.6 shows the aliases supposedly relating to him. Some of the aliases in this table, especially those utilized for PO box and mailing addresses, were used by other agents, and Noulens seems to have just managed these PO boxes and mailing addresses.[45] Noulens seems to have used seven of the aliases in the table regularly while in Shanghai: Hilaire Noulens, Samuel Herssens, Charles Alison, Marcel Motte, Edward Briggs, A. Ruck, and Alfred Julien. How did he utilize these names? Again, we can glean something from the report made by the Special Branch of the SMP and its explanation of his activities following his arrival in Shanghai from Tientsin:

> On March 20, 1930 he removed to the now defunct Strand Hotel, Szechuen Road, where he engaged a room under the name of H. Noulens. On March 21, 1930, he removed to a flat at No. 741 Rue Ratard where he gave his name as Marcel Motte and his nationality as Belgian. On April 25, 1930, he rented a small back room in an office building at No. 235 Szechuen Road where he went under the name of Noulens and posed as a teacher of French and German.
>
> On January 30, 1931, Noulens, under the name of Herssens rented No. 66 Hart Road, and in the following month was issued with a China General Omnibus Season ticket in the latter name. When applying for this pass, Noulens gave his name as Herssens, his nationality as Belgian and declared that his residence was located at No. 66 Hart Road whilst his office address was at No. 40 Kiangse Road.[46]

Noulens relied on the aliases Charles Alison, Edward Briggs, and A. Ruck to rent and use room No. 30-C at 49 Nanking Road.[47] The alias Alfred Julien was utilized for renting a room in the New Bickerton Hotel, at Bubbling Well Road, from 22 December 1930 to 15 January 1931.[48]

Table 3.7 shows the houses and rooms used by Noulens in Shanghai. Among these, only the apartment at 741 Rue Ratard was located in the French Concession; all the others were in the International Settlement and were leased under different names. The contract of the apartment at 741 Rue Ratard was already over at the time of Noulens' arrest, so there were in fact two houses and two rooms that Noulens and his wife used regularly as residences or "working places" in Shanghai. How did they organize their life and activities there?

Living "Underground" in Shanghai

After Noulens' arrest, the Special Branch of the SMP interviewed the coolies and domestic servants who had worked at Noulens' houses and rooms and made reports of their statements. By extracting the narratives

Table 3.7 Houses and Rooms Used by Noulens

Address	*Name*	*Monthly rent (Shanghai tael)*	*Note*
Room No. 4, No. 235 Szechuen Road	H. Noulens	22	Rented from 25 Apr. 1930
Flat No. 30C of the Central Arcade, No. 49 Nanking Road	C. Alison	85	First leased to Mr. Vandolsen for six months from 31 Dec. 1930 and transferred to Mr. Alison on 12 Feb. 1931
No. 66 Hart Road	S. Herrsens	125	Rented from 30 Jan. 1930
No. 74 West End Gardens, Yu Yuen Road	Mrs. M. Motte	90	Rented from 1 Apr. 1931
Flat No. 4 Emerald Building, 741 Rue Ratard	Marcel Motte	65	Rented from 21 Mar. 1930 till 31 Mar. 1931

Source: SMP files, D2510/2, D2510/20, D2527/41.

relating to Noulens' and his wife's life from these statements, we obtain a glimpse of their life "underground" in Shanghai.

Following is an extract from the statement of a coolie at room No. 4, 235 Szechuen Road:

> In January, 1931, the foreigner who occupied room No. 4 his name is Noulens, engaged me to clean his office every morning for $5.00 a month. Who did that work before me I do not know. Noulens gave me a key from his office which I kept until June 16, 1931, when I handed over to a detective. On 24th day of every month at about 9 a.m. I come to Mr. Noulens for my wages. When I was employed at Room No. 7, which is on the same floor and opposite of Room No. 4, I often saw Mr. Noulens. He used to come at about 9 a.m. and to leave after about 10 minutes. Then he came for half an hour or so at 11 a.m. and at about 3 p.m. Sometimes he carried some foreign newspaper with him. A Chinese came see Mr. Noulens almost every day at that time. He came at about 11 a.m. and stayed for 20 minutes or so. He did not carry anything with him. He was about 30 years of age, height 5'11", wore foreign dress.[49]

From this narrative, we learn that Noulens clearly used the room at 235 Szechuen Road as an office for his work and for meeting a Chinese comrade. Another thing we can learn from this account is that he kept regular hours there. Every day, he came to this room at the fixed times of 9 a.m., 11 a.m., and 3 p.m. and met his Chinese counterpart almost every day at about 11 a.m.

The second extract is from the statement made by a coolie at room No. 30-C, 49 Nanking Road:

> At about 7 a.m. daily I have to clean room number 30C which is occupied by the foreigner whom I saw in the room on June 15th 31, in custody of the police. I do not know his name. Since he has occupied room 30C I have only seen him on several occasions when he entered the office alone, each time at about 9.30 a.m. The only other person that I have seen frequenting this room during the tenancy of this particular foreigner is a foreign female whom I have since recognised at Amoy Road Gaol. I have seen her enter on three occasions at about 9.30 a.m.[50]

This room was used as his "private" office, because nobody except his wife went in there. Here again, we see the regularity in habits of the Noulens couple, as they went in this room at 9:30 a.m. In another interview, the same coolie stated that Noulens occasionally stayed there overnight.[51]

The third extract is from the statement made by a domestic servant employed by Noulens' wife at Flat No. 4 Emerald Building, 741 Rue Ratard, and No. 74 West End Gardens, Yu Yuen Road:

> Mr. Motte, whilst residing at 741 Route Ratard, used to leave the house regularly every day, during the office hours. I don't know what he was doing or at what office he was working. I don't know what nationality they were. During my employment 741 Route Ratard, I never saw Mr. and Mrs. Motte being visited by anybody.
>
> * * *
>
> Since we removed to 74 West End Gardens Mr. Motte discontinued his residing with Mrs. Motte and visited her on Saturday afternoons, staying overnight and leaving the house by Monday morning. The residence of Mr. Motte is unknown to me. I had never seen anyone, except Mr. Motte, visiting Mrs. Motte at 74 West End Gardens.
>
> * * *
>
> Very often Mrs. used go out, but I don't know where.[52]

These two residences were intended as private quarters. The Noulens couple avoided any social contact with neighbors and others, and here again Noulens kept regular hours.

The final extract is from the statement made by a domestic servant at 66 Hart Road:

> When I started work, Mr. Herssens, my master, was in the house. He went out at 8.30 a.m. everyday, came back for tiffin at about 1.30 p.m., and went out again after tiffin. He did not return at regular times in the afternoon but usually 7 p.m.
>
> No woman ever lived with my master in the house. However, on several occasions, he returned with a woman to take tiffin together. I have learned that this woman is now in the custody of the Police.
>
> I worked at 66 Hart Road for about 5 months. I did not see anybody call on my master, and I did not know what was my master's profession.
>
> * * *
>
> About the end of January, my master left Shanghai for two months. I did not know where he went to. He returned to Shanghai about March 28 or March 29. During his absence, a foreigner, whose name I did not know, came to live in the house. The description of this foreigner is as follows:- About 22 or 23 years of age, about 5'6" in height, medium build, oval face, dark complexion, speaks English, profession unknown. This foreigner never went out. He spent his time in the house by reading books and newspapers. He left the house upon the return of my master, and I did not know where he went to.
>
> The foreigner who lived temporarily in my master's house was sometimes visited by a foreigner who had lost the two fingers near the thumb of his left hand. This visitor was about 5 feet 9 inches tall, medium build, about 30 years old, chestnut hair, clean shaven, common dress. When this visitor spoke with my temporary master, they did not speak in the English language.[53]

Noulens basically used this house as a weekday residence and also as a safe house for couriers and agents. Interestingly, he did not meet anybody except his wife here, like he did at 74 West End Gardens, and did not establish contact even with the agent for whom Noulens offered this house (or perhaps Noulens met him at another place).

From the above statements, we can reconstruct Noulens' daily life while "underground" in Shanghai as follows.

Every weekday morning, Noulens went to the Bund from 66 Hart Road, and during the daytime he "worked" at his offices at 235 Szechuen

Road or 49 Nanking Road. At about 11 a.m. he met his Chinese "comrade" at 235 Szechuen Road. He came back to 66 Hart Road at about 1 p.m. for lunch, and sometimes his wife had lunch with him. After lunch he went to his offices again and then returned to 66 Hart Road until 7 p.m. On Saturdays he went to 74 West End Gardens in the afternoon, stayed there one night, and returned to his usual schedule.

Rotating between several houses and offices regularly, using different aliases, separating private life and working places, and avoiding any social contact, Noulens relied on these strategies and techniques to conceal his existence and identity. These strategies and techniques were essential for his task as the liaison officer of the Comintern, and Noulens managed them quite well, because the Special Branch of the SMP remained unaware of his existence in Shanghai until information relating to him was obtained from Singapore.

The End of Life Underground: "The Noulens Affair"

Even though Noulens successfully concealed himself and managed his liaison activities, his life underground in Shanghai abruptly ended on 15 June 1931, when he was arrested by the Special Branch of the SMP. How and why was he detected and arrested? The breakthrough came from Singapore.

On 1 June 1931, a French Communist, Joseph Ducroux alias Serge Lefranc, was arrested in Singapore.[54] He was one of three agents dispatched by Noulens,[55] and his mission was to investigate Communist movements in British Malaya, to establish a liaison between the regional headquarters in Shanghai and the Malayan Communist Party "Central," and to make Singapore a liaison center for Communist movements in Southeast Asia and British India.[56] When he was arrested, among the seized documents and papers were memos, one PO box address — "206" — in Shanghai, and a telegraphic address, "Hilanoul." This information was passed on to the SMP, and it was found that the holder of these addresses was Hilaire Noulens and that his address was 235 Szechuen Road.[57]

On 9 June 1931 two Special Branch staff members went to 235 Szechuen Road and confirmed that Noulens was lodged in room No. 4 on the second floor. A name card, "Instructor in the German and French Languages," was tacked to the door, so one of the Special Branch staff members disguised himself as a person who wanted to learn French and visited Noulens in the room. Noulens said that he came from Luxemburg, that he was available only in the evening, and that most of his students were Chinese.

From 10 June, this address and Noulens were monitored by the Special Branch, and subsequently it was found that he also used rooms at 49 Nanking Road and at 168 Szechuen Road.[58] On 12 June, the disguised Special Branch staff member met Noulens again at 235 Szechuen Road. After this visit, Noulens apparently suspected he was being monitored; this is clear from the report made by the Chinese police officer who kept watch over Noulens' movements around 235 Szechuen Road:

> He stood outside the doorway of 235 Szechuen Road for a few minutes and then walked to the north-east corner of Hongkong and Szechuen Roads. Here he remained until 7.10 p.m. when he left and walked to the Central Arcade, No. 49 Nanking Road, after traversing the following roads: North along Szechuen east along Hongkong; south along Museum; east along Peking; south along Yuen Ming Yuen; across Jinkee Road and through an alleyway at the rear of Sasoon Building to Nanking Road where he turned west. He remained in The Central Arcade until 11 p.m. when he came out and proceeded on foot along North Szechuen Road to near Range Road. He then retraced his steps to 235 Szechuen Road where he stood outside for about five minutes and then walked to the Central Arcade.[59]

This report is about Noulens' movements on 14 June, the day before his arrest. Noulens' acts of standing outside the building for a while and taking a roundabout course clearly indicate that Noulens suspected he was being watched. By then, his precautions were to no avail. He was arrested at 235 Szechuen Road on 15 June 1931, and his wife was also arrested at 49 Nanking Road on the same day, when she came to visit Noulens there.

Subsequently, houses at 74 West End Gardens and 66 Hart Road were found by the Special Branch, and these houses and rooms at 235 Szechuen Road, 168 Szechuen Road, and 49 Nanking Road were searched. These searches yielded "211 documents and 1,081 other papers and books. Of the documents which were in English, German, Russian, Japanese, and Chinese, 73 deal principally with 'Red' revolutionary activities in China, 18 with similar work in Japan, 4 with Korea, 14 with the Philippine Islands, 14 with Indo-China, 10 with the Straits Settlements, 1 with Formosa and 1 with Indonesia. The documents indicate that the expenditure of the Shanghai Branch came to about $130,000.00 per month."[60]

Through the "Noulens Case," the British Political Intelligence accumulated a considerable amount of detail about "the progress, aims and methods of Communist intrigue in China, Indo-China, Indonesia, Malaya, Japan, Formosa, Korea and the Philippine Islands."[61] But it also admitted "the efficacy of the system of concealment employed" by staff in the regional headquarters and pointed out that "the detection of Communist agents, when entering a country (especially an international settlement, such as Shanghai), or when established, presents difficulties of an almost insuperable order."[62] The strategies and techniques employed by Noulens to manage the liaison network and to hide his existence and identity were, indeed, so effective that he was able to escape notice in Shanghai. His capture occurred through no fault or negligence of his own, but because of the "indiscreet behaviour"[63] of another agent, Ducroux, in Singapore.

Conclusion: Tasks, Strategies, Skills, Abilities, and Techniques

Noulens' strategies and techniques of keeping various houses and rooms, bank accounts, and postal and telegraphic addresses, and concealing his existence and identity were essential to his work of managing and maintaining liaisons from Shanghai to Moscow, Europe, and East and Southeast Asia. In other words, his tasks required secrecy and invisibility, and he effaced his own tracks under a sheaf of names, addresses, and documents.

Had his tasks and duties been different, they would have required different sets of strategies, skills, abilities, and techniques. Anonymous, transient, and rootless, Noulens carried out activities that can be fruitfully contrasted with the activities of two other activists who subsequently acquired legendary reputations: Nguyen Ai Quoc and Tan Malaka. Both Nguyen Ai Quoc and Tan Malaka were key agents for the regional headquarters of the Comintern in Shanghai when Noulens was the head of the OMS. They were expected to establish and maintain liaisons between Shanghai and Southeast Asia and beyond. In short, they acted as regional facilitators of the liaison network centered in Shanghai. The skills and abilities that were most crucial for their undertakings as regional facilitators were their multilingual capabilities and their extensive and in-depth experiences of activism on the ground, so to speak, in the region.[64]

Nguyen Ai Quoc was undoubtedly one of the most famous Asian revolutionaries during the 1920s and 1930s. He was involved in Communist movements in French Indochina, France, Moscow, Siam, Southern China, and British Malaya, and through his organizational work experiences he developed a network of links with local Communists in several regions. He could speak Vietnamese, Chinese, French, English, and Russian. From December 1929, he was in Hong Kong and in charge of establishing and maintaining liaisons between Shanghai and Southeast Asia, especially

French Indochina and British Malaya. He was involved in the establishment of the Vietnamese Communist Party (renamed the Indochinese Communist Party in 1929), the Siamese Communist Party, and the Malayan Communist Party in 1930 as the representative of the Comintern.[65]

Tan Malaka was the most famous Indonesian Communist during the 1920s and 1930s, and he traveled between the Dutch East Indies, British Malaya, the Philippines, and China. He could speak Malay, Dutch, English, German, and some Chinese (and perhaps some Hokkien as well). In 1931, when he was in Shanghai, the regional headquarters of the Comintern, there had been a plan to send him to Rangoon as an agent for setting up a liaison center there. This liaison center would be a connecting point between India and the Dutch East Indies.[66]

Although Nguyen Ai Quoc and Tan Malaka had skills and abilities that differed substantively from Noulens', secrecy and invisibility were, to an important extent, crucial for all three to undertake their tasks, so they had to employ strategies to conceal their existence and identities. But there was another type of agent who applied a completely opposite strategy. His name was Richard Sorge, and he was also in Shanghai from 1930 till 1933.[67]

Sorge was engaged in military intelligence activity in Shanghai. Unlike Noulens, he registered himself in the German consulate as a journalist immediately after his arrival at Shanghai. He also had another name, Johnson, posing as an American journalist, and he used this name for his clandestine activities. He contributed articles to newspapers in Germany and at the same time gave reports to Moscow. He never tried to hide himself from the public eye. The SMP suspected him of being a Comintern agent in 1932 and monitored him until 1933.[68] When he engaged in conspiratorial activities in Tokyo, he exposed himself to the public more intentionally than he did in Shanghai. He obtained Nazi membership and established a close friendship with the German ambassador in Tokyo. His existence was so open in the German embassy that he had no problem gaining access to confidential information. When Sorge was arrested, many of the staff in the German embassy could not believe that he was an agent. He lived his double life so well that people could not imagine him being someone else.

As agents, Noulens and Sorge applied completely different strategies. The former made himself invisible by using many names and addresses, while the latter led an active social life by relying on only two disguises. These differences in strategy were due to differences in their tasks. Sorge's task, both in Shanghai and in Tokyo, was to collect information. To avoid suspicion, he fully utilized his main front as a journalist, gathering information openly to facilitate his "spying." Noulens was different. Since his task was maintaining and managing an underground liaison network, he needed to conceal himself from the public eye because his disclosure meant the disclosure and destruction of the network.

Revolutionaries and agents who conducted their revolutionary activities underground during the 1920s and 1930s in East and Southeast Asia adopted various strategies, skills, abilities, and techniques according to their tasks and purposes. As the head of liaison officers in Shanghai, Noulens was in charge of maintaining and managing liaisons from Shanghai. An essential feature of his job was to conceal not only these liaisons but also his existence and identity. He conducted these tasks by utilizing strategies and techniques such as keeping and managing various houses and rooms, bank accounts, and postal and telegraphic addresses; utilizing several passports, nationalities, and aliases; and rotating residences regularly. These strategies and techniques were vital for him as an agent, and without looking at them we cannot understand his life underground.

At the same time, unlike the vivid and by now iconic personas of Nguyen Ai Quoc, Tan Malaka, and Richard Sorge, there is a generic quality about Noulens, an absence of personality and distinction that makes it impossible to write a conventional biography of the man. This impossibility of writing about the life of Noulens is a consequence of the tyranny of selection and omission exercised by the police and other archives that we are forced to rely on. But it is also a testament to Noulens' achievement, his complete success in self-erasure, without which the international and regional Communist movement would not have been possible.

Notes

1 For the itineraries and activities of Ho Chi Minh, see William J. Duiker, *Ho Chi Minh* (Crows Nest: Allen & Unwin, 2000); Sophie Quinn-Judge, *Ho Chi Minh: The Missing Years* (Singapore: Horizon Books, 2003); and Pierre Brocheux, *Ho Chi Minh: A Biography*, trans. Claire Duiker (New York: Cambridge University Press, 2007). For those of Zhou Enlai, see Barbara Barnouin and Yu Changgen, *Zhou Enlai: A Political Life* (Hong Kong: The Chinese University Press, 2006); and Gao Wenqian, *Zhou Enlai: The Last Perfect Revolutionary*, trans. Peter Rand and Lawrence R. Sullivan (New York: Public Affairs, 2007).

2 Memoirs of underground or exile lives and activities include Tan Malaka, *From Jail to Jail* [Rougoku kara Rougoku he] (Tokyo: Rokusaisha, 1979, trans. Noriaki Oshikawa); Teikichi Kawai, *Aru Kakumeika no Kaiso* [A Revolutionary's Memoir] (Tokyo: Shin Jinbutu Ouraisha, 1973); and Chin Peng, *Alias Chin Peng: My Side of History* (Singapore: Media Masters, 2003).

3 The Pan-Pacific Trade Union Secretariat was established in 1927, after the Pan-Pacific Trade Union Conference in Hankow. It was under the Red International of Labor Unions (the Profintern), and its missions were publishing journals and papers, providing advice and money to the All-China Labour Federation, and supporting and promoting labor union movements in East and Southeast Asian countries. David McKnight, *Espionage and the Roots of the Cold War: The Conspirational Heritage* (London: Frank Cass, 2002), pp. 104–5.

4 See, for instance, David McKnight, *Espionage and the Roots of the Cold War*; Christopher Goscha, *Thailand and the Southeast Asian Networks of the Vietnamese Revolution, 1885–1954* (Surrey: Curzon, 1999); C.F. Yong, *The Origins of Malayan Communism* (Singapore: South Seas Society, 1997); Alexander Grigoriev, "The Far Eastern Bureau of the ECCI in China, 1929–1931," in *The Chinese Revolution in the 1920s: Between Triumph and Disaster*, ed. Mechthild Leutner, Roland Felber, M.L. Titarenko, and A.M. Grigoriev (London: RoutledgeCurzon, 2002), pp. 156–65; Takashi Tachibana, *Nihon Kyousantou no Kenkyu* [Study of Japanese Communist Party], 3 vols. (Tokyo: Koudansha, 1983); Frederic Wakeman, *Policing Shanghai: 1927–1937* (Berkeley: University of California Press, 1996); and Ban Kah Choon, *Absent History: The Untold Story of Special Branch Operations in Singapore 1915–1942* (Singapore: Raffles, 2001).

5 Frederick S. Litten, "The Noulens Affair," *The China Quarterly* 138 (June 1994): 492–512.

6 Ibid., pp. 497–8, 511–2.

7 There are several studies on the origins of Communist movements in East and Southeast Asia, such as Ruth McVey, *The Rise of Indonesian Communism* (Jakarta: Equinox, 2006, reprinted edition); Yong, *The Origins of Malayan Communism*; Cheah Boon Kheng, *From PKI to the Comintern, 1924–1941: The Apprenticeship of the Malayan Communist Party* (Ithaca: Southeast Asia Program, Cornell University, 1992); Goscha, *Thailand and the Southeast Asian Networks*; Kasian Tejapira, *Commodifying Marxism: The Formation of Modern Thai Radical Culture, 1927–1958* (Kyoto: Kyoto University Press, 2001); Alfredo B. Saulo, *Communism in the Philippines: An Introduction* (Manila: Ateneo de Manila University Press, 1990); Arif Dirlik, *The Origins of Chinese Communism* (New York: Oxford University Press, 1989); and Marilyn A. Levine, *The Found Generation: Chinese Communists in Europe during the Twenties* (Seattle: University of Washington Press, 1993).

8 The Indonesians came mainly from Java and Sumatra. Cheah, *From PKI to the Comintern*, p. 9.

9 Yong, *The Origins of Malayan Communism*, pp. 62, 84; Goscha, *Thailand and the Southeast Asian Networks*, pp. 79, 88–91, 94.

10 Hirohide Kurihara, *The Indochinese Communist Party in the Comintern System* (in Japanese) (Tokyo: University of Tokyo Press, 2005), pp. 55–6; Goscha, *Thailand and the Southeast Asian Networks*, pp. 83–8; Yong, *The Origins of*

Malayan Communism, pp. 9–10, 17–28, 41–4, 53–4, 62–3, 67–9, 71–2, 85–6, 91, 101, 113–4, 121; Fujio Hara, *Maraya Kakyo to Chyugoku: Kizokuisiki Tenkankatei no Kenkyu* [Malayan Chinese and China: Study of Conversion in Identity Consciousness] (Tokyo: Ryukeishosha, 2001), pp. 19–52.

11 Japanese Communists who devoted themselves to the Chinese revolution include Nakanishi Isao and Kawai Teikichi. For their activities, see *Interrogation Papers of Isao Nakanishi* (Tokyo: Akishobo, 1996); and Kawai, *Aru Kakumeika no Kaiso*. While the links forged by Japanese Communists in Asia were primarily limited to China, some Japanese nationalists (or Asianists) had linkages with revolutionaries not only in China, but also in the Philippines, French Indochina, and British India. Why such a contrast between Japanese Communists and nationalists existed is quite an interesting question. In my view, to answer this question we should consider several factors, such as language skill, regional perspectives and experiences, where and how linkages were established, the size and character of Japanese communities in the region, historical timing, and international relations. For how links were made among Japanese Asianists and revolutionaries in Southeast Asia, see Caroline S. Hau and Takashi Shiraishi, "Daydreaming about Rizal and Tetchou: On Asianism as Network and Fantasy," *Philippine Studies* 57, 3 (2009): 329–88.

12 Kurihara, *The Indochinese Communist Party*, p. 3.

13 Jeremy Agnew and Kevin McDermott, *The Comintern: A History of International Communism from Lenin to Stalin* (London: Macmillan, 1996), p. 22.

14 Kurihara, *The Indochinese Communist Party*, p. 57.

15 McKnight, *Espionage and the Roots of the Cold War*, pp. 104–5.

16 Kurihara, *The Indochinese Communist Party*, p. 58; and Shanghai Municipal Police files (SMP files) (Washington, DC: National Archives and Records Administration), D2527/45.

17 McKnight, *Espionage and the Roots of the Cold War*, p. 101.

18 *All About Shanghai: A Standard Guide Book* (reprinted. Original edition Shanghai: The University Press, 1934–35) (Hong Kong: Oxford University Press, 1983), p. 22.

19 Ibid., pp. 29–32, 97–101, 105, 122–5.

20 Kousuke Takahashi and Tadao Furumaya, eds., *The History of Shanghai* (in Japanese) (Tokyo: Toho Shoten, 1995), p. 21.

21 Ibid., p. 22.

22 Statistics Office, Department of General Affairs, Government of Tokyo, "Demographic Change in Tokyo from 1920 to 2005," <http://www.toukei.metro.tokyo.jp/tjinko/2009/to09000001.htm>.

23 *All About Shanghai*, p. 195.

24 Sumio Obinata, *Kindai Nihon no Keisatu to Chiiki Syakai* [Police and Communities in Modern Japan] (Tokyo: Chikumashobou, 2000), pp. 25–6, 112–3, 162, 200, 222–3.

25 Richard Sorge, *Zorge Jiken: Gokutyu Syuki* [Sorge Case: Memoirs Written in a Prison] (Tokyo: Iwanami Shoten, 2003), pp. 122–3.

26 SMP files, D2510/10. According to Litten, Noulens' first visit to Shanghai was in 1928, and at this time he was a plain staff member of OMS in Shanghai. He left Shanghai in July 1929 because the Japanese Communist Manabu Sano was arrested in Shanghai and Noulens had a close contact with him. Litten, "The Noulens Affair," pp. 500–2.

27 Litten, "The Noulens Affair," p. 502; SMP files, D2527/45.

28 SMP files, D2527/45.

29 Litten, "The Noulens Affair," pp. 502–3; SMP files, D2527/41, D2527/45.

30 PO box No. 1941 was owned by the North China Daily News Co., and it was allocated to Noulens as a reader. See SMP files, D2527/41.

31 SMP files, D2510/2, D2527/41, D2527/43.

32 SMP files, D2527/42. In Table 3.3 there are only five addresses, but three of these were registered to two companies simultaneously, so there were eight telegraphic addresses utilized by Noulens.

33 SMP files, D2527/45.

34 Ibid.

35 Together with bank notes of eight bank accounts, six seals and a document that indicated which seals should be used for each bank account were also seized by the SMP. SMP files, D2510/13.

36 SMP files, D2510/4, D2510/95.

37 SMP files, D2527/45.

38 Ibid.; Litten, "The Noulens Affair," pp. 500–1.

39 The Central Committee of the Chinese Communist Party operated in Shanghai until 1933. Patricia Stranahan, *Underground: The Shanghai Communist Party and the Politics of Survival, 1927–1937* (Lanham, MD: Rowman & Littlefield, 1998), p. 151.

40 Tachibana, *Nihon Kyousantou*, vol. 2, p. 83.

41 SMP files, D2510/77. Noulens' wife also seems to have used only one passport for her travel from Belgium to China in 1930.

42 SMP files, D2510/10.

43 Litten, "The Noulens Affair," pp. 494–5; SMP files, D2510/9, D2510/95, D2527/41.

44 Litten, "The Noulens Affair," pp. 497–8, 511–2.

45 For example, the aliases H. Vanutsen and Rudolf Bergmann were assumed by the Special Branch of the SMP to be used by James H. Dolsen. He was a journalist and claimed to be American. He was last seen at 168 Szechuen Road on 14 June 1931, one day before Noulens' arrest. SMP files, D2527/1, D2527/41.

46 SMP files, D2510/10.

47 SMP files, D2510/2, D2527/18.

48 SMP files, D2510/37. Unlike Noulens, his wife seems to have used only two aliases in Shanghai: Mrs. Motte and Mrs. Ruck, mainly the former. SMP files, D2527/45.

49 SMP files, D2510/95.

50 Ibid.

51 Ibid.

52 Ibid.

53 SMP files, D2510/21.

54 For Ducroux's biography, see Laurent Metzger, "Joseph Ducroux, a French Agent of the Comintern in Singapore (1931–1932)," *Journal of the Malayan Branch of the Royal Asiatic Society* 69, part 1 (1996): 1–20. On how he was monitored, detected, and arrested by the British Political Intelligence Services in East and Southeast Asia, see Takeshi Onimaru, "Policing the Comintern Network in Asia: 'The Lefranc Affair' and the British Security System" (in Japanese), *Southeast Asian Studies* 43, 3 (2005): 303–18, and "Identifying Agents' in Asia: The Political Intelligence Services, the Passport Control System, and the Communist International in Asia in the 1920s and 1930s," paper presented at a public conference on "Identifying the Person: Past, Present, and Future," at St. Antony's College, University of Oxford, 26–27 Sept. 2009.

55 The other two were Wong Muk Han and Teo Yuen Foo. Wong was in charge of reorganizing Communist movements in British Malaya, and Teo's mission was to set up the Dutch East Indies Bureau and then to establish a liaison between it and the regional headquarters in Shanghai. Wong was arrested in Singapore with Ducroux, but Teo was not detected by colonial police in Southeast Asia. Yong, *The Origins of Malayan Communism*, pp. 99, 163.

56 Ibid.; Kurihara, *The Indochinese Communist Party*, p. 135; SMP files, D2527/45.

57 Without special attribution to a source, the following descriptions about how Noulens was monitored and arrested were based on reports made by the staff in the Special Branch of the SMP in SMP files, D2510/2, D2510/15, D2510/95.

58 The room at 168 Szechuen Road was rented by Dolsen. SMP files, D2527/1, D2527/41.

59 SMP files, D2510/95.

60 SMP files, D2510/2.

61 SMP files, D2527/45.

62 Ibid.

63 Ibid.

64 For the role they played as regional facilitators in the liaison network from Shanghai, see Takeshi Onimaru, "Shanghai Connection: How the Communist Network in East and Southeast Asia Was Constructed, Maintained and Collapsed," paper presented at International Conference on "Political Networks in Asia" at the National Graduate Institute for Policy Studies, Tokyo, 14 May 2010.

65 This is based on Duiker, *Ho Chi Minh*; Goscha, *Thailand and the Southeast Asian Networks*; Kurihara, *The Indochinese Communist Party*; and SMP files, D2527/45.

66 This is based on Goscha, *Thailand and the Southeast Asian Networks*; Tan Malaka (translated into Japanese by Osikawa), *From Jail to Jail*; and SMP files, D2527/45.

67 The following account of Sorge is based on F.W. Deakin and G.R. Storry, *The Case of Richard Sorge* (London: Chatto and Windus Ltd., 1957); and Sorge, *Zorge Jiken*.

68 SMP files, D3509.

CHAPTER 4

Provincial Cosmopolitanism: Vũ Trọng Phụng's Foreign Literary Engagements

Peter Zinoman

While it is frequently observed that Vietnamese literature was radically transformed under the force of French colonialism during the late nineteenth and early twentieth centuries, the precise character of this transformation and of French influence on Vietnamese literature and intellectual life, more generally, remains poorly understood. This is partially a consequence of the relative paucity of research on modern Vietnamese cultural and intellectual history, but it also owes something to the durability of misleading notions within the existing scholarship about the dynamics of cultural change under colonialism. A good example is the tendency of historians to inflate the significance of overseas travel as a channel for the spread of foreign influence among the Vietnamese elite. This emphasis reflects the coincidence that the handful of modern Vietnamese intellectuals who have been the subject of biographical research in the West — Hồ Chí Minh, Phan Bội Châu, Nguyễn An Ninh, Bùi Quang Chiêu, Nhất Linh, and Trần Đức Thảo, for example — were all shaped to an unusual degree by overseas travel and study.[1] The current academic preoccupation with the global and transnational dimensions of modernity will doubtless reinforce the tendency to highlight those Vietnamese actors and groups that happen to have been forcefully marked by their experiences and engagements abroad.[2]

However, the spread of French influence among the Vietnamese intelligentsia was never simply a function of overseas travel. Even during the "hey day of the Vietnamese student migration" between 1925 and 1930, only a small percentage of the educated elite spent significant time in France.[3] According to Scott McConnell, only 3,000 Vietnamese students attended school in France during the entire interwar period.[4] After peaking at around 1,700 during the late 1920s, the number of Vietnamese enrolled in metropolitan schools declined sharply throughout the 1930s.[5] The low number of students was a consequence of administrative obstacles to overseas study put in place by the colonial state during the 1920s.[6] Candidates for study abroad were required to collect 11 official documents and to secure travel permission directly from the governor general.[7] As a result, only 500 of the roughly 40,000 Vietnamese living in France at the end of the 1930s could be classified as "professionals, intellectuals or students."[8]

Even when informal and undocumented Vietnamese sojourners are taken into account, the fact remains that most Vietnamese intellectuals enjoyed little more than a filtered access to the cultural life of metropolitan France through a dense mesh of geographical distance, slow-moving transportation and communications technologies, and deliberate colonial policies of censorship and obscurantism. As a result, any attempt to understand French cultural influence among the Vietnamese intelligentsia must be careful not to generalize based on how a handful of privileged young men experienced student life on the Left Bank. More typical, and hence more significant historically, were the experiences of colonized intellectuals who never traveled abroad and yet still pursued a passionate interest in the culture and politics of the wider world through dog-eared foreign novels and dated French newspapers. This random and uneven mode of engaging with global modernity engendered an odd sort of provincial cosmopolitanism that dominated local intellectual life in French Indochina and, perhaps more generally, within the colonial world as a whole.

To shed light on the peculiar workings of this characteristic aspect of colonial modernity, this chapter examines explicit engagements with foreign authors and literature found in the work of the interwar Vietnamese writer Vũ Trọng Phụng.[9] The narrow parameters of Vũ Trọng Phụng's life experience and the sweeping breadth of his intellectual horizons make him a quintessential emblem of provincial cosmopolitanism.[10] Six years of colonial schooling had equipped him with a basic foundation in the French language, but it provided little formal training in any academic or professional discipline. Because he never visited Europe, Vũ Trọng Phụng had no opportunity to explore those institutionalized repositories of Western learning — libraries, archives, universities, and museums — that offered the possibility of accessing even a partial record of European intellectual traditions. His knowledge of these traditions, therefore, was dependent entirely on his own opportunistic and unsupervised reading.

This caricature of Vũ Trọng Phụng is from a pamphlet released by the publishing house Minh Đức in Hanoi in 1956 called *Vũ Trọng Phụng Is with Us*.

Portrait of Vũ Trọng Phụng by Vũ Dân Tân (2008).

Given his provincialism and modest class background, it is not surprising that Vũ Trọng Phụng never developed the kind of intimate friendships with cultivated Europeans that played such a formative role in the intellectual development of better-known Southeast Asian thinkers and activists from the late colonial era such as Jose Rizal and Raden Ajeng Kartini.[11]

Nevertheless, Vũ Trọng Phụng's body of work contains direct citations to more than 60 foreign writers from a remarkably diverse array of traditions, movements, and historical eras. The character and intensity of his foreign engagements may also be seen in the translations he published of fiction, drama, and literary essays. When considered as a whole, this mixed bag of references suggests that Vũ Trọng Phụng's familiarity with foreign literature was broad but shallow, eclectic but unsystematic. The mottled and diffuse character of this repertoire of influences confirms the impression that Vũ Trọng Phụng was never a disciple of any particular foreign writer or international literary movement. It also provides evidence that his reading tastes and habits were not conditioned by a discriminating sense of difference between high and low culture or by a studied penchant for any particular literary genre or style. Moreover, Vũ Trọng Phụng's efforts to interpret the foreign texts that he read and to situate their aesthetic and political agendas in relation to local bodies of literature, including his own, point to the difficulties of attempting to align colonial cultural, intellectual, and literary projects with metropolitan counterparts, even those that shared the same name.

Eclecticism of Influence

Perhaps the most striking aspect of the compilation of references to European texts and writers found in Vũ Trọng Phụng's work is its diverse and diffuse character. This eclecticism may be seen in the broad temporal range of the figures that Vũ Trọng Phụng cites and in the wide array of literary movements and traditions that they represent. Several of his essays reveal a passing familiarity with classical Greek playwrights — Sophocles, Euripides, Aristophanes, and Aeschylus — and he refers, on occasion, to Shakespeare and to the giants of French neoclassical drama — Corneille, Racine, and Molière.[12] Most of his points of reference, however, are located in the nineteenth and early twentieth centuries. Included in this mix are a wide array of romantics and neo-romantics, mid-nineteenth-century realists and early twentieth-century social realists, symbolists, naturalists, modernists, and Catholic neo-traditionalists. Vũ Trọng Phụng also cites numerous writers who resist conventional classification (for various reasons) plus a handful of journalists, sexologists, scientists, and social scientists.

Given Vũ Trọng Phụng's oft-noted reputation as a "realist," it is surprising that early nineteenth-century romanticism looms larger in his writings than mid-nineteenth-century realism. Although he alludes, on at least two occasions, to the legal persecution of *Madame Bovary*, Vũ Trọng Phụng betrays no appreciation of Flaubert's pioneering experiments with realist fiction, nor does he once mention Stendhal.[13] More surprising still is the absence of a single reference to Balzac, a curious and paradoxical omission since critics have frequently compared the social-historical project and panoramic scope of Vũ Trọng Phụng's work to *La comédie humaine*.[14]

On the other hand, Vũ Trọng Phụng's familiarity with the major figures of late nineteenth-century French naturalism (often considered a subset of realism) seems more substantial. In 1932, he prefaced his first major published work — the play *Không một tiếng vang* (No Echo) — with an epigram from Zola.[15] Likewise, his 1937 short story "Đi săn khỉ" (The Monkey Hunt) opens with an allusion to Alphonse Daudet's naturalist novella *Tartarin de Tarascon*.[16] But Vũ Trọng Phụng's interest in naturalism is most clearly evident in his engagement with Guy de Maupassant. Among his earliest publications are original translations of the Maupassant short stories "Un fou" and "Solitude," and his novels *Số đỏ and Vỡ đê* refer directly to three others, including "La patronne" and "La crime de Père Boniface."[17] Moreover, in 1931 Vũ Trọng Phụng published a translation of "Le roman," Maupassant's terse and elegant essayistic statement of his literary philosophy and method.[18]

Still, writers associated with late nineteenth-century naturalism attracted less of Vũ Trọng Phụng's attention than the leading lights of early nineteenth-century romanticism. Vũ Trọng Phụng cites influential romantics such as Rousseau, Goethe, Lamartine, Musset, and Chateaubriand, and he exhibits significant interest in Alfred de Vigny.[19] Two of Vigny's major works — *Chatterton* (1835) and *Servitude et grandeur militaires* (1835) — appear repeatedly in his writing. In 1931 Vũ Trọng Phụng published an original translation of remarks made by Vigny about his famous novel *Stello* (1832).[20] The romantic author who appears most frequently in Vũ Trọng Phụng's work, however, is Victor Hugo. Not only does Vũ Trọng Phụng cite Hugo directly more times than any other writer, but his 1936 translation of Hugo's play *Lucretia Borgia* (1832) stands as his only effort to render into Vietnamese a major foreign literary work.[21] Vũ Trọng Phụng's interest in Hugo may also be seen in his 1932 essay "Cái đặc-tính của kịch lãng-mạn" (Special Features of Romantic Drama) — an approving summary of Hugo's famous romantic manifesto that appeared initially as the preface to his play *Cromwell* (1827).[22]

Vũ Trọng Phụng had significantly less to say to about the two literary movements — high modernism and socialist realism — that dominated the interwar era during which he produced all of his work. The influential modernists Gide, Proust, and Malraux garner a single unremarkable reference each, as do the celebrated proto-modernist Baudelaire and the symbolist poet Verlaine.[23] Vũ Trọng Phụng makes passing allusions to social realists such as Romain Rolland and Maxim Gorky, but he never mentions more orthodox French *socialist* realists such as Paul Nizan or Henri Barbusse.[24] Nor does he refer to any of their high-profile Soviet counterparts, some of whom (Gladkhov, for instance) were already developing followings within leftist Vietnamese circles during the late 1930s.

In addition, Vũ Trọng Phụng cites a handful of minor and major writers who resist generic literary classification but who are nevertheless linked by the fact that their work generated controversy and, in some cases, legal persecution for explicit sexual content. Prominent among this group is the prolific but largely forgotten poet and playwright Jean Richepin — a flamboyant member of the short-lived, bohemian "Vivant" group whose work literary historians tend to classify as pre-symbolist or late romantic.[25] Not only does Vũ Trọng Phụng cite Richepin more frequently than any writer with the exception of Hugo and Maupassant, but he published a translation of his polemical defence of obscenity charges launched against his 1876 collection of verse, *Chansons des gueux* (Songs of the Down-and-Out).[26] In a similar vein, Vũ Trọng Phụng refers on three occasions to *Les Demi-Vierges* (1894) — Marcel Prévost's sensational middle-brow novel that explores the dangers posed to late nineteenth-century Parisian society by the newly emergent "modern women."[27] Colette, Francis Carco, and Victor Margueritte fall into the same category: writers better known for the scandalous content of their work than for their membership in any clearly defined literary movement.[28]

In addition to writers and poets, Vũ Trọng Phụng's list of foreign references includes a handful of journalists and social scientists. Prominent among the former are André Viollis and Louis Roubaud, both of whom published widely read exposés of colonial rule in Indochina during the 1930s.[29] He also cites prominent writers of non-fiction reportage, including Albert Londres, Pierre Seize, and Maryse Choisy.[30] Vũ Trọng Phụng's engagement with social science exhibits a special interest in scholars who wrote on colonial issues, such as the influential social geographer Pierre Gourou and a handful of obscure scholar-bureaucrats who conducted policy-driven research on social welfare and public health issues in Indochina.[31] Also notable is the relatively large number of references he makes to Freud and to the pioneers of German sexology Magnes Hirshfeld and J.P. Liepmann.[32]

While Vũ Trọng Phụng's assemblage of foreign references exhibits remarkable breadth, its depth is considerably less impressive. The vast majority of authors and works are mentioned only once, and no single figure, text, or movement garners special or sustained attention. The most widely cited author, Victor Hugo, appears a mere eight times, and the only other figures cited more than twice are Maupassant (six), Richepin (five), Margueritte (four), Vigny (four), Zola (three), Roubaud (three), Prévost (three), and Freud (three). Given the prolific output of many of these figures, Vũ Trọng Phụng's fleeting references to them are insufficient to convey even a general sense of their overall body of work and tend to ignore their most important achievements. Vũ Trọng Phụng's treatment of Hugo's voluminous *oeuvre*, for example, extends only to the curious troika of *Les Misérables*, *Lucretia Borgia*, and the preface to *Cromwell*, and his six citations to Maupassant refer, in seemingly arbitrary fashion, to five relatively obscure short stories plus the essay "Le Roman." In addition to blurring distinctions between reputedly major and minor works, Vũ Trọng Phụng's desultory treatment of his various foreign interlocutors fails to call attention to specific texts as manifestations of larger trends or as turning points within the overall trajectory of a literary career.

Localizing Realism

Vũ Trọng Phụng's selective, decontextualized reading of foreign writers corresponds with his unorthodox understanding of the conventional literary categories of his day and with his unusual interpretations of the relations between these categories and the foreign writers whom he cites. His views on literary realism are a case in point. As has been noted, Vũ Trọng Phụng's disproportionate interest in French romantic writers might be viewed as inconsistent with the commitment to literary realism that he expressed throughout his career. More incongruous still is a brief but curious reference he made to French "realist writers" in a 1937 interview with the critic Lê Thanh. In an epilogue to the interview, Lê Thanh wrote: "Mr. Vũ Trọng Phụng also spoke a lot about realist writers in France — Maupassant, Colette, Richepin and Victor Margueritte — who have had a great influence on him."[33]

As reported by Lê Thanh, Vũ Trọng Phụng's quartet of influential "realists" did not include any of the iconic figures of French realism such as Stendhal, Balzac, Flaubert, or the Goncourt brothers; and the relationship of the four writers whom he did cite to the realist canon is tenuous in some cases, and non-existent in others. Consider Maupassant. Although his work falls well within the broad parameters of the modern French realist tradition, the primacy of Maupassant's association with Zola and the naturalist movement was already well established by the late nineteenth century. As one standard literary history observed of Maupassant in 1899: "... il est le plus naturaliste de nos romanciers, ou plutôt le seul vraiment naturaliste [... he is the most naturalist of our novelists or, better yet, our only true naturalist]."[34] The durability of Maupassant's naturalist credentials may be seen in Olin Moore's description of his work 20 years later as "the purest representative" of naturalism.[35] Nevertheless, Vũ Trọng Phụng preferred to label Maupassant as a realist, and there is evidence that this decision was far from arbitrary. In his partial translation of the essay "Le Roman," Vũ Trọng Phụng erased Maupassant's own distinction between the two movements by translating both realism and naturalism with the same Sino-Vietnamese word "tả thực."[36] This suggests that while Vũ Trọng Phụng was aware of the existence of a distinction between the two movements, he chose to ignore it.

The presence of Colette and Margueritte in Vũ Trọng Phụng's realist pantheon is equally puzzling. Like most successful women writers in France, Colette was never "a member of any of the major literary intellectual circles of her day."[37] Moreover, as the feminist critic Juliette M. Rogers has argued: "Literary critics of Colette's day did not consider her 'outsider' position unusual as many women writers did not fit into their established literary schools of thought in the first decades of the twentieth century in France."[38] Hence, Vũ Trọng Phụng's inclusion of Colette in the realist camp went against the grain of the dominant metropolitan critical discourse on the topic. In a similar vein, Vũ Trọng Phụng's classification of Victor Margueritte as a realist does not reflect his dominant literary reputation at the time, nor does it dovetail with the standard realist pantheon in place during the interwar era when he made his remarks. While realist echoes are clearly present in the label "social writer," which was applied to Margueritte during his lifetime, the author of the infamous novels *Prostitueés* and *La Garçonne* was renowned, among both critics and the reading public at large, less for his putative realism than for the scandalous sexual content of his novels.[39]

But the least likely and most bewildering member of Vũ Trọng Phụng's realist quartet is Jean Richepin. As with Margueritte, the mediocrity of Richepin's work has ensured its exclusion from general discussions of any modern French literary school with the exception of the insignificant non-tradition of "late romanticism." Indeed, the pejorative characterization of Richepin by his biographer Howard Sutton as "a spirited and impenitent exponent" of "a belated Romanticism at once derivative and extravagant" suggests that the writer's poor reputation may, in fact, be connected to his "late romantic" affinities.[40] Moreover, Sutton asserts that "the revision of literary values inaugurated by the Symbolist writers in the latter part of the nineteenth century" precipitated Richepin's abrupt descent into obsolescence.[41] "Following an almost revolutionary transformation of standards," Sutton explains, "he was regarded with indifference or even disdain, as a leading representative of a literature based on false values that a new generation, avid for truth and authenticity, rejected without appeal."[42] Hence, in a further irony, Vũ Trọng Phụng's expression of admiration for Richepin's "realism" during the 1930s occurred decades after the writer's eclipse in France — an eclipse partially fostered by his alleged sins against those hallmarks of classical realism: "truth" and "authenticity."

Given their dubious links to the conventional canons of French realism, Vũ Trọng Phụng's description of these four writers as influential realists requires some explanation. In this regard, the fact that throughout his career Vũ Trọng Phụng identified himself as a realist is probably significant. In a letter addressed to the critic Thái Phỉ and published in *Hà Nội Báo* on 23 September 1936, he wrote:

> In the recent edition of the newspaper *Tin Văn*, you wrote to warn realist writers about the dangers of pornographic literature. The reason that I address you in this letter is not because I accept your charge that my writing is pornographic but because I am a realist writer.[43]

Several months later Vũ Trọng Phụng opened the introduction to his controversial novel *Làm Đĩ* with the pithy assertion: "*Làm Đĩ* is a realist novel."[44] He was equally clear on the subject in his interview with Lê Thanh published the following year. "My literature," he stated, "is realist literature."[45] Given his repeated invocation of this sentiment, one by-product of Vũ Trọng Phụng's characterization of Maupassant, Colette, Margueritte, and Richepin as realists was to establish a fraternal link between their status and reputation and his own.

But what was it about these four disparate figures, in particular, that attracted him to them? Part of the answer may lie in the fact that each of them shared with Vũ Trọng Phụng a history of legal persecution and public condemnation for the crime of *outrages aux bonnes moeurs* (indecency). In 1876, Richepin served one month in prison after obscenity charges were issued against his scatological and sexually explicit collection of poems: *Chanson des gueux*.[46] Similar accusations forced Maupassant to defend his poem "Une Fille" before a magistrate in January 1880, and in 1883 the influential bookseller Hachette banned his volume *La Maison Tellier* from railway kiosks.[47] Controversies over obscenity marked Colette's entire career, from the "scandalous success" of her early Claudine novels to the explorations of homosexuality, eroticism, and promiscuity in later works such as *Sido* and *Le Pur et L'Impur*.[48] Finally, as Mary Louise Roberts has argued, Victor Margueritte's 1922 novel *La Garconne* generated the most sensational literary scandal in interwar France, owing to "the sexual promiscuity of the novel's heroine and its explicit sexual passages."[49]

Vũ Trọng Phụng's literary career was also dominated by scandals and legal persecution surrounding the alleged indecency of his work. As Lại Nguyên Ân has recently shown, formal obscenity charges were first launched against Vũ Trọng Phụng at the outset of his literary career, in response to the publication of one of his short stories in the short-lived Hà Nội journal *Tiếng Chuông*.[50] Vũ Trọng Phụng's trial and subsequent conviction on 22 March 1932 for the crime of *outrages aux bonnes moeurs* (tội tổn thương phong hóa) was covered in the local press and invoked in print repeatedly by his enemies.[51] Later in the decade, Vũ Trọng Phụng's fiction and reportage — especially the novels *The Storm* and *To Be a Whore* and the non-fiction book *Venereal Disease Clinic* — were taken to task by an unlikely alliance of neo-traditionalists, "progressive" social reformers, Marxist puritans, and Catholic conservatives. The bitterness of these attacks is well illustrated in Nhất Chi Mai's essay "Pornographic or Not? One Reader's Opinion," which chides Vũ Trọng Phụng's preoccupation with "rape, prostitution, crime and gambling," criticizes his writing style as "dirty, filthy and without shame," and dismisses his literary "ideology" as "dark, hateful and small-minded."[52]

In his defense, Vũ Trọng Phụng published a handful of letters that likened his own victimization at the hands of his critics to the unfair persecution throughout history of distinguished writers for alleged crimes against morality. It is perhaps no coincidence that three of Vũ Trọng Phụng's four influential "realists" appear in these appeals. "It is not my intention to trick you," he wrote to one of his critics in 1937, "by arguing in the manner of Zola, Flaubert, Baudelaire, Margueritte and Richepin — writers who were once condemned as pornographers but are now celebrated as great writers."[53] In a letter published two weeks later, Vũ Trọng Phụng employed the same tactic and mentioned some of the same figures: "It is because I respect my readers that I refuse to be intimated by old-fashioned conservatives and continue to write in the spirit of Richepin, Margueritte, Carco, Maryse Choisy, and Colette."[54]

Vũ Trọng Phụng's repeated efforts to defend himself in this way suggest that his puzzling characterization of the four "influential realists" might be interpreted as another rehearsal of this same defensive strategy. This argument finds additional support in the fact that Lê Thanh spent the majority of the *Bắc Hà* interview pestering Vũ Trọng Phụng about the obscenity issue. Vũ Trọng Phụng's annoyance with this line of questioning comes across clearly in their first exchange:

> Lê Thanh (LT): Do you try to titillate your readers when you write?
>
> Vũ Trọng Phụng (VTP): How can one titillate a reader? Do you think my readers are so ignorant and childish to permit themselves to be titillated by me?
>
> LT: So can you let us know your motives when you create one of those scenes that many consider pornographic.
>
> VTP: If you tell a story that is basically about a rape, how can you not describe scenes like the ones that appear in my novel *The Storm*. In writing *The Storm*, my only purpose was to offer a snap-shot of present-day society. And when you look at this society, it is hard to view it with optimistic eyes. Today's society is in the process of decay; it is a society the likes of which we have never seen before in our history. Its very atmosphere is rotten and stinking. We live in an era during which those with power and money live only for sensual pleasure. Certainly you have heard stories about members of the nouveau riche who, despite having half-a-dozen wives, still commit acts as indecent as those perpetrated by my character Nghị Hách. Not to mention what they do day and night in cheap and tawdry taverns. Most of our youth are concerned only with play and pleasure. They can no longer bear difficult work or, indeed, anything that requires sitting and thinking hard. They think only of cruising the streets, dancing, singing or going to the cinema.[55]

Later in the interview Lê Thanh returned to the topic, and Vũ Trọng Phụng responded on cue with the by-now-familiar defensive gambit of invoking his own commitment to realism.

> LT: It is a good thing that your novels reflect society. But many critics attack your kind of realist writing for its pornographic tendencies.
>
> VTP: You can't call my kind of literature pornographic! On the contrary, it is more accurate to call it literature that describes obscene scenes. But how can anyone say that I shouldn't describe such scenes? My literature is realist literature and those scenes have really happened; some I have seen with my own eyes. I invite you to report on a province such as Tuyên Quang. You will discover stories a thousand times more obscene than the ones that I describe.[56]

It was within the immediate context of this well-worn defense that Vũ Trọng Phụng drew attention to the "realism" of Maupassant, Colette, Richepin, and Margueritte. This suggests that what appears, at first glance, to have been a statement of literary assessment or classification may, in fact, have been formulated to serve a very different purpose. Indeed, the category of "realism" functioned for Vũ Trọng Phụng less as an aesthetic (or even a political) category and more as an instrument to be deployed in what was essentially a local struggle with his critics. For Vũ Trọng Phụng, the utility of this instrument lay in its capacity to bring him and his work into alignment with a distinguished cohort of international writers, each of whom had also been stigmatized unfairly as a consequence of obscenity charges launched by unsophisticated critics and jealous rivals. As is common in such episodes of strategic "localization" (to invoke O.W. Wolters' use of the term), the power of this instrument was a function of the way that its exotic foreign aura tended to impress and intimidate.[57] The instrument possessed additional potency in the context of its new environment as a result of the educated public's relative lack of familiarity with it — especially the ill-defined and decontextualized incarnation of it presented by Vũ Trọng Phụng. This lack of familiarity with realism prevented Vũ Trọng Phụng's antagonists from challenging the idiosyncratic and tendentious way that he wielded it. Indeed, the fact that none of his critics ever took issue with his highly dubious characterization of Jean Richepin confirms the considerable tactical power of Vũ Trọng Phụng's instrumental localization of French "realism."

It would be an overstatement, however, to suggest that Vũ Trọng Phụng's interpretation of realism was nothing more than a function of the instrumental value it afforded him in debates over the morality of his work. On the contrary, Vũ Trọng Phụng's desultory remarks on "realism" reiterate two definitional axioms that suggest he possessed a rudimentary but nevertheless specific and coherent understanding of the concept. First, and perhaps most important, Vũ Trọng Phụng believed that true literary realism focused on the poor and on marginal members of society. As he bluntly put it in 1932: "Realist literature shines light on the ignobility and bad habits of a society."[58] Not only did Vũ Trọng Phụng state this axiom directly, but he demonstrated a strong commitment to it by consistently placing disenfranchised, impoverished, and criminal characters at the center of his narratives. Vũ Trọng Phụng's second axiom was that realism's quest for representational accuracy demanded a disregard for traditional taboos against the portrayal of ugliness and immorality. In a letter to the critic Thái Phỉ, published in 1936, he wrote: "Realist writers have a right and a duty to describe filthy aspects of human intercourse such as rape, adultery, and incest ..."[59] Vũ Trọng Phụng underlined this point by disavowing poetic euphemism and by insisting repeatedly that things be called by their most common and vulgar name. "We should not be afraid of a truth that is dirty or ugly," he wrote in 1937. "Covering a filthy, gaping wound in silk and velvet will not help to heal it. Rather, it must be exposed and operated upon even if it smells bad and hurts our eyes."[60]

Vũ Trọng Phụng's characterization of realism falls well within the general parameters of metropolitan definitions at the time. However, the particular elements that he underlined — an emphasis on the lower classes and a disregard of strictures on taste and refinement — loomed large in an earlier definition that dated from the first emergence of the concept in France during the 1830s. According to Ian Watt, the earliest formulations of realism highlighted its "low" subject matter, which explains why "the 'realism' of the novels of Defoe, Richardson and Fielding is closely associated with the fact that Moll Flanders is a thief, Pamela is a hypocrite and Tom Jones is a fornicator."[61] The sensational impact of Flaubert's *Madame Bovary* in the mid-1850s, however, triggered a definitional shift away from realism's *subject* and toward its characteristic formal and methodological qualities. As Watt explains: "If the novel were realistic merely because it saw life from the seamy side, it would only be an inverted romance; but in fact it surely attempts to portray all the varieties of human experience, and not merely those suited to one particular literary perspective: the novel's realism does not reside in the kind of life it presents, but in the way it presents it."[62]

In light of the new apprehensions of realism that came to predominate in the wake of Flaubert, Vũ Trọng Phụng's preoccupation throughout the 1930s with the genre's "low" subject matter appears stuck in an early nineteenth-century literary-historical time warp. Formal and methodological dimensions of the concept are absent from his discussion, and he exhibits scant interest in the new prescriptions for realism's proper "political viewpoint" and "class position" advanced by interwar socialist realists. This penchant for selective anachronism stands as an important and distinctive aspect of Vũ Trọng Phụng's habit of mind (it looms large in his views on women, gender, and sexual relations, for example), but it may also be seen as a common intellectual orientation of provincial cosmopolitanism in general.

Translating Romanticism

As with his understanding of realism, Vũ Trọng Phụng's engagement with literary romanticism defies conventional expectations. It has already been noted that in spite of his self-identification as a realist, Vũ Trọng Phụng cites romantic authors more frequently than realist ones. This apparent incongruity is compounded by the fact that three of the four French writers that Vũ Trọng Phụng translated into Vietnamese were well-known romantics or late romantics: Hugo, Vigny, and Richepin (Maupassant was the exception). While Vũ Trọng Phụng's unexpected interest in romanticism begs the question of how he interpreted the aesthetic and political project of the movement, it also complicates a widely held view about the role of French romanticism within Vietnamese intellectual life during the late colonial era.

Many scholars have argued that outside of small leftist circles most interwar Vietnamese writers and intellectuals were ardent disciples of an apolitical version of French romanticism, disseminated by the colonial school system. As the argument goes, romantic writers and works loomed large within an educational curriculum that was designed to conceal France's revolutionary and republican traditions from easily influenced Vietnamese pupils.[63] "In the area of literature," argues Cong Huyen Ton Nu Nha Trang, "what the youth of Vietnam had available, in school and out of school, were works of French classicists and romanticists."[64] Hoang Ngoc Thanh makes a similar point: "In French and Indochinese schools ... the greatest emphasis was given to the French Romantic movement. Such novels as *Graziella* by Lamartine and *Paul et Virginie* by Bernadin de Saint Pierre were made required reading for secondary school students. Romantic, dreamy or gloomy poems like *Le Lac* by Lamartine had to be memorized by heart."[65] Bùi Xuân Bào chides the literature curriculum at l'Ecole Supérieure de Pédagogie de Hanoi for ranging narrowly from "the classicism of Corneille, Racine, Molière and La Fontaine" to "the romanticism of Hugo, Lamartine and Vigny."[66] According to this line of reasoning, colonial educational policy functioned to instill in Vietnamese youth a reverence for neoclassicism and romanticism while concealing from them more contemporary and more politically "progressive" French literary traditions.

A related argument locates the popular appeal of romanticism in the colonial state's efforts to depoliticize Vietnamese society by paying collaborationist intellectuals to publish quiescent periodicals featuring romantic writers and their work. According to this view, the translation and promotion of French romantics in Phạm Quỳnh's *Nam Phong* and Nguyễn Văn Vĩnh's *Đông Dương tạp chí*, for example, was part of a deliberate colonial strategy to distract the reading public from the temptations of anti-colonial politics. For Hoang Ngoc Thanh, "the romantic trend in literature and society" was a direct product of these machinations: "Louis Marty and his able henchman Phạm Quỳnh could not be unaware of the favorable impact, from their point of view, of Romanticism upon the patriotic fervor of Vietnamese youth. The French authorities could not hope for anything better for their interests than having the Vietnamese youth of the time devoting themselves to pathetic love, moaning, weeping or burying flowers."[67]

While evidence indeed exists that the colonial state encouraged a taste for romanticism to combat the radicalization of Vietnamese youth, Vũ Trọng Phụng's interest in the movement does not necessarily confirm this familiar story.[68] After all, the eclecticism of Vũ Trọng Phụng's foreign literary engagements demonstrates clearly that Vietnamese reading habits were never conditioned solely by school curricula. One reason for this is that the emphasis on French-language acquisition within colonial schools diminished the capacity of state-sanctioned translations to serve as a gateway for controlling access to French literature.[69] The importance of reading as a leisure activity for the large French expatriate community in Indochina and the gradual appearance of bookshops, reading rooms, and a small number of public libraries meant that urban Vietnamese especially enjoyed access to a diverse but diffuse assortment of French books and periodicals outside of classroom walls.[70]

The conventional argument is weakened further by its dependence on the simplistic assumption that French romanticism was necessarily a conservative force both cultural and politically. Propagated in Europe by crusading realists[71] and naturalists[72] during the second half of the nineteenth century and by Communist cultural theorists[73] in subsequent decades, this crude assessment of romanticism was taken up within interwar Vietnamese leftist circles[74] and enshrined as an article of faith in cultural manifestos issued by the Vietnamese Communist Party after World War II.[75] But this view disregards the subversive cultural project and radical political influence of romanticism during its early nineteenth-century heyday. Leading romantics were known for denouncing the stale conventions and moral strictures of neoclassicism and for trumpeting the virtues of modernity, individualism, originality, and youth. Moreover, many of the leading early French romantics voiced opposition to the Catholic Church and the French monarchy and provided support for radical political movements such as republicanism and socialism.[76] Given their penchant for unorthodox and anachronistic textual interpretation, on the one hand, and their lack of familiarity with the historical waxing and waning of European critical fashions, on the other, it is not surprising that many Vietnamese provincial cosmopolitans read romantic works according to the radical early nineteenth-century spirit in which they had originally been composed and consumed.

Vũ Trọng Phụng's translations (or summarizations) of works by Hugo, Vigny, and even Richepin are perhaps best understood in this particular light. In "Special Characteristics of Romantic Drama," for example, Vũ Trọng Phụng summarizes the modern virtues of the aesthetic vision expressed in the preface to *Cromwell* and urges his readers to become "disciples" (*do de*) of Hugo.[77] He points approvingly to the tradition-busting significance of Hugo's attack on the classical theatrical "unities" of time, place, and action. He describes Hugo's important notion of the grotesque and explains how it agreeably violates older principles of dramatic decorum (*lois de bienséance*). Most important, he endorses Hugo's call for the juxtaposition of the grotesque and the beautiful on stage as a tactic to enhance dramatic realism. As evidence for the local applicability of Hugo's thesis, he argues that the most beloved character in pre-modern Vietnamese literature — Thúy Kiều — was marked by the romantic co-existence of pious and sensual qualities. In short, Vũ Trọng Phụng's reading of the preface to *Cromwell* calls attention to those "modern" aspects of Hugo that made him a radical figure during the early part of his career and that dovetailed with the oppositional nature of Vũ Trọng Phụng's own political-aesthetic project: his rejection of tradition, his commitment to realism, and his preoccupation with the ugly, shocking, and seamy sides of life. Moreover, in occasional references that appear elsewhere in his work, Vũ Trọng Phụng emphasizes Hugo's promotion of "individualism" and his "humanist" social vision.[78] In Vũ Trọng Phụng's partial and selective formulations, therefore, Hugo's romanticism is not clearly distinguished from the projects of other foreign literary movements (realism and naturalism, for example) whose modernity he explicitly endorsed.

In a similar vein, Vũ Trọng Phụng's translation of Vigny emphasizes selective aspects of his broader vision that corresponded with an important element of his own. In "Three Positions in the World of Literature: A Poet's Lawyer," Vũ Trọng Phụng translates an essay by Vigny that summarizes the central theme of his novel *Stello*, which laments the shabby treatment of artists by all political regimes. This theme is illustrated through a comparison of the wretched predicament of poets under three separate political systems: Gilbert under absolute monarchy, Chatterton under constitutional rule, and André Chénier under a republic. Vigny's flowery language and endorsement of a position that closely resembles art for art's sake sits oddly with Vũ Trọng Phụng's commitment to realism and socially relevant art. But in true provincial cosmopolitan fashion, Vũ Trọng Phụng ignores this contradiction and concludes his translation with a brief editorial statement highlighting the relevance for colonial Vietnam of Vigny's stirring defense of artistic freedom. "Although he made this case over a hundred years ago in nineteenth century France," Vũ Trọng Phụng writes, "Vigny's views on the status of writers ring true in our society as well."[79]

Vũ Trọng Phụng's commitment to artistic freedom also underpins his translation of Richepin. In "A Literary Case," Vũ Trọng Phụng translates and comments upon Richepin's preface to the second edition of *Chansons des gueux*, which rehearses his defense against the obscenity charges for which he was tried, convicted, and imprisoned in 1876. Vũ Trọng Phụng's introduction to the "Preface" celebrates the late-romantic Richepin as a "realist" who specializes in the portrayal of "the ugliness of social reality" and "the base nature of mankind." He then presents Richepin's own words:

> There is no shame in calling things by their true name or photographing things as they truly are. It is those who seek to find filth in nude paintings or sculpture that actually create filth. These are the people who drape a fig-leaf over a nude statue. But it is precisely this fig-leaf that does damage by arousing sexual desire, by making dirty what God intended to be sacred. I dare say that my book *Chanson de Gueux* does not use such a fig-leaf. Although my writing is bold, intemperate even brazen, I reject the charge that it damages morality. The kind of literature that damages morality is the kind that is elegant (bay bướm) and polished (gọt rũa) but relates immoral stories under cover of darkness; that hides in a bouquet of fragrant flowers the head of a poisonous snake.

> It is like a beautiful, elegant and pure looking woman, wearing powder and makeup, walking well-dressed along the streets, timidly displaying "đôi gò bồng đảo" for the world to see, with a beauty mark on her cheek, holding a copy of the Bible, but hiding a copy of a pornographic photo. My writing is not like this kind of literature.[80]

It is striking how Richepin's line of reasoning here resembles arguments that Vũ Trọng Phụng advanced later in his career about the difference between pornography and unvarnished realism. "Filth is not pornography," he wrote in the 1937 letter he published in *Tương Lai* defending his work. "Pornography is something half naked and half covered. It is there in the bourgeois film *Music Hall* and in the obsessions of the magazines *Beauté* and *Sex Appeal*. It is a dancing girl wearing a see-through modern dress. And it is there in so-called 'noble' romance novels."[81] This passage suggests that what Vũ Trọng Phụng shared with Richepin was outrage at the hypocritical moral standards that sanctioned the persecution of writers for graphic descriptions of the "reality" of human sexual behavior while turning a blind eye to soft-core commercial eroticism and the commodification of sexuality by advertising and the mass media.

Richepin concluded by drawing a contrast between the deceitful and manipulative image of a faux-elegant prostitute posing pretentiously as a respectable lady with his own poetic depictions of sexuality, which he likened to a "hearty peasant girl completely nude walking down the street; singing bawdy songs and swearing."[82] "She likes to laugh, speak, dance and sing," Richepin continued, "and she does not conceal her natural gifts unlike those women in silk brocades who expose a fragment of breast, thigh and armpit to attract old men and young boys."[83] Unlike his earlier point about the hypocrisy of conventional obscenity standards, it is difficult to align anything in Vũ Trọng Phụng's writing with the leering prurience of Richepin's late-romantic idealization of the natural sexuality of an uninhibited peasant girl. In his large body of writing on the topic, Vũ Trọng Phụng depicts sex and sexuality as alternatively farcical and grotesque (*Số đỏ* and *Kỹ nghệ lấy tây*), joyless and clinical (*Lục xì* and *Làm đĩ*), or tragic and violent (*Giông tố* and *Cơm thầy cơm cô*). Hence, Vũ Trọng Phụng's essentially conservative, anti-erotic portrayals of human sexuality seem utterly at odds with Richepin's bohemian sensualism. Indeed, given Vũ Trọng Phụng's well-known conservatism on the topic, it is reasonable to expect that he would have expressed disapproval of Richepin's views. This, however, is far from the case. In a brief conclusion to the translation, Vũ Trọng Phụng writes: "Although he was jailed for a month and stripped of his civil rights, Richepin was never the object of public scorn. Among our writers, is there anyone who dares to follow in Richepin's footprints? Go! Go! If you have talent and courage, go!"[84]

Conclusion

While this chapter has treated separately Vũ Trọng Phụng's engagements with realism, on the one hand, and romanticism, on the other, an analysis of his apprehension of the relationship between the two movements provides additional insight into the provincial cosmopolitan character of his thinking. In this regard, it is significant that virtually every European literary-critical tradition tends to define each of these movements, at least in part, relationally with respect to the other. The temporal/historical relationship between the two looms especially large in these definitions since realism as a relatively coherent literary movement in Europe emerged after romanticism and, in many cases, as an explicit response to it. Moreover, ideal-type definitions of realism and romanticism tend to work according to a similar logic by contrasting the characteristic form and content of one movement with the other.

For Vũ Trọng Phụng, however (and for provincial cosmopolitans in general), evidence of an equivalent relational dimension within his understanding of these movements is more or less absent. On the contrary, one of the most striking aspects of his interpretations of the political and aesthetic projects of the various realists and romantics that he cites — and the naturalists and modernists too, for that matter — is the extent to which they tend to overlap and bleed into one another. This is probably because Vũ Trọng Phụng's apprehension of the temporal unfolding of the rise of these movements in Europe was diminished by the fact that they all emerged historically in Indochina, more or less simultaneously, as one of the many abrupt consequences of the colonial encounter. This meant that for Vũ Trọng Phụng and for his generational cohort in general, there was something new, and indeed vaguely modern, about all of these movements regardless of the era in which they originated.[85] Hence, it is possible to add to the list of features characteristic of provincial cosmopolitanism a tendency to ignore the significance of temporal and hence historical and generational relations between them. It is easy to see how this intellectual tendency could work to reinforce other elements of provincial cosmopolitanism discussed in this chapter, such as a predilection for decontextualized readings, a tolerance for anachronism, and a proclivity for the instrumental manipulation of foreign items to serve local purposes. Moreover, this tendency combined with the material, geographic, and institutional conditions of colonial life to reinforce the intellectual eclecticism characteristic of provincial cosmopolitanism.

An appreciation of the depth and character of Vũ Trọng Phụng's provincial cosmopolitanism carries important implications for future studies of his work and of Vietnamese literary and intellectual history more generally. For example, it cautions against efforts to situate him and his peers within the dominant European classificatory system of his day. It also points to the shortcomings of more general efforts to conceptualize Vietnamese cultural politics during the late colonial era as little more than local iterations of more familiar global struggles in the realm of cultural politics. Rather than trying to identify the leading lights of Vietnamese realism, romanticism, naturalism, and modernism or measuring the extent to which interwar intellectuals and activists were collaborationists or anti-colonialists, scholars need to be sensitive to the possibility that Vietnamese cultural politics was dominated by the coexistence of putatively opposite impulses within the thinking of intellectuals and the orientations of collective movements. While it may be premature, given the current state of our knowledge, to advance a definitive characterization of Vũ Trọng Phụng's political or aesthetic project, his idiosyncratic relationship to the dominant metropolitan literary categories of his day suggests that a meaningful assessment of his work will require the development of new and innovative categories and concepts that can only emerge from an analysis of the patterned interaction of local and global forces and dynamics.

Notes

1 On Hồ Chí Minh, see Thu Trang Gaspard, *Hồ Chí Minh à Paris (1917–1923)* (Paris: L'Harmattan, 1992); and Sophie Quinn-Judge, *Ho Chi Minh: The Missing Years, 1919–1941* (Berkeley: University of California Press, 2002). On Phan Bội Châu, see Vĩnh Sính, ed., *Phan Bội Châu and the Đông Du Movement* (New Haven: Council on Southeast Asian Studies, Yale Center for International and Area Studies, 1988). On Nguyễn An Ninh, see Hue-Tam Ho Tai, *Radicalism and the Origins of the Vietnamese Revolution* (Cambridge: Harvard University Press, 1992). On Bùi Quang Chiêu, see R.B. Smith, "Bui Quang Chieu and the Constitutionalist Party in French Cochinchina, 1917–30," *Modern Asian* Studies 3, 2 (1969): 131–50. On Nhất Linh, see Neil Jamieson, *Understanding Vietnam* (Berkeley: University of California Press, 1993); and Greg Lockhart, "Broken Journey: Nhất Linh's *Going to France*," *East Asian History* 8 (1994): 73–95. On Trần Đức Thảo, see Shawn McHale, "Vietnamese

Marxism, Dissent and the Politics of Postcolonial Memory, 1946–1993," *Journal of Asian Studies* 61, 1 (2002): 7–31.

2 Benedict Anderson's recent influential discussion of "long-distance nationalism" is contributing further to this tendency within Southeast Asian studies. "Long-Distance Nationalism," in Benedict Anderson, *The Spectre of Comparisons: Nationalism, Southeast Asia and the World* (London: Verso, 1998), pp. 58–74.

3 Scott McConnell, *Leftward Journey: The Education of Vietnamese Students in France, 1919–1939* (New Brunswick, NJ: Transaction Publishers, 1989), p. 47.

4 Ibid., p. xiii.

5 Ibid., p. 52. On 13 March 1930, only 1,556 Vietnamese students were enrolled in school in the following eight French cities: Paris (1,200), Toulouse (101), Monpellier (78), Marseille (54), Aix-en-Provence (36), Bordeaux (14), Nancy (14), and Arles (13). Trinh Van Thao, *Vietnam du confucianisme au communisme* (L'Harmattan, 1990): 238.

6 Daniel Hémery, "Du patriotism au marxisme: L'Immigration vietnamienne en France de 1926 à 1930," *Le Mouvement Social* 90 (Jan.–Mar. 1975): 21–3.

7 Herman Lebovics, *True France: The Wars over Cultural Identity, 1900–1945* (Ithaca: Cornell University Press, 1992), pp. 114–5.

8 Đặng Văn Long, *Người Việt ở Pháp 1940–1954* [Vietnamese in France, 1940–1954] (Paris: Tủ Sách Nghiên Cứu, 1997), p. 3. The vast majority were soldiers and manual laborers.

9 Obviously, another method to assess the significance of these engagements is to trace their impact within Vũ Trọng Phụng's fiction and literary nonfiction, but that important task lies outside the scope of the present chapter.

10 Biographical data on Vũ Trọng Phụng may be found in Peter Zinoman, "Vũ Trọng Phụng's *Dumb Luck* and the Nature of Vietnamese Modernism," introduction to *Dumb Luck: A Novel by Vũ Trọng Phụng*, ed. Zinoman, trans. Nguyễn Nguyệt Cầm and Zinoman (Ann Arbor: University of Michigan Press, 2002).

11 On Rizal's foreign friendships, see Benedict Anderson, *Under Three Flags: Anarchism and the Anti-Colonial Imagination* (London: Verso, 2005). On Kartini's, see R.A.K. Kartini, *On Feminism and Nationalism: Kartini's Letters to Stella Zeehandelaar, 1899–1903*, trans. Joost Cote Clayton (Victoria: Monash Asia Institute, 1995).

12 The Greeks are mentioned in "Vẽ nhọ bôi hề" [Clown Make-up], *Phụ nữ thời đàm, tập mới* [Women's Contemporary Discussion] (24), Hà Nội, 20 May 1934. Shakespeare, Corneille, Racine, and Molière appear in "Cái đặc-tính của kịch lãng-mạn" [Special Features of Romantic Drama], *Ngọ Báo* [The Daily News] (1337), Hà Nội, 28 Jan. 1932. Shakespeare is also mentioned in *Trúng số độc đắc* [Winning the Lottery] (1939), *Toàn tập Vũ Trọng Phụng tập 4* [Vũ Trọng Phụng: Complete Works, vol. 4] (Hà Nội: Hội Nhà Văn, 1999), p. 201.

13 The Flaubert references are in "Chung quanh thiên phóng sự Lục sì: bức thư ngỏ cho một độc giả" [Around the Reportage *V.D. Clinic*: An Open Letter to a Reader], *Tương lai* [The Future], 11 Mar. 1937, and "Thư ngỏ cho ông Thái Phỉ, chủ báo Tin Văn về bài 'Văn chương dâm uế'" [An Open Letter to Thái Phỉ, Head of Literary News, about the Article 'Pornographic Literature'], *Hà Nội báo* [Hà Nội News] (38), 23 Sept. 1936.

14 Zinoman, "Vũ Trọng Phụng's *Dumb Luck* and the Nature of Vietnamese Modernism," p. 1.

15 Vũ Trọng Phụng, *Không một tiếng vang* in *Toàn tập Vũ Trọng Phụng, tập 5* [Complete Works of Vũ Trọng Phụng, vol. 5] (Hà Nội: Hội Nhà Văn, 1999), p. 194. The epigram "Planter enfin le véritable drame humain au milleu des mensonges ridicules" is from Zola's essay "Le naturalisme au théâtre." Emile Zola, *Oeuvres complétes*, vol. 11 (Paris, Cercle du Livre Précieux: Tchou, 1966), p. 279. Thanks to Anna Gural-Migdal and Alain Pages for help tracking down this reference.

16 "Đi săn khỉ," in *Truyện ngắn Vũ Trọng Phụng* [Short Stories of Vũ Trọng Phụng] (Hà Nội: Hội Nhà Văn, 1996), p. 128.

17 "Un fou" translated as "Điên" appeared in *Ngọ báo* (1204 and 1205), 21 and 22 Aug. 1932. "Solitude" translated as "Hiu quạnh" appeared in *Ngọ báo* (1368), 10 Mar. 1932.

18 Vũ Trọng Phụng's partial summary of "Le Roman" appeared in two installments: "Tư cách nhà phê bình" [The Critic's Personality], *Ngọ báo* (1267), 3 and 4 Nov. 1931; and "Lối viết chuyện của phái tả chân" [The Realist Camp's Way of Writing a Story], *Ngọ báo* (1271), 8 Nov. 1931.

19 Rousseau is cited in *Cơm thầy cơm cô* [Household Servants] (1936), *Toàn tập Vũ Trọng Phụng tập 1* [Complete Works of Vũ Trọng Phụng vol. 1] (Hà Nội: Hội Nhà Văn 1999), p. 349. Lamartine and Musset are cited in the story "Uyên ương" [Mandarin Duck], *Ngọ báo* (955), 13 and 14 Oct. 1930. Chateaubriand is cited in the article "Quanh bài phỏng vấn cùng Ông Lê Thanh" [Around the Lê Thanh Interview], *Bắc hà* (2), 8 Apr. 1937. Goethe is mentioned in the introduction to *Làm đĩ* (1936), *Toàn tập Vũ Trọng Phụng tập 3* [Complete Works of Vũ Trọng Phụng, vol. 3] (Hà Nội: Hội Nhà Văn, 1999), p. 231. Vigny is cited in *Lục xì* [V.D. Clinic] (1937), *Toàn tập Vũ Trọng Phụng tập 1*, p. 393, and in the article "Những tật xấu của danh nhân" [Bad Habits of Famous People], *Tiểu thuyết thứ năm* (45), 31 Aug. 1939.

20 "Ba địa vị trong làng văn: một ông thầy cãi của nhà làm thơ" [Three Positions in the World of Literature: A Poet's Lawyer], *Ngọ báo* (1282), 11 Nov. 1931.

21 Vũ Trọng Phụng published the play under the title *Giết mẹ* [Matricide] in 1936. *Toàn tập Vũ Trọng Phụng tập 5*, pp. 289–400.

22 See note 12.

23 Gide and Malraux are cited in "Để đáp lời báo Ngày Nay: dâm hay không dâm" [A Response to *These Days*: Pornographic or Not], *Tương lai*, 25 Mar. 1937. Proust is cited in the novel *Lấy nhau vì tình* [Marry for Love] (1937),

Toàn tập Vũ Trọng Phụng, tập 4: 43. Baudelaire is mentioned in "Chung quanh thiên phóng sự Lục xì" and "Thư ngỏ cho Ông Phan Trần Chúc" [Open Letter to Phan Trần Chúc], *Đông Dương tạp chí* (35), 13 Jan. 1938. Verlaine is cited in "Để đáp lời báo Ngày Nay: dâm hay không dâm" and in "Những tật xấu của danh nhân."

24 Rolland is cited in *Trúng số độc đắc*, p. 274. Gorky is cited in "Thư ngỏ cho Ông Phan Trần Chúc" and "*Tắt đèn* của Ngô Tất Tố" [Ngô Tất Tố's *When the Lights Go Out*], *Thời Vụ Báo* (100), 31 Jan. 1939.

25 Richepin is cited in "Thư ngỏ cho Ông Phan Trần Chúc," "Chung quanh thiên phóng sự Lục xì," "Để đáp lời báo Ngày Nay: dâm hay không dâm," and in Vũ Trọng Phụng's interview with the critic Lê Thanh: "Chúng tôi phỏng vấn Ông Vũ Trọng Phụng về những tiểu thuyết 'Giông tố,' 'Làm đĩ'" [We Interview Vũ Trọng Phụng about the Novels *The Storm* and *To Be a Whore*], *Bắc Hà* (1), 1 Apr. 1937.

26 "Một cái án văn chương" [A Literary Sentence], *Ngọ báo* (1333), 23 Jan. 1932.

27 Prévost's novel *Les Demi-Vierges* is cited in *Số đỏ, Toàn tập Vũ Trọng Phụng tập 3:111, Giông tố, Toàn tập Vũ Trọng Phụng, tập 2*, p. 400, and *Lấy nhau vì tình*, p. 128.

28 All three are mentioned in "Để đáp lời báo Ngày Nay: dâm hay không dâm." Colette and Margueritte are cited in "Chúng tôi phỏng vấn Ông Vũ Trọng Phụng về những tiểu thuyết 'Giông Tố,' 'Làm Đĩ'." And Margueritte also appears in "Thư ngỏ cho Ông Phan Trần Chúc" and "Chung quanh thiên phóng sự Lục Xì."

29 Roubaud is cited in *Kỹ nghệ lấy Tây* [The Industry of Marrying Westerners], *Toàn tập Vũ Trọng Phụng tập 1*, p. 228, "Hội nghị đùa nhả" [A Conference of Bad Jokes], *Đông Dương tạp chí* (3), Jan. 1938, and "Nghề cạo giấy" (1935) [Clerkship]. "Nghề cạo giấy," first published in the short-lived newspaper *Tân thiếu niên*, has been lost and never recovered, but a brief passage that mentions Roubaud is excerpted in Nguyễn Đình Lạp's "Cường hào" [Powerful and Rich Man], *Quốc Gia*, 16 Sept. 1938. Viollis is cited in "Những việc đáng ghi chép của năm Bính Tý" [Matters Recorded in 1936], *Tuong Lai* (1937?).

30 Seize is cited in *Kỹ nghệ lấy Tây*, p. 228. Choisy is cited in "Để đáp lời báo Ngày Nay: dâm hay không dâm" and in *Cơm thầy cơm cô*, p. 300. Londres is cited in a recently published letter written by Vũ Trọng Phụng to Nguyễn Văn Đạm in 1935: "Nguyễn Văn Đạm: Đôi điều kể thêm về Vũ Trọng Phụng" (Lại Nguyên Ân ghi) [A Little More about Vũ Trọng Phụng (Lại Nguyên Ân transcriber)], Evăn, 15 Nov. 2004.

31 Gourou is cited in "Vấn đề tiểu công nghệ" [The Problem of Small Industry], *Đông Dương tạp chí* (35), 13 Jan. 1938.

32 Hirshfeld is cited in "Thư ngỏ cho ông Thái Phí, chủ báo Tin Văn về bài 'Văn chương dâm uế.'" Liepmann and Freud are both cited in *Làm đĩ* [To Be a Whore] (1936), *Toàn tập Vũ Trọng Phụng tập 3* [Complete Works of Vũ Trọng Phụng, vol. 3] (Hà Nội: Hội Nhà Văn, 1999), pp. 231–5. Freud is also mentioned in Số đỏ: 135 and "Những tật xấu của danh nhân."

33 Lê Thanh, "Chúng tôi phỏng vấn Ông Vũ Trọng Phụng về những tiểu thuyết 'Giông tố,' 'Làm đĩ'."

34 L. Petit de Julleville, *Histoire de la langue et de la littérature française* (Paris: Armand Colin, 1899), p. 214.

35 Olin H. Moore, "The Romanticism of Guy de Maupassant," *PMLA* 33, 1 (1918): 96.

36 For example, one of Maupassant's sentences is: "Mais si nous jugeons un *naturaliste*, montrons-lui en quoi la vérité dans la vie diffère de la vérité dans son livre." Vũ Trọng Phụng's translation reads: "Còn đối với *nhà văn tả thực* ta chỉ nên bảo cho họ biết, nếu phải thế: sự thực ở đời chẳng giống sự thực trong sách anh làm!" Phụng Hoàng, "Tư cách nhà phê bình."

37 Juliette M. Rogers, "The 'Counter-Public Sphere': Colette's Gendered Collective," *MLN* 111, 4 (1996): 736.

38 Ibid.

39 Patrick de Villepin, *Victor Margueritte: La vie scandaleuse de l'auteur de La Garçonne* (Paris: Francois Bourin, 1991). See especially chapter 11: "Pornographe ou écrivain social?" pp. 121–7.

40 Howard Sutton, *The Life and Work of Jean Richepin* (Geneva: Libraire E. Droz *et al.*, 1961), p. 10.

41 Ibid.

42 Ibid.

43 Vũ Trọng Phụng, "Thư ngỏ cho Ông Thái Phỉ, chủ báo Tin Văn về bài 'Văn chương dâm uế'."

44 Vũ Trọng Phụng, *Làm đĩ*, p. 232.

45 Lê Thanh, "Chúng tôi phỏng vấn Ông Vũ Trọng Phụng về những tiểu thuyết 'Giông Tố,' 'Làm Đĩ'."

46 Sutton, *The Life and Work of Jean Richepin*, p. 16.

47 Michael Lerner, *Maupassant* (London: Allen and Unwin, 1975), pp. 107, 153.

48 See Judith Thurman's useful introduction to the recent translation of *Le Pur et L'Impur*. Colette, *The Pure and the Impure*, trans. Herma Briffault, with an introduction by Judith Thurman (New York: New York Review of Books, 2000), pp. vii–xviii.

49 Mary Louise Roberts, *Civilization without Sexes: Reconstructing Gender in Postwar France, 1917–1927* (Chicago: University of Chicago Press, 1994), p. 49. According to Roberts, "The Archbishop of Paris denounced it as obscene and conservative Catholic groups worked to have it seized from bookstores. When the first movie version appeared in 1923, there was such a violent struggle to censure it that the film was shown only once. The translation of the novel into other languages (ultimately 14 in all) caused further uproar, because French conservatives were horrified at the impression of French women it might produce abroad" (p. 48).

50 Lại Nguyên Ân, "Vài tư liệu về việc Vũ Trọng Phụng bị gọi ra tòa năm 1932" [Several Documents Pertaining to Vũ Trọng Phụng's Trial in 1932], talawas, 10 Oct. 2005, <http://www.talawas.org/talaDB/suche.php?res=5638&rb=0106>.

51 As the 1881 and 1898 French laws under which the case was tried stipulated that publishers bore primary responsibility for such crimes, Vũ Trọng Phụng was tried as an accessory only. He was fined 50 francs, but the sentence was suspended by the court. His publisher, Nguyễn Văn Thìn, paid a separate 50 franc fine and spent six days in jail.

52 Nhất Chi Mai, "Ý kiến một người đọc, dâm hay là không dâm," *Ngày nay* (15), 21 Mar. 1937.

53 Vũ Trọng Phụng, "Chung quanh thiên phóng sự Lục xì."

54 Vũ Trọng Phụng, "Để đáp lời báo Ngày Nay: dâm hay không dâm."

55 Lê Thanh, "Chúng tôi phỏng vấn Ông Vũ Trọng Phụng về những tiểu thuyết 'Giông Tố,' 'Làm Đĩ'."

56 Ibid.

57 See "Local Cultural Statements," in O.W. Wolters, *History, Culture, Region in Southeast Asian Perspectives* (Singapore: Institute of Southeast Asian Studies, 1982), pp. 56–68.

58 Vũ Trọng Phụng, "Một cái án văn chương."

59 Vũ Trọng Phụng, "Thư ngỏ cho Ông Thái Phỉ, chủ báo Tin Văn về bài 'Văn chương dâm uế'."

60 Vũ Trọng Phụng, "Chung quanh thiên phóng *sự Lục sì*."

61 Ian Watt, *The Rise of the Novel: Studies in Defoe, Richardson and Fielding* (Berkeley: University of California Press, 1957), p. 11.

62 Ibid.

63 For example, see Gail Kelly, "Colonial Schools in Vietnam: Policy and Practice," in Kelly, *French Colonial Education: Essays on Vietnam and West Africa* (New York: AMS Press, 2000), p. 14.

64 Cong Huyen Ton Nu Nha Trang, "The Role of French Romanticism in the New Poetry Movement in Vietnam," in *Borrowings and Adaptation in Vietnamese Culture*, ed. Truong Buu Lam (Honolulu: Southeast Asian Studies, Center for Asian and Pacific Studies, University of Hawaii, Manoa, 1987).

65 Hoang Ngoc Thanh, *Vietnam's Social and Political Development as Seen through the Modern Novel* (New York: Peter Lang, 1991), p. 91.

66 Bùi Xuân Bào, *Le roman vietnamien contemporain: tendances et evolution du roman vietnamien contemporain, 1925–1945* (Sài Gòn: Long Vân, 1972), p. 79.

67 Hoang Ngoc Thanh, *Vietnam's Social and Political Development as Seen through the Modern Novel*, p. 91.

68 Recent research on the political objectives of the French colonial state's literary and cultural policies in Vietnam may be found in Christopher E. Goscha, "'The Modern Barbarian': Nguyen Van Vinh and the Complexity of Colonial Modernity in Vietnam," *European Journal of East Asian Studies* 3, 1 (2004): 147–51, 161–6.

69 Gail Kelly, "Colonial Schools in Vietnam: Policy and Practice," in Kelly, *French Colonial Education: Essays on Vietnam and West Africa* (New York: AMS Press, 2000), p. 10. Following educational reforms implemented by

Governor-General Sarraut in 1918, 10 of the 13 years of instruction offered by the Franco-Vietnamese school system were carried out in French and "the major emphasis in schooling was language acquisition." Hence, even students who left school after only six years of elementary and primary education and all graduates of primary-superior and secondary school levels attained functional literacy in French.

70 In 1929, a Sài Gòn newspaper published a statistical breakdown of the foreign authors that Vietnamese readers checked out from one of the two city libraries. The data refers to the six-month period between 11 November 1929 and 30 April 1930, and the figures in parentheses signify the number of times that works by each author were borrowed: A. Dumas (931), A. Conan Doyle (427), Gyp (381), A. France (336), Leroux (331), Bordeaux (288), Balzac (272), H. Wells (256), LeBlanc (254), Hugo (247), Prévost (245), Maupassant (238), Victor Margueritte (223). "Người nước ta thích đọc sách gì?" [What Books Do Our People Like?], *Trung lập*, 11 Oct. 1929. For the emergence of public reading rooms during the 1930s, see "Phòng đọc sách Đường D'Arras" [Reading Room of Arras Road], *Cùng-bạn tuần báo*, 8–15 July 1933.

71 Among the most famous early views of romanticism's anesthetizing effects is Flaubert's description of the impact of romantic novels on Emma Bovary.

72 Zola's harsh views on romanticism can be found in his essay "Lettre à Jeunesse." For an English translation, see "A Letter to the Young People of France," in Emile Zola, *The Naturalist Novel*, ed. Maxwell Geismar (Montreal: Harvest House, 1964), pp. 33–43.

73 The most influential early Soviet critique of romanticism's political project was advanced by Georgi Plekhanov in *Art and Social Life*. For relevant excerpts, see *Marxism and Art: Essays Classic and Contemporary*, ed. Maynard Solomon (Detroit: Wayne State University Press, 1979), pp. 128–39. Trần Văn Giàu claims that a French translation of this work circulated in Vietnam during the early 1930s. Trần Văn Giàu, *Triết học và tư tưởng* [Philosophy and Ideology] (Hồ Chí Minh City: Thành Phố Hồ Chí Minh, 1988), p. 440.

74 See the analysis of this topic in the excellent dissertation by Tuan Ngoc Nguyen, "Socialist Realism in Vietnamese Literature: An Analysis of the Relationship between Literature and Politics," PhD dissertation, Victoria University, 2004, pp. 70–3.

75 See Trường Chinh's characterization of romanticism in the polemical cultural manifesto "Marxism and Vietnamese Culture," first delivered at the Việt Minh's Second National Cultural Conference during 1948. Truong Chinh, "Marxism and Vietnamese Culture," in *Truong Chinh: Selected Writings* (Hà Nội: Foreign Languages Publishing House, 1977), p. 244.

76 On the political and social radicalism of romanticism during the early nineteenth century, see David Owen Evans, *Social Romanticism in France, 1830–1848* (Oxford: Clarendon Press, 1951); James Smith Allen, *Popular French Romanticism: Authors, Readers and Books in the Nineteenth Century*

(Syracuse: Syracuse University Press, 1981); and Sandy Petrey, "Romanticism and Social Vision," in *A New History of French Literature*, ed. Denis Hollier (Cambridge: Harvard University Press, 1989), pp. 661–6.

77 "Cái đặc-tính của kịch lãng-mạn."

78 In "Quanh bài phỏng vấn cùng Ông Lê Thanh," Vũ Trọng Phụng writes: "Under the great family regime [chế độ đại gia đình], we must struggle for the individual [cá nhân] like Hugo and Chateaubriand."

79 "Ba địa vị trong làng văn: một ông thầy cãi của nhà làm thơ."

80 "Một cái án văn chương."

81 "Chung Quanh Thiên Phóng Sự Lục Sì."

82 Ibid.

83 Ibid.

84 Ibid.

85 By way of illustration, consider the following passage from the critic Hồ Xanh's review of Vũ Trọng Phụng's novel *Số đỏ*: "In the past ten years, Vietnamese literature has opened wide its door to receive the light of a new era. Faced with the brilliant flowers of the French literary garden, our artists have bowed their heads respectfully and plucked many buds. Each one is beautiful in its own way: classicism possesses a classical beauty, romanticism possesses a romantic beauty, and realism possesses a realist beauty." Here, Hồ Xanh acknowledges the extraordinary cultural character of the late colonial era, during which centuries of French literary history came to be absorbed by Vietnamese "artists" in roughly a decade. Hồ Xanh, "Văn học bình luận: Số đỏ của Vũ Trọng Phụng," *Công Thương Báo* 1, 6 (1–15 May 1938).

CHAPTER 5

Du Ai, Lin Bin, and Revolutionary Flows

Caroline S. Hau

In 1992, the Philippine Bureau of Posts issued a set of stamps in honor of the guerrilla groups that were active during World War II. The stamps, labeled "Philippine guerrilla units of World War II," featured such well-known groups as Vinzons Guerrillas, Anderson's Command, President Quezon's Own Guerrillas, the Luzon Guerrilla Army Forces, and the Cebu Area Command. One unit, however, stood out in the set because it was the only guerrilla group honored that was commanded by and composed almost exclusively of "foreigners." The Wha Chi (Hua Zhi, short for Feilubin Huaqiao Kangri Zhidui, Philippine-Chinese Anti-Japanese Guerrilla Forces) is arguably the best-known organization of the Chinese guerrilla resistance movement in the Philippines.[1]

Even though its contributions to the Filipino narrative of national liberation struggle have been recorded and corroborated by several non-Chinese — including American — sources,[2] the Wha Chi has long been identified with "national democratic," i.e., leftist, activism. Its place in Philippine history has been marked out by its relationship and collaboration with the radical guerrilla Hukbalahap (Hukbo ng Bayan Laban sa mga Hapon, People's Anti-Japanese Army; the name was later changed to Hukbong Mapagpalaya ng Bayan, or People's Liberation Army), which posed a potent challenge against the Philippine state during the first decade following the country's formal independence from the United States in 1946.[3] Some members of the group would go on to help found and organize the Communist Party of the Philippines–New People's Army, still active 40 years after its establishment in 1968.[4]

"Chinese" historical participation in the Filipino revolutionary movement and the contested place of Maoism and China in the development of Filipino Communism are, in fact, integral aspects of the Philippine "revolutionary" experience.[5]

Chinese workers[6] in the Philippines were already organizing in the late 1910s and early 1920s.[7] Tracking the activities of a key Chinese labor leader — who would later appear as a character in Du Ai's novel — provides a telling microcosm of Philippine-Chinese radical history.[8] Xu Jingcheng (1905–71) (Ko Keng Seng/Co Kin Sin, original name Xu Jingbiao but also known by a number of aliases, the most important being Xu Li or Ko Li) was born in Jinjiang, Fujian province, China, on 8 January 1905. At the age of 12 he moved to Hong Kong, where he was taught English (he first read Marx in English translation). He made short trips to the Philippines in 1919 and 1921 before settling down in Manila in 1925. Working as a store employee and a teacher, he led the Workers Association (Gongren Xiehui), which counted shopkeepers, teachers, and store clerks among its members, and was responsible for helping to set up other occupation-based Chinese unions. In 1926 a Young Communist League member, Li Xingqiu, visited the Philippines[9] and initiated contact with Xu, who became a member and later assumed leadership of the Manila branch.[10] Ko eventually served as a member of the Partido Komunista ng Pilipinas (PKP, Communist Party of the Philippines) Central Committee in 1930,[11] and 60 of the 80 YCL members would join the newly established PKP.[12] The political conflict in China extended to the Philippines as local Chinese Communists clashed with Guomindang (Kuomintang) groups. After the December 1927 uprising in China, the Philippine-born Chinese Communist Party member Li Bingxiang (also known as Li Yongxiao and Felipe Lee Yung Shaw [see next section]) returned to the Philippines, established contact with Ko and Li Xingqiu, and helped organize the Philippine Chinese Labor Association (PCLA, Huaqiao Gonghui/Hua Kiao Kong Hue, Overseas Chinese Workers' Union). These three men would be instrumental in forging ties with the Filipino Communist movement.

The PCLA first established ties with the Congreso Obrero de Filipinas and the Partido Obrero but, owing to the racial politics practiced by the COF, were kept at a "segregated distance."[13] It was the founder of the Partido Komunista ng Pilipinas Crisanto Evangelista's group that actively advocated the integration of the PCLA into the Filipino labor movement and worked closely with the PCLA. The PCLA later renamed itself the Philippine Chinese Labor Federation (PCLF, Feihua gelaogong tuanti) as its member unions expanded to 30, with a total membership of 5,000.[14] The PCLF's links with Profitern were coursed through Crisanto Evangelista, and PCLF joined Evangelista in walking out of the COF convention in 1929.

Three of its members would join the board of the newly established left organization Katipunan ng Anak-Pawis ng Pilipinas on 5 May 1929[15] (see Onimaru's chapter on the Comintern network). Close links between the Chinese and Filipino Communists can be seen in the fact that 3 of the 35 members of the newly established PKP Central Committee in 1930 were Chinese: Co Sing Liat, Ko Keng Seng (Xu), and Sun Ping. One of them, code-named "Comrade C" (probably Ko himself), would be a member of the Politburo.[16] A Manila Chinese left leader, a certain "Li,"[17] and an alternate, "Koo" (Ko?), were elected members of the Central Committee in 1938.[18]

At the beginning of World War II, Ko organized the Anti-Japanese and Chinese-Protection Committee (Kangri huaqiao weiyuanhui).[19] The founding members of the Wha Chi guerrilla group were drawn from the ranks of the PCLF, renamed the Philippine Chinese United Workers Union,[20] or Feilubin Huaqiao Gelaogong Tuanti Lianhehui (shortened names Lao Lian Hui in pinyin and Lo Lien Hwe in Hokkien), in 1938 after several more Chinese Philippine labor unions joined the federation. The Wha Chi was organized on 19 May 1942 as a squadron under the Hukbalahap (Hukbo ng Bayan Laban sa Hapon,[21] People's Anti-Japanese Army, renamed Hukbong Mapagpalaya ng Bayan or People's Liberation Army after World War II) Filipino guerrilla army. A number of Wha Chi leaders were involved in training both Chinese and Filipino guerrillas.[22] Squadron 48, named in honor of China's New Fourth and Eighth Route Armies, formally adopted the name "Wha Chi" after it negotiated with the Huks to assume an independent and neutral status as a guerrilla unit. The Wha Chi grew from 52 fighters to a 1944 peak of 700 members forming five squadrons. From February 1942 to the end of the Japanese Occupation in August 1945, it was active in Manila and 14 other provinces in the Philippines, fought in 260 battles and skirmishes, claimed to have killed more than 2,000 enemy soldiers (mostly Filipino constabulary troops under the Japan-sponsored Philippine government), and lost 77 of its own members.[23]

Given that the Philippine state criminalized the leftist forces during most of the Cold War period,[24] the Wha Chi, not surprisingly, was marginalized from official national discourse and from the largely Guomindang-dominated and -policed local Chinese affairs of the time. Not until four years after the Philippines established diplomatic relations with the People's Republic of China in 1975 was a monument to the Wha Chi martyrs finally built in the Chinese cemetery in Manila. With formal recognition of mainland China has come the belated re-recognition of the Wha Chi's "valuable service rendered to America and the Philippines,"[25] couched in the language of bilateral friendship between the Philippines and mainland China in the wake of the Sino-Soviet split. This official recognition glosses over the Wha Chi's historical connections with the global and regional socialist-cum-anti-colonial network that spanned East and Southeast Asia, Russia, and the United States in the first half of the twentieth century.

Ironically, because of the Wha Chi's record of cooperation with Filipino and American-commanded guerrilla units during the war, Wha Chi returnees to China (officially called *guiqiao*, or "returned overseas Chinese") in the grip of the Cultural Revolution suffered the inverse of what their fellow members in the Philippines had gone through. Whereas Wha Chi veterans in the Philippines were branded and hounded as Communists, Wha Chi veterans in China were stigmatized as "reactionary" and "bourgeois-capitalist" overseas Chinese (*huaqiao*) who counted among the "seven categories of sinister people" (along with landlords, rich peasants, counter-revolutionaries, bad elements, rightists, and enemy agents).[26] Far more seriously, they were denounced as "agents of the U.S.–Chiang Kai Shek clique" (*Mei Jiang tewu jituan*); a Gang of Four representative in Fujian province went so far as to compare the Philippine Wha Chi returnees to a lychee tree bearing "fruits with red skin, white meat and black hearts" (*Feilubin huawei shi ge lizhishu, jiechu de guo shi hong pi bai ruo hei xin de*).[27] The fruit of this persecution was extremely bitter — more than 340 cadres in China (nearly 50 per cent of the Wha Chi members) were affected, and in Fujian alone eight (including the commanders of the Second, Third, Fourth, and Manila squadrons) died as a result.[28] The eight cadres were officially "rehabilitated" in November 1978 by the Fujian Committee of the Chinese Communist Party. In 1992, the same year that the Philippine government issued stamps in honor of the Wha Chi, the Office of Overseas Chinese Affairs in mainland China sent formal greetings to commemorate the Wha Chi's 50th anniversary.

For members of the Wha Chi, this vindication of their role in promoting Philippine-Chinese relations underscored the Wha Chi's commitment to, and embodiment of, the "spirit of internationalism" (*guoji zhuyi jingshen*),[29] or what Susan Bayly calls the "socialist ecumene."[30] But what is notable about this internationalism — which found expression in the language of global fraternal community based on revolutionary solidarities, long-distance exchange, and friendship — is that it was fostered within the particularistic context of an anti-colonial Chinese nationalism that not only was related, but also contributed, to the development of Philippine radical nationalism. While the Chinese guerrillas did not think of themselves as "dual" nationalists and their political action derived from, and promoted, a discourse of emancipation that stressed international cooperation and solidarity among leftist groups and forces all over the world, their presence in the Philippines nevertheless opened itself to the possibility of being articulated as an instance of Filipino nationalist action without necessarily precluding their loyalty and commitment to China and world revolution.

In other words, while this kind of Chinese "revolutionary cosmopolitanism" promoted political loyalty to the Chinese state and operated within the framework of nation-states, it was not necessarily chauvinistic; instead, it involved forms of engagement, attachment, identification, and activism that worked both within as well as beyond the bounds of the nation-state and actively contributed to the development of indigenous nationalism and, later, Communism and socialism in Southeast Asia.[31] This revolutionary cosmopolitanism confirms the fact that, as the historian Wang Gungwu has argued, overseas Chinese responses to nationalism not only have a place in the contemporary history of Southeast Asia,[32] they actually play a role in the making and remaking of "national" communities in both China and the Philippines. By affirming the political significance of the historic movement across borders of Chinese people who, in the name of international solidarity, aided Filipino nationalists in fighting for national liberation from the Japanese during the 1940s, this cosmopolitanism poses important questions that force a rethinking of commonsensical notions of nationness and national belonging.

What is striking about this cosmopolitanism is not just the degree to which it was historically compatible with radical popular nationalism, although this does not mean that its relationship with nationalism was tension-free.[33] What is striking about this cosmopolitanism is that the kinds of people, spaces and movements, concerted actions, emotional involvements, solidarities, and networks and connections it entailed operated simultaneously on and across local, national, regional, and international registers. Although this cosmopolitanism was reducible neither to "nationalism" nor to "socialism," it often found itself subject to both (and sometimes either) socialist and nationalist interpellations. Such a cosmopolitanism was rendered legible and accorded recognition in non-Communist Philippines and post-Maoist China only insofar as it could be made to fit within a nationalist narrative of liberation and a socialist-regional narrative of amity and cooperation. And yet these activists moved around in one country and moved across countries, meeting people and establishing local, national, regional, and international networks and connections. What makes their movements politically salient is not that they traveled within and across multiple borders, but the various "meanings and causes on behalf of which those crossings can be pressed into service."[34]

In a region in which nationalism retains its positive associations as a liberatory and mass-mobilizing force, cosmopolitanism has the potential to reinvigorate the theory and practice of nationalism by redefining and remaking the national community; breaching its exclusionary borders; productively contaminating its assumed "purity" of culture and identity; and expanding the grounds and horizons for its dreams, claims, advocacies, and realizations of freedom, equality, and justice. Cosmopolitanism does so by forcefully bringing up the question of the foreigner, the alien who is supposed to remain outside the bounds of the national community, but whose selective inclusion and exclusion expose the limits and potentials of nation-making.

This chapter analyzes three different but related embodiments of revolutionary cosmopolitanism: the overseas Chinese returnee Du Ai, his partner and artistic collaborator Lin Bin, and *guiqiao* like them; the Wha Chi organization, of which Du Ai was a member; and his three-part novel (the third volume of which was written by Lin Bin), *Fengyu Taipingyang* (Storm over the Pacific),[35] which memorializes the wartime adventures of the Wha Chi and Du Ai's experiences. Author(s), organization, and novel map the significance, reach, scope, and — a crucial point often overlooked — limits of the cosmopolitan radical's crossings of borders and journeys across spaces. They reveal the contexts under which different peoples from different countries are thrown together, and explore the possibilities as well as constraints — worked out through the medium of kinship and language — of the friendships, solidarities, and networks that are forged in the course of their being thrown together to create a "community of fate." They expose the intellectual and organizational fault lines running through both Chinese and Philippine revolutionary movements' attempts to graft Communist internationalism onto anti-imperialist nationalism. But they also point to the ways in which these crossings and connections can end up challenging received notions of national belonging and loyalty, revealing the ways in which nationalism bears the trace of what is "alien" and "other" to it and opening nationalism up for reinvention both conceptually and practically.[36]

Biography as Fiction

The Hakka poet, fictionist, and essayist Cao Chuanmei, who took the pen name of Du Ai, was born in Dapu County, in the eastern part of Guangdong province, in 1914. Despite growing up in poverty and being forced to discontinue his studies while in junior high school, he was able to enter Guangdong Zhongshan University's literature department in 1933, graduating in 1937. Joining the leftist writers' organization Lian Meng Guangzhou Fenhui, he edited numerous underground publications.[37]

Du Ai joined the Communist Party in 1936. He went to Hong Kong in September 1937 before landing in Manila in 1940. In the Philippines, he worked for the *Jianguo Zhoukan* and other publications, and on translations from English. Above all, he was deeply involved in the anti-Japanese resistance movement,[38] and may have been sent by the Party to the Philippines to do liaison work. In Manila, Du Ai fell in love with his fellow activist Lin Bin (Lin Caiying, born in 1922 in Xiamen, Fujian province), a third-generation Hokkien *huaqiao* who had come to the Philippines when she was eight years old. She had studied at St. Stephen's High School and the University of Santo Tomas in Manila, and would become Du Ai's most important artistic collaborator. Lin Bin, a critic in her own right, has written extensively on the cultural production of the anti-Japanese movement before World War II, and on literary production by women activists.[39]

Du Ai

Fengyu Taipingyang

As the department head of the Hua Chiao Anti-Japanese Anti-Traitor Alliance (Kang Fan) and a member of the Wha Chi, Du Ai was one of the people who were involved in the May 1943 ten-day siege in Mount Arayat, when Japanese and Filipino constabulary troops encircled the mountain to flush out guerrillas. Returning to Hong Kong in 1947, where he worked at the *Huashang Bao* and other publications, and to Guangzhou just before the "Liberation" in 1949, he served in a number of national and provincial cultural committees and writers organizations. He was at one time chairman of Guangdong province's Department of Culture. Persecuted during the Cultural Revolution, Du Ai began working on *Fengyu Taipingyang* in the last 13 years of his life, after his retirement in 1980.[40] Only two volumes of *Fengyu* were published in his lifetime.[41] Upon Du Ai's death in 1993, Lin Bin assumed the responsibility of completing the last half of the third volume (approximately 160,000 words) by relying on extensive dictation and notes that she had taken on her husband's deathbed.[42] The word count of all three volumes (2002 edition) adds up to 960,000 words,[43] making *Fengyu* one of the longest single works of overseas Chinese fiction in Southeast Asia.[44] *Fengyu*'s significance is enhanced by the fact that no novel-length fiction in Chinese has so far been published in the Philippines.

The Chinese writer Mao Dun, in his preface[45] to Du Ai's collection of fiction *Zai Lusong Pingyuan* (On the Plains of Luzon) (written between 1947 and 1949 and revised in 1956 under the title *Conglin Qu* [The Forest]),[46] notes the depth of Du Ai's immersion in the Philippines and his close interaction with the Filipino people in the common battle against fascism, and comments on the artistic challenge of adequately depicting the intertwining of fates (*mingyun*).[47] Du Ai's journeys from China to Hong Kong to the Philippines and back to Hong Kong and China yielded, at each stop, poems, essays, short stories, and a long novel, but his reputation rests largely on his work for the resistance movement and his depiction of overseas Chinese and Filipino experiences in the Philippines.[48] The fact that Du Ai's Philippine sojourn provided him with the palette to paint from his imagination, observation, and experience is amply borne out by his detailed descriptions of Philippine and Chinese-Philippine everyday life.

Moreover, Du Ai hailed from the Hakka part of Guangdong province in South China. The Hakka have a centuries-long history of migration that links them with neighboring Fujian and Jiangxi, with non-Han minorities in China and the borderlands, as well as Hong Kong, Southeast Asia (particularly Malaysia and Thailand), and the rest of the world. In Guangdong, such links have made the areas near and along the Pearl River Delta sites where distinctions between "Chinese" and "non-Chinese" are far from clear-cut;[49] they add an important geo-historical dimension to Du Ai's social location as a Huanan (South Chinese) writer whose representative works are set in the Nanyang (Southern Ocean) territories, which include the Philippines. The Chinese literary critic Yang Yi explicitly connects the regional Huanan literary imagination to overseas Chinese Nanyang literature by pointing to their use of imagery rooted in a common "dream" of the big ocean (*dahai zhi meng*) and "love" of tropical forests (*redai conglin zhi lian liao*) — imagery that resonates in the theorizing of Southeast Asia as an "area."[50]

Not only can Du Ai's life and career be mapped by his actual movements across national boundaries, his major work also takes journeys as its major theme and source of emplotment. *Fengyu Taipingyang* follows various members of the Wha Chi as they journey (individually or in groups) across different parts of Central and Southern Luzon. The unfolding of the novel's plot — which matches the narrative account of highlights provided by Liang Shangwan and Cai Jianhua's memoirs — is replete with place names that serve as signposts marking Wha Chi's passage through time and space: from the early days of leaving Manila for Bataan to hunt for abandoned weaponry, to the evacuation of Chinese to Laguna and Bulacan, to the establishment of a three-month base at Mount Pasbul (called Mount Lao Qing in the Liang and Cai memoirs) at the border of Pampanga and Bataan, to joining the Huks in attacking the town of Cabiao in Nueva Ecija, to hiding out in Mount Arayat (known as the Yenan of the Philippines). From Nueva Ecija, Squadron 48 moved to Mount Miguel, at the Bulacan-Nueva Ecija border, before venturing southward, marching through the Sierra Madre range and arriving in Laguna. In 26 days alone, for example, the squadron traveled 500 kilometers on foot and marched through 36 towns in Bulacan, Rizal, Tayabas, and Laguna. Going independent with the permission of the Huks, the squadron adopted the formal designation Wha Chi and established friendly relations with other guerrilla units, taking care not to get itself embroiled in inter-guerrilla rivalry and conflict by pursuing a policy of stated neutrality. Working closely with the Hua Chiao Anti-Japanese Committee (Hua Wei), an umbrella organization that included the Hua Chiao Anti-Japanese Anti-Traitor Alliance (Kang Fan) and the *Hua Chiao Guide* (the underground newspaper), the Wha Chi also fielded guerrillas in Manila, to which they returned, in the company of Huk and the US 11th Airborne Division, in February 1945 as the Japanese retreated from the capital.

The novel contains more than 180 named characters, of whom 12 are principal protagonists and many are modeled on or composites of real-life people, representing friends and foes, Filipinos (including different groups of indigenous peoples), Chinese, Americans, mestizos (mixed blood), and, to a lesser extent, Japanese. The two major characters of the novel, Hoster Lee and his sister Li Jinfu (Miss Lee), are experienced travelers:[51] at 18 and 15 years of age respectively, both left the Philippines for China to join the battle against the warlord Yuan Shikai. There, Hoster worked as the translator for Sun Yat-sen's Comintern adviser Mikhail Borodin while his sister, a gifted painter, served in the information unit. When the White Terror broke out in 1927, the siblings escaped to Outer Mongolia, traveled to Soviet Russia, and eventually made their way back to the Philippines via Malaysia.

The real-life people on whom some of the main characters in the novel are modeled (including Xu Jingcheng, discussed in the previous section) also traveled extensively. The careers of two leading Wha Chi leaders exemplify the physical reach and scope of revolutionary cosmopolitanism during the high noon of Chinese anti-colonial and Communist nationalism. Liang Shangwan was born in Kuala Lumpur, Malaysia, and joined the Malaysian Communist Youth League while attending secondary school. Captured in Singapore in 1931 and incarcerated for half a year, he went to China upon his release and then moved to Hong Kong before arriving in Manila.[52] Even more remarkable was Felipe Lee Yung Shaw (Li Yongxiao, Li Bingxiang, 1905–57),[53] the Wha Chi liaison officer who lends his Chinese name and some of the details of his life to Hoster Lee, one of the principal characters in Du Ai's novel. Born in Manila, Felipe Lee spoke Tagalog and studied English and Spanish. After completing his elementary education at the Anglo-Chinese School (the oldest Chinese school in the Philippines), he went to Shanghai for high school. From there he went on to university in Shanghai, where he was exposed to the writings of Marx and Lenin. He was involved in the May 4th Movement and became a member of the Communist Party in 1924. He moved to Beijing but was forced to flee to South China to avoid arrest by the "warlord" government. He ended up in Guangdong, where he worked as an interpreter for Mikhail Borodin, the Comintern adviser to Sun Yat-sen during the Guomindang-Communist United Front of 1924–7. In 1927, when Jiang Jieshi (Chiang Kai-shek) turned against the Communists, Lee Yung Shaw fled to the Shanghai International Concessions, then escaped to Manila. As a Wha Chi guerrilla, he was captured but managed to escape by confounding the

Japanese — with hours of rosary-clutching and unintelligible prayers — into releasing him unharmed (an event dramatized in *Fengyu*).

Du Ai's reliance on the novel form to dramatize the Wha Chi's involvement in anti-colonial struggle in the Philippines sets his project apart from the memoirs, essays, biographical sketches, and historiographies produced by veteran guerrillas and their relatives, and by scholars of overseas Chinese studies. In their illumination of the concrete personal experience of international political solidarity, novels have the capacity to convey the complexity of everyday life while also capturing in prose form the epic quality of armed confrontation and its heroic (and often tragic) consequences. The omniscient narration in *Fengyu* weaves the threads of different characters' lives into a collective biography of the Wha Chi.

Fiction allows the author to take liberties that are not otherwise possible even in auto/biographies and histories that employ fictional devices to flesh out the substance of their subjects. The fictionist creates composites of characters, compresses time and events, rearranges settings, and reorders chronologies to heighten the dramatic impact of the narrative. Fictionalizing characters and events plays on the blurring between truth and untruth and non-truth to produce interpretations of lives and events that can be read against, or in light of, other textual interventions, other accounts. Fiction does not stand in opposition to fact, since it may be employed to tell stories that are too risky or uncomfortable to relay as witnessed "truths." Novels often make claims simultaneously to fictionality and factuality precisely because authors can experiment with journalistic and historical writing and comment on the world in an avowedly fictional work. Novelists draw on a broader notion of factuality, not of history but of "historylike,"[54] to make epistemological, political, and moral claims.

Furthermore, Lin Bin's role in completing Du Ai's project shows the extent to which *Fengyu Taipingyang*, while published under Du Ai's byline, is the work not just of one man, but of his widow — an activist, essayist, and critic in her own right who has played a crucial role in preserving her husband's legacy and documenting the historic contribution of women and writers to Chinese and Filipino revolutionary activism. Traces of Lin Bin can be gleaned from the heroines in the novel and from the novel's frequent references to women warriors such as Josephine Bracken (wife of the martyred national hero Jose Rizal). At the same time, Lin Bin was her husband's first reader and the author of the third volume that completes the novel. This novel, populated by a multiplicity of characters, is itself multiply authored, and the gendered dimension of its production is reflected in the novel's careful attention to the portrayal of its female protagonists.[55]

Founding Communities of Fate

Fengyu Taipingyang poses and answers the question of what possibilities and limits define the Wha Chi's brand of revolutionary cosmopolitanism. The novel points to a degree of interdependence and intimacy between Wha Chi guerrillas and their Filipino counterparts that is unequaled by any existing account of Chinese-Philippine relations.

In fact, the novel suggests that the Wha Chi's freedom of action is largely defined by the cooperation and friendship extended to the Chinese guerrillas by Filipino activists and, above all, ordinary people. Following the declaration of Manila as an open city, for example, 400 Chinese composed mainly of members of the United Workers Union (Lo Lien Hwe) and their families evacuate Manila and head for Barrio Mandili in Cabiao, Nueva Ecija, Central Luzon, in January 1942. In this undertaking they are helped by the progressive organization Kalipunang Pambansa ng Magsasaka sa Pilipinas (National Society of Peasants in the Philippines), which mobilizes civilian population support for the Wha Chi. Wha Chi guerrillas — some of whom helped train the Huk guerrillas — are protected and nurtured by the Filipino population in areas that are under the Huks' sphere of influence, boosting morale and providing food, shelter, medical aid, geographical guidance, intelligence information, and military support: "Once you find the people, you'll find the way" (*zhao dao lao baixing jiu you chulu*).[56] The support of the Chinese in the provision of basic necessities, medicine, and safe houses, as well as arrangement of transportation and communication and smuggling of documents and the *Hua Chiao Guide*, is also instrumental to the Wha Chi's survival in enemy territory. In Mount Pasbul, indigenous Dumagat Aetas guide the Wha Chi through the mountain passes into safety. To quote from the novel: "We fight on Philippine soil. Our main weapon power is Filipino might. We believe [*xiangxin*] in them, we rely [*yikao*] on them. This is our steadfast, unwavering principle [*jiandingbuziyidefangzhen*]."[57]

Because of the Wha Chi's extensive dealings with the Huks and travels through the Filipino countryside in Luzon, multilinguals and interpreters play a crucial role in mediating communication among the Chinese (for example, between Cantonese- and Hokkien-speakers who do not have a command of *putonghua*), between the Chinese and Filipino guerrillas, and between the Wha Chi and the civilian population. *Fengyu* records the continuous shifts in language as people shift linguistic registers and speak in Hokkien, Cantonese, Mandarin, English, Spanish, Tagalog, Kapampangan, Panggalatok, Agta, and Dumagat according to the demands of their interlocutors. The text of *Fengyu* is, not surprisingly, stippled with romanized and phonetic transcriptions of words, phrases, and sentences from different languages. Wha Chi guerrillas such as Paolo, who are unable to understand or speak one or more of the Philippine languages, feel their handicap most deeply. In fact, it was the relative scarcity of translators at a time when the Wha Chi were cut off from communication with the Huks and forced to march through areas outside of Huk influence that made the Wha Chi painfully aware of the limits of their capacity to move and recruit among the native population.

In the theater of war, survival depends on seeming rather than being, and destabilizes assumptions about the givenness of ethnic or cultural identities. Wha Chi survival is conditioned by the guerrillas' ability to evade or overcome the strictures of "Chineseness" and their physical appearance. In some cases, their "Chinese" features work against them, marking them apart from the townspeople. In other cases, the ambiguity of physical appearance puts them in danger as Filipinos have difficulty telling them apart from the Japanese until they open their mouths: "Are you Japanese, or are you Formosans?"[58] In yet other instances, Wha Chi guerrillas avoid capture by melting into the population, wearing civilian clothing, and speaking only English, Tagalog, or other Philippine languages. In a few instances, they disguise themselves as Japanese soldiers to sabotage enemy quarters or trick collaborators.

Translation does not work just to expedite communication but allows speakers to bring into a given language the knowledge, history, and culture encoded in other languages. There are repeated references to Filipino historical figures such as Lapu-Lapu, Melchora Aquino, Josephine Bracken, Antonio Luna, Miguel Malvar, and Jose Rizal, and to Rizal's last poem, avocadoes, mangoes, coconuts, tuba, basi, and balut. Filipino folk songs are sung, dances danced alongside extended quotations from Rizal's last poem. The indigenous Baluga teach the Wha Chi to subsist on cogon grass, while the Huks provide tips on how to walk through mud without slipping. Given that the majority of the Wha Chi guerrillas were in their late teens and early to mid-20s, the Wha Chi journeys are not simply educational (*Bildung*), but also represent rites of passage in which young Chinese acquire the "experience" that molds them into adults.

This mixing of references is rendered early in the novel, when Li Jinfu leads her art class through a history lesson on the heroism of the Philippine national hero Andres Bonifacio, founder of the revolutionary secret society Katipunan:[59]

> "Children, Bonifacio's assassination is similar to what happened in China. When so-called Generalissimo Jiang Jieshi saw that the revolution was being won in Shanghai and Nanjing, he embarked on counterrevolution and massacred many revolutionaries in order to steal the fruit of revolution. Classmates, isn't it hateful?"
>
> "Hateful!" chorused the children.
>
> "Wasn't Katipunan able to kill off the villain and get back the fruit of revolution?" [Asked by a student.]
>
> "Yes, the fruit of revolution has to be taken back. But the situation at the time was complicated. When the power of the Spanish colonizers after three hundred years' rule was waning, Uncle Sam forced his way in and replaced the Spaniards."
>
> When the children heard this, they felt that the Philippines was indeed weighed down by calamity and, with China, formed a pair of suffering brothers [*nanxiong nandi*].

A discussion of the betrayal of the Katipunan and its suppression by the Spaniards serves as a jumping board to a criticism of Chiang Kai-shek's suppression of the Chinese Communists and, further on, a dissection of the current situation in Soviet Russia. References to Rodin's "The Thinker" call up the career of Lenin, who once recommended Rodin's art to a friend.

Analogies abound in the novel, linking and distinguishing disparate personages, events, and territories. Set during World War II, the novel has an epic sweep ranging across the entire world historical stage even as it focuses on the Chinese resistance movement in the Philippines. Comparison juxtaposes insights and analyses and serves to connect the Philippines to China, Russia, and Southeast Asian countries by narrating their histories of struggle against oppression within the framework of a particular leftist vision of international solidarity and nationalist liberation.

The limits of Wha Chi freedom of action are largely informed by the reach of translation. Because of the limited number of translators who could talk to local populations in their own languages, the Wha Chi found itself unable to establish stable bases in areas outside the sphere of Huk influence. And, as we will see below, difficulties in communication between the Huks and Wha Chi militated against the Wha Chi's full incorporation into the Huk battalions and necessitated the Wha Chi's adoption of a policy of logistical self-sufficiency.

The constraints within which the Wha Chi operated as a guerrilla unit are offset in the novel by stirring tales illustrating the close relationships between Chinese and Filipinos. Intimacy is dramatized by *Fengyu* in three forms: love, friendship, and kinship. The novel's narrative of struggle is interwoven with — if not, to use a different metaphor, filtered through — the narratives of at least five pairs of lovers from different class and cultural backgrounds, including two pairs that involve Chinese men and Filipino women. Unlike *huaqiao* novels that stop short of having interracial love end in consummation and marriage — a consequence of the fear that *huaqiao* patriots who fall in love with native women risk being unable to return to China — *Fengyu* painstakingly charts the separations and reunions that bring the lovers together and tear them apart, holding readers in suspense as to the final outcome of these entanglements until the very end of the book. While Marianna loses her beloved Robin Chen on the eve of liberation, Wu Qing and Maria are united in the final chapter.

Like the innumerable friendships that are forged in the exigencies of war, the book imagines people being thrown together, developing ties of friendship and romance, being separated and reunited again and again by developments and changing circumstances. Filipino characters such as the woman warrior Juana (modeled after the Huk heroine Dayang-Dayang), the lawyer Palucha, the Huk liaison officer Juan Talata, the mestizo Custer Silis, among others, slip in and out of the novel, appearing when least expected. An element of surprise, contingency, and incalculability[60] marks all meetings, partings, and reunions, even as it haunts all military encounters. Even family members are separated without guarantees of eventual reunion.

The extent of this interaction does not only involve the sharing of information, experiences, and lives. A Filipino intimate of the Wha Chi, Alis, even begins to dream of tigers after hearing stories from the Chinese guerrillas. Friendships between Filipinos and Chinese in the novel are cemented, apart from the frequent invocation of the standard Tagalog word *kaibigan* (friend, from the root word *ibig*, "love"), by the use of two Filipino honorifics — *kasama* and *kumpadre/kumadre*. Calling each other *kasama* (literally, companion, but also comrade) puts Chinese and Filipinos in a horizontal relation of equals, while *kumpadre/kumadre* draws on the Catholic ritual of baptism to form extended kinship relations by virtue of making the Chinese a godparent to the Filipino's offspring.

This intertwining of lives cuts across state- and society-defined differences of culture and language. Where national states have tended historically to conceive of and model relations among their citizens in terms of the ideology of "the family," *Fengyu* shows that international solidarity may be modeled on ritual kinship beyond what is imagined and policed by the state.

In fact, the incapacity of the state to protect its citizens leads two lovers, Maria and Wu Qing (Puliao), to draw a parallel between the Filipinos' and Chinese people's experience of colonization and to couch this comparison in familial terms:[61]

> Maria was moved by the fact that Chinese and Filipinos did not have control over their own lives ... "This pearl [i.e., the Philippines, "Pearl of the Orient"] is not in our hands, and the fruit in our bowl has been stolen. You have come to a place in the Pacific where orphans live."
>
> Paolo's heart leaped. "We too are orphans. It is often said that the huaqiao [overseas Chinese] are orphans abroad. Our country is a great country, but it is often oppressed by others. Because our government is corrupt, nobody takes care of us."

The Wha Chi's journeys across Luzon provide as well occasions for social mapping of the local terrains, as Chinese guerrillas encounter successions of townspeoples, topographies, climates, flora and fauna, customs, and practices. Songs and stories of heroes and heroines from both countries enliven the tedium in between ambushes on Japanese forces. The Wha Chi's encounter with the Baluga results in friendships that are sealed not only by the exchange of songs, poems, and gifts, but by the blasting away of Chinese prejudice against "tribal" people and Filipino prejudice against the Chinese. Reciprocity is also evident in the Wha Chi's relations with the Huks. Wha Chi guerrillas put their Chinese experiences to good use in the service of the Huks by helping to train Filipino guerrillas and organize squadrons, and serving as model units.

At the same time, Wha Chi experiences in the Philippines make it impossible for them to simply "apply" the techniques of guerrilla training and warfare that they have learned in the course of their involvement in the resistance movement in China. The Wha Chi also learn to adapt their Chinese strategies to Filipino terrain, practices, and contingencies: they modify the rules of the Chinese Red Army to suit Philippine conditions and terrain, even as Mao's works provide inspiration for defensive tactics. The Wha Chi's nationalism is one that is open to the world: "We Wha Chi are the people's army" [*women huazhi shi renmin de jundui*],[62] and "we are with every country's people in the world" [*women she he quan shijiegeguo de renmin zai yiqi*][63] are complementary rather than contradictory principles. Reciprocity also operates in the context of war: Wha Chi arrival in Southern Luzon encourages the Huks to restore their former organizational structure instead of relying on small units following Japanese clampdown on guerrillas, even as Wha Chi aid and are aided by the Huks and other guerrilla groups when they embark on military attacks.

In sum, the Wha Chi experience memorialized by *Fengyu Taipingyang* affirms the necessity of rethinking the concept of communities, not as ideal collectivities that share a common origin or even common destiny, but as *communities of fate* "that already include difference and conflict, where heterogeneous people and groups have been 'thrown together' by history and economy, in situations where their interests or cultural ideals cannot spontaneously converge, but also cannot completely diverge without risking *mutual destruction* (or *common elimination* by external forces)" (emphasis in the original).[64] This community of fate carries with it the hope of bonding, but also the risks of betrayal and rejection, as the Wha Chi pin their survival on their faith in Filipino hospitality, at the same time that they find themselves betrayed by some of their own people and confronting Filipino "enemies." *Fengyu* records numerous instances of reciprocity but is all the same haunted by the pain of setbacks and failure. The community of fate without guarantees is like the war that engenders it, a war that occasions acts of incredible courage, munificence, and self-sacrifice, but also cruelty, cowardice, and self-interest.

China, the "Chinese Question," and the Polycentric Left

After World War II, the paths of the Wha Chi troops diverged as some left for China while others elected to remain in the Philippines. Du Ai's novel ends with some of the patriots leaving for China while others decide to stay in the Philippines to help rebuild the two countries.[65] Those among the Wha Chi patriots who left did not leave the Philippines without transforming Philippine life. They had made the Philippines the site of their self-realization as inter/nationalists and as the sphere of their own transformative activities. In so doing, they also helped to change Filipino perceptions of the Chinese. Luis Taruc in his book *Born of the People* talks about the Wha Chi guerrillas' achievements, which help to countervail the powerful Filipino stereotype of the Chinese as exploitative capitalists.[66]

The funeral procession in honor of the Wha Chi warrior Robin Chen in Manila, for example, draws 1,000 people, including Filipinos who have heard of the "48" (Kwarenta'y Otso) and who pay their respects to the dead through cries of mourning and "Thank you, Chinese friends!" The Wha Chi are hailed as "good intsik [Chinese]" (*hao yingci*) and "our own people" (*zanmen ziji de ren*) and cheered as they march through Filipino towns, stopping along the way to help townspeople capture and dispense justice to brigands and sundry collaborators.[67]

Not everything about Chinese-Philippine relations is rosy, of course, and one risks the danger of idealizing Philippine-Chinese relations forged during the war. Taruc's second book speaks of conflicts of interest between the Wha Chi and the Huks over tactics and strategies:

> When the Japanese war broke out, four of their [Chinese Communist] high-ranking officials joined us in the field. Two of them claimed to have already been given training, one in politics, the other in guerrilla warfare, on the Chinese mainland. They were attached to our Politburo as advisers and acted as liaison officers between ourselves and their own anti-Japanese resistance movement.
>
> Their advice was often resisted by Vicente Lava, who was then our general secretary, and by myself. It seemed to us that their advice was always related to Chinese mainland activities rather than Philippine interests.
>
> First they advised us to attack the Japanese relentlessly. Although we did so, we suspected that their motives were chauvinistic, that their main concern was with the battle then going on in China. It seemed to us that they viewed our struggle only as a diversionary action.
>
> When our fight resulted in a fierce Japanese counter-attack, and we suffered heavy casualties, they switched to a defensive strategy, urging us to hide our guns and return to our barrios. They sent most of the members of their own organization home to China. They called this policy "retreat for defense." But the Filipinos in the field refused to put it into action. We had great respect for the Chinese comrades. But when we realized the extent of their chauvinism and self-interest, our respect quickly diminished.[68]

Taruc's account, which castigates the Chinese Communists for being concerned only with China's affairs, overlooks the internal divisions and debates within the United Front — the uneasy strategic alliance of both Chinese conservative and progressive organizations in wartime Philippines — particularly on the heated and extremely divisive issue of the "Defensive Policy."[69] As recounted in the novel,[70] during the early years of World War II the Wha Chi uphold the United Front by creating a special commission headed by the United Front representative Liu Yiming. Liu advocates the "retreat for defense" policy and, when faced with opposition from Wha Chi leaders, threatens to dissolve the Wha Chi.

The turning point comes when the Wha Chi decide to abolish Liu's position within their organization and carry out their own strategy, in the process forming squadrons in Central and Southern Luzon as well as Manila.

In their memoirs, the Wha Chi officers Liang Shang Wan and Cai Jian Hua corroborate this account by explaining that officers of the Hua Chiao Committee, a leading organization of the Chinese United Front, used the "retreat for defense" policy as a pretext to curtail the activities and argue for the disbanding of the Wha Chi. Only one Wha Chi commander took the policy seriously, while the rest of the officers and members ignored the directive and continued fighting, as did the Huks. Liang and Cai also offer a detailed account of the day-to-day cooperation between Hukbalahap and Wha Chi guerrillas, an account that, despite its taking an "outsider" or "foreigner" position in its depiction of the anti-Japanese struggle in the Philippines, points to a number of important collaborative efforts among Chinese and Filipinos in engaging the enemy forces.[71]

The controversial "retreat for defense" policy did not only mark a crucial episode in the history of the left struggle during World War II. It would be elevated from historical episode to element of theoretical critique that indexed the deepening divisions within the Filipino Communist movement after the war. The "retreat for defense" policy was one of the main issues used by the breakaway Communist Party of the Philippines (CPP) to criticize PKP "errors and weaknesses."

In the document "Brief Review of the History of the Communist Party of the Philippines: On the Occasion of the 20th Anniversary of its Reestablishment," the CPP leader Amado Guerrero repeats the critique thus:

> There was no clear program of anti-imperialist and antifeudal struggle going beyond the antifascist struggle against Japan and no plan to expand the revolutionary forces beyond Manila and Central Luzon. The line of the people's struggle was narrowed to armed resistance against the Japanese occupation forces and their Filipino collaborators.
>
> Even with regards to armed struggle, the leadership of the merger party with Vicente Lava as general secretary adopted the line of "retreat for defense," a policy of reducing guerrilla units into impotent teams of three to five persons and avoiding armed combat with the enemy. This line was proclaimed after the Japanese fascist troops attacked the main base of the Hukbalahap at the foot of a small vulnerable mountain, Mount Arayat in the middle of the Central Luzon plains.

> However, the people's army made significant strides in armed struggle mainly because several platoon-size and company-size units disregarded the policy and spontaneously fought the enemy; and because finally in September 1944 a Party conference declared the "retreat for defense" policy erroneous. But soon after, the US military forces landed to re-occupy the Philippines and arm their puppets.[72]

PKP General Secretary Jesus Lava's version puts it this way:

> It was only late in the 1960s, when the Maoist Chinese Communist Party decided to organize and field its own Maoist Party in the Philippines under the leadership of Joe [Jose Maria] Sison, that the matter was revived with much fanfare and venom to maliciously discredit the PKP, its leaders and its whole history of struggle and sacrifice, but conveniently without any mention of the key role in policy formulation played by the Chinese Maoists themselves.[73]

Lava alleges that conversations with those involved, especially Casto Alejandrino, revealed that, in fact, the policy had first been suggested by a Chinese comrade. Though not put into practice even after it reached lower organs, the policy was judged to be erroneous by the Central Committee in September 1944. Vicente Lava was replaced by a troika that actually included the Chinese member who had originally been involved in the formulation of the policy.[74]

Lava's account reveals the extent to which the acrimonious nature of PKP-CPP relations was informed by the Sino-Soviet split in the mid-1960s, as other Communist parties all over the world found themselves under pressure to "choose" which country they would side with. With Communism now devolving into a "polycentric" movement,[75] internal tensions within the Philippine left resulted in the "re-establishment" of the Communist Party of the Philippines in the late 1960s. Part of the tensions and divisions within the Philippine left at the time came to be articulated with the question of China. The "growing dissidence of the pro-Chinese faction resurrected fears among the old Party leadership of the Chinese Communist Party's interference in the Philippine left's internal affairs."[76] This can be gleaned from a series of charges and countercharges aired in Party publications, with the PKP accusing the CPP of being "local-bred parrots of Peking."[77] PKP articles denounced "Maoist splittism"[78] for sowing "imperialist-inspired disunity"[79] within the international socialist movement and seeking to isolate the USSR and establish "Maoist Chinese hegemony."[80]

Branding "China" as an external, alien power with the capacity to intervene in Philippine politics not only provided the PKP with a potent ideological weapon for delegitimizing the Maoist faction, it also raised the thorny issue of assimilation of the Chinese in the Philippines. Declaring that the great majority of the Filipino-Chinese community "belong to the working and petty-bourgeois classes, with the bulk of the assimilated Filipino-Chinese being service workers, artisans and small shopkeepers," the PKP Eighth Congress then went on to raise the spectre of ascendant, unassimilated Chinese "big bourgeoisie," even after the state embarked on its program of mass naturalization in 1975.[81] Charged with remitting their profits overseas (by implication to their "homeland"), these affluent Filipino-Chinese groups are seen as having "close affiliations" among themselves and an "exclusivist culture," promoted by "allegedly Filipinized Chinese schools."

In creating a schema that correlates assimilation with class belonging, so that working-class and petty-bourgeois "Chinese" were assumed to have assimilated while the rich "Chinese" were not, the PKP — like the nationalist elites and the Cold-War-era Philippine state — ends up re-affirming a necessary link between ethnicity and class: to be Chinese *is* to be rich, and to be rich is to remain "Chinese." The language of the PKP's solution to the Chinese Question mirrors that of the state's, right down to the use of the term "integration":

> The inordinate hold of the Filipino-Chinese bourgeoisie on the economy has therefore become a real problem but it is not the primary one. In the overall struggle of the Filipino people against imperialism, the Filipino-Chinese community can still play a positive role, provided they are integrated into Philippine society and recognize the primacy of national interest. Integration, however, can only result from a long process which begins with the realization that the Filipino-Chinese have a real stake in the overall progress of their country of residence and should cease cultivating feelings of loyalty to China or Taiwan.[82]

The Maoist faction's orientation to Red China, which was easily discernible in its founding documents and organizational tactics and strategies,[83] meant that the new Communist Party of the Philippines could not remain uncontaminated by its associations (in both material and ideological senses) with a "China" in the throes of the Cultural Revolution.

Reacting defensively to the spectre of the "alienness" of Maoist ("Chinese") thought raised by the PKP, "nat-dems [national democrats], unlike their Maoist counterparts in Western countries have consistently refused the label 'Maoist', arguing that it connotes allegiance to an alien, hence sinister ideology"; to be "Maoist" was to be "subservient to a foreign power."[84] Armando Malay argues that the "objective tension thus created between the desire to assuage local Sinophobic sentiments and the simultaneous necessity of establishing Marxist-Leninist legitimacy, for domestic and international consumption, was partially resolved in favor of selective de-Maoization."[85] As part of the effort to Filipinize Maoism, the 1974 party document "Specific Characteristic of Our People's War" sought to identify the specificity of the Philippine context of struggle (for instance, the formation of mobile guerrilla bases and the "centralized leadership, decentralized operations" strategy in keeping with the country's archipelagic and mountainous geography), even though the overall strategy adopted was not "substantially different from the 'protracted people's war'" formulated by Mao Zedong.[86]

Despite this ambivalence toward the Chinese "foreign," the CPP has made efforts to address the issue of anti-Sinicism. Amado Guerrero's *Philippine Society and Revolution*,[87] a key text of the Party, provides a scathing account of "Malay racism bred by foreign and feudal exploiters of the people" and directed against "the Chinese and the Aetas."[88] He criticizes the Magsaysay and Garcia administrations for resorting to "the old colonial and chauvinist trick of attacking Chinese retailers" while "mak[ing] it difficult and expensive for foreign nationals of Chinese descent to become Filipino citizens."[89] At the same time, Guerrero has pointed out how economic legislation against Chinese retailers actually was politically motivated:

> Though the Garcia puppet regime was conspicuously encouraging Filipino merchants to push out merchants of Chinese nationality from the retail business, especially in the rice and corn trade, it allowed the big Kuomintang compradors to have a big share in the import-export and wholesale business and to bring their capital to Taiwan. All Chinese residents in the Philippines were coerced to manifest their allegiance to the Chiang bandit gang or else face reprisal.[90]

The CPP's "Programme for a People's Democratic Revolution in the Philippines"[91] advocates a "class approach" in dealing with naturalized Filipinos and foreign nationals in order to "do away with 'Malay' racism and chauvinism":[92]

> Residents or citizens of Chinese ancestry are very often the target of racist and chauvinist attacks launched by US imperialists, modern revisionists, and other local reactionaries in line with their anti-China,

> anti-communist and anti-people policy. The Kuomintang comprador bourgeoisie should be thoroughly exposed and attacked for its class position and for the fact that it is an accomplice of U.S. imperialism, modern revisionism and all reactionaries.[93]

The Chinese are discussed in a separate section but in juxtaposition with "national minorities" such as the Aetas: both are subject to the racism and discriminatory policies of the state. Moreover, Guerrero gestures toward the implication of the "Chinese Question" in the anti-Communist policies of the government during the 1950s and 1960s. In Guerrero's denunciation of the "big Kuomintang compradors," he is careful not to racialize the compradors as "Chinese." These compradors are, instead, *political* collaborators who benefited from the anti-Chinese legislation of the Magsaysay and Garcia administrations.

The breakaway movement's attempt in the early 1970s to disentangle Chinese ethnic identification with money and citizenship opened up the possibility of reformulating the articulation between nationalism and Communism along non-racist lines. But the CPP's stance on the ethnic Chinese quickly lost its radical edge owing to the state's own changing policies on Chinese integration after 1975. As splits within the CPP in the early 1990s further reinforced the polycentrism of the Philippine left, different splinter groups sought to propound an inclusive framework for thinking about the "Chinese Question," as seen in public statements released by different leftist organizations concerning the kidnapping of Philippine Chinese and the 1998 anti-Chinese riots in Indonesia. Within mainstream politics, left organizations actively courted ethnic-Chinese support for their respective political platforms and projects. The "national-democratic" organization Bayan Muna placed an ad in the *Chinese Commercial News* during the 2001 party-list electoral campaign seeking Chinese "solidarity with us in our struggle" and citing "kababayang Tsinoy" contributions to the economic development of "our country" and the great sacrifices of "Filipino-Chinese brothers who fought hand-in-hand with other patriotic Pinoys to resist Japanese invasion."[94]

Philippine Marxism's dialogue with anti-colonial nationalism has involved grappling with exclusivist nationalist constructions — not all of them emanating only from the state — of the "Chinese" as aliens, as alienating capital, and as alien revolutionaries located outside the bounds of the national-popular community. Although one of the Communist parties has explicitly repudiated anti-Chinese racism in its key document, the contested presence and role of "China" and the "Chinese" in the Philippine revolutionary movement nevertheless illuminates core tensions that underlie the intellectual and organizational divisions within the Philippine left.

Not surprisingly, the recuperation of the Wha Chi guerrillas by both the Philippine state and the Philippine left has meant downplaying the multiple identifications claimed by the guerrillas in favor of a nation-centered narrative of "Chinese" contribution to the Filipino struggle against Japanese imperialism. The continuing vulnerability of the Philippine Chinese to criminal prosecution on charges of subversion has contributed in no small measure to the absence of explicit references to Communism: the characters in the novel are avowedly nationalist while being at pains to deny that they are also Communists, notwithstanding their stated sympathy for Russia and their obvious acquaintance with and citation of Mao Zedong's writings. This downplaying of popular nationalism's articulation (however fraught) with internationalist Communism may also have something to do with the fact that Du Ai began working on his novel less than a year after the revolutionary regimes of China and Vietnam confronted each other over Cambodia and only two years after Deng Xiaoping initiated the reforms that put China on the path of "socialism with Chinese characteristics." By the time the novel was published in the mid-1980s, socialist revolution had come to be defined primarily through its excesses (i.e., the Cultural Revolution) and its "modification" along capitalist lines.

The Wha Chi's multiply identified nationalism/revolutionary cosmopolitanism was rooted in the anti-colonial and anti-imperialist struggle of World War II in which Japan was defined as an "external enemy." This inter/nationalism is not a permanent condition, nor even a stable or easily realized one, because it arises only within a context of political action enabled by a particular (and unique) confluence of historical and political contexts. Rapidly changing regional geopolitics after World War II have rendered this form of dual nationalism/revolutionary cosmopolitanism especially vulnerable to erasure by time and forgetfulness of the people on whose behalf the dual-nationalist revolutionaries undertook political action and made self-sacrifices. The Wha Chi experience highlights the translingual practices (to use a term by Lydia Liu) and political projects that enabled both Chinese and Filipino inter/nationalisms to be shaped in part by their mutual (though also fraught) co-implication,[95] and testifies to the fact that nationalism and revolutionary cosmopolitanism in this region, from their inception, were mediated by a "translated modernity" grounded in contacts not just between "Asia" and the "West," but *within*

"Asia" (for instance, in Japanese mediation of "Chinese" modernity through translation of Western concepts) and *between* "Asia" and the "non-West." But the ways in which these translingual and political projects are remembered, or perhaps forgotten, are shaped by a highly contingent politics of memory that may endow these projects with meanings and significance beyond the stated intentions of those who undertook these projects.

Revolutionary cosmopolitanism shows that the making (and re-making) of national communities depends, in fact, on a historically situated, constitutive experience of the "outside" and of "foreignness," a potentially radical openness to the foreign other that is often ignored, if not repressed by the assertion of unnecessarily monolithic and exclusionary national identities. It highlights the fact that nationalism is not always or necessarily about boundedness, exclusivity, rivalry, and enmity, but that it possesses the capacity for openness, linkages, dialogue, bridges, networks, mutuality, reciprocity, complementarity, and friendship. As the *huaqiao* nationalists and their Filipino friends and comrades shared their languages and experiences, sufferings and dreams, as well as freely and selflessly exchanged their gifts of love, life, and sacrifice, we witness their two national imaginings flow together, mixing and merging into one, and when they diverge, each one already carrying traces of the other.[96]

Notes

This chapter is dedicated to the memory of Lin Bin, who generously shared her insights and writings with me over the years. I thank Liu Hong, Tesa Encarnacion Tadem, and the staff of the Third World Studies Center of the University of the Philippines for their invaluable help in obtaining some of the materials for this chapter; and Hau Chiok and Sy Chiu Hua, as well as Jojo Abinales, Kasian Tejapira, and Shiraishi Takashi for their support and encouragement. The errors in this chapter are my sole responsibility.

1 Wha Chi, the historical spelling adopted by the group in the Philippines, is also known by other spelling variants such as Wah Chi and Hua Chi.

2 For a discussion of the difficulties faced by scholars in constructing reliable accounts of the Chinese (as well as Filipino) resistance movement during the Japanese Occupation, see Yuk-wai Yung Li, *The Huaqiao Warriors: Chinese Resistance Movement in the Philippines 1942–1945* (Quezon City: Ateneo de Manila University Press, 1996), pp. 75–8, 115–6.

3 Benedict J. Kerkvliet, *The Huk Rebellion: A Study of Peasant Revolt in the Philippines* (Quezon City: New Day Publishers, 1979).

4 See Gregg R. Jones, *Red Revolution: Inside the Philippine Guerrilla Movement* (Boulder, CO: Westview Press, 1989). The Huk veteran Cesar Lacara (also

known as Tatang) in his memoirs provides a personal account of Huk co-operation with the Wha Chi when, during the last days of the war, the Chinese forces were sent to Manila to help liberate the city. Lacara's memoirs include a picture of the Wha Chi troops among the gallery of prominent freedom fighters of the left in the Philippines. See Cesar Hernandez Lacara (Tatang), *Sa Tungki ng Ilong ng Kaaway: Talambuhay ni Tatang* [On the Tip of the Enemy's Nose: Autobiography of Tatang] (Metro Manila: Kilusan ng Paglilinang ng Rebolusyonaryong Panitikan at Sining sa Kanayunan [LINANG], 1988).

5 This chapter covers only the role played by the Chinese in the leftist revolutionary movement. For an account of the Chinese contribution to the Philippine revolution of 1896, see Teresita Ang See and Go Bon Juan, *The Ethnic Chinese in the Philippine Revolution* (Manila: Kaisa para sa Kaunlaran, 1996). Further research also needs to be undertaken to extend the account provided by this chapter to cover the political role of the ethnic Chinese in the anti-Marcos, EDSA (Epifanio delos Santos) "People Power," and post-EDSA social movements.

6 Laborers constituted 11.6 per cent of all Chinese in 1903 and worked in the garment, furniture, lumber, laundry, restaurant, sugar, printing, shoe, bakery, paper, construction, and other industries. Small-scale shopkeepers, teachers, clerks, and store employees were also involved in labor-organizing. See Wong Kwok-Chu, *The Chinese in the Philippine Economy 1891–1941* (Quezon City: Ateneo de Manila University Press, 1999), p. 73.

7 The earliest labor union was the Overseas Chinese Labor Party (Huaqiao Gongdang), which counted clerks, teachers, and shopkeepers among its members and published a newspaper, the *Common People's Daily* (*Pingmin Ribao*), from 1919 to 1922, but was not known to have any connection with the Chinese Communist Party (Yung Li, *Huaqiao Warriors*, p. 60).

8 Unless otherwise indicated, the following details are culled from Xu Chengjian, Xu Chengyan, and Xu Chengliang, "Shenqie huanian jingai de fuqin Xu Li (Xu Jingcheng)" [Cherishing Profoundly the Memory of Our Beloved Father Xu Li (Xu Jingcheng)], in *Feilubin huaqiao kangri aiguo yinghun* [Philippine Chinese Martyrs of the Anti-Japanese Resistance], ed. Gong Taoyi (Beijing: Huawen Chubanshe, 2001), pp. 6–13.

9 There is no direct evidence to suggest that the central leadership of the Chinese Communist Party had a systematic program for promoting organizational work in the Philippines, but the argument that Chinese Communist elements in the Philippines were basically "uncoordinated actions of individuals to seek refuge abroad" (see Yung Li, *Huaqiao Warriors*, p. 65) may not strictly apply to all initiatives either.

10 The Partido Komunista ng Pilipinas' official history (*Communism in the Philippines: The PKP*, vol. 1) (Quezon City: Historical Commission, Partido Komunista ng Pilipinas, 1996, pp. 93–4) records the formation in 1926 of the Manila nucleus of the Young Communist League (YCL) of the Communist

Party of China led by a Co Sing Liat, who would later be a member of the Central Committee of the PKP. The biographical account of Xu Jingcheng by his sons (see Xu *et al.* in Gong, *Feilubin huaqiao kangri aiguo yinghun*, p. 6), however, states that Xu (Ko Keng Seng) was the head of the YCL Manila branch. Are Co Sing Liat and Ko Keng Seng the same person?

11 Partido Komunista ng Pilipinas, *Communism in the Philippines*, pp. 93–4.

12 Ibid., pp. 114–5.

13 Ibid., p. 93.

14 Ibid., p. 94.

15 Ibid., pp. 99, 102.

16 Ibid., p. 125.

17 Probably Li Bingxiang.

18 Partido Komunista ng Pilipinas, *Communism in the Philippines*, p. 291.

19 Yung Li, *Huaqiao Warriors*, p. 79.

20 "By March 1930, the PCLF had a membership of around 1,500 workers in 12 unions, plus 200 more in a Chinese Young Workers' Club which included calisthenics, drama, singing and other Chinese cultural groups. By March 1930 also, the Chinese YCL [Young Communist League] in the Philippines had 80 members, of whom 30 were industrial workers, 30 were handicraft workers, 10 were shopkeepers, and 10 were farmers. Of this total Chinese YCL membership, around 60 subsequently became members of the Partido Komunista ng Pilipinas [although they maintained separate all-Chinese nuclei], while 20 others remained as members of the Chinese YCL branch in the Philippines, which was directly under the YCL in mainland China" (Partido Komunista ng Pilipinas, pp. 114–5). See also Yung Li, *Huaqiao Warriors*, pp. 79–81.

21 The Wha Chi leaders are credited with having suggested the name "Hukbo ng Bayan Laban sa Hapon." The Huk leader Luis Taruc had initially favored the name "Philippine Army of Liberation." Antonio S. Tan, *The Chinese in the Philippines during the Japanese Occupation 1942–1945* (Quezon City: University of the Philippines Press for the Asian Center, 1981), p. 125.

22 Khin Khin Myint Jensen, "The Chinese in the Philippines during the American Regime: 1898–1946," PhD dissertation, University of Wisconsin, 1956, p. 284.

23 See Wha Chi, *The Souvenir Issue of the 40th Anniversary of the Philippine Chinese Anti-Japanese Guerrilla Forces* (Manila: Wha Chi, 1982); Liang Shangwan and Cai Jianhua, *Huaqiao kangri zhidui* [Overseas Chinese Anti-Japanese Troops] (Hong Kong: Guangjiaojing Chubanshe, 1980); Liang Shangwan and Cai Jianhua, *Huazhi huiyilu: Ji Feilubin huaqiao kangri youji zhidui* [Remembering the Huazhi: On Philippine-Chinese Anti-Japanese Resistance Troops] (Hong Kong: All Directions Publishing, 1996); Liang Shangwan and Cai Jianhua, *The Wha Chi Memoirs*, trans. Joaquin Sy (Manila: Kaisa para sa Kaunlaran, 1998); Tan, *Chinese in the Philippines during the Japanese Occupation*, pp. 116–27; Yung Li, *Huaqiao Warriors*, pp. 75–114;

Gong Taoyi, ed., *Feilubin huaqiao kangri aiguo yinghun*, and *Feilubin huaqiao guiqiao aiguo danxinlu* [Philippine-Chinese Returnee Patriots] (Beijing: Huawen Chubanshe, 2002).

24 The criminalization of the left may account for the fact that despite their obvious leftist leanings, the characters in *Fengyu Taipingyang*, the novel discussed in this essay, are at pains to deny that they are Communists, notwithstanding their stated sympathy for Russia and their obvious acquaintance with and citation of Mao Zedong's works!

25 I quote Maximo Nocete, a Filipino major writing in 1945 about the Wha Chi, cited in Liang and Cai, *The Wha Chi Memoirs*, p. 105.

26 Theresa Chong Cariño, *China and the Overseas Chinese in Southeast Asia* (Quezon City: New Day Publishers, 1985), p. 44.

27 Liang and Cai, *Huazhi huiyilu*, p. 76, and *Wha Chi Memoirs*, p. 98.

28 Liang and Cai, *Huazhi huiyilu*, p. 76, and *Wha Chi Memoirs*, p. 99.

29 Liang and Cai, *Huazhi huiyilu*, p. 81.

30 Susan Bayly, "Vietnamese Narratives of Tradition, Exchange and Friendship in the Worlds of the Global Socialist Ecumene," in *Enduring Socialism: Explorations of Revolution and Transformation, Restoration and Continuation*, ed. Harry G. West and Parvathi Raman (Oxford, UK: Berghahn Books, 2008), pp. 145–7; and *Asian Voices in a Postcolonial Age: Vietnam, India and Beyond* (Cambridge: Cambridge University Press).

31 This point is elaborated theoretically in Pheng Cheah, "Chinese Cosmopolitanism in Two Senses and Postcolonial National Memory," in *Cosmopolitan Geographies: New Locations in Literature and Culture*, ed. Vinay Dharwadker (New York: Routledge, 2001), pp. 133–69. See also Kwame Anthony Appiah, K.A., "Cosmopolitan Patriots," in *Cosmopolitics: Thinking and Feeling Beyond the Nation*, ed. Pheng Cheah and Bruce Robbins (Minneapolis and London: University of Minnesota Press, 1998), pp. 91–114. For Chinese theorizing of the relationship between Marxism-Leninism and the national question, see Liu Shiaoqi, "Conclusion," in Liu, *Internationalism and Nationalism* (Beijing: Foreign Languages Press, 1952), <http://www.marxists.org/reference/archive/liu-shaoqi/1952/internationalism_nationalism/index.htm>. Liu quotes Mao Zedong as stating that patriotism is not only intimately connected with internationalism, but represents "the application of internationalism in the national revolutionary war."

32 Wang Gungwu, *Community and Nation: China, Southeast Asia and Australia* (New South Wales: Asian Studies Association of Australia, and Allen and Unwin, 1992), p. 54.

33 The current scholarly framing of the nationalism vs. cosmopolitanism debate is forcefully critiqued in Pheng Cheah's "Introduction," in *Cosmopolitics: Thinking and Feeling beyond the Nation*, ed. Cheah and Bruce Robbins (Minneapolis: University of Minnesota Press, 1998). Huynh Kim Khanh has argued in favor of viewing Vietnamese Communism as a fusion of anti-

imperialist patriotism (as opposed to elite-sponsored nationalism) and internationalist Communism in his *Vietnamese Communism 1925–1945* (Ithaca: Cornell University Press, 1982).

34 Bonnie Honig, *Democracy and the Foreigner* (Princeton: Princeton University Press, 2001), p. 80.

35 Du Ai, *Fengyu Taipingyang* [Storm over the Pacific], vol. 1 (Guangzhou: Huacheng Chubanshe, 1985); *Fengyu Taipingyang*, vol. 2 (Guangzhou: Huacheng Chubanshe, 1988), with a Beijing edition published in 1991 by Wenhua Yishu Chubanshe; *Fengyu Taipingyang*, 3 vols. (Zhuhai, Guangdong: Zhuhai Chubanshe, 2002). In this essay, I will rely on the 1985 edition of vol. 1, the 1988 edition of vol. 2, and the 2002 edition of vol. 3. The 2002 edition reprinted the 1985 edition in its entirety, but cut and spliced some parts of vol. 2 and many chapters of vol. 3. See note 37.

36 Caroline S. Hau, "The Question of Foreigners: Bai Ren's *Nanyang Piaoliuji* and the Re/making of Chinese and Philippine Nationness," in *Southeast Asia over Three Generations: Essays Presented to Benedict R. O'Gorman Anderson*, ed. James T. Siegel and Audrey R. Kahin (Ithaca: Southeast Asia Program, Cornell University, 2003), pp. 189–222.

37 The following biographical information is culled from the author's note in *Fengyu Taipingyang*, 2002 edition; Du Ai, "Wo de chuangzuo licheng" [My Creative Path], in *Du Ai Zixuanji* [Du Ai: Selected Works] (Zhuhai: Huacheng Chubanshe, 1982), pp. 1–16; Du Ai, biographical entry, *Guangdong dangdai zuojia zhuanlie* [Biography of Contemporary Guangdong Writers] (Guangzhou: Zhongshan University Press, n.d.), pp. 70–1; and an interview with Du Ai's widow, Lin Bin, in Guangzhou, Guangdong province, People's Republic of China, 30 Sept. 2001. More information about Lin Bin can be found in an interview published in *Shijie Ribao*. See Hu Yaohua, "Yi dangnian, kangriqing yibihaishen: Fang guiqiao nüzuojia Lin Bin" [Remembering the Past, Comradeship in the Anti-Japanese Resistance Is Deeper than the Ocean: Interview with Lin Bin], *Shijie Ribao* [World News, Philippines], 14 July 1995, p. 11. See also "Keji xiandai zhuming zuojia Du Ai" [The Celebrated Hakka Writer Du Ai], in *Kejia wenhua shuju ku* [Digital Treasury of Hakka Culture], 21 Apr. 2008, <http://sglyj.meizhou.gov.cn/modules/data/article.php?storyid=289> [accessed 22 June 2008].

38 Hu, "Yi dangnian, kangriqing yibihaishen: Fang guiqiao nüzuojia Lin Bin."

39 See, for example, Lin Bin, "Zhongguo xinwenxue heshi zoujin Feilubin de jikao" [When Did China's New Literature Enter the Philippines? An Examination], *Shijie Ribao* [World News, Philippines], 17 Feb. 2001, p. 15, and "'Daoguo jiqing' Houji: Feihua xiaoshuo sanwen xuanxu" [Memories of the Archipelago: Preface to *Selections from Philippine-Chinese Novels and Essays*], *Shijie Ribao*, 13 May 2001, p. 15. For discussions of Lin Bin's place in Philippine-Chinese literature, see Jiang Hua, "Kangzhan shiqi de Feihua wenxue (Part 1)" [Philippine-Chinese Literature during the Wartime],

Shang Bao [Chinese Commercial News], 7 Jan. 2001, p. 11, and "Kangzhan shiqi de Feihua wenxue (Part 2)" [Philippine-Chinese Literature during the Wartime], *Shang Bao*, 8 July 2002, p. 7. Evidence suggests that Du Ai may have contracted a first marriage in China before he met Lin Bin.

40 In his preface (Du 1985, vol. 1), Du states that the idea of writing *Fengyu Taipingyang* had already occurred to him in the 1950s, but he only began working on the novel on 1 May 1980.

41 *Fengyu* was also serialized in the Philippine dailies *Shijie Ribao* (vols. 1 and 3) and *Shang Bao* (vol. 2). Lin Bin expressed dissatisfaction with the publisher's extensive editing (and cutting) of chapters in vol. 3 of the 2002 edition of *Fengyu* and planned to republish the novel in its entirety at some point in the future.

42 See Lin Bin's afterword in Du, *Fengyu Taipingyang*, 2002 edition, vol. 3, p. 1217.

43 The 1985 edition (vol. 1) contains 400,000 words and the 1988 edition (vol. 2) 240,000 words. The 2002 combined edition puts the total at 960,000 words. A Beijing edition of vol. 2, published in 1991 by Wenhua Yishu Chubanshe, contains 251,000 words.

44 For a critical evaluation of Du Ai's place in Chinese arts and letters, see Huang Weizong, "Lun minzu wenhua de jianrongxing ji qidianxing zuojia: Du Ai" [On the Synthesis of National Culture and Its Representative Writers: Du Ai], n.d., photocopied manuscript; and Yang Yi, "Du Ai zai Zhongguo xiandai xiaoshuo shishang de diwei" [Du Ai's Place in the History of the Contemporary Novel], n.d., photocopied manuscript.

For literary analyses of *Fengyu*, see Sun Ailing, *Lun guiqiao zuojia xiaoshuo* [On the Novels of Overseas Chinese Returnees] (Singapore: Xinjiapo Yunnan Yuanyashe, 1996), pp. 267–86, 359–62; He Chuxiong, "Daqibangbo de ZhongFei renmin zhantou qingyi de songge: Du *Fengyu Taipingyang* yi, erbu" [An Epic of Chinese-Philippine Comradeship: Reading *Fengyu Taipingyang*, vols. 1 and 2], n.d., photocopied manuscript; He Chuxiong, "ZhongFei renmin bingjian kangjiriben qinlüezhe de shishixing yingxiong lezhang: Ping sanjuanben changpian xiaoshuo *Fengyu Taipingyang* (Part 1)" [Epic of Chinese and Filipino Heroes Struggling against the Japanese Invaders: Critique of the Three Volumes of the Novel *Fengyu Taipingyang* (Part 1)], *Shijie Ribao*, 2 July 2002, p. 21, and "ZhongFei renmin Bingjian kangjiriben qinluezhe de shishixing yingxiong lezhang: Ping sanjuanben changpian xiaoshuo *Fengyu Taipingyang* (Part 2)" [Epic of Chinese and Filipino Heroes Struggling against the Japanese Invaders: Critique of the Three Volumes of the Novel *Fengyu Taipingyang* (Part 2)], *Shijie Ribao*, 4 July 2002, p. 21. See also Li Zhiyuan, "Gaoge fanfa xisi de shenglijin xingqu: Lun *Fengyu Taipingyang* de nüxing yingxiong qunxiang suzao" [In Praise of the Anti-Fascist Victory Anthem: On the Portrayal of the Heroines of *Fengyu Taipingyang*], n.d., photocopied manuscript, pp. 130–8.

45 Mao Dun, "Preface to *Lusong Pingyuan*," in Du Ai, *Zai Lusong Pingyuan* [On the Plains of Luzon] (Hong Kong: Renjianshuwu, 1949), pp. 1–2.

46 For an account of Du Ai's career as a journalist, see Lin Bin, "Laobaoren Du Ai (Part 1)" [Du Ai the Veteran Journalist], *Shijie Ribao*, 4 Aug. 2001, p. 21, and "Laobaoren Du Ai (Part 2)" [Du Ai the Veteran Journalist], *Shijie Ribao*, 7 Aug. 2001, p. 21. Du Ai had worked under Mao Dun in Hong Kong, where the latter was editor-in-chief of the journal *Yuanlin*. See Lin Bin, "Kangri zhanzheng shiqi de Feihua wenxue wenhua huodong" [Philippine-Chinese Literary and Cultural Activities during the Sino-Japanese War], *Shijie Ribao*, 22 May 2001, p. 21.

47 Mao Dun, "Preface," p. 1; also cited in Zhuang Zhongqing, "Mao Dun yu biaoxian Nanyang shehui de wenxue" [Mao Dun and the Literary Depiction of Nanyang Society], *Xiamen Ribao*, 2 May 2001, p. 7.

48 Yang Yi, "Du Ai zai Zhongguo xiandai xiaoshuo shishang de diwei."

49 Scholarship on South China has generally acknowledged that cultural distinctions between Han and non-Han peoples (such as the Yao) are far from simple. See David Faure, "The Lineage as Cultural Invention: The Case of the Pearl River Delta," *Modern China* 15 (1989): 4–36.

50 Yang Yi, "Du Ai zai Zhongguo xiandai xiaoshuo shishang de diwei," p. 167. Yang Yi's "forest and seas" characterization of Huanan writing resonates with Anthony Reid's theorizing of Southeast Asia in geo-climatic terms in his magisterial *Southeast Asia in the Age of Commerce, 1450–1680, vol. 1: The Lands below the Winds* (New Haven: Yale University Press, 1990), pp. 1–10.

51 Unless rendered in pinyin, the romanized names of the characters are based on transliterations provided by Lin Bin (personal communication, 23 Feb. 2005).

52 See author's notes in Liang and Cai, *Wha Chi Memoirs*; and Tan, *Chinese in the Philippines during the Japanese Occupation*, p. 121.

53 See Li Lijun, "Wo de fuqin Li Binxiang (Li Yongxiao) de yisheng" [My Father, Li Binxiang (Li Yongxiao)], in *Feilubin huaqiao kangri aiguo yinghun*, ed. Gong Taoyi, pp. 14–9; see also Tan's account, originally from *Chinese in the Philippines during the Japanese Occupation*, excerpted in Liang and Cai, *Wha Chi Memoirs*, p. 116.

54 Lennard J. Davis, *Factual Fictions: The Origins of the English Novel* (New York: Columbia University Press, 1983).

55 Li Zhiyuan, "Gaoge fanfa xisi de shenglijin xingqu: Lun *Fengyu Taipingyang* de nüxing yingxiong qunxiang suzao."

56 Du, *Fengyu Taipingyang*, vol. 2 (1988), p. 871.

57 Ibid., p. 886.

58 Du, *Fengyu Taipingyang*, vol. 1 (1985), p. 204.

59 Ibid., p. 23.

60 Recalling Jacques Derrida, *The Politics of Friendship*, trans. George Collins (London: Verso, 1997).

61 Du, *Fengyu Taipingyang*, vol. 1 (1985), p. 264.

62 Du, *Fengyu Taipingyang*, vol. 3 (2002), p. 1089.

63 Ibid., p. 1100.

64 Etienne Balibar, *We, the People of Europe? Reflections on Transnational Citizenship*, trans. James Swenson (Princeton: Princeton University Press, 2004), p. 132, citing Herman R. van Gunsteren, *A Theory of Citizenship: Organizing Plurality in Contemporary Democracies* (Boulder, CO: Westview Press, 1998).

65 Du, *Fengyu Taipingyang*, vol. 3 (2002), p. 1201.

66 Luis Taruc, *Born of the People* (New York: International Publishers, 1953), p. 76.

67 Du, *Fengyu Taipingyang*, vol. 3 (2002), chapter 119.

68 Luis Taruc, *He Who Rides the Tiger: The Story of an Asian Guerrilla Leader* (New York: Praeger, 1967), pp. 33–4.

69 See Liang and Cai, *Huazhi huiyilu*, pp. 28–9, and *Wha Chi Memoirs*, pp. 37–8.

70 See chapters 89 and 94 of Du, *Fengyu Taipingyang*, vol. 3 (2002), pp. 907–9, 966–7.

71 Liang and Cai, *Huazhi huiyilu*, pp. 10–3.

72 Amado Guerrero, "Brief Review of the History of the Communist Party of the Philippines: On the Occasion of the 20th Anniversary of Its Reestablishment" (26 Dec. 1988).

73 Jose B. Lava, *Memoirs of a Communist* (Manila: Anvil, 2002), p. 64.

74 Ibid.

75 Peter Worsley, *Marx and Marxism*, rev. ed. (London: Routledge, 2002), p. 4.

76 Armando Malay, Jr., "Some Random Reflections on Marxism and Maoism in the Philippines," *Marxism in the Philippines: Marx Centennial Lectures* (Quezon City: Third World Studies Center, University of the Philippines, 1984), pp. 45–93, esp. 59. Lava's memoirs recount the visit to the Huk camp in 1950 of a representative from the Chinese Bureau, and suggest that tensions between Philippine and Chinese comrades during the war may have been partly fueled by personality clashes: "Our conversation was fruitful, conducted in an atmosphere of friendship. There was no arrogance on the part of the Chinese Bureau representative. Compared to early representatives during the Japanese occupation, this one was unassuming humble and soft-spoken" (Lava, *Memoirs of a Communist*, pp. 169–70). Owing to intense governmental repression, the Huks lost contact with the Chinese for some years. Lava also hints at the rift between the PKP and the "Maoist Chinese Party" in the early years of the Sino-Soviet split over the question of the Chinese Bureau's autonomy and right of say in Philippine affairs: "Perhaps the Maoist Chinese Party did not appreciate our position that the Chinese Bureau in the Philippines should be under the jurisdiction of the Philippine party. Perhaps the Chinese comrades also resented our decision to accept the Chinese Bureau's inclusion into the overseas Chinese committee on condition

that it did not interfere with purely internal problems of Filipinos" (Lava, *Memoirs of a Communist*, p. 322).

77 "Ping Pong Diplomacy," *Ang Komunista* [The Communist] 2, 4 (21 July 1971): 1.

78 "Why the Maoists Lost in 'Liberated Diliman,'" *Siklab* [Blaze], 23 Aug. 1971, p. 2.

79 "Imperialist Uses of the Sino-Soviet Dispute," *Political Review* 1, 1 (Mar. 1971): 6.

80 "Ping Pong Diplomacy," p. 1, and "Issues in the Ideological Dispute between Maoism and the International Communist Movement," *Ang Komunista* [The Communist] 3, 1 (Jan. 1972): 4. Lava argues that the PKP was "neither anti-Chinese nor pro-Soviet" and "not beholden to and certainly not under instructions from any foreign party." In the early years of the split, "due to meager knowledge of real cause of Soviet-Chinese conflict," the PKP was "inclined to take more positions on various issues that coincided with Chinese side ... Perhaps we felt some kind of kinship with the underdeveloped Chinese nation. Indeed, we were influenced by some Maoist perspectives on Marxism-Leninism." Lava, *Memoirs of a Communist*, p. 322.

81 Partido Komunista ng Pilipinas, Eighth Congress, 1980, pp. 20–3.

82 Ibid., p. 23.

83 The most obvious manifestation of this orientation was the keen demand among activists for "Red East" commodities such as Mao's Red Book and Red Army caps.

84 Malay, p. 50.

85 Ibid.

86 Ibid., p. 51.

87 Amado Guerrero, *Philippine Society and Revolution* (Oakland, CA: International Society of Filipino Patriots, 1979), pp. 3, 41, 154–5.

88 Ibid., p. 3.

89 Ibid., pp. 41, 154–5.

90 Ibid., p. 44.

91 "Programme for a People's Democratic Revolution in the Philippines," Appendix 6, in Alfredo B. Saulo, *Communism in the Philippines: An Introduction*, enlarged edition (Quezon City: Ateneo de Manila University Press, 1990), pp. 196–209.

92 Ibid., p. 203.

93 Ibid., pp. 203–4.

94 Bayan Muna, advertisement, *Shang Bao* [Chinese Commercial News], 7 Jan. 2001.

95 Lydia H. Liu, *Translingual Practice: Literature, National Culture, and Translated Modernity. China, 1900–1937* (Stanford: Stanford University Press, 1995). For the Chinese case, see Rebecca E. Karl, *Staging the World: Chinese Nationalism at the Turn of the Twentieth Century* (Durham: Duke University

Press, 2002), pp. 91–2. Tellingly, the seeds for Karl's research on revolutionary dialogue and international solidarity as important components of modern Chinese self-definition and nationalism were planted by her encounter with a group of Filipino Communists who had escaped to China in the 1960s after being hounded by the Marcos government.

96 I thank Kasian Tejapira for allowing me to incorporate his astute reading of, and commentary on, "The Question of Foreigners: *Nanyang Piaoliuji* and the Re/Making of Chinese and Filipino Nationness," an analysis of the Philippine *guiqiao* Bai Ren's novel that raises issues addressed and elaborated in this present study. Kasian presented his comments at the Core University Program workshop at Kyoto University on 25 March 2002. Caroline S. Hau, "The Question of Foreigners," in Hau, *On the Subject of the Nation: Filipino Writings from the Margins 1981–2004* (Quezon City: Ateneo de Manila University Press, 2004), pp. 15–62, 273–82.

CHAPTER 6

"Party as Mother": Ruam Wongphan and the Making of a Revolutionary Metaphor

Kasian Tejapira

Mother as Party

A favorite pastime of my family while stuck in Bangkok's notorious traffic jams on our way to work, school, or home, and with nothing better to do, was to listen to music on the car's cassette player. And among the dozen or so audio cassettes piling up in our car, the one my primary-school-age daughter Kloy liked most was an album titled *Pheuan deuan tula*, or "October Friends," in reference to the generation of radical leftist intellectuals and student activists-turned-Communist guerrillas who were involved in the 14 October 1973 mass uprising against military dictatorship and the subsequent 6 October 1976 right-wing massacre of student protesters and resultant military coup.[1] It was produced by Jin Kammachon, alias Kulsak Reuangkhongkiat, a well-known composer-cum-singer of the famous Kammachon (Proletarian) pop band of leftist medical student activists during the said period, on the occasion of the 20th anniversary of the October 6th Massacre in 1996. Despite the overt radical political content of most of the 14 songs in the album, the alluringly sweet melody and soft tone of their typical light pop music as well as the romantic imagery of their words held a special appeal for Kloy, who kept playing it on the cassette player and asking me time and again about Jin: who he was, whether I knew him, whether and when I could take her to see him, etc.[2]

One particular song in that album struck me as strangely and vaguely familiar in both its words and its melody, as if I had not only heard it but also sung it myself before sometime, somewhere. Touchingly titled "Bunkhun khong mae" (The Debt of Gratitude to Mother), the song opens as follows:

A flock of little birds fly over the sky.
Cool are sparkling dewdrops.
Rice plants bend with the wind.
A fresh whiff of wild flowers emanates from the forest.
Motherly love gives us warmth …

And yet, when compared with my dim recollection of it, there was something different, missing, suspicious, or not quite right about this version, especially the opening words of its chorus: "Bunkhun khong mae mai aj leum dai" (The debt of gratitude to mother is unforgettable). I can swear I distinctly remember having sung the same chorus in the past slightly differently as "Bunkhun khong **phak** mai aj leum dai" (The debt of gratitude to **the Party** is unforgettable).

That slight difference is crucial and provides the very clue to the former avatar of this song. It sent me on a frenetic search of a collection I had been building up of hundreds of memoirs, interviews, pamphlets, propaganda tracts, novels, short stories, poems, songs, newsletters, dissertations, monographs, research reports, audio and video cassettes, CDs, etc., about the now defunct Communist Party of Thailand or CPT-led rural guerrilla movement that raged throughout the country from 1965 to circa 1985, when it collapsed due to internal strife.[3] Eventually, I found what I had hazily sensed. Printed on page 8 of the first volume of a collection of revolutionary songs from the Communist-led *maquis* published underground in 1978 is a song titled "Mai leum bunkhun khong phak" (Let's Not Forget the Debt of Gratitude to the Party).[4] A line-by-line comparison between these two songs reveals a close affinity that couldn't possibly be coincidental (see Table 6.1).

Evidently, lines number 1, 5, 9, and 13 of the two songs show glaring similarities and continuity with minimal changes between them. The word "Party" in the 1978 original is simply replaced by "mother" in the 1996 reworked version (line 9), and the term "the Communist Party" is replaced by "motherly love" (lines 5 and 13). The words on lines 2, 3, 4, 6, 7, 8, 14, 15, and 16 of the original song have been shortened in the later version, while the first note of each of those lines is extended in length and the tempo slowed down. The pitch of the last note on lines 2, 6, and 14 has also been altered from high to low. All in all, the part of the original song that is least changed is the chorus (lines 9 to 12), which remains largely the same in the later version, especially its melody. With all these revisions, the 1978 revolutionary song "Mai leum bunkhun khong phak" (Let's Not Forget the Debt of Gratitude to the Party) has

Table 6.1 Line-by-line Comparison between "Mai leum bunkhun khong phak" and "Bunkhun khong mae"

"Mai leum bunkhun khong phak" (Let's Not Forget the Debt of Gratitude to the Party), 1978	"Bunkhun khong mae" (The Debt of Gratitude to Mother), 1996
1. A flock of little birds fly over the sky,	*1. A flock of little birds fly over the sky.*
2. with radiant golden sunshine above and cool sparkling dewdrops down below.	*2. Cool are sparkling dewdrops.*
3. Bright green rice terraces descend down the hill.	*3. Rice plants bend with the wind.*
4. A fresh gentle breeze brings the scent of all kinds of flowers.	*4. A fresh whiff of wild flowers emanates from the forest.*
5. The Communist Party gives us warmth,	*5. Motherly love gives us warmth.*
6. caring for, sustaining and supporting us in a manner that is hard to find.	*6. Her invaluable breast milk nourishes us.*
7. The Party has saved us from a corrupt society,	*7. The education she provides*
8. and taught, trained and enlightened us ever since.	*8. helps us gain the knowledge to pay back what we owe to this land.*
9. The debt of gratitude to the Party is unforgettable.	*9. The debt of gratitude to mother is unforgettable.*
10. Oh! This new life we've got brings tears to our eyes.	*10. The new life we've got brings tears to our eyes.*
11. We vow to follow the Party forever	*11. We will always remember Mother's teachings*
12. and overturn Thailand with armed struggle so that everyone enjoys a happy life.	*12. and work hard to earn our living so as to enjoy a happy life.*
13. Great is the Communist Party,	*13. Great is motherly love,*
14. like a beacon forever shining in the hearts of Thai people.	*14. as far and wide as the sea,*
15. Let us boundlessly uphold and respect the Party.	*15. like a shining beacon in our heart.*
16. May the Party last long. Long live the Communist Party.	*16. Our debt of gratitude to her is everlasting.*

Note: The comparison does not come across as clearly in the English translation as in the original Thai.

been seamlessly rewritten, refashioned, and transformed into its 1996 apolitical reincarnation, "Bunkhun khong mae" (The Debt of Gratitude to Mother), thus enjoying a cozy, homey afterlife subsequent to and in spite of (or perhaps precisely because of) the collapse of both the revolution and the Party.

It is most likely that Kulsak is also the author-cum-composer of the original song, although Chatchawal's edited volume does not give the name or identity of the author or composer of any song, due to the customary practice of anonymity in the Party's clandestine movement. Kulsak himself simply said in a published interview that "Bunkhun khong mae" was composed afterward, that is, after his sojourn in the *maquis*, and dedicated to his mother in imitation of a very popular old song titled "Kha namnom" (The Value of Mother's Breast Milk).[5] However, Attakan Uppathamphakul, a colleague of Kulsak who was closely involved in the reissuing on CD of Kulsak's album in 2001, has confirmed in a personal conversation with me that my foregoing "Mother as Party" hypothesis is true.

What is the point of the above discussion? Why so much ado about a reworked old song? The point is that the magical metamorphosis of the Communist Party into a mother through Kulsak's reworking of the original song arguably represents the logical conclusion of a potent metaphor in which the formal, organizational relationship between the Party and its members and followers was deliberately imagined as a personal, familial one between a mother and her offspring. Having been authorized and propagated by the Party leadership and become prevalent in the revolutionary movement since the early 1960s, the metaphor induced the rank-and-file members to understand and imagine their individual relationship with the Party as that which normally and customarily obtained with their mother. Hence the possibility in Kulsak's original rendering of describing the reciprocal relationship between the Party and "us" in such cozy terms as "gives us warmth, caring for, sustaining and supporting us," "taught, trained and enlightened us," and, in turn, "the debt of gratitude," "Oh! This new life we've got," "uphold and respect," etc., which are the very predicates typical of a mother and her offspring subjects.

By naturalizing or familiarizing (i.e., manufacturing personal family effects out of) the political, organizational relationship between the Party and its members, the former as an external organization, institute, or group of strangers is thus internalized by the latter as a resident Mother-cum-Moral Subject with the natural, familial authority to watch, guide, and direct their every thought and behavior from within, in the sense that a parent is usually held, according to a traditional Thai saying, as "Phra nai

Ruam Wongphan

jai look" (an icon in the heart of his/her child). Therefore, a Party member in good moral, ideological standing should think of the Party as he/she would think of Mother, love the Party as he/she would love Mother, obey the Party as he/she would obey Mother, be willing to die for the Party as he/she would be willing to die for Mother, and so on. Likewise, whatever the Party says should carry the same weight as whatever Mother says; whatever the Party teaches should carry the same weight as whatever Mother teaches, and so on *ad infinitum*.

The real author of this protean metaphor at the service of the Communist Party of Thailand was the legendary Ruam Wongphan (1922–62).

A Good Son of the Party

Among the internal Party documents that circulated in the revolutionary movement under CPT leadership during its Third Congress, or armed struggle period (1961–82), an outstanding one that helped inspire the comrades' fighting and self-sacrificing spirits in the face of the superior firepower of the reactionary state and formed the basis of their imagined relationship with the Party was Comrade Ruam Wongphan's "Farewell Letter to Mother."

Born to an ethnic Lao Phuan, middle peasant family in Bangplama District, Suphan Buri province, in the central plains of Thailand, Ruam, like many bright, ambitious, overachieving young male upcountry students of his generation — including future Communists such as Jaroen Wanngam, Phin Bua-on, and Phichit Dijai — found peasant life and work too arduous, tedious, and narrow.[6] So, at the age of 18, he ran away from home to the capital city of Bangkok in search of higher education and a new and better life. There he became a temple boy, living with monks he knew at a couple of temples to save on expenses while studying at nearby secondary and commercial schools and taking a menial job at a clinic in the neighborhood. Four years later, in 1944, he managed to enroll at both Thammasat and Chulalongkorn universities as well as land a job as the Thai principal of the Hainanese Qiguang Gongxue, or Sawang Witthaya School. Politically educated and radicalized by certain Hainanese colleagues at the school, who also taught him some Chinese, Ruam joined the Thai Communist Party in 1949 as one among scores of ethnic Thai (in the narrow sense of being neither Chinese immigrant, nor Vietnamese immigrant, nor Sino-Thai comrades who constituted the first-generation Party membership) students and intellectuals who formed the first batch of educated natives to enter the Party in the post-World War II period.

Handpicked by the Party leadership to travel secretly to soon-to-be-liberated China for further political and theoretical training, Ruam abruptly left his bride, Pradit Sutthijit, who was a fellow teacher at the Qiguang Gongxue School. He left in early April 1949, just 15 days after their marriage on 16 March, without any notice. Only when he stopped over in Hong Kong did he write her a letter to say good-bye and that he expected to come back in a year.

Unfortunately, that was not to be. The severe disruption in lines of communication due to the Chinese Communist revolution and the subsequent Free-World blockade of the People's Republic of China meant that the letter would be the only message she got from him for a very long while. For a period of more than a year from 1951 to 1952, Ruam, along with nine other Thai Party comrades including Prasert Sapsunthorn, Nith Phongdapphet, and Sak Suphakasem, attended the Chinese Communist Party (CCP)'s Political School at Zhongnanhai Palace in Beijing. His was the first batch of Thai Communists to receive formal training by the Chinese comrades. Later, with the establishment of the Marxist-Leninist Institute by the CCP and its designation as the new training venue,[7] four other batches of varying numbers of Thai Communist students would follow at irregular intervals in the years to come: the second batch of

50 students from 1953 to 1957, the third batch of 11 starting in 1963, the fourth batch of 10 starting in 1964, and the fifth and last batch of 18 starting in 1965. All in all, about 99 Thai Communists were trained by the Chinese in this program during the 1950s and 1960s, and most of them returned to assume key leadership roles in the Thai revolutionary movement afterward.[8]

According to Phin Bua-on, a second-batch student in the program, every Thai student there had to adopt a Chinese *nom de guerre*, his being Chen Zhong. The curriculum consisted of five main subjects: Marxist philosophy, political economy, military science, history of the Chinese Communist Party, and history of the Bolshevik Party of the Soviet Union. Chinese instructors were responsible for the third and fourth subjects and Soviet ones for the rest. The teaching was conducted through lectures and student seminars given by the respective instructors through an instant interpreter. The textbooks used included Marx's *Capital*, Lenin's *Selected Works*, and Mao's *Selected Works*. After completing the basic curriculum in two and a half years, the students went on to the intermediate level, where they underwent an additional one-year intensive training as "research students" with an emphasis on group discussion rather than lecture attendance. At the end of the program, a select few would be retained at the institute as teaching assistants to pursue advanced studies.

In Ruam's case, when he finished with the CCP's Political School in 1952 and was about to return home, he was suddenly "called upon" to travel to the Sipsong Pan Na area of southern Yunnan, where the local population was largely rural ethnic Tai, presumably to carry out political and organizational work there.[9] This unplanned and unexpected assignment meant it would be six more years before he could go back to Thailand and his unfairly deserted wife. By that time, in 1958, everyone back home had long given up any hope of his coming back and the Revolutionary Group led by Field Marshal Sarit Thanarat had already staged a US- and Palace-backed bloodless coup, on 20 October, to overthrow a constitutional regime and keep Thailand under the staunchly anti-Communist absolutist military dictatorship of Sarit and his successors for another 15 long years.[10]

Fresh from his political and organizational work among Tai peasants in Sipsong Pan Na and fired by his conviction that Mao Zedong's doctrine of peasant revolution was right and applicable to Thailand, Ruam immediately resumed his Party work and set about contacting, educating, mobilizing, and organizing Thai peasants in the countryside.[11] The center of his activities was his home village in Suphan Buri, where he had to overcome the initial disappointment and negative attitudes of many villagers who considered him a failure, someone who had had a rare chance to go to Bangkok for higher education and yet came back with no government position to speak of.

Be that as it may, with his friendly and sincere, cool, calm, selfless, and fearless character, his well-rounded experience and wide-ranging knowledge, Ruam managed gradually to build up his contacts among local peasants, schoolteachers, and workers, win their trust, organize them into study groups, recruit a select few to form Party cells, persuade them to do voluntary irrigation works, and set up a cooperative farm-cum-political school. He had an outstanding ability to clearly and vividly articulate and explain difficult subjects, be it world affairs, national problems, theoretical issues, or practical matters, as well as convince and encourage his audience. His firm and resolute commitment to the cause of national independence and political democracy, peace, and justice, and his constant, cheerful smiles and fascinating stories from new, revolutionary China helped draw people. He extended his clandestine network from Suphan Buri into the surrounding central provinces of Lop Buri, Ang Thong, and Kanchanaburi.

Ruam also invited groups of friends from Suphan Buri to visit him in Bangkok for further discussion while his wife cooked them simple meals. To earn his living and support his family, Ruam turned a small plot of land in his wife's home into a thriving chicken farm where he single-handedly put up the whole wooden structure and learned to breed, raise, feed, cure, and clean some 400–500 hens so as to collect and sell their eggs. He also took especially good care of his wife and in-laws, presumably to make up for his almost decade-long, unceremonious, unilateral absence without leave.

When looked at retrospectively, Ruam's strenuous efforts at mobilizing and organizing peasants in central Thailand during those few years after his return fitted into a larger picture of similar attempts being made by other comrades in other regions of the country, especially the Northeast and the South. Together, they formed part of the multifarious measures being taken by the CPT to lay the actual groundwork for the decade-long theorized, discussed, and anticipated rural armed struggle, including the setting up of the clandestine Voice of the People of Thailand radio station in southern China, and the dispatch of many batches of young peasants to China, North Vietnam, and Communist-controlled areas in Laos and Cambodia to receive training as future guerrilla commanders and medical personnel, etc. The fact that in its modern political history Thailand had hitherto enjoyed merely brief periods of relatively democratic regime (1945–7 and 1955–8, each lasting approximately two and a half years), whereas enduring governments were possible only under military strongmen (namely, Field Marshal Plaek Phibunsongkhram and Field Marshal Sarit Thanarat), had convinced the Party that, as Chairman Mao said and many fraternal parties had heroically and successfully put into practice, "state power grows out of the barrel of a gun," otherwise all the good works and hard efforts carried out by the Party under those brief favorable democratic conditions would just dissipate and come to naught time and again once a military dictator took power.[12]

So, finally, at its Third Congress, convened in September 1961, the Party tacitly decided to resolutely pursue the path of armed struggle. For the first time, the Party leadership itself went into the countryside. In the words of the CPT's only public, official history:

> [The Party] grasped the revolutionary line of encircling the cities from the countryside and better realized the important role played by the farmers in the national-democratic revolution. The party was coming into full maturity.[13]

In retrospect, this fateful decision had far-reaching repercussions for the Party itself in ways that were probably not fully anticipated or recognized at the time. Among the more salient of them were the following:[14]

1. *Ruralization*: It would transform the CPT from an urban party into a rural and even jungle one in terms of its sociopolitical locus and environment. Meanwhile, urbanization and capitalist economic development were proceeding apace in Thai society at large.
2. *Peasantization and minority ethnicization*: It would shift the mass base of the CPT and consequently the class composition of its membership from Chinese workers and petty bourgeoisie plus a number of Thai intellectuals to Thai peasants and ethnic minority hill tribes. Meanwhile, in Thai society at large, rural peasant communities were undergoing clearer class differentiation. Landless or impoverished peasants were migrating to the cities in droves while students, professionals, and the middle class in general were rapidly expanding in both number and kind.
3. *Militarization*: It would change the CPT from a civilian albeit militant political party to a clandestine, underground guerrilla organization in terms of organizational form and culture. In other words, the Party would gradually lose its former character of a mass political organization and assume a new militarized one. Meanwhile, wars,

weapons, military mentality, and a culture of violence were spreading like wildfire in Thailand and Indochina.

4. *Re-sinicization*: At its founding in 1942, the CPT was an overwhelmingly ethnic Chinese party. However, by the end of the post-war decade, with the recruitment of a significant number of bright, young, energetic, capable, and articulate Thai students and intellectuals to its ranks, it managed ethnically and culturally to Thaify itself to a certain extent. The decision of the Third Party Congress to follow Mao's theory of armed struggle would strongly and irresistibly reorient it toward the Red East or China in terms of ideology, theory, and political culture as evident in the early revolutionary songs produced and broadcast by the Voice of the People of Thailand, which were completely under the intoxicating influence of the Chinese Great Proletarian Cultural Revolution. Meanwhile, the Thai state and society were also undergoing profound and extensive Americanization.[15]
5. *Localization*: The pursuing of guerrilla warfare in various scattered rural areas around the country would fragment the CPT and turn it from a once nationally unified and substantially uniform party into one with internally different and regionally varying cultures and styles under the diverse influence of neighboring fraternal Communist parties and states. Thus, the Thai Communists in the North would be strongly influenced by Red China while those in the Upper Northeast would be subject to the seeping influence of Laotian Communists. The Thai comrades in the Lower Northeast would copy many practices and policies from the Khmer Rouge, whereas those in the South would apparently go native[16] and those in the East would turn into copycat local mafia bosses.[17] Meanwhile, the Thai economy and society were being increasingly integrated at the national level and linked more closely with the global economy.

At the Third Party Congress, Ruam, a leader of the postwar, ethnic Thai, and mostly Thammasat University alumni faction in the Party, was also elected to the six-member-strong Politburo and put in charge of Party work in central Thailand. A chain-smoking workaholic who quite often wrote and talked non-stop day and night (his wife couldn't resist quipping that he used cigarettes as a tonic for his brain), he developed tuberculosis shortly thereafter, probably having contracted it while caring for his dying father. With the state authorities becoming alerted to Party activities in Suphan Buri and closing in on Ruam due to the inexperience and carelessness of some green local cadres, the Party leadership, out of concern for Ruam's health and safety, instructed him to take a break, see a doctor, quickly withdraw from the countryside, and refrain from returning there. However, being worried about the continuity of his unfinished work, Ruam unwisely went back to rural Suphan Buri to give parting instructions to his subordinates, only to be informed on by a traitor named Suwan. After being hotly pursued by police through the night, he was finally arrested at noon the following day, 23 February 1962. His house was then ransacked by the police, and his devoted and long-suffering wife, totally shaken up, was detained along with Ruam and his peasant comrades at Division 2 of the Special Branch police.

At this point, Ruam's ironic life journey had come full circle. Had he not escaped from a wretched peasant life to Bangkok in his boyhood, he wouldn't have gained higher education, met the then urban Thai Communist Party, and gone to China to expand his horizons. He would have remained a mere peasant, poor and undereducated, parochial and ignorant. He could possibly have become a devout Buddhist, but hardly ever a committed Communist. And yet, precisely because of his escape, he got a chance to discover Marxism-Leninism and Mao Zedong thought and became a convinced Maoist. His new political creed entailed a radical revalorization of the peasantry, who now constituted the basic and main motive force of the revolution. Having fled to the city in Thailand, Ruam then returned to the countryside via Sipsong Pan Na in China, with a new appreciation of the immense political value and potential for staging a revolution of the very rural class that he had once turned his back on. Ironically, his circular journey was driven by a flow of overseas discourse and ideology whose dynamics eventually brought him via a roundabout route back home to his old roots.

Party as Mother

After a week in detention, having uncompromisingly refused to cooperate with police interrogators and perhaps sensing that his days were numbered, Ruam wrote a farewell letter to his mother on 1 March 1962 and had it smuggled out to his comrades. Less than two months afterward, on the evening of 24 April 1962, he was summarily executed for "having committed acts of communism … unbefitting someone born as a Thai" by order of Prime Minister Field Marshal Sarit Thanarat acting under the notorious Article 17 of the 1959 absolutist constitution of Sarit's own design, which provided for the concentration of executive, legislative, and judicial powers in the hands of the Prime Minister himself.[18]

Ruam's "Farewell Letter to Mother" reads as follows:

Mother, you have tenderly cared for your unborn child with pride in your own flesh and blood. You have infused your freedom-loving, peace-loving and most just blood into your child. And once your child opens his eyes and sees you and the wider world, your lofty virtues are then instilled in your own flesh and blood through your breast milk. Your virtues make up the flesh and blood of your child, turning it into their concentrated embodiment. You grind cooked rice into a pulp with your teeth and feed it to your child until he grows up. Not only have you molded your child's character out of your lofty virtues through your blood vessels, breast and mouth, but you have also taught him to be a moral, truthful, sympathetic and virtuous person all through the years while he is growing up. You hate oppression, exploitation, a greedy scramble and all immoralities. Now, your lofty virtues, pure heart and immaculate body have combined together and solidified in your child. Your lofty virtues in your child have risen to confront your enemy and stood eyeball to eyeball with the enemy of the people. It is out of its fear of your lofty virtues that the enemy is out to destroy and kill your child tonight.

Mother, you already are the conqueror of your enemy.

May your truth last forever.

One child of yours is gone but many more will be born.

Farewell, mother.

From your child,
Ruam
March 1st, 1962. 10.00AM[19]

Needless to say, the figure of Mother that Ruam so affectionately described in his farewell letter quoted above is by no means Rai Wongphan, his biological procreator, but the Communist Party of Thailand, and thus the content of the letter actually portrays an imagined relationship between the Party and himself as a Party member through that metaphor. As told by Ruam, the more salient features of this imagined relationship are as follows:

1. *The religious overtones*: The pregnancy and childbearing described in the letter signify Ruam's own political and ideological rebirth through the educational and organizational labors of the Party. Comparable to this rebirth is the act of religious conversion. Generally held as an important turning point in one's life, it normally involves the notion

of purifying or shedding one's former self and a concomitant moral rebirth and/or change of identity. Symbolic of this process are such rites of passage as ordination (the CPT's equivalent being a ceremony held for new members to swear an oath of allegiance to the Party), change of name (the Party equivalent being the assumption of a *nom de guerre* by new recruits to the guerrilla army), observance of a new code of conduct (the Party's equivalent being the strict adherence to Party and/or army discipline by Party members and guerrilla fighters), etc.

In this connection, a particular sentence Ruam wrote in the letter — "Now, your lofty virtues, pure heart and immaculate body have combined together and solidified in your child" — is noteworthy for the resonance it bears of the Immaculate Conception of Jesus Christ by Mary. In the same vein, an anonymous comrade of Ruam uses the term "Moranasakkhi" (martyrdom) twice to describe his death while Ruam's widow also remarks on her late husband's "lofty priestly virtues."[20]

2. *The ideological bonds*: The Party and its members are united as one through the nourishing link of blood vessels, breast milk, and cooked rice pulp. So much so that they share the same blood and it is impossible to separate or make a distinction between their respective blood. In that sense, it is unthinkable for a member to lead a life outside or apart from the Party.

That common blood is ideological in nature, and it signifies various virtues such as love of freedom, peace, justice, morality, truthfulness, and sympathy; loathing of oppression, exploitation, a greedy scramble, and all immoralities; courage to confront the people's enemy, etc. In sum, the blood ties linking the Party to its members symbolize the unbreakable ideological bonds of Communism and related political virtues between them.

3. *Members as living embodiment and objectification of the Party's abstractions*: The CPT is thus held as the fount and center of the said abstract doctrine and virtues while its members become the living objectification and personification of these abstractions. Hence Ruam's repeated assertion that Mother's (i.e., the Party's) lofty virtues have made up or solidified in the child (i.e., Party member), or Mother (i.e., the Party) has molded the child's (i.e., Party member's) character out of her lofty virtues. The upshot is that Party members are reduced to a mere living embodiment and instrument of the Party's virtues and doctrine.

I believe it was Ruam's 1962 farewell letter that first introduced the Party-as-Mother metaphor into the Thai Communist movement. My doctoral thesis research into Communist literature and Party publications prior to that period has yet to find any comparable instance of it.[21] Besides, at the time the letter was written, both Mother and child were still very young. The CPT had yet to attain the age of majority, having been established only on 1 December 1942, while Ruam himself was just going on 13, having been admitted into the Party around 1949. (Upon becoming a Communist Party member one was considered reborn, politically speaking, and hence started counting the years of one's life anew.) Therefore, it is rather unlikely that the tradition of this metaphor had begun any sooner.[22]

Be that as it may, once begotten by Ruam's farewell letter, the Party-as-Mother metaphor soon grew in both potency and currency and spread throughout the revolutionary movement. Ruam was posthumously honored and hailed by the CPT as a model revolutionary hero whom all Party members and guerrilla fighters should emulate. The story of his life and final sacrifice was made a staple subject of group study and discussion among comrades in the *maquis*, especially on the anniversary of his death. Numerous poems were recited, songs performed, and plays staged in his honor and memory.[23] For instance, Comrade Ming, a post-World War II Thammasat University alumnus who later joined the Communist guerrilla movement on Phu Phayak Mountain in northern Thailand, wrote an oft-recited poem titled "Jak ruam theung mae" (From Ruam to Mother), which was inspired by Ruam's farewell letter:

> Dear Mother …
> Your blood flows through my body.
> Our blood ties are fastened with love.
> Your blood actually forms my body and soul
> and will continue to flow till the day I die.
> Mother, I now see clearly
> that you are as bright as the sun.
> And your heart is the fount that overflows
> with revolutionary virtues.
> You infuse me with your blood
> and keep feeding me till I grow up
> with revolutionary morality
> that sets me against the invader of the Thai nation.
> Till the day when I'm fully grown,
> you have painstakingly taught and trained me,
> nurtured and cared for me,
> implanted in my mind a new, enlightened way of life.

I feel the warmth and safety of your embrace
like nestlings being nestled by their red eagle mother
who glides swiftly unhindered over the sky
from the mountain top to the distant sea.
No jungle is too far for her wings.
Being fearless up in the sky,
proud and strong down on the ground,
she is ready to confront anyone anywhere.
The tasks you assign me,
the commands you give me,
will be bravely and forcefully carried out
regardless of the danger involved.
Mother, the enemy has caught me
and threatened to kill me,
using the carrot and stick approach
to no avail.
Dear Mother, this life of mine is sacrificed for you
with unswerving loyalty.
You are the great pillar and procreator
of our Thai nation.
I will never betray or revolt against you in this life.
Nor shall I turn weak or bad.
I will die standing strong
and never kneel down and kowtow to the enemy.
Farewell Mother, my life is ending
while your blood is gushing
from my bolt upright body
in a shower of bullets.[24]

In the light of this poem and other similar works in the CPT-led revolutionary movement, Kulsak's "Mai leum bunkhun khong phak" (Let's Not Forget the Debt of Gratitude to the Party)-turned-"Bunkhun khong mae" (The Debt of Gratitude to Mother) song mentioned earlier is but a later if better-known product and continuation of the long-standing tradition of Party-as-Mother metaphor begotten by Comrade Ruam Wongphan.

Amazingly enough, when the CPT began to imagine itself as Mother, its arch-enemy, Prime Minister Field Marshal Sarit Thanarat, had been depicting himself as the Father of the Thai nation for some time, as shown in the following extracts from his speeches:

> The Prime Minister is the father of the largest family, bears the greatest responsibility and has to look after the well-being of his fraternal countrymen most closely. (1960)

> Even today, although the system of government is different and one does not use the word "pho" [i.e., father in Thai] as before, I still hold on to our ancient Thai traditional concept of father "ruling" children. (1961)[25]

And, of course, once the Prime Minister is held as "Father," disobeying him would be as bad as disobeying one's father, criticizing him would be as improper as criticizing one's father, electing him to office would be as absurd as electing one's father, and expelling or overthrowing or revolting against him would be as unthinkable as doing the same against one's own father.

It would take the Thai radical students and intellectuals about ten years after Sarit's demise in 1963 to break the spell of his Despot-as-Father metaphor over Thai society and stage the 14 October 1973 popular uprising against his despotic successors. It would take them almost another decade to become disillusioned with Ruam's mesmerizing Party-as-Mother metaphor and rise up to commit matricide against the undemocratic and Sinophile leadership of the CPT in the *maquis* in the early 1980s.

Postscript

The attentive reader may have noticed a glaring discrepancy between the date of Ruam's execution — 24 April 1962 — and the date of publication of his cremation volume — 23 April 1995. During those odd 33 years, Ruam's remains were kept by his widow, Pradit Sutthijit, in a plain coffin at the Makudkasattriyaram Temple in downtown Bangkok, where she regularly paid him a visit. She refused to cremate him, in expectation that someday, somehow, in her own words, truth would prevail, justice would be done, and history would absolve him.[26] Perhaps she was waiting for the CPT-led revolution to win, an extreme unlikelihood after its dissipation and collapse in the mid-1980s.

Shortly after 9 p.m. on 14 September 1994, a group of ex-comrades of the 1970s generation who were attending a cremation ceremony at the said temple happened to stumble upon Ruam's coffin. There lay the remains of the legendary martyr and good son of the Party whom the students had until then simply heard and read about in the *maquis*. A quick inquiry yielded the information that the temple would soon dispose of Ruam's remains in a common cremation with other unclaimed remains. Out of a sense of distant comradeship, respect, and gratitude, they traced and found Mrs. Pradit and obtained her permission to hold a proper cremation ceremony for Comrade Ruam. Meetings were then called, donations collected, plans made, and contributions solicited for a cremation volume.

And yet, how to remember and mourn a Communist martyr after the failure of the revolution and a general disillusionment with the doctrine for which he fought and died? In the end, the ex-comrades, including Mrs. Pradit herself, opted for an uncontroversial solution. Time and again, Ruam is extolled in the cremation volume as a hero and martyr to the cause of democracy, and his life story is simply incorporated into a grand historical narrative of the long and tragic but triumphant struggle for democracy in Thailand.[27]

Thus, in this irony of history, a Communist martyr who could not be remembered nor mourned while the revolution was still raging finally got the proper farewell that he deserved only after — and maybe because — the revolution had already and safely collapsed. However, he ended up being mourned and remembered for something that, strictly speaking, he could not have unreservedly believed in, something he did not actually die for.

Notes

1 Benedict Anderson, "Withdrawal Symptoms," in Anderson, *The Spectre of Comparisons: Nationalism, Southeast Asia and the World* (London and New York Verso, 1998), pp. 139–73.

2 The album was first released under the title *Pheua matuphoom* (For the Motherland) in October 1989 and contained nine songs, including "Bunkhun khong mae" (The Debt of Gratitude to Mother). *Pheuan deuan tula* is thus a reissue to which five new songs were added.

3 Benedict Anderson, "Radicalism after Communism," in Anderson, *The Spectre of Comparisons*, pp. 285–98.

4 Chatchawal Prathumwit, ed., *Bon senthang peun lem 1* [On the Path of Armed Struggle, vol. 1] ([n.p.]: Prachachon Publishing House, 1978), p. 8.

5 Attakan Uppathamphakul, ed., *Phirab khao 3 bot phleng pheua chiwit pheua prachachon* [White Dove, vol. 3: Songs for Life and the People] (Bangkok: Dokya Group Press, 2001), p. 150. Strictly speaking, his statement is factually correct even though it might not be the whole truth. The glossed-over part, which is also the most crucial and telling one, has to do with the song's actual Communist revolutionary pedigree.

6 Pradit Sutthijit *et al.*, *Anusorn neuang nai ngan chapanakij sop nai ruam wongphan* [Cremation Volume of Ruam Wongphan], Wat Makudkasattriyaram, Bangkok, 1995.

7 Thong Jamsri, "Thong jamsri: Lekhathikan phak khommunit haeng prathet thai" [Thong Jamsri: Secretary General of the Communist Party of Thailand],

Sarakhadi 20, 232 (June 2004): 80. There is not much information in the Thai sources that could help identify this obscure "Marxist-Leninist Institute." A recently published interview with the octogenarian Thong Jamsri, a founder (as a delegate to its First Congress in 1942) and current secretary general of the practically defunct CPT as well as a second-batch student at the said institute, tells us that it was jointly set up by the Office of the National Culture Commission of China and the Soviet Union to serve as the training institute for leading members of various national Communist parties around the region. My preliminary research revealed that there used to be an Institute of Marxism-Leninism-Mao Zedong Thought, affiliated with the Chinese Academy of Social Sciences under the State Council of China, until recently, when globalization/neoliberalism put it out of fashion and existence. Whether it was the same institute where the Thai Communists were trained needs further investigation.

8 Wijak Nanthayut, *Senthang chiwit lae lokkathas thang kanmeuang phin bua-on reu amnaj yutthawiwat phoo choo thong thrissadi kan torsoo song naewthang nai kanpatiwat thai* [The Life and Political Outlook of Phin Bua-on Alias Amnaj Yutthawiwat, the Upholder of the Struggle between the Two Lines Banner in the Thai Revolution] (Bangkok: The 25th Anniversary of the October 6th Incident Book Project, 2001), pp. 20–4. The account of the CCP's training program for Thai Communists in this part comes from a posthumous biography of Phin Bua-on (1930–99), a second-batch Thai student at the Marxist-Leninist Institute in Beijing, written by his former junior comrade under a pseudonym. An upcountry, Thammasat University student activist-turned-CPT Politburo member-cum-major theorist during the Third Congress period, Phin was arrested and imprisoned from 1967 to 1969 by the Thai authorities, allegedly tipped off about his whereabouts by a leftist opponent in the Party Secretariat. After his release, Phin turned his back on the Party, cooperated with dovish elements in the state security apparatus, formed a breakaway Marxist faction in open opposition to the Party, and was eventually branded a "revisionist" and formally expelled from the Party in 1976.

9 Pradit *et al.*, *Anusorn*, pp. 30–1. At this point, the account in Ruam's cremation volume is decidedly unclear. For example, by whom was Ruam "called upon" to go to Sipsong Pan Na — the CPT or the CCP? Anyway, it seems reasonable to suppose that Ruam performed the assigned task on behalf of the Chinese Party since the area was part of southern China. The fact that as a Thai he spoke a language relatively similar to the local Tai dialect in Sipsong Pan Na might partly explain why he was chosen. But why did it have to be him and not other Thai comrades? Was it because of his peasant family background? One can only guess.

10 Thak Chaloemtiarana, *Thailand: The Politics of Despotic Paternalism* (Bangkok: Social Science Association of Thailand and the Thai Khadi Research Institute, Thammasat University, 1979); Suphot Dantrakul, "20 tulakhom 2501" [20 Oct. 1958], in Pradit *et al.*, *Anusorn*, pp. 89–106.

11 Pradit *et al.*, *Anusorn, passim*; Wijak, *Senthang chiwit*, pp. 128–9. Phin Bua-on, who took over Ruam's Party responsibility after the latter's arrest and execution by the authorities, gives some relevant information on the subject in his biography by Wijak.

12 These were the lessons from the CPT's history similarly drawn and emphasized by two of the triumvirate of Party leaders during its Third Congress period, i.e., Thong Jamsri and Wirat Anghathawon. See Thong, "Thong jamsri: Lekhathikan phak," 80; and Tho Phianwitthaya (Wirat Anghathawon), trans. Chris Baker, "An Internal History of the Communist Party of Thailand," *Journal of Contemporary Asia* 33, 4 (2003): 527.

13 Voice of the People of Thailand, "VOPT Recounts CPT History Covering 1942–1977," Foreign Broadcast Information Service daily report, *Asia & Pacific* 4, 241 (15 Dec. 1977): J6–J15.

14 Kasian Tejapira, "Jak phleng pheua chiwit theung phleng patiwat" [From Songs for Life to Revolutionary Songs], in *Sailom plian this ... tae duang jit mi dai plian leoi: Phleuk haeng chiwit lae siang phleng patiwat thai* [The Wind Is Changeable ... But the Heart Is Steadfast: Life Crystals and the Sound of Thai Revolutionary Songs], ed. Wat Wanlayangkool *et al.* (Bangkok: The Collective of Thai Revolutionary Songs Project, 2003), pp. 23–37.

15 Kasian Tejapira, *Commodifying Marxism: The Formation of Modern Thai Radical Culture, 1927–1958* (Kyoto and Melbourne: Kyoto University Press and Trans Pacific Press, 2001), chapter 2; Benedict R.O'G. Anderson, "Introduction," in *In the Mirror: Literature and Politics in Siam in the American Era*, ed. and trans. Anderson and Ruchira Mendiones (Bangkok: Editions Duang Kamol, 1985), pp. 9–40.

16 I derive this idea from an acute observation of Chantana Fongthale, alias Anand Hanphanichphan, a Thammasat University student activist-cum-poet and traditional Thai musician in the early 1970s who later joined the CPT-led guerrilla movement in the North in the aftermath of the October 6th right-wing massacre and military coup, in his thoughtful and very well written memoirs of his guerrilla years. See Chantana Fongthale (Anand Hanphanichphan), *Jak doi yao theung phupha ji* [From the Yao Hill to Ji Mountain] (Bangkok: Chabkrae Publishing House, 1993), pp. 51–2, 58–9.

17 The fascinating story of Khongjet Phromnamphol, a Ramkhamhaeng University student activist-turned-Communist guerrilla commander-turned-influential local gunman is told by himself in an unpublished manuscript: "Thap khon daeng (Bantheuk leuad phanom dong rek 2)" [Army of the Reds (Blood-stained Memoirs from Phanom Dong Rek Mountain Part 2)].

18 Kasian Tejapira, "The Emergence of NGO Movement in Thailand and the Sarit Regime," in *The NGO Way: Perspectives and Experiences from Thailand*, ed. Shinichi Shigetomi, Kasian Tejapira, and Apichart Thongyou (Chiba: Institute of Developing Economies, Japan External Trade Organization, 2004), pp. 21–37.

19 Cited in Pradit *et al.*, *Anusorn*, pp. 52–3.

20 Pradit *et al.*, *Anusorn*, pp. 28, 32, 119.

21 Kasian, *Commodifying Marxism*.

22 Although no conclusive evidence has yet been found, it is very likely that Ruam borrowed the Party-as-Mother metaphor from the Chinese Communist Party. In this regard, the following personal e-mail message from Wang Chaohua, a former student leader in the 1989 Tiananmen Square protest and at that time a graduate student in literature at UCLA, dated 3 October 2004, in response to the draft manuscript of this essay and my inquiry, is so eye-openingly pertinent and instructive that I cannot resist quoting it at length here. I would like to express my deep gratitude to Dr. Wang for kindly and generously sharing with me her personal experience and intimate knowledge of Chinese Communist cultural politics:

> … As for the metaphor of the Party as Mother, it was indeed well established in China for many years, definitely before the beginning of the Cultural Revolution in 1966. Another date I can identify is March 1963, when Mao canonized a soldier of the People's Liberation Army, Lei Feng, who died in an accident. In the official media campaign to promote his image following Mao's call for "learning from Lei Feng," it was repeatedly emphasized that Lei loved the most to sing a song that compares the Party to Mother. That would mean the song was there before 1963.
>
> Lei himself was born in Hunan, south-central China, and orphaned at probably eight, if I remember correctly. Thus, in the mushrooming literature after his death, it was often explained that the Party literally gave him a rebirth — fed him and brought him up when he stayed in a state-run orphanage, educated him and gave him a job as a postman while he was growing up, and recruited him into the army and finally the Party (the CCP) while he was serving in China's northeast Liaoning province.
>
> The title of his most favorite song is "Chang zhi shan-ge gei dang ting" (Singing a Song to the Party). The lyrics go like this:
>
> Singing a song to the Party,
> I compare the Party to Mother.
> Mother merely gave birth to my body,
> Whereas the Party's glorious light brightens my heart.
> In the Old Society, when I was lashed,
> Mother knew only weeping [over me];
> It was the Party who called upon me to join the Revolution,
> to seize the whip and lashing back at the enemy.
>
> So this, as far as I can remember it, is a very rough translation. As you can imagine, the metaphor would live on in China's official culture through the Cultural Revolution. However, it didn't come to the whole extent of Ruam's letter until the early eighties, when China was already on the track to

commercialization/capitalist reform. The song that most explicitly explored the relation between the Party to its member as that between a Mother and her child has the title "Party, my dear Mother."

Incidentally, your message came in right after China's National Day on October 1. Someone else happened to write about this song in a Chinese chatroom. So here I'll try some rough translation again, based on the lyrics provided by the internet author:

> Mother, Dear Mother, with your sweet breast milk you bred me to grow up,
> Supported me to learn how to walk, taught me how to speak,
> sang to me to send me to sleep, and worried about me all the time.
> Mother, Dear Mother, how sincere and honest your virtue is!
> Mother, Dear Mother, it was you
> who encouraged me to launch into this revolutionary life, Dear Mother.
> Party, Dear Party, you as Mother bring me up,
> Taught me to be patriotic, and encouraged me to receive education,
> A happy tomorrow is calling on me,
> with you displaying the beautiful future of the Four Modernizations.
> Party, Dear Party, how noble and glorious your image is!
> Party, Dear Party, you indeed are my Dearest Mother, Dear Mother!

23 Pradit *et al.*, *Anusorn*, pp. 67–70, 75–84; Thapluang, "Baebyang khong wirachon patiwat" [The Model of a Revolutionary Hero], *Athipat* 7, 1 (Apr. 1978): 22–4.

24 Ming, "Jak ruam theung mae" [From Ruam to Mother], *Athipat* 7, 1 (Apr. 1978): 25, my own translation; see also Pradit *et al.*, *Anusorn*, pp. 67–70.

25 Cited in Thak, *Thailand*, pp. 165, 166.

26 Pradit *et al.*, *Anusorn*, pp. 116–7, 120.

27 Ibid., pp. 85–6, 117, 120.

CHAPTER 7

Flows and Fallacies: James J. Puthucheary on Race, Class, and State

Khoo Boo Teik[1]

Let us begin with a reading of the history of Malaysia as a matrix of global, regional, and internal flows that shaped its political economy just before and just after Merdeka (Independence) in 1957. A few notes of caution should be sounded here. The reading that is offered here is not comprehensive. It may be said to provide the middle part of a historical progression of myriad flows without appending the earlier or much later terms of the progression. Nor is the treatment of the flows strictly chronological. It may even be thought to be sweeping and vertiginous, but it will, hopefully, not be dismissed as being fanciful.

Inflows, Outflows, and Internal Flows

Many flows washed into Malaya in different ways. There were the imperial incursions of emerging Western powers — Portugal, the Netherlands, and Britain — whose rivalry for the domination of Melaka, and subsequent seizures, "protection," or "indirect rule" of the Malay states culminated in the formation of British Malaya.[2] British Malaya was not intended to be a settler colony in the mold of Britain's "white dominions." All the same, the colony's administration and economic exploitation required the entry and presence of officials, administrators, traders, managers, soldiers, and police. These personnel were assigned from the "mother country," or recruited from parts of Europe and other British colonies (such as India and Ceylon). In the wake of the construction of empire and the penetration of colonial capitalism came waves of mass immigration, notably from the Dutch East Indies, China, and India, that resulted in the multiethnic setting that Furnivall would famously theorize as the "plural society." The mass deployment of immigrant labor and the use of foreign capital in the primary-commodity production and service sectors were superimposed upon a previously native agricultural economy. From this emerged a peculiar socioeconomic structure having enduring political consequences, that is, an ethnic division of labor wherein the "sons of the soil"[3] were largely tied to the soil while immigrants were organized in tin mines and cash-crop plantations. Or else the latter and their descendants inserted themselves into the urban and modern, trading and retail, and even informal sectors of the economy. "Sojourner" in intent and in sentiment bound to the "old country" most of the immigrants certainly were. Yet the reality of their stabilizing domicile and the growing numbers of their young encouraged the implantation of their own systems of community-supported schools having their own "imported" teachers, mediums of instruction, textbooks, syllabi, and examinations.[4] All these "vernacular" schools operated alongside the "native" religious schools, as well as the likewise implanted and burgeoning system of government and Christian mission-run English schools. Over time, the dominant segments of the population — the Europeans, the co-opted Malay aristocracy, and the "King's Chinese" — were habituated to the discourses, traditions, and customs of the British empire, including making pledges of loyalty to the British Crown, organizing the construction of memorials to monarchs and fallen soldiers, and collecting subscriptions to support the wars of the empire. At the same time, however, there was the uncelebrated entry and stealthy diffusion of "subversive" discourses, namely, political ideas spread by "alien" agitators who sought "overseas" Chinese and Indian support for revolutionary or anti-colonial movements "back home." Other organizers fought on labor's behalf, or nurtured anti-imperialist visions in Malaya itself, an Indian variant of the latter being particularly relevant to this essay.[5] Then the last half-century of the colonial period witnessed two global wars. The first war catalyzed a "proletarian revolution" in Russia, the global reverberations of which were eventually felt in Malaya as well. The second war brought a "pan-Asian" imperialism that briefly supplanted British colonialism only to sponsor or be opposed by new social and political forces that espoused competing nationalist ideologies and provoked antagonistic loyalties.

The flows also washed out of colonial Malaya. There were, critically, the exports of primary commodities. Of these, the most lucrative were tin and rubber (some seeds of which had been smuggled from Brazil), the production and export of which restructured the internal economy while remaking the global economy. The surpluses accruing to expanding "foreign investments" in plantations, mines, and trading houses were transferred out during economic booms. Surplus "foreign labor" was repatriated to ease economic crises. Remittances from Malaya helped to support families left behind in China and India, while donations helped to finance political activity in both those countries. World War II and its aftermath created an exodus of many colors, ethnically speaking. European "repatriates" who were able to mostly fled to Britain or India. Some "Chinese patriots" returned to China to participate in the war against Japanese invasion, while other endangered notables evacuated from Malaya to various points of refuge in unconquered China, Australia, or India.[6] After the Japanese capture of Singapore, soldiers of the surrendered British Indian Army and other volunteers formed the Indian National Army, which proceeded to fight the British army in India for Indian independence. Members of the Malay Giyu Gun (PETA)[7] fought in the Dutch East Indies for an Indonesian republic and, perhaps more abstractly, for *Melayu Raya*.[8] No less real, although much less exalted, was the conscription and supply of Indian laborers during the "Japanese Occupation" of Malaya to construct the Siam Railway; thousands of the laborers did not survive their ordeal. Even territories could flow out, as it were, as when the four northern states of the Malay Peninsula — Perlis, Kedah, Kelantan, and Trengganu — were re-ceded to Thai suzerainty at the time of the Japanese Occupation, only to be reabsorbed, after the Japanese defeat, into postwar Malaya. Students were present in the outward movement of people: Chinese students had been going to China (and Hong Kong), Indian students to India, and Malay students to Indonesia and the Middle East. But increasingly "students from Malaya" — Malays, Chinese, Indians, and "others" — went to the "mother country," typically to seek particular forms of professional training, in law and medicine, for example. Their experiences frequently encompassed searches for, if not discoveries of, their personal and collective identities, commitments to causes, and, upon their return, encounters with the social and political realities of Malaya.

Within Malaya the flows were no less important. Under the impact of rising Asian nationalism and the labor movements in Europe, changes to existing forms of labor organization released parts of the working classes from various pre-capitalist institutions of bondage, thus giving some degree of mobility to "free labor." In times of peace, the development of towns, ports, stations, roads and railways had reordered spatial patterns of habitation and production, and laid new networks of transportation. In times of war, the socioeconomic upheavals wrought by military invasion, the repression during the Japanese Occupation, and the conduct of guerrilla warfare further changed the spatial distribution of population and economic activities. Residential patterns were again altered as people were uprooted and dispersed or else they relocated themselves out of necessity, for the sake of survival or to support armed resistance. The postwar return of the colonial state in the form of the British Military Administration and its intensifying clashes with radical nationalists, militant labor, and the Communist Party of Malaya soon provoked an insurrection. Britain's ally during the war but proscribed soon after it, the Communist Party of Malaya abandoned its open struggles in the cities that its guerrillas planned to surround from the countryside. Other Party cadres went underground but set up or infiltrated "open front" organizations. The colonial state arrested radical Malay nationalists and incarcerated them in detention camps. Suspected "Chinese Communist sympathizers," though, were often banished to China — 60,000 of them by James Puthucheary's count. Hundreds of thousands of politically suspect rural or semi-rural residents were forcibly "resettled," that is, fenced behind so-called (Chinese) New Villages. Amidst all this, the mass mobilization among the "free" population had begun. This prelude to pre- and post-independence electoral politics took emerging politicians trekking up and down the country, plying their ideological wares, organizational offerings, and expectations of an independent Malaya.

And so on. Naturally the above division of "inflows," "outflows," and "internal flows," given the appearance of linearity in each case, is made for the sake of convenient description: the people who lived through them would have sensed the flows swirling about them all at once. In personal terms, all would have had to respond with varying degrees of fulfillment, success, or failure. In social terms, some would have actively tried to make history out of the flows, not of their choice, that had washed all over their lives.

James J. Puthucheary (1922–2000) was one such person.

Flows and a Man

Without contriving to fit a personal trajectory neatly or logically with the flows of history, it is plausible to view James Puthucheary's life as an embodiment of many of the flows discussed earlier. He was born in India, of parents who were originally from Kerala, and brought to Malaya at an early age.[9] His father, Joseph Chacko Puthucheary, "had studied at the University of Madras and was well known in the Malayalee community as a brilliant mathematician and linguist"; his mother belonged to a family

James J. Puthucheary

that could "trace their status as head of the Syrian Christian community."[10] James Puthucheary was raised in "the idyllic setting of Johore Bahru of the 1930s,"[11] when the Malay colony of Johore had become an "Unfederated Malay State," and completed his schooling at the Johore English College. Further details of Puthucheary's personal life are not available to the author. Yet, it seems plausible to speculate that the worldview and sensibilities of the mature Puthucheary were shaped by the many-faceted qualities of his youth: of his being a descendant of ancient civilizations but belonging to an immigrant ethnic minority group, growing up in Malay-Muslim Johore but living next to cosmopolitan Singapore, and studying in English schools that, more than the "vernacular schools," facilitated friendship with peers of "different races." Much later, when recalling his days in India in the late 1940s, Puthucheary remarked that he "used to dream of Johor Bahru ... used to think of [his] old friends."[12]

Puthucheary was not involved in the war over Malaya that ended in Singapore's surrender in 1942. However, in 1943, the year Subhas Chandra Bose visited Malaya to galvanize support for the Indian National Army (INA) and the Indian Independence League,[13] Puthucheary joined the INA. His participation came almost casually: invited by a friend to a "meeting of Indians," he found himself working with the Indian Independence League for a year, after which he joined the INA.[14] He did not regard his enlistment as an act of an Indian nationalist per se; rather, he saw himself joining a global anti-imperialist movement, one opening to which was constituted by armed struggle against the British rule of India.[15] After some training, he was made a second lieutenant in the Azad Guerrilla Regiment of the INA. In April 1944 his regiment saw action against the British forces in Imphal and Palel, located within the state of Manipur and just inside India. The Imphal campaign was the INA's first and best-known campaign. It involved a long siege of Imphal and Palel that ended in military disaster for the INA. The INA troops were weakened by the inadequacy of supplies, battered by enemy fire, and hampered by the monsoons.[16] Like many of his fellow soldiers, Puthucheary was afflicted with malaria. "The only one in his platoon to survive,"[17] he managed to retreat to Mandalay and to Rangoon. He did not surrender but went to live in the countryside. Then he met and provided information to "Abdul Rashid … the man who really made the INA an important factor in Indian political life."[18] Shortly after, Puthucheary, given some letters to Bhulabhai Desai, an Indian National Congress leader prominent for defending three INA officers court-martialled for treason in October 1945, was "taken in a Dakota plane by a British Indian Air Force officer" to India.[19] There, Puthucheary hid, recuperated, contacted INA members, joined meetings and demonstrations for Indian independence, and "became impressed with the Left, particularly the communists, who stood out as the most dedicated."[20]

Even in 1947, he regarded himself as being "unformed" in his political ideas: "I had gone [to India] as an Indian nationalist" and "had become vaguely sympathetic to the Communists," who impressed him by their "capacity to work" and their dedication to their purpose which was "far greater than all the multitudes of parties and factions in India."[21] He most sympathized with the Communists, because "the Indians shot up some of the [Communist] leaders in 1947," which was "so vicious, that the language of argument ceased and the language of violence took over in order to intimidate the Communists."[22] But in 1985, 22 years after he had been detained in Singapore on "pro-Communist" charges, he was insistent: "I didn't have any Communist association."[23] He was "certainly an admirer of Gandhi"; but being a "transient Indian" who "didn't come from deep Indian roots," Puthucheary did not take to the "pseudo religious mythology."[24] During the terrible time of Partition, Puthucheary worked with an ambulance service aiding a refugee camp that was located on the Indian side of the cleaved Punjab.[25] By then he knew that the unity of India was not tenable. It would remain a painful subject over which he would not be effusive in future; in fact, he largely "blacked it out." Even if he had earlier cast aspersions on the intents and outcomes of the colonial communal electoral system enacted by the British, on the infrequent occasion that Puthucheary was to refer to Indian independence again, he maintained that Partition could have been averted had the Indian National Congress been more conciliatory toward the Muslim League. At any rate, he maintained that someone like Nehru "could have done more."[26]

Puthucheary began university in India, attending Jaipur Engineering College, but only for a few months — because "I was not meant to be an engineer"[27] — and spent a year at Sungari College, founded by Rabindranath Tagore. Eventually, he decided that he was not an Indian: "Politically I felt as an Indian," but "I had been de-culturalised almost completely."[28] He made some very good friends, but "they didn't talk the same language" or else "the words were the same" only they meant different things for him, so that a "great gulf" existed between them.[29] And, thus, it was "no great wrench" for him to leave India when asked to return by his father, who was "fed up" with his wanderings.[30]

Puthucheary left India for Singapore in 1948. Back in Malaya, Puthucheary worked with ex-INA personnel who channeled their political commitments into organizing left-wing anti-imperialist and trade union activities. After June 1948, when the Communist Party of Malaya launched its insurrection, many of those organizers "were detained and banished" while others who "escaped and went underground … were killed in military operations or executed for the alleged offence of bearing arms."[31] Puthucheary decided against joining the insurrection despite the persuasion of his close childhood friend William Kuok Hock Ling (who was later killed in military action).[32] Instead, Puthucheary entered Raffles College, University of Malaya, then sited in Singapore. Here he helped to found a student newspaper (*The Undergrad*). He also became one of the leaders of the student movement and, in 1949, the first secretary general of the University of Malaya Students Union. Here, too, he met and cooperated with a range of "leftists" — in the Malayan Democratic Union, the Anti-British League, and circles of nationalist Malay journalists.[33]

In January 1951 Puthucheary, along with "a large group of English-speaking intellectuals,"[34] was arrested by the Special Branch police and imprisoned without trial on St. John's Island. He was released from prison in June 1952 and returned to the University of Malaya. A year later he helped found the university's Socialist Club and produce its organ, *Fajar*.[35] But on 28 May 1954, three weeks after the fall of Dien Bien Phu, members of the *Fajar* editorial board, including Puthucheary, were arrested and charged with sedition. By then, the university's "left-wing intellectuals were expanding their influence and establishing relationships with the Chinese Middle School students."[36]

Of Puthucheary during this period, it has been observed that he was a

> young man who added significantly to the momentum of 1952 ... Detained in the Anti-British League raids of January 1951, he was released along with fellow student Abdullah Majid on 23 June 1952. It was not long before he met Lee [Kuan Yew] and company at Rajaratnam's house. Puthucheary was a capable organizer with outspoken views. He provided a springboard for Lee and the others into the University undergraduate world and its small and faction-ridden coterie.[37]

This relationship with "Lee and company" brought far-reaching repercussions — for the politics of Singapore and Malaya, and for Puthucheary personally. The *Fajar* defendants were represented by Lee Kuan Yew in a trial that brought Lee a resounding reputation as a lawyer for the left. In 1954 Lim Chin Siong, the popular leader of the "Chinese left" and the trade unions in Singapore, Lee, and others formed the People's Action Party (PAP). After obtaining his degree in economics, Puthucheary went to work with the Singapore Shop and Factory Workers Union, the largest union in Singapore.[38] He was soon active in the PAP as well. Puthucheary suffered a second round of detention without trial in 1956 when the "left-wing" leaders of the PAP were arrested. In prison, Puthucheary "sat for the intermediate examination for the Bachelor of Law degree of the University of London."[39] And here, where the prison "conditions were not as bad as they could have been" — because "civil servants began to show more 'flexibility' as the PAP's political fortunes went up"[40] — Puthucheary wrote *Ownership and Control in the Malayan Economy* (hereafter *OCME*),[41] the pioneering radical critique of the Malayan political economy.

Puthucheary was released in 1959, the year the PAP took power in Singapore on the backs of the anti-colonial, trade union, and student movements. He was appointed the manager of the Industrial Promotion Board,[42] chairman of the Central Provident Fund, and chairman of the Tariff Advisory Committee. But since "he did not fit into the mould of the [PAP],"[43] that is, the regime now headed by Lee Kuan Yew, Puthucheary resigned from these appointments in 1961. He returned to the university, this time to read law. Meanwhile, the merger of Singapore with Malaya (and Sabah and Sarawak) to form Malaysia had become the political issue of the day, critically an issue that split the PAP. The party's rump, led by its "right wing," controlled the government and wanted merger. The party's breakaway "left wing," reconstituted in a new party, Barisan Sosialis (Socialist Front), opposed merger — at any rate on the proposed terms of merger.[44] Puthucheary evidently supported merger in principle but would not support the PAP rump in practice. On 1 February 1963, "he finished writing his last exam [*sic*] paper."[45] At four o'clock the next morning, he was arrested and again detained without trial, this time under "Operation Cold Store" — the mass arrest of the PAP's principal opponents,[46] including some of the island's most prominent political leaders.

Only ten months later was Puthucheary freed. In that he was less unfortunate than some of his fellow detainees, who were to be incarcerated for many more years without any trial under the Internal Security Act (ISA). But the PAP government banished Puthucheary from Singapore. Thus, he "relocated" to Kuala Lumpur, where his wife, Mavis, lived with their two children, the younger of whom was an infant son born while the father was imprisoned.[47] He joined Skrine and Co., one of the leading law firms in Malaysia.

In 1964 he placed his anti-imperialist credentials at the service of the Malaysian government, at the latter's request even though Prime Minister Tunku Abdul Rahman had considered Puthucheary to be a "Communist." At a time when certain anti-colonial quarters inside and outside the country criticized the new Federation of Malaysia — particularly its incorporation of Sabah and Sarawak — for being an imperialist contrivance, Puthucheary traveled to the Afro-Asian Solidarity Conference in Ghana as a member of an official Malaysian delegation that included younger ruling party politicians such as Mahathir Mohamad and Musa Hitam.[48] The trip was a failure. The Malaysian delegation did not receive the accreditation it sought to present "Malaysia's case" at the conference.

Puthucheary's next involvement with the Malaysian government came in the wake of the interethnic violence of 13 May 1969. When "May 13" happened, Puthucheary was away, on the east coast of Peninsular Malaysia.[49] Soon there were several telephone calls to his home in Kuala Lumpur. The calls were made by Abdullah Ahmad, whom Puthucheary had met at university and who was now Deputy Prime Minister Tun Abdul Razak's intermediary to bring Puthucheary for closed-door political and policy discussions. A political casualty of May 13, Tunku Abdul Rahman remained Prime Minister in name although real power had passed to Razak, the director of the National Operations Council, which ruled the country while Parliament was suspended under Emergency regulations. The somewhat "aloof" Razak had read *OCME* and been interested in the author's analysis of the economy and related matters in economic development. In his discussions with Razak and the latter's coterie of advisers and protégés, Puthucheary contributed his knowledge of economics and ideas for development to the eventual formulation of the New Economic Policy (NEP). It may be said that *OCME*'s underlying concerns with poverty, foreign control of the economy, and interethnic inequalities presaged the NEP's turn away from *laissez-faire* capitalism to direct state intervention and massive public investment in order to "eradicate poverty" and, critically, to alter the structure of ownership and control of the Malaysian economy.

Puthucheary was also engaged in discussions over the NEP's thrust of affirmative action and its effects on interethnic relations and "national unity." Once James and Mavis Puthucheary visited Mahathir at the latter's home. Then Mahathir was not just out of Parliament after being defeated in the 1969 general election; he had been expelled from the United Malays National Organization (UMNO) for his open attacks on the party's president, Tunku Abdul Rahman. Within UMNO, though, Mahathir, the author of *The Malay Dilemma*,[50] was an influential "Malay nationalist" ideologue whom Razak wanted to include among the younger generation of Malay politicians, technocrats, and administrators Razak was grooming to implement the NEP. Perhaps, Mavis speculates, the purpose of the Puthuchearys' visit to Mahathir was to enable James to pass Mahathir a message from Razak. If it was so, it was James' "small role in the rehabilitation of Mahathir." On another occasion, Mahathir sought Puthucheary's opinion on the viability or desirability of a "Malay-only government." Puthucheary replied that he "didn't care about ethnicity so long as the government did a good job of governing fairly and justly." This reply was evidently bandied in some UMNO circles that wanted to exclude the Malaysian Chinese Association (MCA) from the post-1969 government. Any such exclusion of the MCA would have demolished the interethnic power-sharing foundation of the Alliance, the coalition of UMNO, MCA, and the Malaysian Indian Congress that ruled from 1957 to 1969. The exclusion was not carried out, but its advocates within UMNO had argued that the MCA's poor performance in the 1969 election showed that the Chinese electorate did not support the Alliance and, therefore, did not deserve to be represented in the Cabinet. However, Mavis Puthucheary recalled, "after Mahathir returned to government, James' role [in policy discussions] tapered off."

Razak died in 1976. But very soon after his deputy, Hussein Onn, became Prime Minister, several Razak advisers or protégés, including Abdullah Ahmad and two of Puthucheary's fellow detainees in 1951 — Abdullah Majid and Samad Ismail — were arrested and imprisoned under the ISA. These detainees were charged with being "Communists" in a witch hunt that accompanied a power struggle within the UMNO. Several non-UMNO left-wing or opposition political leaders were detained at the same time, presumably to render the entire witch hunt less bizarre, less farcical, or less centered on UMNO itself. Within the prison camp, certain interrogators attempted in vain to get some of the detainees to implicate other UMNO leaders, notably Mahathir and Musa Hitam. There was, too, an attempt to incriminate Puthucheary falsely,[51] but he was spared another round of incarceration. He spent the rest of his career in law.

To all intents and purposes, and his involvement in the NEP discussions notwithstanding, Puthucheary's active participation in politics had ended in 1963, 20 years after he enlisted in the INA. During that period, he had pursued his politics relentlessly, risking his life abroad and, at home, suffering indefensible deprivations of his liberty by the colonial, the Labour Front, and the PAP governments in turn.

James Puthucheary died on 3 April 2000, before reaching his 78th birthday.

The Critique of Fallacies

At Puthucheary's memorial service, when he was invited to make an unscheduled speech, Prime Minister Mahathir Mohamad paid a brief but emotional tribute to Puthucheary. One can see that the two men held to anti-imperialism and economic nationalism and that they had contributed, albeit differently, to the NEP's formulations and its expanded role for state intervention. But by the time Mahathir pushed his privatization and Malaysia Incorporated programs, he had left little room for the underlying class and poverty concerns that Puthucheary had expressed in *OCME*. Besides, Mahathir was a steadfast opponent of the left and, in power, a wielder of the ISA in times of political crisis. All considered, Mahathir's tribute was no mean acknowledgment of the quality of a man who bore "no cowardly past" and of the earnestness of his struggles.

In any case, as several assessments of *OCME* have recorded, correctly and authoritatively, there is the lasting impact of Puthucheary's intellectual achievement, seen chiefly in the enduring legacy of *OCME* and the inspiration the book gave to later studies of the Malaysian economy.[52]

Here, one might perhaps add a different appreciation of Puthucheary's ideas. A large part of the work of many kinds of radical, dissident, anti-establishment, committed, or concerned scholars — indeed, perhaps all manner of "public intellectuals," to use a fashionable term that assumes nothing about the "correctness" of anyone's political persuasion — necessarily involves making critiques of ruling ideas, mounting challenges to hegemonic discourses, and subverting dominant narratives. It might even be said that the generic objective of such efforts in ideological combat is the apprehension, interrogation, demolition, and substitution of "ruling fallacies," that is, fallacies about a society that help to coax consent from those who are ruled. Whether or not they succeed, those who work in that general manner may perforce become "discourse-criminals," to adapt Kasian Tejapira's irreverently suggestive terminology, who attract the unwelcome scrutiny of "discourse-police"[53] and often the ruthless repression of the regular police.

Puthucheary was one such "discourse-criminal," perhaps doubly so. He was most definitely a determined hunter of fallacies in different forms, so to speak. A nationalist and scholar, he strove to expose the ruling fallacies about colonial political economy. Indeed, the text of *OCME* is peppered with his critiques of false beliefs, "optical illusions," false assumptions, misconceptions, false corollaries, and erroneous ideas. On the question of Malay rural poverty, for example, which was a severe problem to which he paid considerable attention, Puthucheary argued:

> The belief that the [Malay] Reservations would protect the Malay farmer was based on two fallacies. One was the general view that Malay farmers fall into debt through thriftlessness and indolence. The second fallacy was the assumption that if non-Malays were prevented from treating the land as a pledge for debt, Malays would be able to borrow less and land would remain in the possession of the farmer (*OCME*, 10–1).[54]

But as a democratic socialist, too, Puthucheary criticized the "counter-hegemonic fallacies" of a broad left-wing movement that was trying to resolve one of the intractable ironies of Malaysian political history at a crucial conjuncture.

The irony was this: Ideologically, three great currents of Asian nationalism, originating in China, India, and Indonesia, had washed over colonial Malaya only to leave behind no ideological synthesis that could truly be called Malaysian nationalism and popularly sustained as such. In the absence of that ideological synthesis, Malaysia's multiethnic society was captive to insecure or self-serving perceptions of interethnic differences and competition. For the individual citizen, the historical legacies, social divisions, and political developments that formed a "plural society" made it immensely difficult to internalize the idea of a Malaysian nationality (conceived as a deeply felt and closely held identity). At the level of political economy, the chief obstacle was structural: an ethnic division of labor was rigidly embedded in the uneven development wrought by colonial capitalism. At the global level, if it may be expressed so, there was the additional problem of how to develop a nation and an economy out of colonial strictures and neocolonial limitations.

Consequently, a problematique of "ethnicity, class, and state" informed the entire course of pre- and post-Independence Malaysian politics. Finding no easy solution to this problematique, theorists and practitioners on all sides of urgent political contests were liable, for whatever other reasons, to lose their balance and play fast and loose with that problematique, offering fallacies that would eventually fail.

On one side, successive colonial and independent regimes stressed the centrifugal tensions of ethnicity. In now well-rehearsed views, the success of the Alliance-led independence movement was attributed to an interethnic compromise — the Merdeka compromise — forged by the nation's "founding fathers," who laid the basis of nationhood. However, because it was bound to an elite political compromise, and not the integration of the communities it led, the nationalism of the ruling Alliance coalition was superficial and fragile. Thus, the Alliance's nation-building was undermined by the clashes of mass expectations, at once economic, cultural, and political,[55] that dominated post-1957 politics. In the event, May 13 put paid to the "Alliance formula" — itself a fallacy separating "politics for the Malays" from "economics for the Chinese."

On the other side was a broad left-wing movement that emphasized the unifying contradictions of class for radical anti-colonial and anti-capitalist struggles. But the various parties of the left, no matter their choice of armed struggle or constitutional politics, were themselves rooted in, and practically captive to, ethnically demarcated constituencies. To put it crudely, the Communist Party of Malaya was "Chinese," while the Socialist Front was a coalition of the "Chinese" Labor Party and the "Malay" Partai Rakyat Malaya (Malayan People's Party). To that extent, the failure of the left, apart from being due to concerted repression and internal weaknesses, say, was attributable to its "counter-hegemonic fallacy": as it was, "class-oriented" Party programs substantively reflected the ethnic concerns of their respective, unassimilated, mass constituencies.

In short, could anyone resolve this Janus-faced problematique in practice? Could anyone solve both a "national question" involving the rights of the ethnic communities and a "class question" involving the conditions of peasants and workers? By the late 1950s, Puthucheary had decided his own answers.

In his "Statement of Political Belief," Puthucheary explained that he had broken with Communism although "the urge to join up with those who are fighting [colonialism] hardest is irresistible" since it "often appears that to refuse to join such allies is to be dishonest to one's anti-colonial principles."[56] Two events caused him to "reassess my whole attitude to the MCP."[57] The first was Hungary (in 1956), but it "had no bearings on the question,"[58] presumably because Puthucheary's left-wing commitments were not Communist as such but rather anti-imperialist. The second was Malaya's attainment of independence, so that with "the British today hav[ing] opted out of the struggle," the "continuation of a struggle between a government supported by almost the entire Malay population and a group whose support comes entirely from a section of the Chinese" would spark off "a communal struggle which can do incalculable harm to the country."[59] By Puthucheary's evaluation, the Malays now — and critically — held political power but "Malay problems do not attract the attention they deserve and at best solutions are attempted by people who do not understand even the nature of the problems correctly."[60]

"To the vast majority of Malays," Puthucheary contended, "European capital is a vague entity" since "Europeans very rarely have entered into exploiter-exploited relations with Malays as they have with Indian tappers and Chinese workers."[61] To Li Dun Jen's important observations about absentee European capital in the colonial Malayan economy,[62] one supposes that Puthucheary's reply could be cast, in current jargon, simply as the "absence," meaning the physical absence, of European capitalists and not the embedded presence of capital of European origin. Quite the reverse, however, "Chinese traders constitute [the Malays'] exploiters, the people who take away a large part of their meagre produce, who possess comparative wealth in the midst of their poverty."[63] Puthucheary accepted that the counter-insurgency known officially as the Emergency, with its "separation of Chinese into new villages," had not "dissociat[ed] the individual exploiter from the community" but, on the other hand, "the pride in the achievements of China have made the Chinese a more cohesive community and increased the identification of the exploiters with the community."[64] For these kinds of reasons — there were others related to issues of language and culture — Puthucheary repeatedly warned that any "coup d'etat by the other [non-Malay] communities" or "revolution based upon the support of Indians and Chinese, however non-communal its aims may be," would only "lead to a civil war, which will, though it may be fought for ideological reasons, in effect be a war between the two major communities."[65]

But in *OCME*, Puthucheary strove to restore a balance to such ethnic perceptions of economic realities. In the capitalist sector, rather than the "subsistence sector" where most Malays were active,[66] "the [European] agency houses ... associated with some of the very large European-owned banks ... control not only the commanding heights of Malaya's economy, but also much of the plains" (*OCME*, p. xiv). As such, even the "very large number of Chinese traders ... engaged in buying and selling" and the "ubiquitous activity of the Chinese middleman" did not validate "the popular misconception that commerce is controlled by the Chinese" (*OCME*, p. xv). Indeed, only "the lack of understanding of the extent of control that [European-owned] agency houses, mining agencies and import agencies have over the economy" and "an incomplete understanding of the [subsidiary] position of Chinese-owned capital" (*OCME*, p. xvi) prevented people from seeing that "*the commonly held belief that Chinese dominate the economy is false*" (*OCME*, p. xix).[67] Neither in *OCME* nor elsewhere did Puthucheary display a lack of awareness of non-Malay poverty. Of "Chinese poverty in the midst of Chinese wealth in Singapore," he said that it "illustrate[d] an important common fallacy" — that "creating a few Malay capitalists ... making a few Malays well-to-do" would "raise the economic status of the Malays" (*OCME*, p. 180). Puthucheary concluded *OCME* pointedly: "*Exploitation and poverty are class problems, not communal problems*" (*OCME*, p. 174).[68]

Yet — and this, of course, was a crucial qualification full of political implications — Puthucheary conceded that the "communal identification of poverty and exploitation is inescapable," and many Malays held simply that "the Malays are poor, the Chinese are rich" (*OCME*, p. 180). Moreover, it was "difficult to imagine that the poverty of a very large section of the Malays can be solved by any ... minor adjustment to free enterprise" since "the logic of development through free enterprise would be to enrich those who already possess capital" (*OCME*, p. 180). Puthucheary concluded *OCME* with the warning that "we cannot get the development we need by relying on the market mechanism," because "the sort of development that will take place will be lopsided and communal — with political consequences that will be dangerous" (*OCME*, p. 181). Neither in *OCME* nor in a later critique of development theory did Puthucheary urge a determinedly socialist solution beyond a nationalist, anti-colonial, and social democratic path of development. In the latter essay, "Causes of Underdevelopment," written in 1964, however, he recommended economic development directed by state intervention: "if the 'vicious circle of poverty' that keeps underdeveloped countries where they are [is to be broken], there has to be massive government effort in areas which [have] been in many countries the preserves of private enterprise."[69] This direction of state-led economic development was not different from the general scope of responsibilities Puthucheary had assumed in his various government appointments in Singapore before he broke with the PAP.

Five years later came May 13. Afterward, the *laissez-faire* capitalism of the Alliance was replaced by the "massive government effort" of the NEP. What Puthucheary had called "the communal identification of poverty and exploitation" the official statement of the NEP would in time characterize as "the identification of race with economic function." It was then that Puthucheary was drawn into the discussions on how Razak's NEP regime would implement "the development we need." At its core, the NEP was targeted to "eradicate poverty" and to "abolish the identification of race with economic function." The former was presumably an objective that Puthucheary would naturally support, the latter having a direct link to *OCME*'s critique of the existing patterns of ownership and control in the Malaysian economy. What Razak had in mind for the NEP was state capitalism, which he went as far as to defend as a form of "nationalist socialism" that required a drastic switch from the "market mechanism":

> In the era of the 1950s and 1960s, we yielded to private industry to achieve the goals of that era, but now we have "State Participation" to achieve the goals and objectives that are different and are suitable to our situation and aspirations of the Bumiputera.[70]

This far from exhaustive treatment of Puthucheary's stance on ethnicity, class, and state may be summed up thus: In facing the fallacies present on different sides, Puthucheary inserted in turn "ethnicity" into the "Communist program," "class" into *Ownership and Control in the Malayan Economy*, and "state" into the NEP. Each time, it may be said, he was striving to restore a missing element to the "ethnicity-class-state" leitmotif of the Malaysian political economy.

Only Problems that He Could Pose

Viewed impartially, Puthucheary's 20 years of politics were lined with defeat — INA, and an Indian independence scarred by Partition;[71] a total of six years of detention without trial, the collapse of the left in Singapore and his own banishment from the island; and his return to a Malaysia that was quickly truncated by Singapore's secession in 1965 and soon after contorted by the interethnic violence of 1969. In Singapore, whose government of one-time comrades did not lift Puthucheary's banishment until 1990, the PAP's once-touted "socialism that works" has not laid to rest the old perception that "the Malays are poor, the Chinese are rich."[72]

Consequently, Malay politicians in Malaysia routinely use Singapore as a reminder of the "fate in store" for the Malays were they to lose or forsake their political supremacy in Malaysia. As for Malaysia, not even Puthucheary's involvement in the massive post-May 13 state-led social engineering to rectify the imbalances in the problematique of "ethnicity, class, and state" could be said to have led to unqualified success. The extent of poverty eradication under the NEP was impressive by Third World comparisons, but the simultaneous creation of a Malay capitalist class engendered many kinds of difficulties and consequences. For instance, Samad Ismail recalled of Puthucheary's commitments and recommendations for economic development that:

> James was pursuing the view long held by left wing nationalists among the pre-Emergency progressive forces that political equality would only be meaningful in a society with equitable distribution of economic wealth among Malays and Chinese. Government intervention was, to his mind, a less painful method of redistributing economic wealth. He was later quite disappointed that the strategy gave rise to racialist and chauvinistic tendencies among the Malay elite.[73]

And on this last point about the NEP implementers' increasingly ill disguised "tilt towards interethnic imbalances," Puthucheary was sufficiently disappointed to have concluded that "the NEP created more problems in the end."[74] Thirty years of state intervention to abolish the "identification of race with occupational function" left Mahathir — the most influential ideologue of the "Malay dilemma" and the principal practitioner of "constructive protection" for the Malays — with a pre-retirement lament in 2002 that the Malays faced a "second dilemma."[75] There was, ironically, a conjunction of ethnicity, class, and the state in the powerful multiethnic politico-corporate empires that emerged under the state intervention of Mahathir's "Malaysia Incorporated" regime. But those economic empires were emblematic of nothing so much as enormous social inequalities rather than Puthucheary's vision of "democratic socialism."

Knowing what Puthucheary had tried, in theory and in practice, how familiar it is to find that although the forms of the problems he confronted and conditions have changed, many of those basic problems have flowed to this day, if not unsolved then imperfectly resolved. Naturally the situation is different from when Puthucheary wrote *OCME*. First the NEP "*bumiputera* trusts," then a new class of Malay capitalists, and subsequently Mahathir's state-capital alliance (Malaysia Incorporated) have succeeded in seizing the commanding heights of the national economy *vis-à-vis* foreign direct investment. Yet, the issue of foreign ownership and control of the economy remains, only this time it is mediated by processes of "globalization" sanctified with the neoliberal idolatry of the "market mechanism." The NEP has also substantially reduced poverty and "interethnic imbalances." Yet divisive ethnic perceptions of economic realities persist, except that these perceptions have become more preoccupied with interethnic competition and "meritocracy." Only "a civil war between the two major communities" has not happened, although shades of it loomed during May 13. That was the worst fear of a man who began his immersion in politics with the anti-imperialist INA only to witness his dream of Indian independence drowned in Partition's inter-communal bloodbath, and who, upon returning to Malaya, would have been appalled to hear of the Malay-Chinese conflicts that took place just before and just after the Japanese occupation of Malaya and which, it has been estimated, produced more casualties than the violence of May 13.[76]

From all this, one can read an account of Malaysian history, of course. However, one could extend Puthucheary's analyses and critiques to the historical, and persisting, problems that the colonized in many different parts of the world have encountered: foreign control of the national economy, the limitations to autonomous development, the conflicts between the state and the market, and the entanglements of ethnicity and class in conditions of widespread poverty.

Déjà vu? It is pointless to claim moral victory in defeat. It would be patronizing to do so on Puthucheary's behalf. Still, it was not defeat through and through. Personal talents and many kinds of flows enabled Puthucheary to view and to explain with exceptional clarity and sensitivity major sociopolitical issues that afflicted Malaya as much as they continue to afflict comparable postcolonial situations in Asia and Africa. For James J. Puthucheary, as for many others who perform the role of "discourse-criminal," there can be no dishonor in setting tasks that one cannot solve.[77]

Notes

1 I am grateful to Mavis Puthucheary for lending me some materials by and on her late husband, James Puthucheary, talking to me at length, and correcting an earlier draft. I wish to thank Ch'ng Kim See and the staff at the library of the Institute of Southeast Asian Studies, Singapore, and Jomo K.S. for their kind assistance. Tan Pek Leng most helpfully obtained for me a National Archives of Singapore transcript of a 1985 interview with James Puthucheary.

Cheah Boon Kheng, Caroline Hau, Kasian Tejapira, Khoo Khay Jin, and T. Rajamoorthy made critical comments that were invaluable for a revision of the original draft. I am solely responsible for any errors in this essay.

2 These flows should not be reflexively equated with colonial rule. Of uncolonized Siam, it has been noted: "Economically, the Chakri rulers linked resource-rich Siam to the burgeoning global chain of colonial commodity production as the British Empire's most important rice depot; as Siam's biggest landlords and real-estate developers, they enriched themselves enormously in the process. Politically, they visited and learned from the British and Dutch colonial authorities' methods of governing India, Singapore, and Java and applied that knowledge to the administrative reform of their relatively weak and decentralized traditional patrimonial kingdom into an authoritarian and centralized modernizing auto-colonial state. And culturally, they inhabited a mental, intellectual, and discursive 'civilized' world wishfully close to their sovereign counterparts in the European metropolises and far from their compatriots in the villages. Regarding themselves subjectively as almost a supra-ethnic or supranational cosmopolitan ruling caste, they lorded it over the Siamese nation-people as colonial masters with a royal Thai face." See Kasian Tejapira, *Commodifying Marxism: The Formation of Modern Thai Radical Culture, 1927–1958* (Kyoto: Kyoto University Press, 2002), pp. 5–6.

3 The Malay term is *bumiputera*, which was officially used after 1969 to denote and differentiate citizens of the Malay and other indigenous communities from the non-*bumiputera*, or citizens belonging to or descended from immigrant communities.

4 In the case of the system of Chinese schools already well established with community support before World War II, see Tan Liok Ee, *The Politics of Chinese Education in Malaysia* (Kuala Lumpur: Oxford University Press, 1997). For an overview of Tamil schools, see S. Arasaratnam, *Indians in Malaysia and Singapore* (Kuala Lumpur: Oxford University Press, 1970), pp. 178–95.

5 On labor organization, see Michael Stenson, *Industrial Conflict in Malaya* (London: Oxford University Press, 1970), and *Class, Race and Colonialism in West Malaysia: The Indian Case* (St. Lucia: University of Queensland Press, 1980). See C.F. Yong, *The Origins of Malayan Communism* (Singapore: South Seas Society, 1997) for a study of the origins of Communism in Malaya. In the case of Communist organizers, not just Chinese or Indian but also Indonesian revolutionaries found their way to Malaya.

6 An account of the escape of Tan Kah Kee, a "wanted man" because of his anti-Japanese activities, who departed Singapore two weeks before the British surrender and was hidden by friends in Sumatra and Java until Japan's defeat, is given in C.F. Yong, *Tan Kah-kee: The Making of an Overseas Chinese Legend* (Singapore: Oxford University Press, 1987), pp. 286–93.

7 Soda Naoki, *Melayu Raya and Malaysia: Exploring Greater Malay Concepts in Malaya* (Kyoto: Kyoto University Research Paper, 2002), p. 19.

8 Of Ibrahim Yaakob, the leader of the Giyu Gun, Farish A. Noor said: "His personal experience of migration to the metropolis was but one of thousands, which eventually led to the emergence of a previously unknown constituency: the urban-based Malays of the Colonial metropolitan centers who, for the first time, found themselves freed from the shackles of court and tradition of the *Kerajaans* and in an environment where they, too, were foreigners." See Farish A. Noor, *The Other Malaysia: Writings on Malaysia's Subaltern History* (Kuala Lumpur: Silverfishbooks, 2002), p. 81.

9 This biographical brief is based on Dominic Puthucheary, "James Puthucheary, His Friends and His Times," in *No Cowardly Past: James Puthucheary, Writings, Poems, Commentaries*, ed. Dominic Puthucheary and Jomo K.S. (Petaling Jaya: Insan, 1998), pp. 3–37.

10 Puthucheary, "James Puthucheary," p. 22.

11 Ibid., pp. 20–1.

12 Lim How Seng, *Interview with James Joseph Puthucheary*, 15 June 1985, Political Developments in Singapore, 1945–1965, Transcript of Oral History Interview, National Archives of Singapore, Reel No. 1, p. 4, <http://202.172.178.226/DJVUServer/djvuview.jsp?file=/cord_data/570/OHC000570_001.djvu> [accessed 19 Aug. 2009].

13 "The initial impact of Bose's personality on the Indian community of Malaya was terrific. He was undisputedly a born leader of men and a dynamic personality, possessed of a moving power of oratory. He toured the country making rousing speeches to groups of Indians. Malayan Indians, unused to such political oratory, were swept off their feet and responded warmly. Volunteers flocked to the movement. Branches of the [Indian Independence] League were established in every major town and even in the plantations. Recruitment to the I.N.A. picked up. Differences among officers and civilians were forgotten when they were confronted with Bose's supreme confidence. After his addresses to Indian prisoners of war, thousands enlisted. Discreditable methods were used to persuade enlistment. These were overlooked, and eyes were firmly set on the final objective. The slogan *Chalo Delhi* (Let us go to Delhi!) was on everybody's lips" (Arasaratnam, *Indians in Malaysia and Singapore*, pp. 105–6).

14 Lim, *Interview with Puthucheary*, p. 1.

15 Interview with Mavis Puthucheary, Bangi, Selangor, Malaysia, 29 May 2004. Compare with note 21, which refers to James Puthucheary's recollection that he went to India as an "Indian nationalist."

16 For an account of the campaign, and the military and political maneouvrings preceding it, see Joyce C. Lebra, *Jungle Alliance: Japan and the Indian National Army* (Singapore: Donald Moore for Asia Pacific Press, 1971), pp. 174–93.

17 Puthucheary, "James Puthucheary," p. 25.

18 Lim, *Interview with Puthucheary*, p. 2.

19 Ibid., p. 3.

20 Puthucheary, "James Puthucheary," p. 25.

21 Lim, *Interview with Puthucheary*, pp. 4–5.

22 Ibid., p. 5.

23 Ibid., p. 3.

24 Ibid., p. 5.

25 Interview with Mavis Puthucheary, 29 May 2004.

26 When she returned from a trip to India in 1953, Mavis Puthucheary proudly showed James a photograph of herself with Nehru, only to have James pooh-pooh it because "Nehru could have done more." Ibid.

27 Lim, *Interview with Puthucheary*, p. 3.

28 Ibid.

29 Ibid.

30 Ibid.

31 Puthucheary, "James Puthucheary," p. 27.

32 William Kuok, from the very wealthy Kuok family, spurned an offer of safe conduct out of the jungles that was made by an influential intermediary friendly to the family. For a poem to William Kuok's memory, see James Puthucheary, "An Epitaph," in *No Cowardly Past: James Puthucheary, Writings, Poems, Commentaries*, ed. Dominic Puthucheary and Jomo K.S. (Petaling Jaya: Insan, 1998), p. 199.

33 Samad Ismail, "Our James," in *No Cowardly Past: James Puthucheary, Writings, Poems, Commentaries*, ed. Dominic Puthucheary and Jomo K.S. (Petaling Jaya: Insan, 1998), pp. 55–62, gives a short recollection of the author's encounter with Puthucheary.

34 Samad, "Our James," p. 57.

35 Malay for "Dawn."

36 Puthucheary, "James Puthucheary," p. 13.

37 James Minchin, *No Man Is an Island: A Study of Singapore's Lee Kuan Yew* (Sydney: Allen and Unwin, 1986), p. 65.

38 For different assessments of the union and anti-colonial activities bringing together unionists and students, especially in 1954–5, see C.M. Turnbull, *A History of Singapore 1819–1975* (Singapore: Oxford University Press, 1977), pp. 261–2; Minchin, *No Man Is an Island*, p. 77; and Lee Huay Leng *et al.*, "Riding the Tide of Idealism: An Interview with Han Tan Juan," *Tangent* (Singapore) 6 (Apr. 2003): 212–4.

39 *The Straits Times*, 17 June 1959.

40 Mavis Puthucheary provides a longer account of the conditions of prison life experienced by Puthucheary and his fellow detainees then — but "I do not want to give the impression that life in prison was a bed of roses" — in "Remembrance: James J. Puthucheary," *BERITA* 28, 2 (2nd quarter) (2004): 1–3.

41 J.J. Puthucheary, *Ownership and Control in the Malayan Economy* (Singapore: Donald Moore for Eastern Universities Press, 1960).

42 The *Singapore Tiger Standard*, 17 June 1959, reported Puthucheary "waving a booklet of the PAP's five-year plan" at a press conference held the previous day.

43 Puthucheary, "James Puthucheary," p. 28.

44 A summary account of the political complexities of Singapore's relationship to the Malaysia proposal is given in Minchin, *No Man Is an Island*, pp. 110–22.

45 Puthucheary, "James Puthucheary," p. 28.

46 T.J.S. George, *Lee Kuan Yew's Singapore* (Singapore: Eastern Universities Press, 1984), pp. 68–70; Minchin, *No Man Is an Island*, pp. 127–8.

47 Puthucheary's detention made it "necessary" for the Singapore government to terminate Mavis' position in the civil service, so Mavis was personally informed by Lee Kuan Yew, who had called her for a meeting in his office. Interview with Mavis Puthucheary, Penang, 11 Nov. 2003.

48 In July 1981 Mahathir became Prime Minister and appointed Musa to be his deputy.

49 Interview with Mavis Puthucheary, 29 May 2004. The information on Puthucheary in the rest of the paragraph is drawn from this interview, as are various quotes (where applicable).

50 For a detailed analysis of *The Malay Dilemma* that might help an interested reader compare and contrast Mahathir's and Puthucheary's ideas on the Malaysian political economy, see Khoo Boo Teik, *Paradoxes of Mahathirism: An Intellectual Biography of Mahathir Mohamad* (Kuala Lumpur: Oxford University Press), pp. 24–34.

51 Puthucheary, "James Puthucheary," p. 35.

52 Charles Hirschman, "Ownership and Control of the Malayan Economy Revisited," in *No Cowardly Past: James Puthucheary, Writings, Poems, Commentaries*, ed. Dominic Puthucheary and Jomo K.S. (Petaling Jaya: Insan, 1998), pp. 77–83; Ozay Mehmet, "James Puthucheary: A Pioneering Intellectual of Malaysian Economic Development Strategy," in *No Cowardly Past: James Puthucheary, Writings, Poems, Commentaries*, ed. Dominic Puthucheary and Jomo K.S. (Petaling Jaya: Insan, 1998), pp. 84–8.

53 Kasian, *Commodifying Marxism*, p. 194.

54 After this paragraph comes Puthucheary's rebuttal against these fallacies.

55 The expectations were *economic* because *laissez-faire* capitalism could not match the social pressures being exerted by a marginalized Malay peasantry (which sought release from rural poverty), a combination of Malay bureaucrats, intelligentsia, and middle class (which wanted an end to their relative backwardness *vis-à-vis* their Chinese counterparts and Chinese capital in particular), and the non-Malay middle and working classes (that refused to accept that their opportunities for employment, education, and upward mobility could be prejudiced by the constitutional safeguards of certain "Malay special rights"). The expectations were *political* because they crystallized during the 1969 general election into a democratic revolt against the Alliance

"formula." The expectations were *cultural* in that the latent, set, and imagined fissures of the "plural society" were acutely felt in the areas of language, culture, and citizenship, areas susceptible to partisan emotion during the formative experience of "nationhood" still haunted by the collective memories and complex demands of prewar Malay, Chinese, and Indian nationalism. See Khoo Boo Teik, "Politics after Mahathir," in *Modern Malaysia in the Global Economy: Political and Social Change into the 21st Century*, ed. Colin Barlow (Cheltenham: Edward Elgar, 2001), pp. 135–46.

56 James Puthucheary, Letter to Lee Kuan Yew, 2 Sept. 1957, reprinted as "James Puthucheary: A Statement of Political Belief," *The Straits Times*, 23 Jan. 1962.

57 Puthucheary, Letter to Lee Kuan Yew.

58 Ibid. Without elaboration, Puthucheary dated his break "with his political friends" to 1951 (Puthucheary, Letter to Lee Kuan Yew). In this regard, it may be worth recalling an incident from his 1951–2 experience as a political prisoner on St. John's Island: one of his fellow detainees, following a heated argument, attempted to knife Puthucheary. The details of the incident are not quite clear, but Samad Ismail, another detainee who disarmed the attacker, thought that the incident might have arisen after Puthucheary's criticisms of the "ideological standards of the more militant Chinese detainees," some of whom had accused Puthucheary of "ideological weakness and even of disloyalty to the cause." See Samad, "Our James," p. 60.

59 Puthucheary, Letter to Lee Kuan Yew. The "group" presumably referred to the Communist Party.

60 Ibid.

61 Ibid.

62 Li Dun Jen, *British Malaya: An Economic Analysis*, 2nd rev. ed. (Kuala Lumpur: Insan, 1982), p. 171.

63 Puthucheary, Letter to Lee Kuan Yew.

64 Ibid.

65 James Puthucheary, Letter to Wang Gungwu, 1958, reprinted as "On the Future of Socialism in Malaya," in *No Cowardly Past: James Puthucheary, Writings, Poems, Commentaries*, ed. Dominic Puthucheary and Jomo K.S. (Petaling Jaya: Insan, 1998), pp. 146–60.

66 He meant that the generally impoverished Malay peasants operated close to subsistence level, not that their production was not commodified.

67 Emphasis in original.

68 Emphasis in original.

69 James Puthucheary, "Causes of Underdevelopment," in *No Cowardly Past: James Puthucheary, Writings, Poems, Commentaries*, ed. Dominic Puthucheary and Jomo K.S. (Petaling Jaya: Insan, 1998), pp. 105–26. The brackets contain plausible corrections to errors in the source.

70 Tun Abdul Razak, Speech at the Development Seminar organized by UMNO Youth, Morib, Selangor, 25 July 1971, reprinted in *Dasar Ekonomi Baru:*

hikmat, kebajikan dan peranan parti (Petaling Jaya: UMNO), pp. 3–21. Indeed Razak, a Fabian and a member of the Labour Party in his student days in Britain, was not afraid to defend the NEP as a form of "nationalist socialism" although it meant stretching the meaning of "socialism." Intriguingly, Puthucheary, in his Letter to Lee Kuan Yew, had referred to the work of the "early Fabians" in helping British socialists to "identify their socialism and take an interest in discussing and understanding its salient features."

71 K.K. Ghosh, *The Indian National Army: Second Front of the Indian Independence Movement* (Meerut: Meenakshi Prakashan, 1969), pp. 266–7, argues that the INA found victory in defeat when popular Indian revulsion at the postwar trial of INA officers hastened Britain's withdrawal from India.

72 For instance, see Lily Zubaidah Rahim, *The Singapore Dilemma: The Political and Educational Marginality of the Malay Community* (Kuala Lumpur: Oxford University Press, 1998), pp. 19–26. Also see Alfian Bin Sa'at, "The Racist's Apology," *Tangent* (Singapore) 5 (Oct. 2002): 217–20, for a concise and candid airing of "ethnic grievances" replete with images of the marginalization and minoritization of the Malays in Singapore. A "reflection" on Alfian's article is given by Ng How Wee, "Accomplices in the Construction of a Racialist Discourse: The Institutions of the State and the Economy," *Tangent* (Singapore) 5 (Oct. 2002): 203–12.

73 Samad, "Our James," p. 62.

74 The quotes are from Mavis Puthucheary (Interview with Mavis Puthucheary, 29 May 2004).

75 Khoo Boo Teik, *Beyond Mahathir: Malaysian Politics and Its Discontents* (London and New York: Zed Books, 2003), pp. 188–99.

76 Cheah Boon Kheng, *Red Star over Malaya: Resistance and Social Conflict during and after the Japanese Occupation, 1941–1946* (Singapore: Singapore University Press, 1983), pp. 210–40.

77 An updated tribute to Puthucheary's political thought and activities was supplied by Tengku Razaleigh Hamzah, one of Razak's protégés in the NEP project. Speaking at the launch of the second edition of *No Cowardly Past* in Petaling Jaya, Selangor, on 22 March 2010, Razaleigh noted: "James Puthucheary lived what is by any measure an extraordinary and eventful life. He was, among other things, a scholar, anti-colonial activist, poet, political economist and lawyer. The thread running through these roles was his struggle for progressive politics in a multiracial society. His actions were informed by an acute sense of history and by a commitment to a more equitable and just Malaysia. James was concerned about economic development in a way that was Malaysian in the best sense. His thinking was motivated by a concern for socioeconomic equity and for the banishment of communalism and ethnic chauvinism from our politics." See Tengku Razaleigh Hamzah, "No Cowardly Past," *razaleigh.com*, 23 Mar. 2010, <http://razaleigh.com/> [accessed 25 Mar. 2010].

CHAPTER 8

K. Bali: Sino-Thai Peranakan in Search of Sabah Nationhood

Yamamoto Hiroyuki

In July 2005, a Malaysian film titled *Sepet* won the Best Film and five other awards at the 18th Malaysian Film Festival. The film is about the love story between a Malay-Muslim girl and a Chinese boy in the beautiful countryside of Ipoh, Malaysia. In spite of severe criticism by old-guard thinkers who accused the film of being derogatory to the Malay/Muslim community, the film was popular among the Malaysian as well as foreign public. Some reviews lauded the film for painting a lively picture of multi-cultural Malaysian life, but I would argue that the film gained popularity because it succeeded in portraying "another Malaysia," a Malaysia that does not exist. The leading characters in the film are a reversal of what we see in everyday Malaysia: boy tries to gain girl's favor, housemaid instructs her master, and the like.

Art and literature, no matter how realistic, are works of imagination. This imagination is often fostered and strengthened by the creator's own experience. In the age of nationalism, in which culturally and hereditarily defined human categories were given significance to distinguish friends and foes, people with hybrid cultural backgrounds, or Peranakan as they are called in Malay, were often forced into the margins of society, which in turn led them to set out on journeys in search of places where they could live without bothering about their backgrounds.

This chapter focuses on one such person, K. Bali, a journalist and man of letters working in the Malay language in North Borneo (currently the state of Sabah, Malaysia), who started his career in the 1950s. He was born a Sino-Thai Buddhist in a village near the Malaya-Thai border and in his 20s went to North Borneo, where he lived as a Malay-Muslim.

K. Bali's *Memoir*

Being the editor of the only Malay daily publication in the state at the time, K. Bali played a very important role in fostering the idea of "Sabah nationhood" among the Malay-reading people of North Borneo. K. Bali's name, however, barely appears in the scholarship on the history of North Borneo. What we can find, at most, regarding K. Bali are some articles on Malay literature on the state, which treat K. Bali as not much more than a pioneer who brought Malay literature into North Borneo in the 1950s.[1] Most of these articles rely on K. Bali's personal documents, which are held by the Sabah State branch of the Institute of Language and Literature (Dewan Bahasa dan Pustaka, DBP).[2] The documents are based on interviews with K. Bali conducted by the DBP in 1993, and on related documents provided by K. Bali himself. What I would like to draw attention to here is some very important information that was carefully omitted from the documents. Among other things, K. Bali was not born a Malay Muslim but a Buddhist with a Hokkien-speaking Chinese father and a Siamese mother. The same documents were collected and published as K. Bali's *Memoir* in 2002, but the memoir itself contains the same omissions.

In this chapter, I shall trace the first half of K. Bali's life by cross-checking the description provided by the *Memoir* with K. Bali's personal documents and interviews with relevant persons in both Tendong, Kelantan, where K. Bali was born, and Sungai Padi, Thailand, where he spent his teenage years.[3] Influenced by Indonesian nationalism, K. Bali envisioned the possibility of, and sought to bring into being, a society free of discrimination against ethnicities and classes. Consequently, he left Malaya for Thailand, then moved to North Borneo. Interestingly, at the pivotal points of his journey, K. Bali was helped by two prominent personalities of Peranakan background, Kasma Booty and Donald Stephens, as we shall see in this chapter. I shall also examine the concept of "bangsa Sabah" (Sabah nationhood) proposed by K. Bali, a concept formulated out of the experiences of his journey in search of the "ideal" homeland.

Peranakan Chinese in Kelantan

K. Bali was born in 1927 in Tendong village, in the district of Pasir Mas, Kelantan.[4] Tendong is well known for its Peranakan Chinese, or localized Hokkien-speaking Buddhist Chinese who often marry local-born Buddhist Siamese. They live in a settlement beside a Malay settlement in the village, and habitually speak Malay with a Kelantanese accent.[5]

There is no better example of such couples than K. Bali's own parents. K. Bali's father, Tenh Ah Gan, was a Hokkien-speaking Chinese and was called Bali in the village, in the tradition of village Chinese acquiring a Malay nickname. K. Bali's mother was a local-born Siamese whose family originated from Pulau Sentul, Narathiwat, south Thailand.

K. Bali's parents had three sons, of whom K. Bali was the second-born.[6] K. Bali was named Tenh Beng Chuan and called Kote by the villagers.[7] As with other village Chinese boys and girls, K. Bali and his brothers were brought up as Buddhists by their parents and were taught Hokkien by their father, Siamese by their mother, and Malay by the villagers.

K. Bali grew up in the village, in an environment where the Peranakan Chinese mixed freely and intimately with neighboring Malays. He was treated as their brother, since there were no differences between K. Bali and his Malay friends in the village other than religion and his ethnic origin.

This sense of brotherhood was bolstered by Indonesian nationalist thought. K. Bali entered primary school in 1939, when he was allowed to study at a Malay-medium Tendong primary school in the village. It had been common for the village Chinese not to send their children to school, as had been the case with K. Bali's parents, but more parents had begun sending their children to school by K. Bali's time.[8] One day K. Bali was taken by his friends to school, and there he showed a talent for drawing. The headmaster, impressed, allowed K. Bali to attend classes. K. Bali studied there until he had to leave school to help his mother, after his father died in 1944.[9]

In school, K. Bali encountered Indonesian nationalism through books and magazines brought in from Indonesia. Indonesian nationalism rested on three pillars. First, the peoples in the region called Indonesia were, regardless of their differing backgrounds, integrated into a single nation called "bangsa Indonesia" (Indonesian nation). Second, the Indonesian nation had struggled to oust the Dutch colonialists and attain self-rule. And third, the Indonesian nation sought to transcend internal differences such as class and ethnicity. The pillars informed K. Bali's reflections on his status as a Malay-speaking Sino-Siamese Buddhist in the Malay-Muslim-dominated society of Malaya, and inspired him to dream of realizing "bangsa Malaya" in Malaya by applying the tenets of Indonesian nationalism.

But postwar Malaya followed a different course and succeeded only in deepening the ethnic polarization between Malays and non-Malays. The Malayan Union's plan, proposed by the British in 1945, had included the treatment of all the inhabitants in Malaya as equal citizens; but this provision encountered strong criticism from the Malays, who claimed that non-Malays were of foreign origin and therefore should not be treated as rightful citizens of the country. Kelantan, too, was swept by the tide of ethnic polarization.[10] When Harold MacMichael arrived in Kelantan on 14 December 1945 to collect signatures from the Sultans in support of the Malayan Union's plan, about 30,000 Malays gathered in front of the palace at Kota Bharu bearing slogans such as "Tanah Melayu untuk Melayu" (Malaya is for Malays). The protest campaign against the plan took place nationwide and spurred the establishment of the ethnic-based political party United Malays National Organization (UMNO), in May 1946. In a way, the idea of "bangsa Malaya" was rejected by the Malays to make way for "bangsa Melayu" (Malay nation).

During this time of increasing ethnic polarization, K. Bali lived as a "Chinese." In 1946 he enrolled in a Chinese school instead of the Malay school he had attended before the war. This was because his father was of Chinese descent, though K. Bali and his father could neither read nor write Chinese. K. Bali could expect to be accepted as Malay by the Malay community if he became Muslim, but this would affect his family ties.[11]

Under these circumstances, in 1948 K. Bali — at the age of 20 — decided to leave his village and move to Sungai Padi, a Malay-dominated village in the south of Thailand. There he became a Muslim and started his new life as a Malay by using his pen name, K. Bali.

The Malay Muslim Community in Sungai Padi

Sungai Padi, which once flourished with rubber plantations, is located about ten kilometers north of Sungai Kook, Thailand's border with Malaya (Malaysia). There, K. Bali was allowed to attend the third year of Paluru Iterus Primary School, where he was educated in Thai. After finishing primary school in March 1950, K. Bali entered Pracha Nukheroh Secondary School. He attended classes in the morning and gave private lessons in Malay and Thai to Malay students in the evening.[12] At night he worked in a cinema in Sungai Padi, drawing publicity posters, serving as a ticket-taker, and sometimes watching films for free.

Malay cinema had begun to recover from the devastation caused by the Japanese Occupation. Among the first films of postwar Singapore, *Chinta* and *Chempaka* gained popularity in 1948 and gave birth to new film stars such as P. Ramlee and Kasma Booty.[13] K. Bali not only enjoyed watching the films but also imported some ideas from the films into his writings.[14] Kasma Booty, who had a big following among film buffs, later played an important role in K. Bali's life: she was instrumental in enabling him to visit North Borneo.

In Sungai Padi, K. Bali lived in the Malay community. Nobody questioned his family background, because he was fluent in Malay. He had disclosed his family background and his real name only to his very close friends. In 1953 K. Bali formally converted to Islam. The conversion was done by Mek Knua, who taught Islam in Sungai Padi and was K. Bali's "mother" in Sungai Padi.[15]

News of K. Bali's conversion was delivered to his family in 1953 by the man himself.[16] On his return from Tendong to Sungai Padi, K. Bali wrote a poem titled "Restu dari Langit" (Sanctuary from Heaven):

> Remembering my mother
> Rouses my passion
> Mother advised me
> On my seeing her
>
> "Son, do not set out on a journey
> But if you take your journey

Never suffer from hunger in a foreign land
When you die, you must die with satisfaction."

Yet, I shall go on journeying
Even if I am far away from home beyond the ocean
I wish for Mother's sanctuary
Sanctuary from heaven

The poem gives the impression that K. Bali's mother has died, but K. Bali's mother actually died 32 years after the poem was written. If the poem gives such an impression, it should be interpreted as an expression of Bali's preparedness for the end of his life as the Buddhist Tenh Beng Chuan, and, in the same way, for his new journey in life as a Muslim.

From Tendong to North Borneo

K. Bali started his career as a writer while in Sungai Padi.[17] His first published poem was "Keindahan Sungai Padi" (The Beauty of Sungai Padi), which appeared in the March 1951 issue of *Hiboran* magazine. His first novel was *Jangan Pisang Berbuah Dua Kali* (Do Not Have a Banana Tree Produce Fruit Twice [Do Not Repeat the Same Mistake]), published in August 1952 in *Hiboran*. *Hiboran Filem*, *Fashen*, *Tunas*, *Mutiara*, and other magazines in Singapore and Malaya carried his works. K. Bali wrote poems in Thai too.[18]

By this time K. Bali had established himself as a man of letters by following in the footsteps of Indonesian writers who struggled for independence with their pens. This can be seen in his adopted Muslim name, Abdul Rahim, which is a homage to "the father of Malay journalism," Abdul Rahim Kajai.[19]

His new life as a Malay in Thailand, however, did not last long. K. Bali was ousted from Thailand under suspicion of writing an article with political intent for a Malay newspaper. He returned to Kelantan in 1954. It was Kasma Booty who helped K. Bali continue his journey to seek his ideal homeland. At the time, she was the head of a touring theater, Booty Surya Negara. On her tour of Kelantan in 1955, Kasma Booty was visited by K. Bali, who pleaded for a job. Kasma Booty, a Dutch-Indonesian Peranakan, welcomed K. Bali to the theater. K. Bali worked as information agent for the theater, drawing publicity pictures and sending articles to local newspapers.

K. Bali seemed to have entertained hopes of migrating to Singapore, where ethnic polarization appeared to be less severe than in Malaya. In any case, joining the touring theater brought K. Bali to North Borneo on a casual visit.

Booty Surya Negara arrived at Jesselton, the capital of British North Borneo, in February 1956. The theater performed at towns and estates along the west coast of the colony before returning to Jesselton in April.[20] During the tour, K. Bali was amazed to find that North Borneo was free of ethnic polarization and that people lived in harmony in spite of ethnic diversity. Moreover, he found that Malay was widely used as the lingua franca of the region: it was commonly and well accepted by people of various ethnic origins and spoken with different accents, depending on the speakers' backgrounds. Here K. Bali saw the possibility of establishing a "bangsa" with Malay as the common language, just like bangsa Indonesia and bahasa Indonesia.

On arriving at Jesselton in April 1956, K. Bali visited Donald Stephens in his office at the *North Borneo News and Sabah Times*. Stephens, who later became the first chief minister of North Borneo (Sabah) following independence from Britain in 1963, was born in 1920 in Kudat, North Borneo. Both his parents were children of unions between white men and local women. Because they were unwanted by their fathers and they were brought up in isolation from the local communities, Stephens' parents could not identify themselves as either European or with any local community in the country. This led Stephens' father to foster the idea that they did not belong to any of the ethnic groups in the country, but instead identified themselves as North Borneans. Stephens inherited this idea and struggled to bring the idea into fruition, first by establishing an English-language daily[21] in 1953 and later by participating in politics through the establishment of a political party in 1961.[22]

On seeing Stephens in April 1956, K. Bali spoke passionately about North Borneo, where peoples of different ethnic origins lived in harmony, and asked Stephens to employ him to oversee the Malay section of his newspaper. Owing to financial constraints, Stephens was at first reluctant to do so, but he was eventually persuaded by Fauzi Patel, the only other staff member of the newspaper. Patel was in charge of almost all the work in the office. At that time Patel had difficulty in handling the Malay section since he was only beginning to learn the language, so he persuaded Stephens to employ K. Bali to edit the Malay corner.[23]

K. Bali followed Booty Surya Negara and left North Borneo on June 4 for Singapore, since he had to complete his contract with the theater. His farewell message, which read "I shall return as long as I am alive," appeared in the Malay corner on 12 June 1956. The line was taken from his poem "Debar Berombak" (Pulsing Heartbeat).

"Debar Belombak" is a poem in which *adik* (younger brother/sister), on setting out for his/her journey, endures the pangs of separation from *abang* (elder brother). *Adik* confesses that he/she is "struck by admiration for the *abang*'s philosophy of life" and is "fascinated by the conscientious efforts of *abang*," and *adik* tells *abang*, "I shall return as long as I am alive."

The poem implies the parting of a couple, as the word *abang* is commonly equated with "darling" when used by a woman to address her partner and *adik* also has the same meaning when used by a man to address his partner in Malay. But if we take *abang* and *adik* literally, we picture a younger brother saddened by separation from his elder brother and telling him that he will return as long as he is alive. This reveals the built-in message of K. Bali: K. Bali admires Stephens' philosophy of life as well as Stephens himself, who with his mixed Western and Peranakan background envisioned making North Borneo a land free from ethnic discrimination, and K. Bali is fascinated by Stephens' conscientious effort to realize his vision by publishing a newspaper and propounding his ideas to the English readers of the country.

K. Bali's Concept of Bangsa Sabah

K. Bali returned from Singapore and took charge of the Malay section of the *North Borneo News and Sabah Times* on 22 August 1956. From then on, he enthusiastically introduced the idea of Indonesian nationalism through the Malay section.

One of his attempts was to rename North Borneo "Sabah." Indonesian nationalists called their homeland "Indonesia" instead of the name given by the colonialists, "Dutch East Indies." By the same token, K. Bali sought a local name for North Borneo and found "Sabah," an old appellation for the west coast of North Borneo coined by the Brunei court and meaning "downstream" (of the Brunei River).[24] There were some companies, including Stephens' *North Borneo News and Sabah Times*, that used the word Sabah, but most people were unsure of what Sabah meant.

K. Bali went further by calling the people of North Borneo "bangsa Sabah" and the Malay language used there "bahasa Sabah," just as the Indonesian nationalists called themselves "bangsa Indonesia" (Indonesian nation) and their Malay language "bahasa Indonesia" (Indonesian language).

K. Bali's concept of bangsa Sabah crystallized in an article he wrote on 16 September 1959 titled "Malay Language: High-classed or Low-classed?" In this article, K. Bali argued in favor of the importance of the Malay language. This article contained two important points regarding K. Bali's ideas on bahasa Sabah and bangsa Sabah. First, K. Bali made clear that the Malay language was important not because it was the mother tongue of Malays but because it was the common language of the peoples of North Borneo. He wrote: "The right to use Malay is not limited to Malays. The right of use of the language is open to more than 80 million people who live in the Malay archipelago, which consists of Indonesia, North Borneo, Sarawak, Brunei, Singapore, the Federation of Malaya and south Thailand." Furthermore, K. Bali noted the fluency in Malay of the people of North Borneo and stated that "the people in this country, of any ethnic groups, can use Malay, not bothering if it is called high-class Malay, low-class Malay, bazaar Malay, mixed Malay or any kind of Malay."[25] By stating this, K. Bali raised his objection to the then-dominant idea that Malay was the language of civilization and that those who were fluent in Malay (such as those in Malaya and in Indonesia) were more civilized than those who lived in other regions.

Second, K. Bali firmly denied the idea that the Malay language used in North Borneo should be judged by the standards set in Indonesia or Malaya. K. Bali gave as examples words such as *siring* (edge), *sungkai* (fast-breaking by sunset), *jaraya* (high street), and *tagar* (rust), Malay terms found in North Borneo but not in Malaya, and wrote that "these words will never be brought from Malaya even if we wait for ten years from now," and "to develop our Malay vocabularies, we should not just wait for them to come from Malaya." In speaking thus, K. Bali championed the Malay language used in North Borneo by arguing that it had its own individuality and value. While K. Bali admitted that the development of the Malay language in North Borneo lagged behind that of Malaya and Indonesia, he insisted that the lag could be redressed by developing the Malay of North Borneo, not by learning from other territories, including Malaya.

With these two points, K. Bali declared his opposition to the idea of the Malay language as a tool to demarcate and differentiate its users from each other. He emphasized, instead, the alternative idea of language as a tool to integrate people with different, heterogeneous cultural backgrounds.

K. Bali's idea stimulated the local peoples in North Borneo, especially the Muslims. In the early days, the ethnic identities of non-Malay Muslims such as Bajaus were given negative connotations in North Borneo; if a

Muslim was not Malay, he/she was not considered "civilized." Consequently, it was common for educated Muslims to hide their ethnic origins at their workplaces in North Borneo. This situation changed after K. Bali introduced the idea of bangsa Sabah in the mid-1950s.[26] It led to the emergence of a Bajau identity in 1960 among the Muslim-majority ethnic group in North Borneo. This indicated that the people of North Borneo embraced K. Bali's message that they should not judge themselves by the standards of neighboring regions but should have confidence in who they were, a message that still resonates among the people of Sabah today.

Postscript

In response to the rising tide of nationalism, K. Bali pursued a kind of nationalism that would be realized in a certain territory. What made him different from other nationalists of the time was his subject position as a member of a minority. Being a member of a minority group, K. Bali needed some twist in his advocacy of nationalism; otherwise, he would have ended up being absorbed into the majority.

To avoid absorption into the majority, K. Bali traveled from one country to another. As nationalism takes hold within a specific territory, it does not pay much attention to the similarities or commonalities between "its" society and other societies beyond "its" territorial boundaries. Traveling enables a person not only to imagine but to see and experience for himself or herself another society, other societies, across boundaries, even in cases where there is a continuity between societies on both sides of the borders. This double vision of nationalism is what led K. Bali to travel in search of a place where his ideal nationalism could be realized.

K. Bali arrived in Sabah in 1956 and advocated Sabah nationhood, but he did not bring to full fruition his vision. K. Bali's concept of nationalism was idealistic, and for that reason not easily realizable. This leads us to the conclusion that K. Bali's pursuit of nationalism, because it could not be fully realized, meant that his journey in search of an ideal home would never end.

Serving as editor in various newspapers in Sabah until 1995, K. Bali left Sabah and returned to Tendong village in 1998, one year before he passed away on 17 June 1999. There are a number of theories as to why he "returned home" before his death. My argument is that K. Bali did not "return home" but happened to pass away on his travel in search of his ideal nationalism. K. Bali's travel in search of a place where unbounded nationalism could flourish never ended.

List of K. Bali's Published Works

1. Novels/Novellas
   1966. *Bulan Muda Hati Muda*. Ipoh: Pustaka Muda.
   1967. *Hanya Tinggal Kenangan*. Singapore: Pustaka Abadi.
   1969. *Bogel*. Singapore: Pustaka Abadi.
   1969. *Sarini*. Singapore: Pustaka Abadi.
   1991. *Syurga Idaman*. Kuala Lumpur: Penerbitan Nusantara.
2. Anthologies of short stories
   1970. *Ombak dan Angin*. Singapore: Pustaka Abadi.
   1970. *Dari Syurga ke Neraka*. Kuching: Biro Kesusasteraan Borneo.
3. Collections of poems
   1968. *Pantun Indah, Dendang Sabah*. Singapore: Pustaka Abadi.
   1970. *Pantun Perindu*. Singapore: Pustaka Abadi.
   1973. *Yang Terkasih: Kumpulan Sajak 1971*. Singapore: Pustaka Abadi.
   1973. *Debar Berombak*. Kuching: Biro Kesusasteraan Borneo.
   1993. *Restu dari Langit*. Kuala Lumpur: Dewan Bahasa dan Pustaka.
4. Books on history, geography and culture of North Borneo
   1964. *Memperkenalkan Brunei*. Kota Bharu: Pustaka Aman Press.
   1966. *Sayang Sarawak*. Kota Bharu: Pustaka Aman Press.
   1966. *Kumpulan Penjodoh Bilangan*. Singapore: Pustaka Abadi.
   1967. *Kesah Sejarah Perang "Si-Gunting"*. Singapore: Pustaka Abadi.
   1968. *Ringkasan Ilmu Alam Baharu Sabah*. Singapore: Pustaka Abadi.
   1968. *Ringkasan Sejarah Sabah*. Singapore: Pustaka Abadi.
   1970. *4 Sukubangsa Sabah*. Singapore: Pustaka Abadi.
   1985. *Peristiwa-Peristiwa Berdarah di Sabah* (by Ismail Abbas and K. Bali). Kuala Lumpur: Dewan Bahasa dan Pustaka.
   1990. *Si Gunting*. Kuala Lumpur: Dewan Bahasa dan Pustaka.
   1992. *Antanum*. Kuala Lumpur: Dewan Bahasa dan Pustaka.
   1993. *Diari K. Bali*. Kuala Lumpur: Dewan Bahasa dan Pustaka.
5. Other writings
   1959. *11 Wanita Pejuang Dunia*. Penang: Sinaran Bros.
   1959 (1963). *Riwayat Hidup: Seniman Agung Pelukis Dunia*. Penang: Sinaran Bros.
   1967 (1974). *Rahsia Memikat Wanita*. Singapore: Pustaka Abadi.
   1971. *Rahsia Petua Firasat dan Pantang Larang*. Singapore: Pustaka Abadi.
   2002. *Memoir Karyawan Tamu DBP Cawangan Sabah: Dari Tendong ke Borneo*. Kuala Lumpur: Dewan Bahasa dan Pustaka.
6. Comics
   1960? *Samseng di Kota Bangkok*. Singapore: Pustaka Abadi.

1969. *Menanti Kembali*. Singapore: Pustaka Abadi.
1969. *Berlumoran Darah di Pekan Tua* (by Zaidin Johan and K. Bali). Singapore: Pustaka Abadi.
1974. *Tinggal-lah Bunga*. Singapore: Pustaka Abadi.

Notes

1 See, for example, the papers in Penulis dan Penulisan di Sabah, *Penulisan Sastera terhadap Kebudayaan Nasional, 3–6 Disember 1978, Kota Kinabalu* (Kota Kinabalu: Persatuan-Persatuan Penulis, Yayasan Sabah, Dewan Bahasa dan Pustaka, Kementerian Kebudayaan Belia dan Sukan Negeri, 1979). The article by Solehan Solehan Ishak, "K. Bali: Profile of a Theatre: Activist Brief Biography," *Sumber* (Universiti Kebangsaan Malaysia) 4 (1988): 115–24, treats K. Bali in regard to drama.

2 See Sitti Hadiah Haji Abd. Mutalib, "K. Bali," *Jambak 3*, ed. Ahmad Kamal Abdullah and Zaiton Ajamain (Kuala Lumpur: Dewan Bahasa dan Pustaka, 1995), pp. 159–73; and Abd. Naddin Shaiddin, "K. Bali dalam Kenangan," *Dewan Sastera* (Aug. 1999): 46–9.

3 K. Bali's personal belongings were donated by his family to Pustaka Noor Zahra' (Noor Zahra Memorial Library) in Kota Bharu, Kelantan, upon his death in June 1999. I am grateful to the library for allowing me to use the materials, which include photo albums, autograph books, memo pads, and other documents.

4 The description of K. Bali is based on information obtained at the Dewan Bahasa dan Pustaka (Sabah branch) and K. Bali's *Memoir*, and confirmed through the interviews in Tendong and Sungai Padi in February and September 2000.

5 For the Chinese and the Siamese in Kelantan, see Mohd. Yusoff Ismail, *Buddhism and Ethnicity: Social Organization of a Buddhist Temple in Kelantan* (Singapore: Institute of Southeast Asian Studies, 1983); Manning Nash, *Peasant Citizens: Politics, Religion, and Modernization in Kelantan, Malaysia* (Athens: Center for International Studies, Ohio University, 1974); Tan Chee Beng, "Peranakan Chinese in Northeast Kelantan with Special Reference to Chinese Religion," *Journal of the Malayan Branch of the Royal Asiatic Society* 55, 1 (1982): 26–52; Tan Goe Sim, "Latarbelakang Masyarakat Cina di Kelantan," *Warisan Kelantan* 15 (1996): 93–120; Wee Khoon Hock, "Kelantan and the Chinese Kelantanese," in *Kelantan Zaman Awal*, ed. Nik Hassan Shuhaimi b. Nik Abd. Rahman (n.p., 1987), pp. 216–28; and Robert L. Winzeler, "The Rural Chinese of the Kelantan Plain," *Journal of the Malayan Branch of the Royal Asiatic Society* 54, 3 (1981): 1–23.

6 Some articles and documents state that K. Bali was born in 1933, but Nasran, K. Bali's son, states that K. Bali's year of birth was 1927. This was also confirmed by Leo A.W.S., a teacher and poet in Kelantan who maintained

close relations with K. Bali in the 1990s. Leo A.W.S. had a chance to see K. Bali's identity card (interview with Leo A.W.S, 2000, Kota Bharu). K. Bali's younger brother was born in 1929 (interview with Mek Wee, 2000, Tendong).

7 "Kote" is the Kelantanese spelling for "kotel" (bitsy).

8 According to Winzeler, who undertook research on school attendance by Peranakan Chinese in Tendong, only 2 out of 17 children (6 boys and 11 girls) born before 1929 attended primary school, while 17 (13 boys and 4 girls) out of 22 children (16 boys and 6 girls) born between 1930 and 1944 attended primary school. Among the 17 boys and girls, 14 attended Tendong Primary School. Robert L. Winzeler, *Ethnic Relations in Kelantan: A Study of the Chinese and Thai as Ethnic Minorities in a Malay State* (Singapore: Oxford University Press, 1985), p. 48.

9 K. Bali's father died of malaria on 22 August 1944 (interview with Ting Lai Hong, 2000, Tendong). Some articles on K. Bali inaccurately state that K. Bali was brought to Thailand by his father. Mek Knua, K. Bali's "mother" in Sungai Padi, confirmed that K. Bali arrived in Sungai Padi by himself (interview with Mek Knua, 2000, Sungai Padi).

10 On the postwar political development of Kelantan, see Clive S. Kessler, *Islam and Politics in a Malay State: Kelantan 1838–1969* (Ithaca: Cornell University Press, 1978); Nash, *Peasant Citizens*; and Nik Mohamed Nik Mohd. Salleh, "Tentangan Orang-Orang Melayu Kelantan terhadap 'Malayan Union,'" *Warisan Kelantan* 5 (1986): 84–126.

11 Although Malays and Peranakan Chinese lived in harmony in the village, conversion from Buddhism to Islam would create difficulties for the converted person in retaining their family ties. See Winzeler, *Ethnic Relations in Kelantan*, p. 51.

12 Laohakul, K. Bali's classmate at Pracha Nukheroh, recalled that K. Bali was good at many subjects and that he talked about his excitement over what was happening in Indonesia (interview with Laohakul, 2000, Sungai Padi).

13 Kasma Booty was an actress who was lauded all over the Malay world during the 1940s to 1960s. She was born in Medan, Sumatra, in 1932. Her biological father was Dutch, but she was brought up by her mother and adoptive father. Kasma Booty joined a touring theater led by Booty Jacob, where she learned singing and dancing. After the Japanese Occupation she married Booty Jacob and moved first to Penang, then to Singapore, where she debuted as an actress in a Malay film titled *Chempaka* at age 16. Kasma Booty had appeared in about 20 films by 1967, before she retired from the screen. See Ahmad Sarji, *P. Ramlee: Erti yang Sakti* (Selangor: Pelanduk Publications, 1999), pp. 121–3.

14 For example, K. Bali's novel *Bulan Muda, Hati Muda* shares similar settings with *Juita*, a film co-starring Kasma Booty and P. Ramlee. In another novel, *Hanya Tinggal Kenangan*, the lead character moves from Singapore to North Borneo with his beloved daughter Chempaka, the same name as Kasma Booty's character in her debut film.

15 Interview with Safiin, 2000, Sungai Padi, and interview with Mek Knua, 2000, Sungai Padi.

16 Interview with Ting Lai Hong, 2000, Tendong.

17 K. Bali recalled in his *Memoir* that the wellspring of his writings was his stint at the labor union in Sungai Padi, where he lived and worked. However, I could not find out more about the labor union in Sungai Padi when I visited there in February and September 2000. According to Safiin, K. Bali lived on the upper floor of a shophouse near Pracha Nukheroh Secondary School (interview with Safiin, 2000, Sungai Padi).

18 Some poems written in Thai were published in *Peluim Cit* magazine. Sitti Hadiah, "K. Bali," p. 162.

19 Abdul Rahim Kajai was born in Kuala Lumpur in 1894. His father worked as an agent for pilgrims at Mekkah, a job that he also took on after his father's death. After World War II, Abdul Rahim Kajai returned to Malaya and devoted himself to journalism. He took charge of Malay newspapers such as *Saudara*, *Majlis*, *Warta Malaya*, *Utusan Melayu*, as well as *Berita Malai* under the Japanese Occupation. Abdul Rahim Kajai died in December 1943. For more detailed information, see Abdul Latiff Abu Bakar, *Abdul Rahim Kajai: Wartawan dan Sasterawan Melayu* (Kuala Lumpur: Dewan Bahasa dan Pustaka, 1984).

20 K. Bali's accounts of his journeys from 8 February until 4 April appeared in the Malay corner of the *North Borneo News and Sabah Times* and were later collected and published as *K. Bali's Diary*. They are also included in the *Memoir*.

21 The newspaper was called *Sabah Times*. It later merged with an English weekly newspaper in the colony, *North Borneo News*, and changed its name to *North Borneo News and Sabah Times*.

22 For more details on Donald Stephens' background, see Hiroyuki Yamamoto, "From Bornean Federation to Malaysia: Analysis of Stephens' Plan for Merdeka," *MANU* (Universiti Malaysia Sabah) 2 (1999): 59–80, and "'Foreigners' Nationalism' in Malaysia: Donald Stephens and K. Bali in Making of Sabah Nationhood," *Sejarah* (Universiti Malaya) 9 (2001): 49–70, for Stephens' program for the independence of North Borneo.

23 Interview with Fauzi Patel, 2000, Kota Kinabalu. The account was confirmed by Benedict Stephens (Stephens' brother) in an interview (2000, Kota Kinabalu).

24 It is believed that Stephens promoted the use of the name "Sabah." This is plausible, considering that the name Sabah was publicly promoted in the title of Stephens' newspaper, the *North Borneo News and Sabah Times*. We may also recall that it was Stephens who first proposed the change of name from North Borneo to Sabah in the legislative council of North Borneo. But in the beginning, Stephens did not see the significance of the name Sabah and merely considered it to be an old name for a part of North Borneo. It was K. Bali who stressed the significance of the name Sabah through the Malay section of the newspaper and the influence of Stephens.

25 See also *North Borneo News and Sabah Times*, 28 July 1958.

26 Another important idea that was introduced into North Borneo during the same period was the ideology of Ikhwan al-Muslimin (Muslim Brotherhood) via *Qalam* magazine. For detailed information on *Qalam* and Muslim Brotherhood, see Hiroyuki Yamamoto, "The Muslim Brotherhood Movement among Malay-speaking Muslims in the 1950s," in *Reconfiguring Nation-States: Flows and Movements in Southeast Asia*, ed. Noboru Ishikawa (Kyoto: Kyoto University Press, 2008).

CHAPTER 9

Narrating Migration, Reading a Political Itinerary: Connie Bragas-Regalado, Overseas Filipino Worker

Odine de Guzman

In 2004, Connie Bragas-Regalado stepped up her political work by becoming the first overseas domestic worker to be a congressional candidate in a national election. The standard bearer for the party-list Migrante Sectoral Party, Connie was the chair of United Filipinos in Hong Kong (UNIFIL-HK) and a contract domestic worker in Hong Kong since 1991, when she was chosen by the different chapter-members of the largest overseas Filipino workers (OFW) group and sectoral party to represent them in Congress.

Two reforms in the electoral laws of the country facilitated this route to Congress: Republic Act 7941 and Republic Act 9189.

Republic Act 7941, or "The Party-List System Act," mandated by the 1987 Philippine Constitution and enacted by Congress in 1995, sponsors the proportional representation in the House of Representatives of marginalized and underrepresented sectors in society through the election of their respective parties. It provides for as much as 20 per cent of the total number of members of the House for party-list representation.

A party-list group may be described as a national, regional, or sectoral party, an organization, or a coalition of parties.[1] Each party, coalition, or organization submits a list of nominees from which comes its representative(s) in Congress; members of the parties or organizations select the nominees. A party or organization gets elected when it garners at least 2 per cent of the total votes cast for all party-list organizations, which earns it a seat in the House; additional seats may be earned in proportion to the total number of votes each party or group obtains.[2]

The second electoral reform was the passage of Republic Act 9189, or "The Overseas Absentee Voting Act of 2003,"[3] which provides for qualified overseas Filipino citizens to exercise their right to vote in absentia. First implemented during the May 2004 elections, the law allows for citizens abroad to participate in the election of president, vice-president, senators, and party-list representatives.

Briskly implemented within a year's time, RA 9189 is a testament to the economic and political force overseas Filipino workers have become in recent years. Surely, the sheer number alone of OFWs, which in 2004 was more than 5 million, is a strong enough magnet for the ambitions of politicians in the home country to woo the migrants as potential voters in their favor, notwithstanding the maintenance of remittances worth billions of dollars — US$8.5 billion in 2004.[4] Yet despite what could be self-centered political interests and some substantive weaknesses both in laws and in their implementation, clearly these reforms have opened parliamentary participation to groups that have been, in practice, hitherto barred from the electoral process and the largely elite-dominated legislature.

This exploratory chapter traces the itinerary of the overseas Filipino worker Connie Bragas-Regalado to examine the ways by which her direct experience of overseas domestic work has not only set her political route but has also set her apart from the usual politician because of the particular standpoint she brings to the fore. This standpoint, which I propose to call an OFW standpoint, also lends her entry into the political mainstream via the party-list system its transformative potential. Taking off from the notion of the "everyday world as problematic,"[5] I read particular instances in the biographical narrative of Connie's to examine how these recorded instances in her everyday life could have forged a certain perspective, a standpoint, on contemporary Philippine labor migration that could prove highly important for public policy formulation.

Reading the biographical narratives of Connie and the conditions of the social and work experiences of other women migrant domestic workers in Singapore and Hong Kong against the official account and policies on labor migration can reveal the process(es) under which Connie matured in her political work and under which conditions migrant domestic workers' activism remains, and/or discontinues to be, committed. Additionally, such an alternative angle of vision — that which produces a certain standpoint, an OFW standpoint, in this case — also reveals the "realities" that may have been obscured by the visions of traditional politicians who craft the laws that impact on OFW lives.

Connie reading letters of distressed migrant workers (Photo used with the permission of Migrante International)

Connie with members of Migrante Sectoral Party on 20 November 2009, filing of petition for a temporary restraining order on their de-listing by the Commission on Elections.

(Source: <http://migrante-ksa.blogspot.com/2009_11_01_archive.html>. Used with permission of Migrante International)

OFWs: Contemporary Labor Migrants

Statistically, OFWs are both emigrants (overseas Filipinos) and contract workers (overseas Filipino workers), both of whom could be documented or undocumented. Contract workers, who are often the referents of the general term OFW, are further classified as sea-based and land-based. A common factor that binds most emigrants and contract workers is the need to support family members in the home country. The OFWs, the *bagong bayani* or the new economic heroes, were initially called OCWs, or overseas contract workers, a term that is descriptive of a temporary employment status, which is usually fixed terms of six months to two years. But because of the growing prominence of overseas work and of the sense of being neither here nor there implied by the term "OCW," not to mention the sense of restriction imposed on contractual work, the term has fallen out of favor in both government and media parlance. "OFW" — with the insertion of "Filipino" adding a national ring to the phrase, as befits new heroes — is now the preferred version.

Like many other OFWs working as domestic workers, Connie finished college and had been a government employee before she decided to work overseas, knowing that her and her husband's income would not suffice for the growing needs of their family.[6] At that time, Connie and her husband, who was an employee with the National Food Authority, had two small children. Originally from Southern Leyte in the Visayas, Connie's natal family spent time in Kidapawan, South Cotabato, Mindanao, where she completed secondary schooling. She obtained a bachelor's degree in social work at the University of Southern Philippines in Cebu. At this point, she decided to go back to Mindanao and took a post at the Department of Social Work and Development Region XI office. As if following the circularity of fate, she was assigned to South Cotabato, where she later on settled down to begin a family.

Eventually, her young family would experience financial insecurity and she and her husband would make the rational decision to find better employment elsewhere.

The first time Connie set out to be an overseas contract worker, her life trajectory echoed that of the growing number of Filipino women as well as their husbands (like Connie's) who left the Philippines for better economic opportunities offered by neighboring industrializing countries.

Philippine Overseas Labor Migration: A Brief Overview

In the 1970s, the oil crisis brought unprecedented trouble for the Philippine economy and created a compelling need for many Filipinos to leave the country for better employment. As the crisis pulled economies such as the Philippines' to collapse, it shored up the economies of oil-producing states such as those in the Middle East, which then opened a new destination for Filipino labor migrants. By the 1980s, the booming economies in the region, such as those of Hong Kong, Singapore, and Taiwan, changed the direction of Filipino labor migration altogether. Until the 1970s the established destinations for the majority of Filipino migrants were the United States and its territories. By 2005, the top ten destinations of Filipino workers were Saudi Arabia, Hong Kong, the United Arab Emirates, Taiwan, Japan, Kuwait, Qatar, Singapore, Italy, and the United Kingdom.[7]

Although overseas labor migration is not new for Filipinos, the current experience presents new and disturbing trends. The scale of migration is massive and unleashes "brain drain" risks,[8] with 4 million contract workers all over the world as of 2008. Second, the movement is highly encouraged by the government (from the administration of Ferdinand E. Marcos onward) to help address continuing unemployment problems and trade deficits[9] through remittances sent home; government records put the estimated figure for 2009 at US$17 billion.[10] A supposed stopgap measure of the mid-1970s, it has become a permanent strategy of sorts. Third, this contemporary experience is described as a "feminization" of international labor migration. It is increasingly services-oriented and female-dominated.

Women's entry in the contemporary international labor migration program of the government sends contradictory messages about their empowerment in society. On the one hand, the increasing number of women labor migrants — which was 72 per cent of the total deployed newly hired land-based workers in 2005[11] — is a huge step away from the dependent, adjunct status of the majority of women migrants, who were wives and daughters up to the middle of the 1960s. The participation of women as migrant workers has grown solidly from 12 per cent in 1975 to 73 per cent in 2003.[12] This has allowed more women to earn more abroad than they would have done locally, a fact that affords them financial independence from male family members, and sometimes greater autonomy and independence when they become the main family providers.

On the other hand, the out-migration of large numbers of women is also a sign of the continuing limited share of work available to women in the local production process: employment opportunities remain restricted, and income remains insufficient. Additionally, the majority of female overseas workers are in "traditional," "feminine," reproductive work such as domestic work, including caregiving to the young and elderly, and cultural entertainment, where the pay is lower and the nature of work exposes many to a higher incidence of abuse, especially physical and sexual abuse. On top of this, women's participation in the international labor market entails many instances of deskilling, such as the case of Connie and the commonly known cases of public school teachers working as domestic workers in Hong Kong.

Narrating Migration, Reading an Itinerary

Against this background, the life narrative of Connie Bragas-Regalado, as well as those of the millions of other OFWs, underscores the saliency of the feminist adage "the personal is political," of how personal lives are governed by political, external forces. While a decision to work overseas in the end is one's own to make — to borrow a Marxian concept — personal decisions are not made independent of one's historical circumstances. Thus, in the case of OFWs, the continuing limited job opportunities in the country, the rising cost of living, and the aggressive marketing of overseas labor migration by the government are all major compelling, and external, factors that to a certain extent influence, if not predetermine, many people's life decisions. In addition, these factors, which are almost always presented as if they were a natural part of the normal course of things, can likewise contribute to the development of a national consciousness that sees and accepts overseas migration as inevitable if one expects a comfortable life.[13] At the same time, the feminist expression also reminds us that the seeming individual and personal circumstances of labor migrants, for example the kind of work available or a domestic worker's fate at the hands of her employers or recruiters, are not simply determined by their inadequacies or capability but also by the prevailing institutionalized notions about women, Third World women, domestic work, reproductive work, and even the prevailing economic and political relationships between nation-states. Consequently, in the women's quest for a better life, forces such as the national government and the demands of international capital have already affected many Filipinos' contemporary itineraries. Hence, the expression "the personal is political" implies that to improve individual personal life and experience, political structures and sociopolitical relationships need to be addressed and changed collectively.

This reading is an attempt to make sense of an individual experience of labor migration in the context of the wider labor export program of the Philippines and contract labor flows in the Asian region. It illustrates the ways in which the country's labor migration policies have influenced the life course of a migrant worker, Connie Bragas-Regalado: it plots the ways in which Connie went with the migration flow set up by the government, and how in the course of events she and her peers ended up countering this setup through political activism. Their political work served as levees that somehow stemmed the outflow of people and managed the surge of the social costs of labor migration and their impact on individual actors by directing government attention to these.

This reading is also an attempt at capturing what C. Wright Mills has eloquently described as the "sociological imagination," the intersection of public issues and personal problems, of biography and history.

The study of individual, personal lives is part and parcel of history. In the Philippines, biography has, until the last two decades, quite often been appreciated as an expansion of the study of the motivations and consequences of decisions made on behalf of the nation. More properly, biography is undertaken to gain a critical understanding of the nation's great heroes and leaders. It is not only the case that biography, or the study of the *bio*, of life, has concentrated on the lives of "great" people, but that these "great" people have been predominantly men as well.

The study of lives from a feminist purview challenges many of the received assumptions of biography. It redirects attention to the study of women's lives and underscores the fact that women also live exceptional lives worthy of academic and literary attention. Feminist biography does not shy away from focusing on the "great" people; when it does, however, the biography does not always concentrate on an autonomous individual but brings to bear as well the narratives that tell the life of a group or collective. Moreover, according to Liz Stanley, feminist biography disrupts the traditional biographical practice in terms of chronology and reality, especially when an understanding of the subject is attained in the context of her social networks and life situation as conditioned by social position.[14]

The analytic tool of auto/biography, one form of narrative writing that is mostly associated with feminist biography and which also informs this present study, is also "concerned with epistemological matters: with issues and claims surrounding what is seen to be knowledge; and consequently [it illuminates the study of] 'lives' as a means of bringing into focus the relationship between individuals and social structure."[15]

From this purview, the study of lives from the standpoint of the non-dominant has the potential to "create [a] more inclusive, more human conception of social reality."[16]

Taking off from the Hegelian insight on the dialectic between master and servant, standpoint theorists believe that "societal inequities generate distinctive accounts of nature and social relationships [and that] the perspective from the lives of the less powerful can provide a more objective view than the perspective from the lives of the more powerful."[17] To boot, the distinction in perspective, and consciousness, between the more powerful — the master — and the less powerful — the servant — develops from the way the relations between them are organized. In this allegory of the relations between the consciousness of the master and the labor of the servant, Hegel illustrates how the object of the desire of the master is available to him simply and directly, as opposed to seeing the same relations from the perspective of the servant. The master's object of desire is available to him straightforwardly — "from appetite to consummation" — through the labor of the servant, who has produced the object for the master. By this, the servant has conformed to the will of the master and in the process brings to fruition the master's consciousness through the servant's work. All this is invisible from the master's standpoint. "The servant in relation to the master does not constitute a distinct subject, a consciousness distinctly and authentically present who looks back and reflects the master's will and has no autonomous existence. The servant's labor is present in the relation of the master to the object of his desire, the object of consciousness. The invisibility of that relation from the master's standpoint is a product of the organization of the relation between master and servant."[18] Accordingly, the master does not see this organization from his standpoint: it is not visible from his location in the relation. From the location of the master, within his consciousness, present are himself, the object and a servant — "who is merely a means." In contrast, from the location of the servant, there are the master, the servant's labor producing the object, and the straightforward relation between master and object. The set of relations, in its entirety, is visible.[19]

Marx and Engels' explication of the Hegelian allegory establishes a basis for grounding an understanding of political economy in the standpoint of the working class that stems from an explanation of the relations between the consciousness of the ruling and ideological consciousness. Through the narrative of the master and slave, Marx, accordingly, illustrates the difference between forms of consciousness arising from the experience of ruling and those that arise from the experience of doing the work to make possible the conditions of ruling. "Ideological forms of consciousness are definite practices of thinking about society that reflect the experience of ruling."[20] Just as with the Hegelian allegory, the practices that make the experience of ruling are invisible from the standpoint of ruling; they are visible and complete only from the standpoint that makes the conditions of ruling possible: that is, from the standpoint outside the ruling class.

Moreover, as Marx asserted, consciousness and standpoint, being "grounded in the work and activity of actual individuals producing their existence under definite material conditions," provide a basis for a political economy of labor.[21]

In putting forward a feminist sociology and an explication of epistemology and women's standpoint, feminists have extended the Hegelian dialectic and the subsequent formulation of the proletarian standpoint by Marx and Engels to an analysis of the external location of women in the relations of ruling — outside the frame of ruling and outside the dominant discourse that forms the governing modes of knowledge, which has predominantly been male.[22]

In this further extension of the master-servant dialectic, I offer an examination of the relations of ruling from the standpoint of Filipino overseas domestic workers: a standpoint that views the relations of ruling from the embodied location of class, gender, and, subsequently, race. Foreign contract domestic workers may be said to be multiply removed/outside the relations of ruling from the standpoint of two masters, with whom they simultaneously have relations because of their transnational location, namely, the sending state/nation and its ruling class and the receiving nation and its ruling class/state. On the one hand, as the less powerful members of a sending state (or nation), they do have continued relations with the ruling class of the sending state, and continue to make the conditions of their rule and the experience of ruling possible in that equation. On the other hand, as concurrent new members of the less powerful in a receiving state (or nation), they do enter into relations with the ruling class of this other state, and their labor (though absent from the view of the rulers) in this relation makes possible the conditions of rule and the experience of ruling in this other equation. In this second equation, the relations of ruling, i.e., the relations of exclusion, put them outside the frame of ruling that is predominantly a male, non-laboring class, and racially different and dominant. Situated thus in this location of consciousness, foreign migrant domestic workers can have an experience and a complete vision of the relations of ruling not only from the standpoint of the less powerful but also from the standpoint of whose labor has produced the object(s) of desire of two masters, of two systems of organization.

In this journey of millions, the everyday world is undoubtedly political, and certain instances in the everyday may be understood as those particular locations that serve as starting points for a more nuanced understanding of social relations.

Briefly in this narrative, I use the concept "everyday world as problematic" following the explication of Dorothy E. Smith, who has framed it as follows: "where the everyday world is taken to be various and differentiated matrices of experience — the place from within which the consciousness of the knower begins, the location of her null point."[23] Accordingly, the everyday world — that where we are physically and socially, and which we experience directly — is the location where "our experiences arise [as] conditions, occasions, objects, possibilities, relevances, presences [and are] organized in and by the practices and methods through which we supply and discover organization."[24] This location is also "necessarily local and historical."[25] As with other standpoint theorists,[26] Smith is explicit in stating that while the sociological problematic is located in the everyday, this does not mean that investigation is confined to it: "the everyday world is organized by social relations not observable within it."[27]

Beginning sociological inquiry from this location, however, also allows for an understanding of the bifurcating of consciousness, as these knowers are those members of society whose position in it is "outside [the] abstracted ruling apparatus" and "who know society from within their experience of it as an everyday world."[28]

Destination: Singapore. Occupation: OCW

When Connie Bragas-Regalado first set out to become an overseas contract worker in 1983, she did so as a tourist in Singapore. At that time, the practice was for potential workers to enter the city-state as tourists while placement agencies looked for employers. Accordingly, until the late 1980s, foreign labor migrants coming from Southeast Asia usually entered Singapore on tourist visas, and when they found employment they changed their visa status. This was generally allowed, with the Singaporean government imposing only a few regulations, largely because of the high demand for labor. Eventually, the practice was amended and foreign domestic workers could only be allowed entry on tourist visas as long as they obtained "in-principle approval from a licensed recruiter before entry."[29] The potential workers waited in the home country while they were being selected based on their résumé and picture or video presentation. Concurrently, foreign domestic workers continued to enter through informal channels; usually they were contracted through friends and relatives who would bring them to recruiters in Singapore in exchange for a commission of S$100 from the agency and one month's salary from the recruit.

In reality, many Filipino contract workers pay exorbitant fees to have their papers fixed and get a placement. In many instances, the fees for documentation and placement commission and other fees are often left at the discretion of recruiters, making it easy for them to impose fees they deem necessary. For example, for her 1983 placement in Singapore Connie put in more than PHP 50,000, although official receipts from the transactions would reflect only PHP 12,000.[30]

In the late 1970s the Philippines became a "non-traditional" source of foreign domestic workers for upper- and middle-class families in Singapore, supplanting the "traditional" sources of Malaysia and Indonesia. Accordingly, this began with the enterprising Singaporean male tourists, mostly independent taxi drivers and hawkers, who went to the "then sex tourist capital of Southeast Asia" — Manila. These men established links in Manila and brought back with them "*some girls* for placement in the domestic labor market."[31] These dealings were also said to be the forerunner of the recruitment industry: among the penalties the Singaporean government imposed on offending citizens were the payment of a fine and the filling of an application for a license to operate an employment agency.

With the ballooning presence of foreign workers in the city-state, the government introduced regulatory measures to control the influx of foreign domestic workers in the mid-1980s. Higher penalties and stricter control of employment recruiters were incorporated in the Employment Agency Act of 1984, while new guidelines on the recruitment of foreign domestic workers were enforced. They included the following: the imposition of a levy on the employer of the domestic worker; the issuance of the work permit for a duration of two years, subject to one year's renewal and further renewal at the discretion of the ministry; in-principle approval and a security bond of S$5,000 to be executed before the issuance of the work permit;[32] pregnancy tests every six months; and prohibition of marriage to Singaporeans.

Even with the Employment Act of 1984, the government did not regulate the "actual terms and conditions of the employment of foreign domestic workers."[33] It became incumbent upon sending states, such as the Philippines, to establish and lobby for standards for their citizens. This, of course, was not always forthcoming. As Connie recounted, unless concerns of migrant workers were police matters, the Singaporean government did not get involved and left the matter to be resolved by the migrant workers and their recruiters or employers. A case in point is the issue of not being given a day off, which can be a breach of contract since a weekly day off or holiday — usually a Sunday — is normally provided in a contract; or not being given food, another matter that is part and parcel of the stay-in work arrangement.[34] It was not until 1987 that the Philippine government instituted a standard employment contract for Filipino workers in Singapore.[35]

In 1988 the Singaporean government began to be concerned about the number of foreign domestic workers, who at that time numbered 150,000, or 25 per cent of all foreign workers. To curb the increasing number, the government increased the levy on employing foreign domestic workers from S$120 in 1987 to S$160 beginning January 1989 and subsequently to S$200 by the end of the year. Regardless of the increases in levy, which were carried out twice in 1990 — to S$230 and then S$250 — the demand for foreign domestic workers did not decrease. In 1990, it was estimated that one in every 15 households had a live-in foreign domestic worker; this figure was said to be among the highest in the world. Again the government increased the employer levy — in 1992 to S$300 and in 1995 to S$330; by this time, the estimate was that one in eight households had a live-in foreign domestic worker.

Concurrent with the receiving government's concern about the growing number of foreign workers, sending governments such as the Philippines begin to worry about the growing number of reports of abuse of their nationals in the receiving country. At certain points, these became so alarming that the Philippine government twice imposed a ban on the deployment of domestic workers to Singapore.

The first was in 1987, amidst numerous reports of abuse of Filipino domestic workers; this ban was lifted in mid-1989. Although the entry of Filipinos continued, the ban significantly lowered the recorded number of Filipino domestic workers. The records put the numbers at 4,706 for 1989 and 4,698 for 1990. In contrast, the number for 1987 was at 17,601.[36]

The second ban, in 1995, was a result of the diplomatic crisis brought about by the execution of Flor Contemplacion. In actual terms, the Philippine ban did not really affect the law of supply and demand, as migrant workers from other countries — Indonesia, Sri Lanka, Myanmar, and others — simply filled in the gap left by the Filipinos.

In a rather unexpected move by the Singaporean parliament, in April 1998 legislation was passed to increase penalties for abuse of domestic workers. In addition, in what may be seen as a way of "public criticism, several [parliamentarians] urged Singaporeans to try to see maids as lonely, overworked human beings."[37]

A View from Below

> "*Araw-araw may dinadalhan ako ng pagkain kasi ang ipinapakain sa kanila ay panis* [Every day I brought food to other Filipino domestic helpers because they were only given spoiled food]."
>
> – Connie

Although she was relatively fortunate in her two-year work experience in Singapore, Connie was not oblivious to the plight of her compatriots. In interviews, she described her stay as rather uneventful. She had two employers: the first went bankrupt and let her go; the second, an American household, paid her more than the usual salary received by domestic workers at the time.

In her daily routine Connie vicariously experienced the troubles of fellow Filipino domestic helpers. One of the most common difficulties cited by contract domestic workers in various case studies and media interviews was the issue of food. They said that food was either inadequate (*lugaw lang*, only porridge) or they were charged for it when it was supposed to be part of their salary package. Many of these narrations bordered on the unbelievable. Connie herself recalled: "*Araw-araw may dinadalhan ako ng pagkain kasi ang ipinapakain sa kanila ay panis* [Every day I brought food to other Filipino domestic helpers because they were only given spoiled food]."[38] Yet to read this narrative in the context of the Singaporean parliamentarians' reminder to "see maids as lonely, overworked human beings"[39] provides a plot, and a coherent narrative story, to both contentions voiced by stakeholders at opposite ends. On the one hand, entreating fellow citizens to consider foreign hired help as "lonely" and "overworked" — thereby stressing the need to be more understanding and patient, perhaps — is sensitive and magnanimous. On the other hand, to have to issue a reminder can only suggest that employers indeed had been impatient and demanding of their employees. To have to put out a reminder that employers were dealing with "human beings" implies that the employees were not being treated as such. It also suggests something more disturbing: that the workers were not considered human beings in the first place.

In this narrative context, the national reminder to treat foreign workers better accentuates the intersection of issues of gender, class, and race. Foreign migrant domestic workers, in the worst cases, must deal with these intersecting issues as they deal with loneliness and long hours. Historically, domestic work, in the Philippines as in most other countries in Asia, has not been considered real wage work. The nature of domestic work being part of the reproduction process — where accordingly no special skills and training are necessary — and thus not directly contributive to the process of accumulation and exchange, gives it a low value, if it is considered work at all. Since it is largely categorized as "reproductive" work, the logical best persons to take on the work are women, whose "natural" role as mothers and caretakers of the family makes them best suited for the task. Yet despite the social relegation of women as a singular category to the secondary, reproductive sphere, not all women are equally subordinated. Some women perform domestic tasks out of love and for free, within their own homes, while others perform the same tasks as a job for a small wage, outside their own homes. Conversely, some women, who belong to families, or to men, with better access to the means of production, are able to pass their domestic tasks to other women, whose family's limited access to resources requires them to venture out of the reproductive sphere to find gainful employment. But because domestic work is basically an exercise of one's natural role, the women doing the job are hardly considered workers. The fact that this kind of work is performed in the private sphere of an individual's house even adds to the sense that it is not really work in the formal sense. The low status accorded to women and reproductive work in a productive economy makes domestic work one of the least-valued jobs.

In contemporary industrializing economies, women's participation in the productive sphere has not only become acceptable but necessary, especially in smaller nations such as Singapore. Consequently, the task of reproductive work is not redistributed to the whole community nor absorbed by the state. Instead, the sexual division of labor is maintained together with the valuation previously assigned to reproductive work — their women now are more valued citizens doing important, productive work — with the reproductive task relegated to guest women workers: foreign workers whose economic need compels them to go overseas to seek low-status work, such as domestic work. Thus, on top of the historical low value accorded to domestic work on account of the gender and class of the workers, racial difference, compounded with sexual and class bias, increases the low, nay, inferior status accorded to domestic work by foreign migrants.

In contrast, employers gain status in what foreign workers lose. Anecdotal narratives circulating among migrants and advocates include children of employers comparing *their* employees to cars. Filipinas are Mercedes-Benz, Singaporean children reportedly claim. In Malaysia, where among foreign domestic workers Filipinas command the highest pay, the social implications are different when one *has* a Filipina rather than an Indonesian.

While all these are borne out on the individual level, they do inform international dynamics. The Philippines' lesser economic position compared to Singapore is emphasized in this relation. In fact, this relation operates on that premise.

The economic relationship between the Philippines and Singapore lies partly in the flow of people, where highly skilled to unskilled labor (from engineering and IT technocrats to nursing/health-care professionals and domestic workers) from the Philippines go to Singapore, usually on a temporary basis, to fill in these work positions that are necessary for the continuation of the processes of production in the Lion City. The flow of Filipino labor to Singapore, on the other hand, is equally necessary for the Philippine state for the employment and remittances gained from this relationship.

As of December 2006, the estimated number of Filipinos in Singapore was 120,000, of whom 3.6 per cent (4,320) were permanent migrants and 45.4 per cent (54,480) were temporary migrants, with women comprising 76 per cent of the total temporary migrants, while 51 per cent (61,200) were believed to be irregular/undocumented, and 79 per cent of whom were women.[40] The majority of workers were domestic helpers, at 80,000 (66 per cent); there were no recorded male domestic workers. In contrast, there were 6,700 nursing/health-care assistants, 60 per cent of whom were women; 12,700 IT and computer programmers, of whom 20 per cent were women; 6,000 engineers, 10 per cent of whom were women; 5,200 architects/draftsmen, 5 per cent of whom were women; and an all-male aircraft technicians and mechanics staff of 2,500.[41]

Within ASEAN, Singapore was the largest foreign direct investment source of the Philippines from the years 2000 to 2006. The recorded main export markets of Singapore for 2005 were Malaysia, the United States, China, Japan, Taiwan, Indonesia, Saudi Arabia, and South Korea; and Singapore's main sources of imports for the same year were Malaysia, the United States, China, Japan, Taiwan, Indonesia, Saudi Arabia, and South Korea.[42]

While the exchange between the Philippines and Singapore is mutual, it is not necessarily equal. If the present statistics are any indication of the geopolitical relations of 1995, it can be said that the execution of Flor Contemplacion and the reactions of both governments to the whole affair are illustrative of the organization of relations between the Philippines and Singapore. In recalling the outcome of the execution, we find, on the one hand, the Philippines indignant and recognizing the need to freeze diplomatic relations, and on the other, Singapore being detached and seeing only the need to move on from the situation. The severance of diplomatic ties with Singapore did not alarm the Singaporean government so much; neither did it threaten their economic prospects. Other than what Gloria Macapagal-Arroyo calls "OFIs — overseas Filipino investors," the Philippines does not have any other tangible investments in Singapore. The Philippine "investments" are the intangibles that are often overlooked precisely because of the terms of relationship between the two nation-states. Within this relationship, the Philippines falls on the servant's end of the dialectical materialist equation. Philippine labor (as well as that of other developing countries such as Indonesia), in this sense, is that which directly creates and makes possible the object of desire of the Singaporean nation-state, and such labor is embodied by the migrant Filipino "everyperson" (originally, "everyman"). It is indispensable labor but invisible from the point of view of the dominant. And so it makes it rather incomprehensible from the dominant's point of view for the servant — the Philippines — to be making a big deal about the incident with the domestic helper.

The 1995 affair provides the Philippines a stage, a heuristic platform, through which to view its actual, real relations with its neighboring state.

The consciousness, and eventual standpoint, Filipino migrant workers develop out of their everyday experience of overseas labor migration can also be claimed to be ontologically based. Their understanding of their relations with their employers, and of migrant domestic workers with their host country, is informed not only by what they perceive from their specific location in the relationship but also by how the relationship impinges upon their bodies, their being. Race, as already explained, plays a big role in where migrant domestic workers are relegated in the larger scheme of things. But in addition to this, migrant domestic workers are made to experience racial difference bodily.

The experience of hunger is something concrete. To experience it through control and deprivation of food because one's employers believe it proper to limit one's intake of food or to "give only spoiled food" is a direct affront to one's being, which can also make one's body physically weak or sick. Forced hard work, to the point of numbing the body, is another source of understanding of one's actual place in the lived social relations. It solidly grounds one's understanding of the situation in something concrete — on one's body. Understanding is, as it is said, grounded on what you know with your bones.

Balikbayan(i): From OCWs to OFWs, the New Breed of Heroes

Seeing firsthand the situation of many fellow Filipinas in Singapore, Connie Bragas-Regalado decided to go home when her expatriate employers left Singapore. Upon her return, Connie became a *balikbayan*, just like the hundreds of other domestic workers from abroad on their return from their contracts. In the eyes of her family, she was the dutiful daughter, wife, and mother who came home to her family with a better fortune for a more hopeful future. In the eyes of the nation-state, she was a good citizen who persevered to find employment elsewhere, sent home money, and in time would be one of its new heroes.

In Philippine mythology, the idea of the *balikbayan* connotes a sense of triumphant return. The word comes from the terms "*balik*," to return, and "*bayan*," hometown or nation (in more contemporary translation). It is part of the narrative of the transformed, more enlightened hero: the hero who left would have returned victorious from trials, more learned and strengthened by what he (in the legends it was usually a "he") had gone through. The leaving and return are part of the rites of passage of coming to maturity and leadership.

In contemporary times, the idea of the *balikbayan* has became popularly associated with the returning Filipinos based in the United States, who might also be described as among the first- and second-wave migrants of the early 1900s and 1960s. Many of them were already immigrants to the United States, if not US citizens. They would come for short visits to their extended families and hometowns. They were literally returning from a long sojourn back to their families. They were also mostly returning home triumphant — with tales of what they had become and achieved in the United States, complete with their fresh American smell, accent and twang, and, of course, numerous gifts for everyone in the *bayan*.

Until the 1980s, the *balikbayans* were mostly this cohort; by the late 1980s, a new one would emerge, bringing a new resonance to the theme of the triumphant returnee. They would be actually and politically recognized as "heroes."

Amidst the rising criticism over the reported abuse of women migrant workers in 1988, publicists for the Aquino government floated the notion of the overseas contract worker as "*bagong bayani*" partly to divide attention away from the harshness that became the reality of the OCWs — in particular those of the cultural workers in Japan and domestic workers in the Middle East. In part, it was to highlight the material rewards that families and the state could reap from overseas work as a way of dodging public criticism over the ineptness of government in handling the crises. While the Aquino government's ban on the deployment of workers as a response to the growing public concern over the increasing incidence of abuse was not very astute, as NGOs noted, its decision to revive and put the spin on the concept of "OCWs as new heroes" proved to be extraordinary, having influence even more than a decade later. The beginnings of the accolade "new economic heroes" can be traced back to the labor export program of the Marcos era, although it was not until the crises of the late 1980s and 1995 that it gained national currency.

Consonant with the remittance and *balikbayan* programs of the 1970s, the *Bagong Bayani* Awards were organized to contribute to capturing gains from remittances of overseas migrants. A 1989 POEA flyer for the "*Bagong Bayani* Awards" read: "The *Bagong Bayani* Awards (BBA) is an annual search for the country's outstanding overseas contract workers. Initially launched in 1984, it is a celebration of the Filipino workers' role as a new breed of heroes, fostering goodwill among the peoples of the world, enhancing the image of the Filipino as a competent and responsible worker, and greatly contributing to the nation's foreign exchange earnings."

Fortunately for the government, the news of abuses and deaths allowed it to infuse a new meaning to the phrase *bagong bayani*; from a wholly remittances-driven interest, the crises turned it toward a national appreciation for people's sacrifices made on behalf of the nation.

With the declaration of the month of December as "The Month of Overseas Filipinos" through Proclamation No. 276, signed on 21 June 1988 by Corazon C. Aquino, the place of OCWs (who would later be called OFWs — overseas Filipino workers) in the national heroes' echelon was secured. And the events of 1995 made the heroism of the OFWs more apparent than ever: in the imaginary of the Catholic Filipino, what greater sacrifice could there be than death that was tantamount to martyrdom?

A Look at the Everyday Life of a *Bagong Bayani*

Upon a closer look at the story of Connie's return, we might ask, what heroes' welcome did she really come home to?

On her return home, Connie had to contend with being a single mother as well as provider for her elderly parents. In the course of her stay in Singapore, her husband had also decided to go abroad for employment. He went to Saudi Arabia and, eventually, got involved with another woman. This caused their marriage to fall apart.

But, as Connie noted, such a turn of events was not new for OFWs. She lightheartedly explained: "*Yung mga hiwalay kapag tinatanong kung nasaan ang mga asawa, ang sagot ay 'sumakabilang bahay na'*! [Whenever the separated are asked about their spouses, the reply would be 'They have moved to the next house!']."[43] The play on words in this is rather naughty as well as indicative of the women's candid acceptance of the situation. The phrase "*sumakabilang bahay na*" is a play on the original expression "*sumakabilang buhay na*," or to have passed on to the next life/afterlife. The twist is in substituting *bahay* (house) for *buhay* (life), which in this retelling becomes "passed on to the next house," or in this case "moved on to the next/other house," while somehow being indirectly able to express the sentiment that the husband has passed on.

Many OFW women and wives of OFW husbands face the harsh reality of their husbands leaving them for another woman as a consequence of living apart from each other because of the need to find employment overseas. This has become part of everyday reality for many women OFWs and relatives of male OFWs. And while it happens that women OFWs can also leave their husbands or take on lovers when they are abroad, in a patriarchal society like the Philippines, it is more likely that husbands are freer to do so. This is especially true for wives of OFW husbands, where the wives are restricted and policed by traditional mores and by the home community itself. Whereas social norms and expectations of the dutiful wife and mother censure women's actions, desires, and even thoughts, there is no harsh policing of men's actions, desires, and decisions. Thus, it becomes seemingly easy for women to accept their husband's infidelity and eventual separation from the family, because the social structures are mostly skewed to support men's tendency to infidelity and women's to piety.

Coupled with sarcasm and irony, many OFW women are resigned to spousal separations being facts of a migrant's life. The fact that people's lives have been transformed by overseas labor migration somehow cancels out the supposed rationale propagated by the dominant discourse on the OFW: work and sacrifice for family. Interestingly, though, through this example the women are seen to be rather stoical and practical about their circumstances, contrary to gender expectations of women being emotional and dependent on men.

In these instances, too, the impact and outcome of overseas labor migration are mostly consigned to the private domain; the state does not meddle in these familial affairs.

Table 9.1 Number of Overseas Filipino Workers by Relationship to Household Head and Sex: 2000

Relationship to HH	*Total*	*Male*	*Female*
Philippines	992,397	498,843	493,554
Head	305,996	272,939	33,057
Spouse	141,246	8,765	132,481
Son	156,456	156,456	–
Daughter	257,807	–	257,807
Others	130,892	60,683	70,209

Source: NSO 2000 in Ericta *et al.*, 2003.

By common knowledge, Connie, as is the case with many other women OFWs, went on with her life despite the less than warm homecoming she got and the attendant role of single mother and primary income earner of an extended household.

In an analysis of the 2000 Census (see Table 9.1), Carmelita N. Ericta, administrator of the National Statistics Office, surmises that respondents to the census regarded overseas workers as heads of household even though they were absent, because they had higher earnings compared to the rest of the household members. Thus, 30.83 per cent of all overseas workers were considered heads of household. Yet this is mostly applicable only to male overseas workers. And so of the total male population of overseas workers, 54.7 per cent were reported as household heads. Female overseas workers were mostly recorded as daughters of a household head at 52.2 per cent and spouses of a household head at 26.8 per cent. In contrast, of the total male overseas workers, only 1.75 per cent were reported to be the spouse of a head of household.[44]

Of married overseas workers, women make up 40 per cent.[45] Meanwhile, statistical records still reflect a more patriarchal view of gender relations in households even though in reality many women OFWs are now part of the growing number of Filipino women who are de facto heads of household in that they are major income earners. For example, of the young women classified as "daughter" in the statistics above, many are actually major income earners in the family as they finance the building of the family house as well as a father's small business, such as operating a public utility vehicle or a "buy and sell" venture. Yet among OFWs in the 2000 Census, women comprised only 10 per cent of the reported number of heads of household;[46] in the country, 13.5 per cent of household heads are women.[47]

The Migration Chain, Circle, Cycle

The 1990s did not stem the tide of impoverishment for many Filipinos. Economic hardship continued for the majority of people, as the promise of greener pastures elsewhere remained the only hope. As with so many others, Connie — a *balikbayan*, labeled the country's "new hero" — seemed to have no other option but to work abroad. And so she did, leaving her children with her parents and younger sister; she flew to Hong Kong one day in March 1991.[48]

Among the successes of the declaration of the national *bagong bayani* was the creation of the mentality of equating overseas work with perseverance, valor, hope, and fortune, and therefore working overseas meant being responsible and devoted to one's family. The *bagong bayani* would naturally brave new worlds, suffer loneliness and separation for the sake of their families, if need be over and over.

Contemporary overseas labor migration from most developing countries is described as "circular," i.e., non-settlement, and cyclical, i.e., the workers go home and return for another contract.[49]

In the Philippines this phenomenon can also be described as sequential within a family, where, say, siblings in a family of seven can be distributed — at one time or one after the other — in four different countries, such as Hong Kong, Saudi Arabia, Italy, and the United Arab Emirates, with the fifth sibling probably on layover from a contract in Brunei (such as the case of a taxi driver in Manila I interviewed). In some cases this can also be intergenerational, with a parent and older children both labor contract migrants. The concept of the *bagong bayani* has also developed another sequential order — one that once again contradicts its rationale of being for the improvement of family financial prospects: children of migrants ending up being contract migrants as well, for example, a daughter of a domestic worker becoming one herself despite the mother's best efforts to send her child to school for a more promising future.

New Contract: OFW, Hong Kong-bound

On her second sojourn, Connie decided to go to Hong Kong in the belief that the then British colony would have better migrant labor policies. The fact that Hong Kong was near the Philippines was another consideration.[50]

Hong Kong, however, would prove to be formative for the political growth of Connie, who had joined the women's group Gabriela and participated in organizing peasant communities in Southern Mindanao when she came back from Singapore.[51] Compared to Singapore, Hong Kong was indeed democratic and thus allowed workers, including foreign migrants, to congregate and form organizations. And so while migrant labor policies were not entirely equitable, migrants had some form of recourse: a redress mechanism was in place, and protest rallies were allowed.

Thus, when Connie arrived in 1991, Filipino migrant workers were already among the better-organized groups. In fact, even among overseas Filipino labor migrants in general, the Hong Kong-based Filipinos were among the pioneer groups who initiated protests against President Ferdinand Marcos' policy of forced remittance through the banking system. From the initial 1984 alliance of 11 organizations that formed the United Filipinos Against Forced Remittance (UNFARE) to oppose Executive Order 857, United Filipinos in Hong Kong (UNIFIL-HK) was established in May 1985. Other than promoting and defending the rights of Filipino migrants in Hong Kong, UNIFIL-HK allied with organizations of other Asian migrants in Hong Kong such as the associations of Nepalese, Indonesian, Sri Lankan, and Thai workers, thereby expanding its political reach as well as demonstrating that Filipino migrants' issues were not isolated. The coalition of Asian migrant workers made it apparent that issues faced by migrant workers cut across cultures, and that these were factors of international and regional unequal power relations more than single-nation inadequacies.

Historically, Hong Kong had been an in-migration area for mainland Chinese, especially as a consequence of the political turmoil of 1949 and the 1960s' Cultural Revolution. However, the labor shortage in the 1980s precipitated the entry of foreign migrants; foreign women domestic workers had been in demand since. In the late 1980s, Hong Kong opened up to more labor migrants, especially with the big construction projects under way. In 1989, the foreign workforce program was implemented to allow for the entry of additional labor, while the Special Scheme for the New Airport Project brought in even more foreign workers. Yet this was highly regulated: construction companies needed to secure approval from the Immigration Department, which set limits on what specific skills could get in and on the conditions of their stay: short-term and "will depart upon the completion of the airport in 1998."[52]

Like construction workers, domestic workers were highly regulated; their legal status was contingent on their work contract, which bound them to the employer who contracted them and to the specific job for which they came. They could not be hired for any other kind of work. Moreover, given the contractual nature of the work, which was normally for two years, they did not have the right to remain in the country indefinitely, and neither could they gain residency or bring in their dependents. The Department of Immigration issued the work contract and had the following conditions: foreign domestic helpers were to get a minimum salary;[53] they were to be given proper accommodation, food, and medical treatment when necessary and have access to the legal system for labor, criminal, and other cases. For example, they could file for labor claims for contract violations; conversely, their employers could too.[54] Under Hong Kong government policy, foreign domestic workers were allowed to form unions to lobby for issues concerning them,[55] although since the 1997 turnover they can be arrested and deported for militant action.[56] In 1987, the Hong Kong government introduced the "New Conditions of Stay" for foreign domestic workers. Two provisions of the policy were discriminatory: the "two-week rule" and the prohibition from changing employers.[57] The two-week rule stipulated that foreign domestic workers had to go back to their country of origin within two weeks if their contract had been terminated, regardless of the validity of their work visa. This rule exposed migrants to arbitrary termination by the employer as well as binding them to unfair treatment, below-minimum-wage salary, and other restrictive treatment for fear of being terminated; employers did not need to provide justification for the termination, while employees needed to provide proof of abuse to win their case. The new policy was implemented amidst allegations by employers that foreign domestic workers were "job hopping" and "moonlighting," that is, they frequently moved from one job to another and were employed in more than one place.[58]

Other restrictive measures imposed upon foreign domestic workers were the proposed wage cut in 2001, which was meant, together with other civil service cuts, to ease the annual budget deficit. Workers, migrants and locals, won a victory this time, when the government backed down on the proposed measures amidst widespread street demonstrations. In 2003, however, the workers were no longer victorious. A two-pronged tax scheme, consisting of a wage cut and employer levy, was implemented on 1 April to address the budget deficit, despite the street demonstrations of 12,000 domestic workers. The proposed tax set an employer tax of HK$9,600 on the start of each two-year contract and a HK$400 per month reduction in the worker's salary. Accordingly, the set salary deduction was equivalent to some 11 per cent of the worker's minimum wage of HK$3,670. While many foreign domestic workers were not even paid the minimum wage, the new scheme effectively imposed an implicit income tax on their wages, which fell below the income tax exemption of HK$9,000 or less for all earners, as this levy could easily be passed on to the domestic worker by the employer.[59] Because employers pay the government the full amount of the levy for new hires at the beginning of the contract, this opened another avenue for employee abuse, particularly if the contract was pre-terminated. On top of the usual possibility of non-payment or withholding of a portion of the salary, employers could also eventually charge the pre-terminated worker for the levy.

At the end of 1997 the total number of documented foreign domestic workers was 171,333, which was double the number for 1988. Eighty per cent of these were Filipinos. Accordingly, the number of Filipino domestic workers increased from 128,800 as of December 1996 to 146,400 as of June 1997.[60]

Meanwhile, the arrest of illegal workers continued. In 1997, 2,087 were arrested on suspicion of illegality; and in 1998, 2000 workers were arrested.[61]

As of December 2001, there were 154,744 Filipinos working as domestic helpers and 65,027 Indonesians. Overall, there were 230,476 foreign domestic workers at the end of the year, comprising 6 per cent of the labor force.[62] Other nationalities that had a significant increase in their number were Indonesians and Indians, while a smaller number of workers came from mainland China, Sri Lanka, Pakistan, and Nepal.

One year into her Hong Kong stay Connie joined UNIFIL-HK, and two years later she was elected chairperson of the organization of 8,000 members.[63] This, however, was not her first entry into migrant public life: her initial associational involvements were with church activities and ministries among fellow migrants. Not someone to be self-involved and isolated, Connie found herself participating in a Lutheran Church service on her first free day. This started her involvement in ministering to migrant workers, which eventually led to her becoming a member of the Board of Social Ministry of the Church of All Nations, which she attended.

Connie was an indefatigable leader of UNIFIL-HK, and among the challenges and restrictive measures she and the organization dealt with were the 1997 turnover of the British colony to China, the wage cut of 2001, the tax schemes of 2003, as well as the continuing opposition to the 1987 "two-week rule" that indirectly negated worker rights accorded foreign migrants. Many of these struggles were bravely voiced out in the streets of Central.

Connie's political work during her 13 years in Hong Kong clearly illustrates that despite the colony's democratic principles, foreign migrant workers' rights needed to be fought for and defended, if these were to be exercised at all.

Next Leg: Manila. Balikbayan. Occupation: Political Worker

In the lead-up to the 2004 national elections, Connie as the chair of UNIFIL-HK was chosen by the different Filipino migrant organizations under the Migrante Sectoral Party banner to represent them as the first candidate in the party-list elections.

As a full-time political worker, Connie believes this to be a harder job than domestic work because her primary responsibility is to see that Filipino migrants all over the world are protected by the law.

Conclusion

The idea of travel is almost always assumed to be central to the life narrative of a migrant. Connie's experience of migration, as a contract labor migrant, however, posits another perspective on "travel" and the appreciation of travel literature: on the one hand, mobile; on the other, immobile. The immobility comes from the fact that for most of an overseas domestic worker's stay in her destination, she is, for the greater part, stuck in her employer's residence as a consequence of the terms of her contract and the limitations of her resources. Because of these factors, many an overseas Filipina domestic worker may remain at "home" despite being away. This sense of "remaining at home" can be understood literally, but also metaphorically, in terms of desires and belonging, and also, loosely, politically, in the sense of remaining nationals of another nation: most of the migrant's rights — worker's and civil rights — are guaranteed only by her country of origin. She hardly has rights in the new country, where she is also not really expected to belong. In this light, the experience of migrancy — like Connie's and those of the million other overseas domestic workers — can be described as that of a "traveling nation," where the subjects — mostly a group, or a collectivity, of people — move about the world as they remain confined within the borders of their nation.

A traveling nation, circumscribed as it is politically, however, is not necessarily insular. The fact of migrancy brings about "a double perspective," as Edward Said has suggested of a migrant intellectual, for being in constant dialogue with two homes, with two sets of a sense of belonging (or, sometimes, non-belonging).

It is this two-pronged sense of experience and perspective borne out by migrancy that this chapter has explored in the narrating of the biographical narratives of Connie. The perspective resulting in this particular location is also what Connie contributes in her political participation.

The crucial intersection of a gendered, racial, class position can produce an understanding of, as well as a standpoint, on issues specific to overseas migrant domestic workers. Connie Bragas-Regalado brings this potential standpoint with her in her entry into the formal political sphere and differentiates herself from the usual seasoned politician. This particular intersection of experience and perspective is also what gives Connie's entry into the political mainstream its transformative potential: the promise of influencing structural change by directly addressing issues from within and from a perspective of a fuller understanding of their complexities. In feminist discourse, transformative politics is understood as the "use of power to promote peace and development through participatory and consultative processes, with the poor and other marginalized sectors in the forefront of democratic aspirations."[64] Connie's political entry "from below" also anticipates the opportunity to bring in more diverse voices in the legislature.

The reading of selected narratives from the everyday world location of Connie illuminates another angle of vision and its resultant bifurcating of consciousness; through this I demonstrate the lack of sync between government laws and the "realities" of many OFWs. In the process, such an illustration can plot the misinformed decisions government takes with regard to its overseas labor migration policy. It needs to be noted, however, that whether or not the Philippine government's decisions were made based on misinformation or were clearly meant to serve other interests, is another matter for discussion. What I contend is that to take off from the premise that government works for its modern heroes clearly shows the disjunction between what the state claims and what it legislates.

Let me end by quoting a 2005 editorialized poem published in the newsletter of the Migrante Sectoral Party.[65] This poem encapsulates the knowledge and sentiment of the OFW Sectoral Party, of which Connie Bragas-Regalado is the chairperson, regarding government policy on overseas labor migration.

"You only know how to count"

You only know how to count
the following:
the USD8.5 billion remittances
every year
the aid funds from the
American and Japanese
governments

the millions of pesos that are
slowly being stolen from the
funds at the OWWA
and from those who were
forced to find work outside of
the Philippines.
You are not worried
about the thousands of
Filipinos jailed overseas
about your open support to
the US' wars against other
nations
even if these will endanger
our lives
about the thousands of
distressed Filipinos neglected
by host nation governments
and your administration
you continue to go with the
laughter of Bush
and continue with your
paeans of "new hero" labels
to us.
Do not ever think, that there
is no payback
in and out of the beloved
Motherland
for the exploited people will

not forever remain silent.

Epilogue

The results of the 2004 national elections put the Migrante Sectoral Party (MSP) at number 34 in the ranking of party-list candidates. The party garnered a total of 110,506 votes, which was 0.8686 per cent of the total votes cast.[66] While the Commission on Elections accredited MSP, with its first nominee, Connie Bragas-Regalado, to participate in the May 2007 mid-term elections, the party did not push through with its participation; members questioned the commission's disqualification of MSP from the

2010 national elections.[67] Inability to get a seat in two succeeding electoral exercises disqualifies a party from participating for the third time in a row.

One of the problems that beset the party was the low turnout of overseas absentee voters,[68] which could have been due to insufficient information dissemination to migrants in different parts of the world, poor access to registration and polling venues, and limited time allotment for registration and voting. The last two items seem especially relevant for overseas domestic workers since they live with their employers and cannot come and go as they please; they have only one free day a week, usually Sunday. Registration and polling places are generally located in major cities, which could be some distance away from where groups of overseas Filipinos are located; this is especially true in countries such as Saudi Arabia. Aside from travel time, the other issue is cost of travel.

As an organization of itinerant people, MSP benefits from using technology: it has a Facebook account, <www.facebook.com/migrantepartylist>, and a Twitter account, <https//twitter.com/migranteparty>.

Connie Bragas-Regalado continues to be chairperson of the Migrante Sectoral Party and works, and travels, to struggle for and promote Filipino migrant workers' concerns.

Notes

This chapter comes from my doctoral dissertation, which was supported by a research grant from the University of the Philippines Diliman: the OVCRD PhD Incentive Award. Thanks to Caroline S. Hau for her encouragement to pursue this project and for her helpful feedback on this version.

1 RA 7941 defines these as: "[a] political party [is] an organized group of citizens advocating an ideology or platform, principles and policies for the general conduct of government and which, as the most immediate means of securing their adoption, regularly nominates and supports certain of its leaders and members as candidates for public office. It is a national party when its constituency is spread over the geographical territory of at least a majority of the regions; a regional party, when its constituency is spread over the geographical territory of at least a majority of the cities and provinces comprising the region. A sectoral party refers to an organized group of citizens belonging to any of the sectors, whose principal advocacy pertains to the special interests and concerns of their sector[, while] a sectoral organization refers to a group of citizens or a coalition of groups of citizens who share similar physical attributes or characteristics, employment, interest or concerns [and a] coalition refers to an aggrupation of duly registered national, regional, sectoral parties or organizations for political and/or election purposes." See Republic Act

No. 7941 "An Act Providing for the Election of Party-List Representatives through the Party-List System, and Appropriating Funds Therefor," 1995.

2 One of the current points of contention in the law, however, is the provision that puts a limit on the number of seats or representatives each party or group can have in Congress, regardless of the number of votes it wins. Presently, this limit is set at three representatives per party or group, which has somehow controlled the effectiveness of some groups' ability to win votes. An example is the case of the leftist party-list group Bayan Muna (People First), which in 2001 garnered 11.29 per cent of the total votes cast and could have sent as many as six representatives to Congress. Because of the large number of votes Bayan Muna (BM) garnered in 2001 and the "cap" placed on the number of seats each qualified party/organization could occupy, Bayan, whose political party BM represented its entire network of organizations, decided to divide its probable share of votes by having its affiliate organizations form separate political parties/party-list groups. They were hoping to maximize their opportunities for increasing parliamentary representation on behalf of the cause-oriented movement. MSP, the political party of Migrante International, is one of these offshoot parties. See Alexander Martin Remollino, "Electoral Firsts: Militant Political Parties Vie for More House Seats," *Bulatlat.com* 3, 49 (18–24 Jan. 2004), <http://www.bulatlat.com/news/3-49/3-49-electoralfirsts.html>.

3 Republic of the Philippines, "Republic Act 9189 An Act Providing for a System of Overseas Absentee Voting By Qualified Citizens of the Philippines Abroad, Appropriating Funds Therefor, and for Other Purposes," 2003.

4 POEA, "OFW Global Presence: A Compendium of Overseas Employment Statistics 2005" (Mandaluyong City: Republic of the Philippines, Philippine Overseas Employment Administration, 2005).

5 Dorothy E. Smith, *The Everyday World as Problematic: A Feminist Sociology* (Boston: Northeastern University Press, 1987).

6 Biographical data on Connie Bragas-Regalado was collated from various news/feature articles and from the website of the MSP.

7 POEA, "OFW Global Presence: A Compendium of Overseas Employment Statistics 2006" (Mandaluyong City: Republic of the Philippines, Philippine Overseas Employment Administration, 2006).

8 For example, the health sector, where there is a growing demand for trained medical personnel to work mostly as nurse aides and caregivers in industrialized countries; as of 2003, there was one government doctor for every 28,493 Filipinos and one government nurse for every 16,986 Filipinos. See Blanche S. Rivera, "Nurses, Teachers Warned Anew on Illegal Recruiters," *Philippine Daily Inquirer*, 11 Jan. 2005, pp. A1, A4; and Blanche S. Rivera, "Government Hopes to Lure Back Overseas Nurses," *Inquirer News Service*, 30 Aug. 2004, <http://www.inq7.net/globalnation/sec_new/2004/aug/30-02.htm>. See also "Higher Pay for Medical Practitioners a Way to Stop 'Brain Drain':

Sen. Manny Villar," *Silangan Shimbun*, 18 Oct. 2004, <http://www.silangan-shimbun.com/Ocober2004_update/182004.htm>. Fuel for debate for some time was the news about the student who got the top score in the medical licensure board examination only to decide to take up a nursing post in New York instead. See "Editorial," *Philippine Daily Inquirer*, 29 Feb. 2004; Volt Contreras, "Doctor-Topnotcher Leaving as Nurse," *Inquirer News Service*, INQ7.net, 29 Feb. 2004, <http://www.inq7.net/nat/2004/feb/29/nat_10-2.htm>; Volt Contreras, "Top Doctor Pursues Nursing Job in US," INQ7.net, 16 Mar. 2004, <http://www.inq7.net/nat/2004/mar/16/nat_4-1.htm>.

9 See Graziano Battistella and Anthony Paganoni, eds., *Asian Women in Migration* (Quezon City: Scalabrini Migration Center, 1996); Joaquin Gonzalez III, *Philippine Labour Migration: Critical Dimensions of Public Policy* (Singapore: Institute of Southeast Asian Studies, 1998); Sydney Jones, *Making Money off Migrants: The Indonesian Exodus to Malaysia* (Hong Kong: Asia 2000 Ltd and Center for Asia Pacific Social Transformation Studies, University of Wollongong, 2000); Kanlungan Center Foundation, "Fast Facts on Filipino Labor Migration" (Quezon City: Kanlungan Center Foundation, 2001); Wilhelmina S. Orozco, "Economic Refugees Voyage of the Commoditized: An Alternative Philippine Report on Migrant Women Workers" (Quezon City: Philippine Women's Research Collective, 1985); Mary Ruby Palma-Beltran and Aurora Javate De Dios, eds., *Filipino Women Overseas Contract Workers: At What Cost?* (Manila: Goodwill Trading Co., Inc., 1992); Asia Pacific Mission for Migrants (APMM), "Development Aid and Forced Migration," paper presented at the Reality of Aid Meeting, 22–24 June 2003, Manila.

10 POEA, *2009 Overseas Employment Statistics* (Mandaluyong: Philippine Overseas Employment Administration, Republic of the Philippines, 2009). Total remittances are recorded from 2004 as follows: 2004, US$8.5 billion; 2005, US$10.7 billion; 2006, US$12.7 billion; 2007, US$14.4 billion; 2008, US$16.4 billion.

11 POEA, "OFW Global Presence," 2005.

12 POEA InfoCenter, "Deployment of Land-based Newly Hired OFWs by Skills Category and Sex, 1992" (Tables 1992 to 2001), updated 9 Sept. 2002 (Mandaluyong City: Republic of the Philippines, Philippine Overseas Employment Administration, c. 2000–1), <http://www.poea.gov.ph/stats/st_dlbnh_sex92-2001.html> [accessed 26 Jan. 2003].

13 Incidentally, this idea is also reported among the sentiments of labor migrants from other non-/less-industrialized countries and communities in Asia. Take, for example, Indonesia, Sri Lanka (e.g., the documentary *When Mother Comes Home for Christmas*, directed by Nilita Vachani, 1996), and Fujian, China, where one potential labor migrant was quoted as saying: "If you are from Fujian, everyone expects you to go overseas. Fortune only comes from leaving home." See Hannah Beech, "Dreams of Leaving," *Time*, 30 Apr. 2007, pp. 42–7.

14 Liz Stanley, "From 'Self-made Women' to 'Women's Made-selves'? Audit Selves, Simulation and Surveillance in the Rise of Public Woman," in *Feminism and Autobiography: Texts, Theories, Methods*, ed. Tess Cosslett, Celia Lury, and Penny Summerfield (London: Routledge, 2000).

15 Ibid., p. 41.

16 The Personal Narratives Group, ed., *Interpreting Women's Lives: Feminist Theory and Personal Narratives* (Bloomington: Indiana University Press, 1989), p. 3.

17 Em Griffin, "Standpoint Theory of Sandra Harding and Julia Wood," in *A First Look at Communication Theory*, 7th ed. (New York: McGraw-Hill, 2009), pp. 441–53.

18 Smith, *Everyday World as Problematic*, p. 79.

19 Ibid.

20 Ibid., p. 80.

21 Ibid.

22 The list of feminist standpoint theorists usually includes Dorothy E. Smith, Nancy Hartsock, Sandra Harding, Patricia Hill Collins, to name a few. This particular usage is influenced largely by the work of D.E. Smith.

23 Smith, *Everyday World as Problematic*, p. 88.

24 Ibid., p. 89.

25 Ibid.

26 For example, see the works of Nancy Hartsock, *Money, Sex, and Power: Toward a Feminist Historical Materialism* (Boston: Northeastern University Press, 1983), and *The Feminist Standpoint Revisited and Other Essays* (Boulder, CO: Westview Press, 1998); and Sandra Harding, *Whose Science? Whose Knowledge? Thinking from Women's Lives* (Ithaca: Cornell University Press, 1991).

27 Smith, *Everyday World as Problematic*, p. 89.

28 Ibid., p. 88.

29 Diana Wong, "Foreign Domestic Workers in Singapore," in *Asian Women in Migration*, ed. Graziano Battistella and Anthony Paganoni (Quezon City: Scalabrini Migration Center, 1996), p. 94.

30 Rowena Carranza, "HK Migrant Takes Road to Congress," *Bulatlat.com* 4, 2 (8–14 Feb. 2004). See also Migrante PartyList website, <http://migrante.150m.com/>.

31 Wong, "Foreign Domestic Workers in Singapore," p. 92; emphasis mine.

32 Data as of 1996.

33 Wong, "Foreign Domestic Workers in Singapore," p. 93.

34 Carranza, "HK Migrant Takes Road to Congress."

35 Wong, "Foreign Domestic Workers in Singapore," p. 94.

36 POEA Employment Statistical Compendium, 1982–1993 in Wong, "Foreign Domestic Workers in Singapore," p. 97.

37 Graziano Battistella and Maruja Asis, eds., "Singapore," *Asian Migration News*, 15 Aug. 1998, <http://www.scalabrini.org/~smc/amnews/amnarch.htm>.

38 Carranza, "HK Migrant Takes Road to Congress."

39 Battistella and Asis, "Singapore."

40 Office of Pacific and Asian Affairs, DFA 2007. See also POEA, "Overseas Employment Statistics: Deployment per Country per Skill per Sex, 2006," Philippine Overseas Employment Administration website, <http://www.poea.gov.ph/html/statistics.html>.

41 Ibid.

42 Ibid.

43 Carranza, "HK Migrant Takes Road to Congress."

44 Carmelita N. Ericta *et al.*, "Profile of Filipino Overseas Workers," paper presented at the Statistical Research Center Annual Conference, Quezon City, Oct. 2003.

45 Ibid.

46 Ibid.

47 National Statistics Office, "Gender Quickstat (an update of the most requested sex-disaggregated statistics) as of 1st quarter 2007," page last revised 13 Feb. 2008, <http://www.census.gov.ph/data/quickstat/qsgender07q4.html> [accessed 27 June 2008].

48 Carranza, "HK Migrant Takes Road to Congress."

49 Supang Chantanavich *et al.*, *Female Labour Migration in South-East Asia: Change and Continuity* (Bangkok: Asian Research Center for Migration, Institute of Asian Studies, Chulalongkorn University, 2001).

50 Carranza, "HK Migrant Takes Road to Congress."

51 Ibid.

52 Asian Migrant Centre, "1997 Country Profile: Hong Kong," <http://is7.pacific.net.hk/~amc/papers/AMY98HK.htm>.

53 HK$3,860 in 1997.

54 Asian Migrant Centre, "1997 Country Profile: Hong Kong."

55 Cheng Shu-Ju Ada, "Migrant Women Domestic Workers in Hong Kong, Singapore and Taiwan: A Comparative Analysis," in *Asian Women in Migration*, ed. Graziano Battistella and Anthony Paganoni (Quezon City: Scalabrini Migration Center, 1996), pp. 115–6.

56 Ho Jun-Bo, "First Blood to the Hong Kong Migrant Workers' Struggle," 12 Feb. 2002, <http://www.marxist.com/Asia/hong_kong_first_blood0202.html>.

57 Asian Migrant Center, "CMR May Day 2001 Statement," 1 May 2001, <http://www.asian-migrants.org/news/98869909818798.php>.

58 Ibid.

59 Asian Monitor Resource Centre, "Huge Tax on Foreign Domestic Workers," Hong Kong (2003; posted 27 Sept. 2007), <http://www.amrc.org.hk/alu_special/regional_roundup/hong_kong_11>.

60 United Migrant Workers, "The Two Week Rule," Hong Kong Human Rights Monitor (1997), <http://www.hkhrm.org.hk/english/reports/enw/enw0796d.htm> [accessed 28 Apr. 2004].

61 Battistella and Asis, "Singapore."

62 Migration Dialogue, "China, Hong Kong, Taiwan," *Migration News* 9, 3 (Mar. 2002), <http://www.migration.ucdavis.edu/mn>.

63 Carranza, "HK Migrant Takes Road to Congress."

64 CAPWIP, the Center for Asia-Pacific Women in Politics, quoted in Carolyn I. Sobritchea, keynote speech presented at the Institute of Politics and Governance Bai Awards, 12 Apr. 2007.

65 Migrante Sectoral Party Executive Board, "You Only Know How to Count," *Migrante Newsletter*, Apr. 2005.

66 COMELEC, "May 10, 2004 National and Local Elections National Board of Canvassers for Senators and Party-List Representatives National Tally Party-List Canvass Report No. 20 (By Rank) as of June 2, 2004, 3:00 PM," COMELEC website, <http://www.comelec.gov.ph/results/2004natl/partylist.html>.

67 Ellson A. Quismorio and Shianee Mamanglu, "Migrante Party-list Questions Comelec Delisting," *Manila Bulletin*, 15 Oct. 2009, <http://mb.com.ph/node/224909/migrante-partyli>. See also Comelec, "Election Results May 14, 2007 National and Local Elections National Board of Canvassers for Senators and Party-List Representatives National Tally Party-List Canvass Report No. 33 as of June 11, 2008, 10:00AM," <http://www.comelec.gov.ph/results/2007natl/partylist.html>.

68 See, for example, Rev. Fr. Jessie Somosierra, Jr., "OAV Delayed in Italy, Low Turn Out in Hong Kong," GMA News.TV (16 Apr. 2007), re-posted on <http://frjessie.wordpress.com/2007/04/16/oav-delayed-in-italy-low-turn-out-in-hong-kong/>.

CHAPTER 10

The Making of a Jihadist: Itinerary and Language in Imam Samudra's *Aku Melawan Teroris!*

Shiraishi Takashi

He was a man of many names: Abdul Azis, Abu Umar, Ir. Imam Samudra, Fais Yushar, Heri, Hendri, Kudama. His aliases were necessary to his work in the jihadist underground, though his e-mail address was not something one would normally expect of a jihadist: dafi_lover@lovemail.com.[1] A leading member of Jemaah Islamiyah (JI) and an "architect" of the Bali bombings that killed almost 200 people on 12 October 2002,[2] he was arrested on 21 November 2002 in a bus on his way to Pekanbaru (perhaps to Malaysia). He was sentenced to death on 10 September 2003 and executed on 9 November 2008.

A series of studies conducted by the Brussels-based International Crisis Group (ICG) have shown that JI is a reincarnation of Darul Islam (DI) in a post-Afghan global and regional jihadist era, that is, a movement that took shape within the context of the Indonesian nationalist movement and revolution went global and regional and became connected with non-Indonesian jihadist movements in Southeast Asia, Central Asia, and the Middle East. This chapter is not specifically concerned with the question of how and why DI went global and regional, since this topic has been covered by Sydney Jones, whose research is by far the best. Instead, what I find striking about Imam Samudra is the thinness of the language with which he makes sense of his own life, mission, and journey. By examining Imam Samudra's memoirs, *Aku Melawan Teroris!*, this chapter shows how thin his language is and asks where this thinness of language comes from.

Imam Samudra, key suspect in the 2002 terrorist bombings on Bali island, gestures as he shouts "Go to hell Australia" at a local police headquarters in Denpasar, Bali, Indonesia, Sept. 9, 2003. Samudra, who is awaiting execution, has warned that al-Qaida would be "very likely" to launch revenge attacks if authorities kill him, a magazine reported in June 2006. (AP Photo/Divo Aditya)

JI was established in 1993 in Malaysia by Abdullah Sungkar and Abu Bakar Ba'asyir. Both Abdullah Sungkar and Abu Bakar Ba'asyir founded an Islamic boarding school, Pondok Ngruki, in Sukoharjo, Solo (Central Java), in 1971. They joined Darul Islam in 1976,[3] were imprisoned in the late 1970s and early 1980s, and fled to Malaysia in 1985. In coordination with DI leaders in Indonesia, they started sending DI and other young Islamist activists to Afghanistan to wage jihad against the Soviets in 1985. Between 1985 and 1995, more than 200 men underwent military training and saw action in Afghanistan, while many more were trained in Mindanao (southern Philippines) between 1996 and 2000.[4] The Afghanistan veterans were trained in the camps of the Saudi-financed Afghan mujahidin leader Abdul Rasul Sayyaf, where they learned jihadist ideology, established international contacts, and acquired military skills.[5] From 1996 to 2000, JI established a military camp inside the Moro Islamic Liberation Front's Camp Abu Bakar complex in Mindanao, where Afghan-trained veterans instructed the younger generation of mujahidin.[6]

JI grew out of DI in Malaysia in 1993, after Abdullah Sungkar fell out with Ajengan Masduki, the head of DI.[7] Many of the Afghan veterans elected to follow Abdullah Sungkar and join JI. JI bears the clear imprint of Abdullah Sungkar's teachings, which held that "any accommodation with a non-Islamic political system could contaminate the faithful and was forbidden."[8] After Abdullah Sungkar's death in 1999, Abu Bakar Ba'asyir became Amir (head), but hardliners represented by such people as Riduan Isamuddin alias Hambali, Ali Gufron alias Muchlas, Abdullah Anshori alias Abu Fatih, and Abdul Azis alias Imam Samudra opposed his appointment because he was deemed too weak and accommodating.[9]

JI members were spread across Indonesia, Malaysia, Singapore, and the southern Philippines. JI has links with al-Qaeda and alliances with Islamist organizations in Thailand and Burma.[10] There is no doubt that JI was in communication with al-Qaeda and obtained financial assistance from the latter. Nevertheless, JI remained an independent organization and made its own operational decisions. It is organized as a military organization with a territorial command structure. The JI network is built on jihadist ideology, military training, kinship, and school connections, with the boarding school Pesantren al-Mukmin, better known as Pondok Ngruki, in Solo as the center.[11]

Though JI aims at establishing a caliphate in Southeast Asia, its major goal is to create an Islamic state in Indonesia.[12] It emphasizes Salafi teachings, which advocate a return to the "pure" Islam practiced by the Prophet and the two succeeding generations of Muslims, and to jihad. Practically all the leaders in the central command as well as many of those involved in JI's bombing operations were trained in Afghanistan. An ICG report states, "Afghanistan had a huge influence in shaping their world-view, reinforcing their commitment to jihad, and providing them with lethal skills."[13] Activists had been sent to Afghanistan at least seven years before the formal establishment of JI. In this sense, JI in fact signified the institutionalization of the network, with Afghan veterans serving as hubs.[14]

Imam Samudra was one of these veterans.[15] But unlike many others, he chose to make his position public by granting interviews and publishing his writings, though, understandably, his police interrogation papers were the least revealing of the papers that I have read. His autobiographical notes were published in 2004 under the title *Aku Melawan Teroris!* (I Resist Terrorists) by the Solo-based Jazêra. His editor, Bambang Sukirno, suggested the title because, according to him, "the title reflects the content better than [Imam Samudra's original title] *Catatan Harian* [Diaries]": that is, Imam Samudra and his fellow jihadists' actions "were retaliations against the terrorist actions committed by America and its allies against the Islamic community [umat Islam]."[16]

Imam Samudra's book consists of two parts. The first 50 pages deal with his life, but the narrative ends in Afghanistan when he is only 20 years old. The rest of the 200 pages consist of a series of arguments accounting for his jihadist actions. This composition alone suggests the centrality of his Afghan experience in shaping his life. Indeed, his journey to Afghanistan (from which, it seems, he never came back, at least mentally and spiritually) may be said to have been the defining moment in his life, and the single most instrumental event that shaped the meaning, purpose, and perhaps even ultimate end of his life and being.

Speaking of his death sentence, Imam Samudra says: "This is the law of kafir rulers which has to be resisted continuously."[17] The struggle will continue, for "this is like dust for mujahid who are fighting outside [Ini cuma setitik debu bagi para mujahid yang sedang berjuang di luar]." It is easy to say that he is only a jihadist and dismiss him as not worthy of serious consideration, as if we already know who or what a jihadist is — a "terrorist" who has not shown any remorse over the killings he committed at the trial. But Imam Samudra has told us enough about himself to allow us to understand how and why he became a jihadist. What is more interesting, however, is that we can learn something more from his own writings than what he intended.

A Life Defined by an Itinerary

Born Abdul Azis on 14 January 1972 in Serang, the provincial capital of Banten in West Java, Imam Samudra was the son of Ahmad Syihabuddin bin Nakha'i and Embay Badriyah binti Sam'un, and the grandson of a successful merchant, pious Muslim, and haji. *Aku Melawan Teroris!* ends before his marriage, following his return from Afghanistan, to Zakia Daradjad binti Syaiful Fauzan, his former high school classmate.

Afghanistan looms large in his imagination and self-definition. In the *Tempo* interview, he responds, in answer to the question "Why did you choose the path of struggle [jalan perjuangan] like this?":

> Initially I had read a book, *Allah Has Descended on Afghanistan* [Allah Turun di Afghanistan]. It was about the syuhada [religious warriors, martyrs or witnesses] in Afghanistan. There are people who were run

> over by tanks, but were not dead, perhaps because the time had not yet come [for them to die]. There are also stories from syuhada's graves [makam para syuhada], every Monday and Thursday people can be heard chanting [Allah Akbar]. Or a story about mujahidin troops holed up in a mountain without any food. Suddenly helicopters emerged which dropped food for Russian troops which were also holed up in another part of the mountain. But thanks to Allah's decree [takdir], food was dropped where the mujahidin were ...
>
> Stories like this fascinated me [membuat saya tertarik], many stories which are proper [shahih], virtuous [fadhilah] or about the excellence of martyrs. As soon as the blood is spilled on earth, it said, all the sins are forgiven. Even before the body falls [on the ground], [he is] welcomed by a beautiful woman [bidadari] whose fragrance exceeds the world and all of its contents [wanginya itu melebihi dunia dengan segala isinya]. An instant before he is mortally wounded, his place in the heaven is secured. With this conviction, I have never retreated.[18]

Imam Samudra says he read the book when he was in his second year of junior high school. He obtained the book from his cousin Ahmad Sobari, who was martyred in Afghanistan. Imam Samudra says he wanted to go to Afghanistan, and he did in 1990. Afghanistan transformed him: "The way you think [Fikrah]. The way I think changed a lot there." He adds: "Before I went to Afghanistan, I still respected Amien Rais [a prominent Islamic intellectual and politician] and others like him. After I understood, I now put everything into the trash can." In Afghanistan, he "met people who were most hated by the United States, such as Syekh Abdurrasul Sayyaf [the head of the Afghan mujahidin faction]. Even though he was greatly hated by America, he was a first-class person [orang nomor wahid] in Afghanistan. I was taken aback [terkesima], but not bewitched [tersihir] [by him]. I obtained a lot of truth from him. Aside from him, there were also many friends from [the] Arab [world]. They directed me toward the right way of thinking."

Imam Samudra admits that "[a]s a matter of fact there still was *clash*[19] in my mind. For instance, I still thought at that time that jihad was dakwah [proselytizing]. So there was serious conflict. But then I read a hadith, and this was a proper [sahih] hadith which says that the toughest [yang terberat] are the truest [yang terbenar]. And they are definitely hated by infidels. So I started to go to the salafus sholeh school ['school which seeks to return to what is seen by its adherents as the purest form of Islam, that practiced by the Prophet Mohammed and the two generations that followed him']."[20]

Citing a verse from the Qur'an, "And fight those until there is no fitnah," Imam Samudra states that there is only one path — the path of jihad. He relies on ulama Ibnu Katsir's exegesis of the Qur'an to interpret fitnah, defining it as polytheism (kemusyrikan) and not upholding the law of Allah (tidak menegakkan hukum Allah). "So," he continues, "to eliminate fitnah, there is only one method, by jihad [untuk mengeliminasi fitnah itu, hanya ada satu cara, dengan jihad]."

We will come back to his notion of fitnah. The above quotations are lifted from the *Tempo* interview, when Imam Samudra was still working on his memoirs in prison. *Aku Melawan Teroris!* emphasizes Afghanistan, which now serves as the organizing principle of his life narrative.

There are three points that stand out in *Aku Melawan Teroris!*. In the first place, Imam Samudra takes pride in having come from a deeply pious Bantenese Muslim family. He points out that from his mother, Embay Badriyah binti Sam'un, he, "Praise be to God," inherited "the blood of a mujahid and at the same time ulama," Ki Wasyid, a leading figure in the Cilegon revolt in 1888.[21] Whereas Indonesian nationalist historiography makes Ki Wasyid a figure of pre-nationalist anti-colonial resistance against the Dutch, Imam Samudra views the revolt as a "holy war against the colonizers [jihad fi sabilillahsalah melawan penjajah ini] fought under the direct leadership of Ki Wasyid," thus underscoring his own jihadist lineage.[22]

In the second place, Imam Samudra describes his school years as replete with dangers, tests, and temptations. He recalls that, as an "ultranationalist" [ultranasionalis] elementary school student, he and his school team "won a P4 [Panca Sila] contest at the sub-district level (*fair*)." But at the district level, they were defeated, "Praise be to God." He muses:

> Imagine if we had won at the district level, then at the provincial level, and then at the national level. Perhaps I would now be the attorney for Edi Tansil [the convicted Sino-Indonesian banker] or Sofyan Wanandi [the Sino-Indonesian Catholic businessman, known to be anti-Muslim]. I could also have been the Chief Justice who would pass the 'death sentence' on Theo Syafi'i [one of Megawati's top lieutenants with military and Catholic background, also known to be anti-Muslim] or even the Chief Justice trying the Bali bombings case ...[23]

His schooling, he says, threatened to lead him astray from Islam. When he graduated from elementary school, he wanted to register at a state junior high school and a junior high religious school [MTS Insaniyah] in Serang. He had thought of attending the state junior high school to get an education in worldly affairs while attending the junior high religious school for religious education "for the life hereafter [untuk akhirat]." He was ranked fourth among the 240 students who were admitted to the state junior high school. But, to his disappointment, he was placed in the evening class in his first year — he had to go to school in the evening and was therefore unable to do his evening prayers. "This meant that I was 'ready to be processed' ['siap diproses] at that time to become a Secular man [manusia Sekuler], a Pancasilaist [manusia Pancasilais] who is obliged to tolerate all sorts of incorrectness."[24]

One time during the fasting month, Imam Samudra attended a one-day religious course, Pesantren Ramadhan, organized jointly by the Islamic educational associations Muhammadiyah and Persis (Persatuan Islam). The religious teacher at the school had taught him that girls walked on the left side of the hall while boys walked on the right. But the religious teacher (ustadzah) at the pesantren told him that it was a sin (haram), forbidden in Islam, for men and women to walk in rows, and quoted passages from the Qur'an and hadith to support this argument.[25] This came as a "shock" and made Imam Samudra "sad." He says this was "the first spiritual conflict I experienced [konflik batin pertama yang kualami]," for he "had been used to mingling and playing with girls whose aurat [private parts of the body, such as hair, not to be exposed in public] were exposed. I had been freely shaking hands with them without feeling any sin."[26] The reason he was so shocked was that he had been going astray without being aware of it.

This was the "*starting point*" that made him "understand how beautiful Islam is, how wonderful Islam is, how perfect Islam is. I understood there and then that Islam is the only path toward the glory of life in this world and the hereafter." Before that, to him "Islam was just a ritual [Islam itu sekedar ritual]." From then on, however, he started to understand "what life means and what ibadah [devotion to God] means." He now states that "his past was wrong" as he became aware that he was in a secular world, Dunia Sekuler, a world full of fitnah that distanced him from the Qur'an and hadith, from Islam.[27]

He graduated with honors from the state Islamic high school (MAN, Madrasah Aliyah Negeri) in Serang, Banten. While still a student, he became close to one of his teachers, Kyai Saleh As'ad, who had been a Darul Islam leader in Banten in the 1970s. He was reportedly radicalized under Kyai Saleh As'ad's tutelage. In 1988, two years before his graduation, he became the head of a Banten-wide madrasah association, HOSMA (Himpunan Osis Madrasah Aliah). He used this association to promote

Darul Islam ideas among students, through halaqah study-circle groups. He was particularly effective in recruiting new cadres through pengajian (religious lectures) he organized at the Darul Ilmu MAN, close to his own school in Serang.[28]

The third point that stands out in the book is Imam Samudra's encounter with the activist Jabir and his journey to Afghanistan. After his graduation from the state Islamic high school in 1990, he told his police interrogators he was "motivated" to deepen his Islamness (ke-Islam-an) by reading books about Darul Islam, the Afghan resistance against the Russians, and the *Pleasure of Becoming a Martyr* (Nikmatnya menjadi Syahid).[29]

He met Jabir at the Al Furqan mosque in Kramat Raya, Central Jakarta, which belonged to the Dewan Dakwah Islam Indonesia. Jabir came from Bandung. The two men talked in Indonesian Sundanese [bahasa Indo-Sunda]. According to the police interrogation, Imam Samudra said Jabir asked him about his intent (niat) for jihad and he replied that he "was really, really [betul-betul] prepared to do jihad, so I would not go to school any more," even though he had been admitted to the Institut Agama Islam Negeri Bandung in the field of Arabic literature and to Lembaga Ilmu Pengetahuan Islam dan Bahasa Arab.[30] After Jabir assessed (mengorek) Imam Samudra's background, Jabir told him, "There will be departures [pemberangkatan] this year. Want to join?" Imam Samudra asked, "You mean Afghanistan?" "He [Jabir] only answered, 'Dik [younger brother], this is all, hurry up and look for the fare, about 300,000 rupiah, Insyah Allah, if you are sincere, Allah will make your matters easy' [Dia hanya menjawab, 'Dik, udah dech, cepetan cari ongkos sekitar Rp 300 ribu, Insyah Allah kalau antum ikhlas, Allah akan memudahkan urusan antum']."

Imam Samudra got the money from his mother. He also had a passport photo taken. Three days later, he met with Jabir again. After he obtained his passport, the same week, they went to Dumai, Sumatra, and stayed there overnight. The next day they crossed over to Malacca, Malaysia. The route was the same one that Indonesian workers took to enter Malaysia. "There were not a few who were denied entry by the Malaysian immigration, even though they had official papers and the money to show [uang tunjuk], that is money which is enough to stay while in Malaysia [uang jaminan selama tinggal di Malaysia]." They did not have any trouble entering Malaysia. A few days later they left Subang Jaya International Airport and flew to Karachi.[31]

This was not the first time that Jabir visited Pakistan and Afghanistan. He was there in the mid-1980s as one of the first activists who were sent by Abdullah Sungkar. He trained in the Sayyaf camp and took part in the battle of Jaji, near Khost, together with Hambali, Zulkarnaen, Mukhlas, and others.[32] It is not clear whether Jabir stayed with Imam Samudra all the way, though most likely he did not. Like Imam Samudra, Jabir alias Enjang Bastaman came from a family with a strong Darul Islam legacy. His father was a member of DI, while his brother was arrested and imprisoned because of his involvement in the Komando Jihad during the 1970s.[33] Born around 1960, he was a graduate of Pondok Ngruki (c. 1990) and was educated at Perguruan Tinggi Dakwah Islam, in Tanjung Priok, Jakarta. A close friend of Hambali, he had trained in Afghanistan, lived in Malaysia, and visited Thailand. In 1996 he returned to his hometown in West Java, Ciamis, to get married and brought his wife to Malaysia that same year. He returned to Indonesia just before his first child was born, in 1998, and stayed in the Bandung area thereafter. In 2000 he reportedly moved to Tasikmalaya (also in West Java) but maintained regular contact with JI people in Malaysia. He was killed in Bandung in the Christmas Eve bombing operation in 2000.[34]

Under police interrogation, Imam Samudra claimed that he did not have any models (Imam Samudra uses the word "*figure*") but had looked up to Jabir as a guide (berpedoman), and that if there was any Amir, it should have been Jabir who died a martyr (mati sahid fisabilillah). He denied Abu Bakar Ba'asyir had any influence on him. He said he had known Abu Bakar Ba'asyir as Abdu Samad and he was not all that impressed by the one lecture (ceramah) of Ba'asyir's that he attended because the lecture "tends to be good for old people or drug addicts, while I had already been reactive and had known [how to use] the internet to learn more broadly about the Islamic world [cenderung cocok untuk orang-orang tua atau orang yang terkena Narkoba, sedangkan saat itu saya sudah reaktif dan telah mengenal internet untuk mengenal dunia Islam secara luas]." Through the Internet he learned about the oppression of Muslims, in the form of images of Muslims killed, maimed, imprisoned, and abused. Imam Samudra was dismissive of Ba'asyir because the latter only addressed spiritual questions (masalah ilmu hati) and called for reciting the Qur'an (banyak berzikir kepada Allah) without touching on the social problems of a society oppressed by infidels (tidak menyentuh masalah-masalah social masyarakat yang teraniaya oleh orang kafir).[35]

We will never know whether he meant what he said. One wonders whether he admired Jabir and did not appreciate Abu Bakar Ba'asyir very much because Jabir was dead and Ba'asyir was still alive. Or he might well have wanted to protect Abu Bakar Ba'asyir by distancing himself from the JI Amir. In any case, it is hard to believe that Jabir did not occupy an important place in Imam Samudra's life. Jabir was the one who broached the idea of going to Afghanistan with Imam Samudra. He did not merely encourage Imam Samudra to go. The fact that Imam Samudra looked up to Jabir means that the former's Afghan experience is inseparable from his memories of the latter.

When Imam Samudra went to Afghanistan to do jihad in 1990, funding for his travel was provided by Saudi foundations such as the Muslim World League (Rabitat al-Alam al-Islam), whose vice-president was Mohammed Natsir, a widely respected Islamic leader who had been a leading Persis activist in the 1930s; a Masyumi party leader; a former prime minister of Indonesia in the 1950s; and founder in 1967 of the Dewan Dakwah Islamiyah Indonesia, the Indonesian Islamic Propagation Council.[36] All recruits were sent to Maktab al-Khidmat, a "service center" in Peshawar (Pakistan), for logistical support. The service center was headed by Abdullah Azzam, a Jordanian-Palestinian whom Osama bin Laden regarded as a mentor and who became the chief ideologue of al-Qaeda. All the activists Abdullah Sungkar sent to Afghanistan went through Abdullah Azzam's service center to Camp Saddah, the Sayyaf facility in Khumran Agency in Parachinar, Pakistan, on the border with Afghanistan. Sayyaf, the leader of the Afghan faction called the Islamic Union for the Freedom of Afghanistan, was a proponent of strict Salafism and enjoyed the full support of the Saudi religious establishment at that time.[37]

Activists sent by Abdullah Sungkar underwent three-year training in Afghanistan, though shorter courses were also available. ICG reports that the religious instruction was very much focused on Salafi teachings, that it emphasized aqidah (faith), tauhid (oneness of God), and, most important, jihad. Classic Salafi texts such as those by Ibn Taymiyya were taught. Abdullah Azzam's writings, also used as texts in the camp, were "a modern echo" of Ibn Taymiyya's arguments that jihad meant armed struggle and that it was legitimate to wage jihad against Muslims who deviated from the true Islam or refused to enforce the Islamic law.[38]

Imam Samudra went to the camp in Afghanistan, following the route and path that had long been in place before 1990. On their arrival, Jabir and Imam Samudra were picked up by a man named Sofyan at Karachi International Airport. After staying overnight in Karachi, they rode seven hours on a bus in the early morning to Peshawar, the Pakistan-Afghanistan border area. They were accompanied by one of Sofyan's men, a longtime Pakistan resident who acted as a guide. Passing through "beautiful" (indah) mountains and riding a bus with passengers, the majority of whom "spoke languages of the planet that I had not known at all [berbahasa 'planet' yang tidak pernah kukenal sama sekali]," Imam Samudra was dressed in Afghan style (which covered his entire face except his eyes) and did not say a word. Had he spoken, "people would have known who I was." Jabir led the party, which included two Arabs.[39]

The next day they crossed the Pakistan-Afghanistan border to Khost. It took four hours to reach the camp, Muaskar Khilafah. "There I began life which was entirely new and very new [Di situ aku memulai kehidupan yang sama sekali baru dan sangat baru]. It was life which was really, really clean, though I won't say it is 100 percent sterile [steril]."[40] Imam Samudra was one of 25 men who were sent by Abdullah Sungkar for training in the camp.[41]

There is a striking passage in Imam Samudra's memoirs about the camp, his paradise:

> Indeed, [it was] a new stage [babak] of life that made me so happy. Our "music" was a volley of bullets [rentetan peluru], mortar explosion, and boom of zigoyak and da-scha-ka [anti-aircraft guns]. Our "songs" were nasyid (a kind of a capella) inciting the spirit of jihad.[42] Our "hummed songs [senandung]" are the rebounding by turns of verses of the Qur'an which never stopped for 24 hours. There was no women's voices, no small children's cries, let alone jahiliyah [ignorant/unaware] music, the calls of satan.[43]

He was trained in shooting, usage of anti-tank mines, throwing grenades, and making bombs. After seven months in the camp, he was sent to the front.

> Those who came to such an "odd" [aneh] place like this were only those who were ready to kill or be killed, ready to wage jihad to uphold the Allah's word[44] ... In Khost as well as in other jihad fronts in Afghanistan, death felt so close [kematian terasa begitu dekat]. Enemies were everywhere. Death could come to you at any time.[45]

Imam Samudra was only 20 years old when he went to Afghanistan. *Aku Melawan Teroris!* ends there and does not chronicle his life after Afghanistan. It is almost as if he had nothing more to tell, or else found it unnecessary to write on. No doubt this is in part because he did not (or was advised by legal counsel not to) discuss what he did in the jihadist underground. But it is also clear from the way he looks back at his life in the camp in Khost that he had reached the stage at which he felt he was in the camp, and close to death, wherever he went, and hence Allah was close to him, almost with him.

We do not know much of his life after his return from Afghanistan. We only have conflicting information about the length of his stay in Afghanistan. He told his police interrogators that he stayed there for three years until 1993, while the ICG reports that his stay was cut short by the conflict between Abdullah Sungkar and Ajengan Masduki and that he stayed there for only seven months.[46] In any case, Imam Samudra was back in Malaysia and most likely joined Jabir, who lived there for most of the 1990s. In early 1994 Mohammad Nasir bin Abas (alias Khairudin alias Sulaeman alias Leman alias Maman alias Nasir Abas alias Husna alias Abu Husna alias Eddy Mulyono alias Malik), who said he trained Imam Samudra in the camp in 1990–1, met him again in Banting, Selangor. He also said that he met Imam Samudra in 1997 in Sandakan, Sabah, on his way to the Abu Bakar camp in Mindanao.[47] Imam Samudra was active in Malaysia during those years as a JI member, and Ahmad Sajuli bin Abd. Rahman (alias Fadlul Rahman alias Fadlul alias Uyong alias Mat) claimed under interrogation that when he joined the JI Fiah Hunai-KL in 1995, Imam Samudra, together with Hambali, Abu Bakar Ba'asyir, Abdullah Sungkar, and others, was active in the JI proselytizing campaign.[48] Imam Samudra himself said that he was in Banting in 1998, peddling cloth and Muslim dresses.[49] Ferial Muchlis bin Abdul Halim, another JI member, stated that Imam Samudra was an active member of Wakalah Selangor in the field of proselytization.[50] Faiz bin Abu Bakar Bafana said that Imam Samudra participated in the October 2000 meeting with himself, Mulkifli Marzuki, Muklas, Hambari, Dr. Azahari, and others to discuss bomb attacks against churches on Christmas Eve.[51] And indeed he was centrally involved, along with Hambali, Faiz Bafana, Jabir, and others, in the Christmas Eve bombings that year which took place in 11 cities in Indonesia, killing 19 and injuring 120, and in which Jabir was killed due to the premature explosion of the bomb he was assembling.[52]

From 2000 until his arrest in 2002, Imam Samudra went back and forth between Malaysia and Indonesia, mostly between Banting, where he lived most of the time after his return from Afghanistan, and Serang, his hometown. His most important contact in Serang was Ustadz Heri Hafidzin, a close friend and former high school classmate. Heri Hafidzin introduced Imam Samudra to young members of religious study sessions (halaqah), where a small number of people sat around in a circle and discussed Darul Islam ideas. Ring Banten, the group Heri Hafidzin and Imam Samudra led, organized its own military training in Pangdeglang and invited JI members as instructors, even though it was not part of the formal JI structure.[53] Some Ring Banten members were eventually sent to the Abu Bakar military camp in Mindanao for further military training, while others participated in a gold-store robbery in Serang in August 2002, masterminded by Imam Samudra. The robbery was meant to raise funds for the October 2002 Bali bombing operations (even though the participants themselves thought it was to raise funds to support the Muslims in the Ambon religious conflicts).[54]

Imam Samudra's Case for Jihad

In *Aku Melawan Teroris!* Imam Samudra provides an extensive argument about jihad and the justness of the Bali bombings as jihad. Here again his Afghan experience is central to his view of jihad.

He begins his explanation with an obvious statement (at least for Muslims): that the Qur'an and hadith are the absolute truth (kebenaran mutlak [*absolute*]). The problem is, he says, as the world develops, as the population grows, as Satan's deceit becomes more sophisticated (tipu daya syetan semakin canggih), and as generations change, the desire to come back to the Qur'an and hadith eventually demands interpretation or exegesis (keinginan kembali kepada Al-Qur'an dan Sunnah pada akhirnya menuntut adanya interpretasi atau penafsiran).[55] These days there is no one who has the right to say that his exegesis of the Qur'an and hadith is the most correct. Those whose interpretation is correct and truest (benar dan paling benar) are the Prophet and His companions. Those who follow the footsteps of the Prophet and His companions are called Ahlussunnah wal-Jama'ah.[56] And "in the field of jihad he sticks to the instructions [fatwa] of ulama mujahid, those who directly jump into and are involved in jihad [terjun langsung dan terlibat dalam jihad] such as Syaikh Aiman Azh-Zhawahiri, Syaikh Sulaiman Abu Ghaits, Syaikh Usamah Bin Ladin, Syaikh Dr. Abdullah Azzam, Syaikh Maulani Mullah Omar ..."[57]

The reason is simple and straightforward:

> How can ulama who have never waged jihad and jumped into the field of battle possibly understand the problem and details of jihad? [Para ulama yang tidak pernah berjihad dan terjun ke medan pertempuran, bagaimana mungkin akan mengerti permasalahan dan seluk beluk tentang jihad?] Ulama mujahid [ulama who engages in jihad or "struggle"], whose cloth is mixed with the dust of jihad [debu-debu

> jihad], whose sweat is mixed with the smell of gunpowder and mortar, whose ears are not foreign to the sound of bullets, whose heart sometimes gets bitter [ketar-ketir] when encountering and fighting enemy troops, who witnesses pools of blood everywhere, who suffers injuries as the Prophet suffered broken teeth when [he was hit] by an enemy spear in Uhud, they certainly understand better, appreciate better, and are better qualified [lebih pantas] to respond to [menjawab] the problem of the Islamic community, above all concerning jihad.[58]

He continues: "In Islam, those who in the field of jihad are on guard at the fortresses of defense and on alert at the front are normally called ahluts-tsughur. And ulama who are in those positions are called ulama ahluts-tsughur."[59] He argues that "[i]n the Prophet's time, all were ahluts-tsughur. They were not just giving lectures, writing books, and submerged in piles of books. The Prophet certainly wasn't like that." Instead, the Prophet was the Messenger and model for devotion: "He did not just proselytize. He was a war commander who was at the battle front."[60] And Imam Samudra quotes a verse from the Qur'an: "And fight them (the infidels), until there is no more fitnah, and make all religions (which are there) the religion of Allah" (Al Anfal: 39).[61]

Imam Samudra mentions Syaikh asy-Syahid Dr. Abdullah Azzam, Syaikh Aiman Az-Zawahiri, Syaikh Sulaiman Abu Ghaits, Syaikh Mullah Omar, and Syaikh Usamah bin Ladin as ulama ahluts-tsughur. "Israel and America have created the image that those ahluts-tsughur are a bunch of cruel and sadistic monsters, whereas as a matter of truth it is they [Israel and the United States] who are cruel and sadistic. It is they who are *Drakula bin Monster*."[62]

This should be clear to any true Muslim, according to Imam Samudra:

> Muslims who are not imprisoned by the fetters of ethnicity, by the handcuffs of nationalism, by the fanaticism of nationality and by the sentiment of *political willing* [*sic*] should understand and realize the real problem. They should know that the world has now entered into the 10th phase of the New Crusades [Perang Salib Baru]. And men of jihad, mujahid who are willing and able to leave the families and countries they love, who are ready to sacrifice their bodies and souls to seek the will of Allah and the heaven will understand that ahluts-tsughur are ahluts-tsughur.[63]

Yet at present, he says, "religious consideration [pertimbangan keimanan] has been lost to people. As if in darkness [sekeping gulita] people hardly have eyes any more. People are surrounded with fitnah. There is not even a ray of light. There are only a few who can see the truth."[64] He cites a verse from the Qur'an:

> And why do you not want to fight in the path of Allah and (defend) the weak, men, women, and children, who all pray: Lord, get us out of this country, whose people are cruel, and give us a defender from Your side, and give us a rescuer from Your side. [Dan mengapakah kamu tidak mau berperang di Jalan Allah dan (membela) orang-orang yang lemah baik laki-laki, wanita-wanita, maupun anak-anak, yang semuanya berdoa: "Wahai Rabb (Tuhan) kami, keluarkanlah kami dari negeri ini, yang dzalim penduduknya, dan berilah kami pelindung dari sisi Engkau, dan berilah kami penolong dari sisi Engkau."] (An-Nisa: 75)[65]

Interestingly, when he talks about men, women, and children who are weak and ill-treated, he visualizes images — for instance, babies without heads and hands; girls without legs and ears; and those who were killed, injured, and maimed by the US bombings in Afghanistan — that he saw over the Internet.[66]

> Indeed, the cruelty and savagery of America and its allies against the enemy nations [bangsa-bangsa musuh] will never be solved at the negotiating table, let alone the U.N. The savagery of the colonizer nations [bangsa-bangsa penjajah] which have preyed on millions of Muslim souls with the most cruel slaughter, starting from Iraq, Afghanistan and Somalia to Indonesia can only be faced with the way of jihad.[67]

It is clear who "our" target is: the colonizer and criminal nations (bangsa-bangsa penjajah dan penjahat itu).[68] Imam Samudra continues:

> The wounds of Palestine have not yet dried, the cries of mustadh'afin (weak people) in Afghanistan have not stopped. The crying and sobbing of small babies without heads, without ears, without arms and legs, remain in the air. Who cares for them? Who can eradicate their miseries? Who wants to take arms and reciprocate life with life? No *answer*? No *action*? O, *muslim*? *Are you chichen* [*sic*]? La hawala wala quwwata illa billah ...[69]

According to Imam Samudra, the bombings in Bali were directed against the enemies who brought all these sufferings to Muslims: the United States and its allies. "They" call the act "terror." But it is defense and self-respect of Muslims (sebuah pembelaan dan harga diri kaum muslimin).[70] There is no distinction between military and civilian. "Whether they like it or not, all the citizens of America and its allies are obedient tax payers. This also means that they are involved in the process of funding the war.

When an infidel woman intentionally opens and exposes her private part [auratnya] in front of Muslims, she means to try to disperse the concentration of Muslim troops and at the same time try to destroy their *moral*."[71] So "[n]ow we plunge into Indonesia, especially in Bali. Just from the perspective of eastern customs, we can see how the process of degradation has taken place in Kuta, Sanur, and their vicinity. Zionist and Salibist whites [bule-bule Zionis dan Salibis] proudly exhibit their bestiality, as they please … Anyone who still has *filter* in his heart will certainly understand that their act destroys the *moral* of Indonesian nation whose majority is Muslim. Islam considers the act of infidel whites in Kuta, Sanur, and their vicinity a repudiation that has to be prohibited… Phenomena such as this is not without *planning*, not without strategy, and does not happen by accident."[72]

It should be clear by now that Imam Samudra sees the attack of Drakula bin Monster — the United States and Israel — on Muslims everywhere as part of Drakula bin Monster's grand strategy. But despite his conscious Islamism, his Muslim-infidel categories are informed by ideas of nationality, and his language is contaminated by the nation and its categories. Hence his assimilation of Bali, where the majority is not Muslim, into the Islamic world, in the name of Indonesia and its Muslim majority.

It should also be clear that Imam Samudra's language does not have any sociological categories that allow for a political-economic and sociological analysis of the world. He thus sees only Muslim men, women, and children suffering at the hands of infidels, and calls for jihad. But this kind of thinking is not the only way to read the world, even when one starts with the assumption that the Qur'an and hadith are the truth. Almost a century ago, in Kauman, Solo, which is not very far from Pondok Ngruki of Sukoharjo, the center of jihadist learning, the leading nationalist/Islamist/Communist leader Haji Misbach wrote:

> But you readers must remember that once we are united in our harmony, we are bidden by God in the Koran as follows:
>
> [lines in Arabic script]
>
> It Means: Call what is right right, call what is error error, even if the one in error hates you.
>
> It is clear that we human beings are bidden to take care that no one shall continually do actions that are not right. If we have faith, then certainly we will no longer hesitate to heed God's commandment. Even if we are hated by those who act in error, we are still bidden to correct them, irrespective of their nation or whether their rank is high or low …

> To be sure, it is difficult for us to do this at present, for in the world of today the land of Java is filled with nothing but OPPRESSION UPON US. No matter how the oppressed cry out, it seems that they are not HEEDED. All that is offered us is might. If we are unwilling to be PUT UNDER THE YOKE, then the weapons of that might confront us. That is why [conditions in the] Indies today are like the conditions in MECCA in olden times. For where life was indifferent to the oppression around it, there God spoke. Put into Malay, He said, more or less: *Why are you all unwilling to fight the perang sabil [Holy War], and help those men, women, and children who are in wretchedness and who beseech Allah thus: Lord God! May the Lord deliver us His servants from this city of Mecca where men only torment one another! And may the Lord grant us a Mukmin [guide] who will lead us and help us.*
>
> Well! It is now clear enough that God's command obliges us to help whoever is oppressed — to the point that if the oppression is not stopped beforehand, we are obliged to fight.[73]

Here Misbach draws a parallel between the Indies in which he lived and in which "the government only protects the capitalists [kaum kapitalisme], while peasant people or Kromos remain their prey," and Mecca in the olden times, and quotes the Koranic verse calling for perang sabillilah — fighting for the cause of Allah. In his view, then, oppression was not simply a matter of Muslims suffering at the hands of infidels. It was capitalist exploitation of people who were colonized and under infidel rule.

In the same way, Misbach understood fitnah sociologically. Fitnah commonly means "slander, calumny, and libel" in Indonesian/Malay. In Islam, however, the basic idea of fitnah is that of temptation, permitted or sent by God to test the believer's faith, which for the man wedded to his desires would have the appearance of an invitation to abandon the faith. Fitnah, therefore, has the sense of both temptation and a trial of faith. However, fitnah is not a matter of an inner secret temptation but of external circumstances. He who makes fitnah is therefore attempting to distance Muslims from Allah, and he who fights fitnah is proving his faith as mukmin (the faithful). Misbach saw fitnah in the Indies in which he lived in "the greed of capitalism and imperialism," for greed was believed to distance Muslims from God.[74]

Imam Samudra also talks about fitnah often. He says, for instance, that in the present, people are "in the darkness of fitnah" and that only a few can see the truth.[75] Or is it something Jews and Salibists do to Muslims?[76] Or is it "sinful business [bisnis-bisnis haram]" "masked" as tourism and entertainment which destroys morality and morale and undermines Islam?[77] Instead of capitalism and imperialism, Imam Samudra sees a Zionist and Crusadist conspiracy in fitnah.

Conclusion

In a series of excellent works on JI, Sydney Jones argues that JI can only be understood as part of the larger Darul Islam network and its history. She calls it an "extended family," which now consists of

> Darul Islam itself, JI, the Majelis Mujahidin Indonesia, Laskar Jundulloh, the Banten group, and Angkatan Mujahidin Islam Nusantara (AMIN), to name a few, not counting innumerable DI veterans who have their own large followings but operate completely outside any formal structure. These people know and visit each other, go to school together, intermarry, and keep in touch across generations. They also feud, bicker, and not infrequently, inform on each other. But the network endures, even as its component parts are constantly changing.[78]

The network "also includes fellow travelers: anyone who took part in hijrah with DI, to Jakarta, Lampung, Malaysia, Mindanao, or other places of refuge; anyone who trained with DI in Afghanistan or with DI-JI in Mindanao; any member of JI; anyone who fought alongside DI or JI in Ambon or Poso; anyone who regularly attended DI or JI pengajians; anyone imprisoned for trying to establish an Islamic state; and anyone who went to one of the handful of schools associated with JI."[79]

Imam Samudra was born into this network and spent his life moving and acting within this network. His parents were supporters of Persis, founded in 1923, which called "for cleansing Islam of innovations and for the application of the principles of the Qur'an and the hadith to contemporary conditions."[80] He attended the Madrasah Aliyah Negeri (MAN) I in Serang, where he was active as the head of Himpunan Osis Madrasah Aliyah, a Banten-wide association of madrasahs, and he was reportedly radicalized by one of his high school teachers, the former Darul Islam leader Kyai Saleh As'ad.[81] He was admitted to Lembaga Ilmu Pengetahuan Islam dan Arab, the Institute for the Study of Islam and Arabic, a branch of the Imam Muhammad bin Saud University in Riyadh, to study Arabic literature.[82] And he had a fated encounter with Jabir at the mosque in Central Jakarta, which is closely affiliated with the Dewan Dakwah Islam Indonesia. The latter was founded in 1967 by Mohamed Natzir, who started his long Islamist career as a Persis activist and who served as vice-president of the Karachi-based World Muslim Congress and as a member of the Jiddah-based World Muslim League (Rabithah al-Alam al-Islam).

But by the time Imam Samudra was born into this network, the tradition of Islamic Communism that Haji Misbach started had long been lost, even in Kauman, where the latter lived the greater part of his life. In the meantime the network has been threatened by the secular world around it under the long reign of Suharto. The contamination is most visible in Imam Samudra's language, though he seems not to have been consciously aware of this. As we saw in numerous quotations from his book, his language is studded with English words: "*bad habitual*," "aku *full* belajar," "sekolah *enjoy*," "aku belum mengerti apa itu *rangking* [*sic*]," "*No answer*? *No action*? O, muslim? *Are you chichen* [*sic*]?"[83] We have also seen how he believed he narrowly escaped corruption in the secular school he attended. He had been unaware that shaking hands with female students was a sin, and had not felt it to be a sin. He grew up learning to be wary and fearful of contamination.

The ever-present threat of contamination was the reason he was so happy at the camp in Afghanistan, where no women's voices, children's cries, or kafir music could distract him from pursuing his mission. But Imam Samudra's almost unconscious usage of English and his reliance on the conventions of e-mail communication and downloaded images from the Internet were symptomatic of his inability to see the language he used from a distance. Not surprisingly, he equated national categories with religious categories. His language did not allow him to see the world in ways other than Drakula bin Monster and its allies oppressing Muslims.

Haji Misbach had the ability to use the different languages of Islamism, Marxism, and nationalism to analyze Indonesia and the world in a far more sophisticated way than Imam Samudra managed. But historical trajectories have erased Haji Misbach's language and the political possibilities it posited. If we ask what the most devastating legacy of Suharto's New Order is, Imam Samudra's life tells us that it may well be the erasure or suffocation of a rich political, intellectual, and above all linguistic critical tradition. The attenuation of language that characterizes Imam Samudra's writing points to a real narrowing of political choices and options, and will likely have consequences that are far more destructive, irresoluble, and long-standing than have hitherto been imagined.

Notes

1 Kepolisian Negara Republik Indonesia Korps Reserse Polri, *Berita Acara Pemeriksaan* (*Saksi: Faiz Abu Bakar Bafana*), 22 Oct. 2002. *Daf'i* (from *daf'ul*) in Arabic means "to give" and in the context of Imam Samudra's e-mail address might mean "one who loves to give." But there is a possibility

that Imam Samudra meant "dafi_lover" as an insider joke. I thank Wahyu Prasetyawan for his help with the translation.

2 "Imam Samudra: Demi Allah, Tak Akan Selasai" [Imam Samudra: For the Sake of God, This Will Never Be Over], *Tempo* (19 Oct. 2003).

3 Darul Islam was a movement initiated in 1947 by Kartosuwirjo with the aim of establishing an Islamic state in Indonesia. For a mapping of the DI network, see International Crisis Group, "Recycling Militants in Indonesia: Darul Islam and the Australian Embassy Bombing," Asia Report no. 92, Feb. 2005.

4 International Crisis Group, "Jemaah Islamiyah in Southeast Asia: Damaged but Still Dangerous," Asia Report no. 63, 26 Aug. 2003, p. 2.

5 ICG, "Jemaah Islamiyah in Southeast Asia," p. 3.

6 Ibid., p. 1.

7 ICG, "Indonesia Backgrounder: How the Jemaah Islamiyah Terrorist Network Operates," Asia Report no. 43, Dec. 2002, p. 3.

8 Ibid., p. 4.

9 Ibid., p. 3. This internal division deepened when Abu Bakar Ba'asyir established, with Irfan Awwas Suryahardy and Mursalin Dahlan, the Majelis Mujahidin Indonesia (MMI, Indonesia Mujahidin Council) in August 2000.

10 ICG, "Indonesia Backgrounder," p. 1.

11 ICG, "Jemaah Islamiyah in Southeast Asia," p. 1.

12 Ibid.

13 Ibid., p. 2.

14 Ibid.

15 An ICG report states that when Abudullah Sungkar and Ajengan Masduki had a falling out, Sungkar accused Masduki of having Shi'ite and Sufi tendencies and therefore of having strayed from Salafi teaching. Sungkar then went to Afghanistan and asked all the people at the Sayyaf camp to choose between him and Masduki. Imam Samudra reportedly refused to choose because he had been sent by Gaos Taufik, who was on good terms with Masduki. As a result, the ICG says, Imam Samudra's stay in Afghanistan was cut short and he stayed there only seven months (see ICG, "Jemaah Islamiyah in Southeast Asia," pp. 6, 9). But judging from his police interrogation and his *Tempo* interview, he most likely spent three years in Afghanistan, which casts doubt on the ICG report. See "Imam Samudra: Demi Allah, Tak Akan Selasai"; and Kepolisian Negara Republik Indonesia Korps Reserse Polri, *Berita Acara Pemeriksaan (Saksi: Abdul Azis als. Imam Samudra)*, 28 Nov. 2002.

16 Bambang Sukirno, "Pengantar Editor," in Imam Samudra, *Aku Melawan Teroris!* (Solo: Jazêra, 2004), pp. 9–10.

17 "Imam Samudra: Demi Allah, Tak Akan Selesai."

18 "Imam Samudra: Demi Allah, Tak Akan Selesai." Quotations from the next three paragraphs are from this interview.

19 Italicized words in all Imam Samudra quotations in this essay indicate original English phrasing.

20 ICG, "Indonesia Backgrounder," p. 2.

21 Imam Samudra, *Aku Melawan Teroris!* p. 22.

22 Ibid., p. 23.

23 Ibid., pp. 26–7.

24 Ibid., pp. 29–30.

25 Ibid., pp. 32–3.

26 Ibid., p. 33.

27 Ibid., p. 34.

28 ICG, "How the Jemaah Islamiyah Terrorist Network Operates," p. 22.

29 Kepolisian Negara Republik Indonesia Korps Reserse Polri, *Berita Acara Pemeriksaan* (*Saksi: Abdul Azis als. Imam Samudra*).

30 Ibid.

31 Imam Samudra, *Aku Melawan Teroris!* pp. 42–3.

32 ICG, "Jemaah Islamiyah in Southeast Asia," p. 4.

33 Ibid., p. 8.

34 ICG, "How the Jemaah Islamiyah Terrorist Network Operates," pp. 6, 15, 17, 34.

35 Kepolisian Negara Republik Indonesia Korps Reserse Polri, *Berita Acara Pemeriksaan* (*Saksi: Abdul Azis als. Imam Samudra*).

36 ICG, "Jemaah Islamiyah in Southeast Asia," p. 3.

37 Ibid.

38 Ibid., p. 5.

39 Imam Samudra, *Aku Melawan Teroris!* p. 46.

40 Ibid.

41 ICG, "Jemaah Islamiyah in Southeast Asia," p. 6.

42 *Nasyid* comes from the Arabic word *annasyid*, which means "(singer of a) religious song." It now stands in Southeast Asia for an a capella song genre that uses mainly vocal harmonies and is predominantly performed by male vocalists. Bart Barendregt, "The Art of No-Seduction: Muslim Boy-Band Music in Southeast Asia and the Fear of the Female Voice," <www.iias.nl/iias/show/id-56157/framenoid=42832>.

43 Imam Samudra, *Aku Melawan Teroris!* p. 46.

44 Ibid., p. 49.

45 Ibid., p. 50.

46 It should be pointed out that the chronology does not fit well with the ICG report. Imam Samudra went to Afghanistan sometime in 1990, while the split between Abdullah Sungkar and Ajengan Masduki took place sometime in 1992. Even if Abdullah Sungkar visited the camp in Afghanistan right after his fallout with Ajengan Masduki and forced all the activists there to choose between him and Ajengan Masduki — which Imam Samudra allegedly refused, as a result of which the ICG report argues that he cut short his stay there — he should still have been there for more than a year, not seven months. See ICG, "Jemaah Islamiyah in Southeast Asia," pp. 6, 9.

47 Kepolisian Negara Republik Indonesia Korps Reserse Polri, *Berita Acara Pemeriksaan* (*Saksi: Mohammad Nasir bin Abas*), 13 Nov. 2002.

48 Kepolisian Negara Republik Indonesia Korps Reserse Polri, *Berita Acara Pemeriksaan* (*Saksi: Ahmad Sajuli bin Abd. Rahman*), 30 Oct. 2002.

49 Kepolisian Negara Republik Indonesia Korps Reserse Polri, *Berita Acara Pemeriksaan* (*Saksi: Abdul Azis als. Imam Samudra*).

50 Kepolisian Negara Republik Indonesia Korps Reserse Polri, *Berita Acara Pemeriksaan* (*Saksi: Ferial Muchlis bin Abdul Halim*), 31 Oct. 2002.

51 Kepolisian Negara Republik Indonesia Korps Reserse Polri, *Berita Acara Pemeriksaan* (*Saksi: Faiz Abu Bakar Bafana*).

52 ICG, "How the Jemaah Islamiyah Terrorist Network Operates," p. 5.

53 ICG, "Recycling Militants in Indonesia: Darul Islam and the Australian Embassy Bombing," Asia Report no. 92, 22 Feb. 2005, pp. 27–9. The ICG reports that Abu Gali, Imam Samudra, Ustadz Heri Hafidin (head of proselytization and cadre development), and Abdul Fata (head of military training) were central to Ring Banten. All belonged to the DI network, though it is not clear whether Abu Gali, Heri Hafidin, and Abdul Fatah were JI members. See ICG, "Jemaah Islamiyah in Southeast Asia," p. 22.

54 ICG, "How the Jemaah Islamiyah Terrorist Network Operates," p. 23. See ICG, "Jemaah Islamiyah in Southeast Asia," p. 22.

55 Imam Samudra, *Aku Melawan Teroris!* p. 59.

56 Ibid., p. 63.

57 Ibid., p. 64.

58 Ibid., pp. 67–8.

59 Ibid., p. 68. The term *Ahl al-thughoor* or *ahluts-tsughor* historically refers to those who defended Islam's frontier zone in the early centuries of the religion's expansion. Contemporary jihadists use it to mean those who fight to defend the Muslim community. Anthony Bubalo and Greg Fealy, "Joining the Caravan: The Middle East, Islam and Indonesia," Lowy Institute Paper 05, Lowy Institute for International Policy, 2005, <www.lowyinstitute.org/PublicationGet.asp?i=229>.

60 Ibid., p. 69.

61 Cf. the translation (by M. Asad) of the same verse available online: "And fight against them until there is no more oppression and all worship is devoted to God alone," <http://www.islamicity.com/QuranSearch/>.

62 Imam Samudra, *Aku Melawan Teroris!* p. 70.

63 Ibid., p. 72.

64 Ibid., p. 86.

65 Ibid., pp. 97, 162. Cf. the translation (by M. Asad) of the same verse available online: "And why should ye not fight in the causes of Allah and of those who, being weak, are ill-treated (and oppressed)? — Men, women, and children, whose cry is: 'Our Lord! Rescue us from this town, whose people are oppressors; and raise for us from thee one who will protect; and raise for us from thee one who will help!'" <http://www.islamicity.com/QuranSearch/>.

66 Imam Samudra, *Aku Melawan Teroris!* pp. 100, 102.

67 Ibid., p. 97.

68 Ibid., p. 103.

69 Ibid., p. 106.

70 Ibid., pp. 114–5.

71 Ibid., p. 147.

72 Ibid., p. 149.

73 Misbach, "Orang bodo djoega machloek Toehan, maka fikiran jang tinggi djoega bias didalam otaknja," Islam Bergerak, 10 Mar. 1919. Quoted in Takashi Shiraishi, *An Age in Motion: Popular Radicalism in Java, 1912–1926* (Ithaca: Cornell University Press, 1990), p. 149. Italics in the original.

74 Ibid., p. 259.

75 Imam Samudra, *Aku Melawan Teroris!* p. 86.

76 Ibid., p. 94.

77 Ibid., p. 158.

78 ICG, "Recycling Militants in Indonesia," p. 1.

79 Ibid., p. 31.

80 ICG, "Why Salafism and Terrorism Mostly Don't Mix," Asia Report no. 83, 13 Sept. 2004, p. 5.

81 ICG, "How the Jemaah Islamiyah Terrorist Network Operates," p. 30.

82 ICG, "Why Salafism and Terrorism Mostly Don't Mix," p. 6.

83 These examples are from only two pages: Imam Samudra, *Aku Melawan Teroris!* pp. 25, 106.

CONTRIBUTORS

Odine de Guzman is an associate professor in the Department of English and Comparative Literature at the University of the Philippines (UP) and deputy director for research and publication of the UP Center for Women's Studies. She is the editor of *From Saudi with Love: 100 Poems by OFWs* [overseas Filipino workers] (2003) and *Body Politics: Essays on Cultural Representations of Women's Bodies* (2002). Her research interests include women's autobiographical and biographical writing, Philippine feminist and gender studies, and OFW culture and discourse.

Caroline S. Hau is an associate professor at the Center for Southeast Asian Studies, Kyoto University. Her books include *Necessary Fictions: Philippine Literature and the Nation, 1946–1980*; *On the Subject of the Nation: Filipino Writings from the Margins, 1980–2004*; and (editor) *Intsik: An Anthology of Chinese Filipino Writing*.

Kasian Tejapira is an associate professor of political science at Thammasat University, in Bangkok. He is the author of numerous academic publications and a dozen books in both Thai and English. He is also a noted columnist and was formerly a radical activist and guerrilla fighter in the jungles of northeastern Thailand.

Khoo Boo Teik is an executive senior research fellow at the Institute of Developing Economies, in Chiba, Japan. He has authored two books: *Paradoxes of Mahathirism: An Intellectual Biography of Mahathir Mohamad* and *Beyond Mahathir: Malaysian Politics and Its Discontents*.

Resil B. Mojares is a professor emeritus at the University of San Carlos, Cebu City, Philippines. He has served as visiting professor at the University of Hawaii, University of Wisconsin-Madison, University of California at Los Angeles, Kyoto University's Center for Southeast Asian Studies, and the Asia Research Institute at the National University of Singapore. His books include *Origins and Rise of the Filipino Novel* (1983);

Waiting for Mariang Makiling: Essays in Philippine Cultural History (2002); and *Brains of the Nation: Pedro Paterno, T.H. Pardo de Tavera, Isabelo de los Reyes and the Production of Modern Knowledge* (2006).

Onimaru Takeshi obtained his PhD in area studies from the Graduate School of Asian and African Area Studies, Kyoto University, in 2005. He is an assistant professor at the National Graduate Institute for Policy Studies, in Tokyo. He specializes in political history and international relations in East and Southeast Asia and has done research on British political intelligence activities against the Communist International and regional Communist movements in East and Southeast Asia in the 1920s and 1930s. He is also working on regional and national strategies against avian influenza in East and Southeast Asia.

Lorraine M. Paterson completed her PhD in history at Yale University in 2006. Since the autumn of 2004, she has been teaching in the Department of Asian Studies at Cornell University. At Cornell she is a member of both the Southeast Asia Program and the East Asia Program, and her classes include Asian Biographies and Memoirs, Literature of Southeast Asia, and The Chinese of Southeast Asia. Her chapter comes from her doctoral research, which has been revised into a book manuscript titled *Tenacious Texts: Biography, Travelogue, and the East Asian Imaginary in French Indochina*. Her current project is on political exiles deported by the French colonial government from Indochina to various parts of the French colonial world.

Shiraishi Takashi is a professor at the National Graduate Institute for Policy Studies, in Tokyo, and president of the Institute of Developing Economies, in Chiba, Japan. His publications include *An Age in Motion: Popular Radicalism in Java 1916–1926* (available in Indonesia as *Zaman Bergerak*); *Indonesia: Kokka to Seiji* (Government and Politics in Indonesia); *Umi no Teikoku* (The Making of a Region); *Network Power: Japan and Asia*; and *Beyond Japan: The Dynamics of East Asian Regionalism*, the last two of which are co-edited with Peter Katzenstein. He is the editor of *Indonesia* (Southeast Asia Program, Cornell University) and editor-in-chief of *Japan Echo*.

Yamamoto Hiroyuki, an associate professor at the Center for Integrated Area Studies, Kyoto University, is the author of *Decolonization and Nationalism: The Origins of Nationhood in British North Borneo* (in Japanese, 2006).

Peter Zinoman is an associate professor of history and Southeast Asian studies at the University of California at Berkeley. He is the author of *The Colonial Bastille: A History of Imprisonment in Vietnam, 1862–1940* (2001) and the editor and co-translator of *Dumb Luck: A Novel by Vũ Trọng Phụng* (2002). His recent publications include "Nhan Van Giai Pham and Vietnamese Reform Communism in the 1950s: A Revisionist Interpretation," *Journal of Cold War Studies* 12, 4 (Fall 2010). He is also the founding editor-in-chief of the *Journal of Vietnamese Studies* and is currently writing a book about the life and work of Vũ Trọng Phụng.

INDEX